Buddhist and Western Psychology

Buddhist and Western Psychology

Edited by Nathan Katz

Prajñā Press

Boulder   1983

Prajñā Press
Great Eastern Book Company
P.O. Box 271
Boulder, Colorado 80306

9 8 7 6 5 4 3 2 1
First Edition
Printed in the United States of America.

AN IMPRINT OF SHAMBHALA PUBLICATIONS, INC.

Publisher's Note

This format is intended to reduce the cost of publishing certain works in book form. Detailed editing and composition have been avoided by photographing the text of this book directly from the editor's computer-prepared material.

Library of Congress Cataloging in Publication Data
Main entry under title:
Buddhist and Western psychology.
    Bibliography: p.
    Includes index.
    1. Buddhism—Psychology—Addresses, essays,
lectures.   I. Katz, Nathan.
BQ4570.P76B82   1983   150.19'0882943   82-12325
ISBN 0-87773-758-4

In Memoriam

Rune E. A. Johansson

May 17, 1918–March 26, 1981

CONTENTS

PREFACE

Way back in 1900, in a virtual dark age of Buddhist studies in
the west, the publication of a translation of the Dhamma Sangani[1] of
the Pāli Abhidhamma Piṭaka caused quite a stir. Caroline A.F. Rhys-
Davids, the translator, chose to explore the text from an explicitly
psychological perspective. "I was at once attracted," she wrote, "by
the amount of psychological material embedded in its pages. . . .
Even a superficial inspection of [this text] . . . should yield
great promise to anyone interested in the history of psychology"
(xvi). Indeed it should, but what has become of that promise? What
became of the hope that, as more Buddist texts became available in
editions and translations, as scholarship progressed, we would find
our understanding of the psyche enhanced?
   While this volume might count as a bit of evidence that this hope
persists, it seems to be the case that there has been a shift of attention, a subtle deflection of thought on the part of scholars of
Buddhism. This shift has effectually defined a new "field" of study:
namely, Buddhism itself; and it has had the net effect of discouraging efforts in more organic disciplines, such as psychology, philosophy, aesthetics or hermeneutics. For example, were one to
enquire of an academic involved in researching and teaching about
Buddhism what the object of his or her study was, the response would
most likely be, "Buddhism." However, I would argue that this response is far from the obvious one; in fact, it is one that manifests
a discourse, that it is an ideological rather than a descriptive
designation. I would argue that, depending on our academician's
interests, a more appropriate response would be in terms of traditional disciplines, such as psychology or philosophy. I would argue
that "Buddhism" as an object of study is a contrivance at best and
the reflection of a pernicious cultural imperialism at worst.
   In a recent and important work, Edward Said[2] has argued that concomitant with the rise of European imperialism was a change in
western perception of Asian cultures. Justifying an activist manipu-
lation of Asian economic structures and political systems was a deni-
gration and trivialization of Asian cultures, which became embedded
in the western mind as a "discourse" in Michel Foucault's sense.
This discourse, which Said aptly labelled "Orientalism," holds Asia
as inarticulate, monolithic, passive and reactionary—qualities so
ensconced in our perceiving as to repeatedly validate themselves in
scholarship, in a nostalgia for simpler times in "traditional" cultures, in power politics, and in the way we go about doing Buddhist
studies. If we can artificially construct a "field" of enquiry along

x

mere geographic parameters, we can thereby avoid any genuine inter-
cultural dialogue. Thus, the Dhamma Sangani becomes an historical
curiosity, a piece in our puzzle as to the nature of early Buddhism,
a mute "object" to be vocalized by our scholarship. It ceases to be
a compelling system of psychology, as it apparently was for Mrs.
Rhys-Davids.

In the history of Buddhist studies in the west, there have always
been those who have held comparative, issue-oriented studies--such as
this volume--to be specious. These objections have come, at times,
from Buddhists themselves, from western devotees of "Oriental wisdom," but most often from philologically-trained professional Orien-
talists. All of these positions serve to support and maintain that
artificial bifurcation of our world into an east and a west, the essential underpinning of Orientalist epistemology, although the first
is an understandable, albeit inappropriate, reaction to it.

I am grateful to some turns of contemporary feminist theory for
pointing out the insidious dialectic of what may be termed "the ped-
estal effect."[3] This dialectic serves to oppress by intermittently
denigrating and idealizing a particular group. Overarching this den-
igration and idealization remains one constant: trivialization.
Paradigms for this dialectic are found in the Biblical view of women
as either the Virgin Mary or the prostitute Mary Magdalene; antisem-
ites see Jews as either Judas or Jesus; and the Orientalist discourse
sees a given Buddhist text as an historical-philological "object"
while the devotee sees it as "Truth"--equally inauthentic options
perpetuated by this a priori discourse.

For these reasons, the very ambitious hope behind this anthology
on Buddhist and western psychology is that it might help us to see
through Orientalist discourse. Thus, for one thing, the discipline
orientation: this book is about psychology, not about "Buddhism."
Thus, I would hope, there is an intellectual honesty in considering
issues from alternative perspectives and not reducing one system to
the other. Thus, there is the tacit assumption that insights into
the human condition are relevant and meaningful to other humans quite
apart from any bifurcation of our planet into east and west, that as
humans we share more than we exclude by being Indians, Americans or
Swedes.

In his introductory essay to this anthology, the Venerable
Trungpa, Rinpoche points out what should be obvious but is not, that
both Buddhist and western systems of psychology have much to learn
from each other, both in terms of theory and praxis. It is hoped
that this dialogical, antireductionist thrust is carried out by our
authors, all of whom are trained in the languages and textual history
of Buddhism and some of whom are practicing psychotherapists as well.

Of our authors, four have been true pioneers in comparative psychology, and I am especially honored to have them included in this
book. Richard J. DeMartino's essay in Zen Buddhism and Psychoanalysis was one of the first such attempts in modern scholarship.
Padmasiri de Silva's Buddhist and Freudian Psychology was the first
systematic, comparative elaboration of the two psychological systems.
Herbert V. Guenther's work, especially Philosophy and Psychology in
the Abhidharma, sets a standard for the exegesis of Buddhist texts as
informed by western theoretical disciplines. Finally, the late Rune
E.A. Johansson's The Psychology of Nirvana was a trailblazing attempt

by a western experimental psychologist to understand fundamental Buddhist matrices. As Dr. Johansson died shortly after completing his essay, this anthology is respectfully dedicated to his esteemed memory.

I am grateful, first and foremost, to the contributors who have presented us with diligent comparative analyses. These days there is a great deal of pop psychology in Buddhism and pop Buddhism in psychology. This anthology is intended for a more serious reader.

My appreciation also goes to the Venerable Chögyam Trungpa, Rinpoche who is also a pioneer in envisioning a professional clinical psychology program designed to draw upon insights from the Tibetan Buddhist tradition and psychoanalytic theory.

My thanks go to Mr. Larry Mermelstein of the Great Eastern Book Company of Boulder, Colorado, for his encouragement in all stages of production of this anthology; to Ms. Ellen S. Goldberg whose professionalism and diligence as copy editor greatly enhanced the technical coherence of this anthology; to Ms. Donna Chenail and Ms. Rosemary Lane who produced the manuscript so beautifully; and to Andrew S. Levin and Stephen D. Sowle for proofreading the text.

Nathan Katz
Williamstown, Massachusetts
June, 1981

1. Caroline A.F. Rhys-Davids, trans., A Buddhist Manual of Psychological Ethics (Dhamma-Sangani) (London: Royal Asiatic Society, 1900).
2. Edward W. Said, Orientalism (New York: Vintage Books, 1979).
3. Betty Friedan, The Feminine Mystique, 2nd ed. (New York: Dell Publishing, 1974).

Buddhist and Western Psychology

Introductory Essay:
THE MEETING OF BUDDHIST AND WESTERN PSYCHOLOGY

Venerable Chögyam Trungpa, Rinpoche

I: Experience and Theory

Traditional Buddhist psychology emphasizes the importance of direct experience in psychological work. If one relies upon theory
alone, then something basic is lost. From the Buddhist viewpoint,
the study of theory is only a first step, and must be completed by
training in the direct experience of mind itself, in oneself and in
others.

In Buddhist tradition, this experiential aspect is developed
through the practice of meditation, a first-hand observation of mind.
Meditation in Buddhism is not a religious practice, but rather a way
of clarifying the actual nature of mind and experience. Traditionally, meditation training is said to be threefold, including śīla
(discipline), samādhi (the actual practice of meditation) and prajñā
(insight).

Śīla is the process of simplifying one's general life and eliminating unnecessary complications. In order to develop a genuine mental discipline, it is first necessary to see how we continually
burden ourselves with extraneous activities and preoccupations. In
Buddhist countries, śīla might involve following a particular rule of
life as a monk or a nun, or adopting the precepts appropriate to a
Buddhist layperson. In the Western secular context, śīla might just
involve cultivating an attitude of simplicity toward one's life in
general.

Second is samādhi or meditation, which is the heart of Buddhist
experiential training. This practice involves sitting with your
attention resting lightly and mindfully on your breath. The further
discipline of meditation practice is to note when your attention has
wandered from the breath, and to bring it back to breathing as your
focus. An attitude of bare attention is taken toward the various
phenomena, including thoughts, feelings and sensations, that arise in
your mind and body during practice. Meditation practice could be
called a way of making friends with oneself, which points to the fact
that it is an experience of nonaggression. In fact, meditation is
traditionally called the practice of dwelling in peace. The practice
of meditation is thus a way of experiencing one's basic being, beyond
habitual patterns.

Śīla is the ground of meditation and samādhi is the actual path
of the practice. The fruition is prajñā, or the insight that begins
to develop through one's meditation. In the experience of prajñā,
one begins to see directly and concretely how the mind actually functions, its mechanics and reflexes, moment to moment. Prajñā is traditionally called discriminating awareness, which does not mean
discriminating in the sense of developing bias. Rather prajñā is un-

biased knowledge of one's world and one's mind. It is discriminating in the sense of sorting out confusion and neurosis.

Prajña is immediate and nonconceptual insight, but at the same time it provides the basic inspiration for intellectual study. Because one has seen the actuality of one's own mental functioning, there is a natural desire to clarify and articulate what one has experienced. And there is a spontaneous curiousity about how others have expressed the nature and operation of mind. But at the same time, while one's immediate insight leads to study, it is necessary to maintain an ongoing discipline of meditative training. In that way, concepts never become merely concepts, and one's psychological work remains alive, fresh and well grounded.

In the Buddhist culture of Tibet, where I was born and educated, a balance was always maintained between experiential training and theory. In my own upbringing, time was allotted in our regular monastic schedule to both study and meditation practice. During the year, there would also be special times set aside for intensive study, and also for meditation retreats. It was part of our Buddhist tradition that such a balance was necessary for genuine learning to occur.

When I came to the west, to England in 1963, I was quite surprised to find that in western psychology, theory is emphasized so much more than experience. Of course this made western psychology immediately accessible to someone from another culture such as myself. Western psychologists do not ask you to practice, but just tell you what they are about from the very beginning. I found this approach very straightforward and something of a relief. But at the same time, one wonders about the profundity of a tradition that relies so heavily on concepts and opens its doors so easily.

On the other hand, western psychologists do seem intuitively to recognize the need for greater emphasis on the direct experience of mind. Perhaps this is what has led so many psychologists to take an interest in Buddhism. Especially in relation to Zen, they are attracted to the enigma of it. And they are tantalized by the flavor of immediate experience, the possibility of enlightenment, and the impression of profundity. Such people seem to be looking to Buddhism for something they find lacking in their own traditions. This interest strikes me as appropriate and in this respect Buddhism has something important to offer.

One important question always seems to come up when western psychologists begin to study Buddhism. Does one have to become a Buddist in order to learn about Buddhism? The answer is that of course one does not, but it must be asked in return, what does one want to learn? What Buddhism really has to teach the western psychologist is how to relate more closely with his own experience, in its freshness, its fullness and its immediacy. To do this, one does not have to become a Buddhist, but one does have to practice meditation. It is certainly possible to study only the theory of Buddhist psychology. But in doing so, one would miss the point. Without experience to rely on, one would end up simply interpreting Buddhist notions through western concepts. A good taste of meditation is actually necessary in working with oneself and others. It is a tremendous help, whatever interest one may take in Buddhism as such.

Sometimes it is very hard to communicate to westerners the im-

portance of the experiential dimension. After we had started Samye
Ling, our meditation center in Scotland, soon after I came from India
to England, we found that a great many people with psychological
problems came to us for help. They had been in all sorts of different therapies, and many of them were quite neurotic. They looked on
us as physicians carrying out medical practice, and wanted us to cure
them. In working with these people I found that there was a frequent
obstacle. Such people often wanted to take a purely theoretical approach, rather than actually experiencing and working with their
neuroses. They wanted to understand their neuroses intellectually:
where they themselves went wrong, how their neuroses developed and so
on. They often were not willing to let go of that approach.

II. The Training of a Therapist

In the training of a psychotherapist, theoretical and experiential training should be properly balanced. We combine these two elements in our Naropa Institute Psychology program: one begins with a
taste of meditation, then applies himself to study, then experiences
meditation more fully, then does more intensive study and so forth.
This kind of approach actually has an interesting effect: it enhances one's appreciation of what one is doing. The experience of
one's own mind whets the appetite for further study. And the study
increases one's interest in observing one's own mental process
through meditation.

In addition, when study is combined with meditation practice it
has a different flavor. Where direct experience is lacking, study
tends to be mainly memorizing terms and definitions, and trying to
convince oneself of their validity. When balanced with meditative
discipline, study takes on much more life and reality. It develops
clarity about how the mind works and how that knowledge can be
expressed. In this way, study and practice help one another enormously, and each becomes more real and satisfying. It is like eating
a sandwich—because of the bread, you appreciate the meat much more.

One question comes up when you try to balance the experiential
and theoretical sides of training. How much time should be spent on
each? Generally I would say it should be roughly equal. But at the
same time, the amount of hours put into practice, for example, is not
as important as the attitude with which it is done. If the trainee
is wholehearted enough, and if his practice is sufficiently intent,
then his meditation will have its proper role and permeate his study
and daily life.

All of this is not to say that there is no experiential training
in western psychology. But, from the Buddhist viewpoint, it is
greatly underemphasized. And when it does occur, it seems to happen
almost exclusively in the interpersonal situation of people talking
to one another, such as the classical training psychoanalysis. Some
western psychologists have asked me whether the direct experience of
meditation practice is really necessary. They have wanted to know
whether the "interpersonal training" is not enough. To this I would
answer that the interpersonal training is not adequate in itself.
First, it is necessary to study and experience one's own mind. Then,
one can study and experience accurately the mind in the interpersonal

one can study and experience accurately the mind in the interpersonal situation.

We can see this by looking at how the Buddhist tradition of abhidharma works. First, there is an exploration of how the mind evolves in itself and how it functions. The expression of this is the first half of the abhidharma. The second half is concerned with how that mind begins to respond to things from outside itself. This parallels how a child develops. In the beginning, he is mainly concerned with himself. Later, in adolescence, his world begins to grow bigger and bigger.

In order to understand the interpersonal situation correctly you have to know yourself in the beginning. Once you know the style of the dynamics of your own mind, then you can begin to see how that style works in dealing with others. And, in fact, on the basis of knowing oneself, the interpersonal knowlege comes naturally. You discover that somebody has developed his own mind. Then you can experience how the two minds interact with each other. This leads to the discovery that there is no such thing as outside mind and inside mind at all. So "mind" is really two minds meeting together, which is the same mind in some sense.

Therefore the more you learn about your own mind, the more you learn about other peoples' minds. You begin to appreciate other worlds, other peoples' life situations. You are learning to extend your vision beyond what is just there in your immediate situation, on the spot, so your mind is opened that much more.

And that reflects in your work with others. It makes you more skillful in deeds, and also gives you more of a sense of warmth and compassion, so you become more accommodating of others.

III. The Viewpoint of Health

Buddhist psychology is based on the notion that human beings are fundamentally good. Their most basic qualities are positive ones: openness, intelligence and warmth. Of course this viewpoint has its philosophical and psychological expressions in concepts such as bodhicitta (awakened mind), and tathāgatagarbha (birthplace of enlightened ones). But this idea is ultimately rooted in experience--the experience of goodness and worthiness in oneself and others. This understanding is very fundamental and is the basic inspiration for Buddhist practice and Buddhist psychology.

Coming from a tradition that stresses human goodness, it was something of a shock for me to encounter the western tradition of original sin. When I was at Oxford University, I studied western religious and philosophical traditions with interest, and found the notion of original sin quite pervasive. One of my early experiences in England was attending a seminar with Archbishop Anthony Blum. The seminar was on the notion of grace and we got into a discussion of original sin. The Buddhist tradition does not see such a notion as necessary at all, and I expressed this viewpoint. I was surprised at how angry the western participants became. Even the Orthodox, who might not emphasize original sin as much as the western traditions, still held it as a cornerstone of their theology.

In terms of our present discussion, it seems that this notion of original sin does not just pervade western religious ideas. It actually seems to run throughout western thought as well, especially psychological thought. Among patients, theoreticians and therapists alike there seems to be great concern with the idea of some original mistake, which causes later suffering—a kind of punishment for that mistake. One finds that a sense of guilt or being wounded is quite pervasive. Whether or not such people actually believe in the idea of original sin, or in God for that matter, they seem to feel that they have done something wrong in the past and are now being punished for it.

It seems that this feeling of basic guilt has been passed down from one generation to another and seems to pervade many aspects of western life. For example, teachers often think that if children do not feel guilty, then they won't study properly and consequently won't develop as they should. Therefore many teachers feel that they have to do something to push the child, and guilt seems to be one of the chief techniques they use. This occurs even on the level of improving reading and writing. The teacher looks for errors: "Look, you made a mistake, what are you going to do about it?" From the child's point of view, learning is then based on trying not to make mistakes, on trying to prove you actually are not bad. It is entirely different when you approach the child more positively: "Look how much you have improved, therefore we can go further." In the latter case learning becomes an expression of one's wholesomeness and innate intelligence.

The problem with this notion of original sin or mistake is that it acts very much as a hinderance to people. At some point it is of course necessary to realize one's shortcomings. But if one goes too far with that, it kills any inspiration and can destroy one's vision as well. So in that way, it really is not helpful, and in fact it seems unnecessary. As I mentioned, in Buddhism we do not have any comparable ideas of sin and guilt. Obviously there is the idea that one should avoid mistakes. But there is not anything comparable to the heaviness and inescapability of original sin.

According to the Buddhist perspective there are problems, but they are temporary and superficial defilements that cover over one's basic goodness (tathāgatagarbha). This viewpoint is a positive and optimistic one. But, again, we should emphasize that this viewpoint is not purely conceptual. It is rooted in the experience of meditation and in the healthiness it encourages. There are temporary habitual neurotic patterns that develop based on past experience, but these can be seen through. It is just this that is studied in the abhidharma: how one thing succeeds another, how volitional action originates and perpetuates itself, how things snowball. And, most importantly, abhidharma studies how through meditation practice this process can be cut through.

The attitude that results from the Buddhist orientation and practice is quite different from the "mistake mentality." One actually experiences mind as fundamentally pure, that is, healthy and positive, and "problems" as temporary and superficial defilements. Such a viewpoint does not quite mean "getting rid" of problems, but rather shifting one's focus. Problems are seen in a much broader context of health: one begins to let go of clinging to one's neuroses and to step beyond obsession and identification with them. The emphasis is no longer on the problems themselves but rather on the ground of experience through realizing the nature of mind itself. When problems are seen in this way, then there is less panic and everything seems more workable. When problems arise, instead of being seen as purely threats, they become learning situations, opportunities to find out more about one's own mind, and to continue on one's journey.

Through practice, which is confirmed by study, the inherent healthiness of your mind and others' minds is experienced over and over. You see that your problems are not all that deeply rooted. You see that you can make literal progress. You find yourself becoming more mindful and more aware, developing a greater sense of healthiness and clarity as you go on, and this is tremendously encouraging.

Ultimately, this orientation of goodness and healthiness comes out of the experience of egolessness, a notion that has created a certain amount of difficulty for western psychologists. "Egolessness" does not mean that nothing exists, as some have thought, a kind of nihilism. Instead, it means that you can let go of your habitual patterns and then when you let go, you genuinely let go. You do not recreate or rebuild another shell immediately afterward. Once you let go you do not just start all over again. Egolessness is having the trust to not rebuild again at all, and experiencing the psychological healthiness and freshness that goes with not rebuilding. The truth of egolessness can only be experienced fully through meditation practice.

The experience of egolessness encourages a real and genuine sympathy toward others. You can not have genuine sympathy with ego because then that would mean that your sympathy would be accompanied by some kind of defense mechanisms. For example, you might try to refer everything back to your own territory when you work with someone, if your own ego is at stake. Ego interferes with direct communication, which is obviously essential in the therapeutic process. Egolessness, on the other hand, lets the whole process of working with others be genuine and generous and free form. That is why in the Buddhist tradition it is said that without egolessness, it is impossible to develop real compassion.

IV. The Practice of Therapy

The task of the therapist is to help his patients connect back with their own fundamental healthiness and goodness. Prospective patients come to us feeling starved and alienated. More important than giving them a set of techniques for battling their problems, we need to point them toward the experience of the fundamental ground of health which exists in them. It might be thought that this is asking a great deal, particularly when we are working with confronting someone who has a history of problems. But the sanity of basic mind is actually close at hand and can be readily experienced and encouraged.

Of course, it goes without saying that the therapist must experience his own mind in this way to begin with. Through meditation practice, his clarity and warmth toward himself is given room to develop, and then can be expanded outward. Thus his meditation and study provide the ground for working with disturbed people, with other therapists, and with himself in the same framework all the time. Obviously, this is not so much a question of theoretical or conceptual perspective, but of how we personally experience our own lives. Our existence can be felt fully and thoroughly so that we appreciate that we are genuine, true human beings. This is what we can communicate to others and encourage in them.

One of the biggest obstacles to helping our patients in this way is, again, the notion of a "mistake," and the preoccupation with the past that results from this. Many of our patients will want to unravel their past. But this can be a dangerous approach if it goes too far. If you follow this thread, you have to look back to your conception, then to your family's experiences before that, to your great-grandfathers and on and on. It could go a long way back and get very complicated.

The Buddhist viewpoint emphasizes the impermanence and the transitoriness of things. The past is gone, and the future has not yet happened, so we work with what is here: the present situation. This actually helps us not to categorize or to theorize. A fresh, living situation is actually taking place all the time, on the spot. This noncategorizing approach comes from being fully here, rather than trying to follow up some past event. We do not have to look back to the past in order to see what we ourselves or other people are made out of. Things speak for themselves, right here and now.

V. Buddhism and Western Psychology

In my days at Oxford and since then, I have been impressed by some of the genuine strengths of western psychology. It is open to new viewpoints and discoveries. It maintains a critical attitude toward itself. And it is the most experiential of western intellectual disciplines.

But at the same time, considered from the viewpoint of Buddhist psychological tradition, there is definitely something missing in the western approach. This missing element, as we have suggested throughout this introduction, is the acknowledgment of the primacy of immediate experience. It is here that Buddhism presents a fundamental challenge to western therapeutics, and offers a viewpoint and method that could revolutionize western psychology.

PART ONE

Psychological Implications of Pāli Buddhism

DEFENSE MECHANISMS ACCORDING TO PSYCHOANALYSIS AND THE PĀLI NIKĀYAS

Rune E. A. Johansson

There are some basic similarities between psychoanalysis and early Theravāda Buddhism.[1] Both are practical methods aiming at a transformation of human personality. Both use psychological analysis in order to understand human nature and the causes of suffering. Both formulated a dynamic theory of human suffering and found a way to escape it, although their definition of suffering was different: psychoanalysis referred to neurotic states involving ineffectiveness and unhappiness, while Buddhism included the general human condition of frustration and unsatisfactoriness. Sigmund Freud, the originator of psychoanalysis, found that many neurotic symptoms basically are defense reactions, caused by early frustrations of needs. Such defenses are not considered so important in the Buddhist theory, but they have actually been described in the Nikāya literature. Since this has not been generally recognized, I shall in this article point out the parallels I have observed. My first task will be to define the different types of psychoanalytic defense mechanisms, and then I will discuss the Buddhist equivalents and their psychological background.

Most of the so-called defense mechanisms were first described by Sigmund Freud. His more casual and scattered observations were followed up by his daughter Anna Freud,[2] who gave them a more detailed—but not very systematic—discussion. Their importance as personality building factors has since then been generally recognized by psychologists, and they are now frequently discussed without using the special psychoanalytic terminology in which they were first clothed. I shall mainly follow the systematic exposition of R. B. Cattell.[3]

Three factors are said to form the background of the defense mechanisms: the needs, frustration, and the ego. In the beginning there were the needs. Freud of course mainly stressed and explored the sexual need, but there are many others, like hunger, thirst, needs to impress and dominate but also to please and obey. Needs that are satisfied without problem do not seem to create any modifications of behavior and personality, but most needs sometimes meet a barrier. Frustrating experiences of this type may lead to anger and intensified attempts to break the barrier. Or the person may look for some way around the obstacle; this is sometimes called the most intelligent way of reacting to frustration.

If the barrier proves unbreakable, the frustration becomes definitive. This may mean prolonged anger and aggressiveness, but usually

another problem solver takes over, the ego. In psychoanalytic terminology, the ego is one of the three main components of personality,
the others being the id and the superego. This division cannot be
observed in the child from the beginning, because it is a result of
experiences and development. The child is first dominated by the id,
i.e., the unconscious, egoistic, unmodified drives. By the ego is
meant the conscious, realistic, organized, goal-pursuing mental activity which usually leads our personal life. According to Cattell,
it is what we usually call "the will."[4] But behind the ego there is
still the id, containing unknown needs and forgotten experiences.
Above it a superego is formed, i.e., a conscience formed through col-
lisions with the value system of the social environment.

The Defense Mechanisms

Since the ego is "placed, as it were, between the devil of the id
demands and the deep sea of the superego punishment, while on a third
front it faces the intransigent facts of reality,"[5] it is frequently
threatened by frustrations and conflicts. It has also an image of
itself which is particularly sensitive and has to be protected: the
self is a valuable object, it "stands for" something and has a certain prestige in the social environment. Its "honor" has to be safe-
guarded. So on several levels and in several respects it has to be
bolstered and defended. Some of the devices resorted to are called
defense mechanisms.

1. Repression. One device is to forget the whole experience and
act as if the need never existed. It is usually easier to recollect
pleasant experiences than situations in which we have been unsuccessful, especially if the fault has been our own. Psychoanalytic investigations have shown that the experiences which originally caused
neurotic symptoms are usually forgotten. Anna Freud suggested that
repression is our first line of defense against anxiety, and this
would explain why there usually is an element of repression in all
the following types of mechanisms. Since consciousness is the main
function of the ego and since conflicts are intolerable, the most
primitive "solution" would seem to be expulsion, just as we tend to
disregard facts that do not agree with our general attitudes and sen-
timents.

2. Regression. When a child is not permitted to run out and
play with his friends, he may respond by a violent temper tantrum and
break his toys: this type of reaction is common among small children, but when it occurs at a more mature age it is called regression. Ross Stagner reports:

A girl who was about to enter upon a marriage most distaste-
ful to her, for example, suddenly started acting like a twelve-
year-old. She wore her hair in pigtails and tied it with
ribbons, talked in a childish treble, skipped about, and
showed interests appropriate to that early age.[6]

This reaction is a kind of withdrawal from the situation, playing a
role that is not concerned with problems of the type experienced.

3. <u>Isolation or restriction of the ego</u>. A person may try to avoid all situations connected with the problem that seems to be unsolvable and intolerable. A child who has great problems with learning to read may try to avoid all situations that call for reading. Attempts to create watertight compartments between different aspects of life are not uncommon examples of isolation: a man may, for example, try to avoid all social contacts in order to escape temptations of a type that once involved him in an impossible situation. Isolation is a method to protect the ego from embarrassment; but this type of withdrawal need not be regressive.

4. <u>Denial</u>. In some cases, the real nature of a problem or a frustrating experience is simply not experienced but denied and transformed by <u>fantasy</u>. A man returning from a meeting where he has been severely criticized, may tell himself with satisfaction: "How beautifully I solved this problem"--although it will soon turn out that it is far from solved. He has denied the problem by excluding it from consciousness. Another example would be a man who has been so frustrated during his earlier life that he refuses to recognize friendliness in others: friendly words may, for instance, be heard as ironical. Anna Freud relates the case of a small boy who hates his father and feels great anxiety because of it.[7] His anxiety is first displaced: he is not longer afraid of his father but of animals. Then it is denied and he indulges in fantasies about a lion (a symbol of his father) who is dangerous and frightens everybody; but he himself has complete power over it and it obeys him in everything. Consciously he no longer hates his father and feels no anxiety.

5. <u>Projection</u>. An internal threat may be experienced as a threat from without. If a child feels frustrated by his parents and therefore more or less unconsciously aggressive toward them, he may later feel that his environment hates him and wants to hurt him. He then projects his own aggressiveness to others and accuses them of exactly the feeling he has himself. The ego can be experienced as undivided and free from conflicts since the threat has been projected to the outside world.

6. <u>Compensation</u>. If a need has to be denied, its energy can sometimes still be used by being tranferred to a different activity which may give great satisfaction. A boy who is constantly frustrated in his reading lessons may compensate by developing his muscles through physical exercises. And a man frustrated in love may try to write poetry instead. Compensation frequently leads to useful achievements, and it can be recognized as a defense only from the peculiar intensity or even fury with which the activity is sometimes resorted to.

7. <u>Reaction formation</u>. Again, a need may be denied and transformed into its exact opposite: it is said that nobody is so virtuous as a converted sinner. A person with strong aggressive tendencies may become particularly sensitive to cruelty and may devote much time to preventive measures against cruelty, and a child who is very fond of playing in mud and dirt may strongly combat these tendencies and later become exaggeratedly concerned with cleanliness. This defense mechanism also, like compensation, can sometimes be recognized from a certain fanaticism and narrowness in outlook. The ego is made stronger by exclusion and concentration.

8. <u>Rationalization</u>. Sometimes an unacceptable need can be given

free rein or a frustrated need can be given up, if a rational explanation can be invented: in this way conflict can be avoided and the
self-image can be kept undamaged. An aggressive parent may punish
his children severely and then explain that it is for their own good;
unfortunately he has to be strict. A boy who could not win a contest
may say that the conditions were unfair or that he really did not
want to win because his real interests were in a different field.

9. Identification. As a protection against anxiety one can imitate some person in the environment and try to speak and behave like
him. Children often find that trying to act like father gives a
feeling of importance and security, and later, political leaders,
movie stars, sportsmen, and literary figures will function as ideals.
This is how one's character is usually formed and lifelong attitudes
begin. Sometimes this development may result in too unrealistic life
styles as when people identify with Napoleon or believe themselves
to be incarnations of God. Anna Freud relates a case of a small girl
who was afraid of ghosts and dared not walk through a dark hall.
Finally, she found a way and started to run through the room, gestic-
ulating wildly. She explained that she was playing that she herself
was a ghost. By identifying with the enemy she could feel safe.

10. Aggressiveness. As we have seen, aggression is the natural
reaction when a barrier is met. In this situation it is usually not
called an ego defense. But a frustrated ego may develop a certain
pugnacity, a habit to assert the self aggressively and hit back at
every opportunity. In this case, aggressiveness may be called a defense mechanism, since it is a sign of a threatened ego that finds
that its integrity may be best defended by attack.

The Buddhist Theory of Motivation

All the defenses mentioned are then considered to originate from
a frustrated need and to be a device of the ego to save its integrity
and self-image. Has then Buddhist psychology any equivalents to
these concepts? Yes, Buddhism has a complicated theory of motivation, of which we shall mention only a few points, and we find equivalents to the ego and self-image.[8] The fact of frustration was of
course well known.

The most general term for "need" is tanhā, literally "thirst,"
which is the motivational term included in the famous causal series
called paticcasamuppāda, "dependent origination." Here it is derived
from sensation (vedanā) and is described as the force behind the col-
lecting and building activity (upādāna) which ultimately leads to
suffering and rebirth. Mainly, it seems to refer to a craving for
experiences, love, and prolonged life, not so much to the forces behind activity. It has therefore a certain resemblance to Freud's
term libido, which refers not only to sexual desire but also to a
much more general "vital energy." Very common is an enumeration of
three motives to immoral activities: desire (rāga), hatred (dosa),
and illusion (moha). The first of these frequently refers to sexual
desire but also to desires of all types, even to desire for the
Buddhist doctrine (dhammarāga).[9] In the place of rāga, we sometimes
find lobha, "greed."

The corresponding forces behind good activity are usually expressed negatively as alobha, adosa, amoha, "absence of greed, of hatred, of illusion."[10] It is, however, not certain that we should read this to mean that only an absence is meant, since positive terms can also be found: cāga, "renunciation" and "generosity"; mettā, "friendliness"; and paññā, "wisdom."

Freud considered his basic drives as "instinctive" and therefore inherited. The Buddha seems to have preferred a "two-stage theory." On one level, all motives are derived from perception. We are seduced by the pleasant and unpleasant things we see, hear, etc. Without a pleasant experience there would be no desire. This is expressed in the paticcasamuppāda series, referred to above: thirst is conditioned by sensation (which is usually colored by feeling; the word is vedanā, commonly translated by "feeling"). And in A,I,200, desire (rāga) is said to arise because of "the quality of beauty" (subhanimitta), hatred (dosa) because of "the disgusting quality" (patighanimitta) of things, and illusion (moha) because of "improper attention" (ayonisomanasikāra). Behind a motive there is always a perception with a certain feeling (which in reality belongs more to the thing than to personal qualities).

But this does not mean that we are free from responsibility. Behind the perceptual reactions we have dispositions (anusaya) to desire, to repugnance (patigha), and to ignorance (avijjā).[12] These are present, although dormant, in the small child, but as his perceptual abilities develop, they will be activated and release the whole motivational process. The desires can therefore also be said to belong to a person's nature, where a person "endowed with strong desire (hatred and illusion) in his character" (ekacco pakatiyā pi tibbarāgajātiko hoti) is referred to.[13] Although perception is seductive or repulsive and a natural man follows these cues, he is free to disregard them and can even eradicate the dispositions.

In A,IV,236 the reasons why people give gifts to monks will be analyzed here, with two enumerations of eight reasons given (the first of them is also found in D,III,258). Here they will be quoted in full.

First enumeration:

    (1) One gives a gift with devotion (āsajja, literally "sitting on"), (2) one gives from fear (bhaya); (3) one gives thinking: "He gave to me"; (4) one gives thinking: "He will give to me"; (5) one gives thinking: "It is good to give"; (6) one gives thinking: "I cook but they do not; it would not be correct of me not to give to those who do not cook when I cook"; (7) one gives thinking: "If I give this gift, a nice reputation will be spread about me"; (8) one gives in order to adorn his mind and equip his mind (cittālankāracittaparikkhāratthaṃ).

Second enumeration:

    (1) One gives a gift from affection (chandā); (2) one gives from hatred (dosā); (3) one gives from illusion (mohā); (4) one gives from fear (bhaya); (5) one gives thinking: "My ancestors used to give and do like this, and it would not be

correct of me to neglect an old family tradition"; (6) one gives
thinking: "If I give this gift, I shall be reborn in the happy
heaven-world when my body has dissolved after death"; (7) one
gives thinking: "If I give this gift, my mind (citta) will find
peace, and I will feel satisfaction and happiness"; (8) one gives
in order to adorn his mind and equip his mind.

This is a very interesting document in the history of psychology
since it betrays sharp observation and realistic analysis of human
motivation. To give gifts to monks was considered a meritorious deed
rewarded in the next existence, if not already in this. But it was
clear to the Buddha, that a good and generous heart was not the only
motive for giving. The enumerated motives can be divided into five
groups:
    1. A number of feelings are mentioned. A gift can be given from
positive feelings of devotion and concern for the plight of the re-
ceiver. I have taken this to be the meaning of āsajja, which
literally means "sitting on," "approaching." In different contexts,
the connotation may rather be "demonstratively" or even "insult-
ingly."
    Another emotional motive is chanda (from second enumeration, rea-
son [1]), which I have rendered by "affection," corresponding to the
synonym given by a commentary, pema. This word is, however, also
somewhat doubtful. In itself, chanda can refer to both positive and
negative motives, and a translation like "from ambition" or even
"from goodwill" would probably be possible. But here, and in many
other contexts, we find it replacing rāga in the triad mentioned
above, rāga, dosa, moha. This triad is always used to express repre-
hensible motives, and so we can feel certain that even here unsuit-
able feelings are referred to, probably personal love or even sexual
desire for the monk, to whom the gift is given.
    A gift can also be given from fear (first enumeration, reason
[2]). One can be afraid of blame from others or of punishment in the
future, as explained by the commentary.
    2. A colder and more businesslike attitude can be found in some
of the motives given. One can give because one has already received
some gift or other favor (first enumeration, reason [3]) or because
one expects to get one in the future (first enumeration, reason [4]).
Even rewards in a future life (second enumeration, reason [6]) can be
taken into consideration. If nothing else, a happy state of mind
(second enumeration, reason [7]) can be expected as reward.
    3. The pleasure mentioned in the second enumeration, reason [7]
probably has something to do with the superego development. It gives
pleasure to do one's duty as implanted during the early years. This
sense of duty is more clearly expressed in the first enumeration,
reasons [5] and [6]. The same is expressed in the second enumeration, reason [5], which points out the importance of habit and tradition.
    4. The remaining points are more interesting from the psycholog-
ical point of view. First we have the two remaining members of the
triad mentioned above. How can a gift be given from hatred? The
most reasonable explanation seems to be that it refers to the hatred
and aggression concealed in the unconscious id of a person. One can
hate monks and what they stand for because of early frustrations or

because of one's own shortcomings with regard to the same ideals. But by means of reaction formation this hatred can be transformed into the opposite attitude unconsciously. Maybe the act of giving will then be performed more demonstratively or even fanatically than would seem natural. Or the hatred behind the generosity could be directed toward the self. A man hating himself unconsciously could compensate this by generosity. In these cases there would be no conscious knowledge of the real motive behind the gifts. But it is also possible to feel hatred and express it by giving in an ironic or condescending way.

One can misunderstand the effects of a gift or one's own motives to give: in this case illusion can be said to motivate the gift. To give is not always a merit, according to the Buddhist view, but only when the intention is good. Evidently this can be misunderstood. And private motives, like inferiority complexes, a wish to make a good impression, an expectation of rewards can remain unconscious, and the giver will act motivated by an illusion.

5. So far we have not mentioned the Freudian concept of ego, although it must have played its part in the processes called reaction formation and compensation above. Its existence and importance is, however, more stressed in the two remaining points, the first enumeration, reasons [7] and [8]. What does it mean to give in order to adorn and equip the mind? The word for mind is citta, which in many respects corresponds to the ego as Freud defined it, since it is "a personal psychological factor responsible for the unity and continuity of the human being but without any suggestion of permanent substance," and "a conscious center of activity, purposiveness, continuity and emotionality."[14] So the points in the first enumeration, reason [8] and the second enumeration, reason [8] sound nearly like a definition of the defense mechanism, although they cover all types of self-assertion not included among the psychoanalytic defenses; giving in order to bolster and defend the ego, by means of compensating for defects and rationalizing inferior motives, and in order to stress one's importance or opulence would belong here. One typical example is given as the first enumeration, reason [7]: one can give in order to get a pleasing reputation among people. This would result in an improved self-image.

Frustration and Defenses in Buddhism

So far nothing has been said about the element of frustration which the psychoanalysts have found behind all defense reactions. The Buddha's point of departure was suffering and he defined it in terms of frustration: "to wish for something and not obtain it is suffering" (yam p'iccham na labhati tam pi dukkham).[15] But how do people react to frustration? Another remarkable text gives the answer.[16] Eight ways of reacting are described

1. The monks reprove a fellow monk for some offense, and he, when reproved by them, pleads forgetfulness saying: "I do not remember, I do not remember" (... na sarāmi, na sarāmī'ti asatiyā 'va nibbetheti).

To be reproved by the Order of monks is of course a frustration, and this monk replies that he does not remember. This is a defense, and it may be that he has really forgotten. In this case we have the defense mechanism of <u>repression</u>. If his defense is a conscious lie, it is of course still a defense but not a defense mechanism in the psychoanalytic sense, since these are always unconsious transformations of forces in the id.

> 2. The monks reprove a fellow monk for some offense, and he, when reproved by them, blurts out at his reprover: "What right have you to talk, you stupid fool? Do you really think you must speak?" (<u>... codakam yeva paṭippharati 'kiṃ nu kho tuyhaṃ balassa avyattassa bhanitena, tvam pi nāma bhanitabbam maññasī 'ti?</u>).

This is evidently a case of <u>aggression</u>, i.e., the most original and "natural" way of reacting to frustration.

> 3. The monks reprove a fellow monk for some offense, and he, when reproved by them, retorts to the reprover: "It is <u>you</u> that has committed such and such an offense, so <u>you</u> must first make amends!" (<u>... codakass'eva paccāropeti 'tvam pi kho 'si itthannāmam āpattim āpanno, tvam tāva pathamam paṭikarohī'ti</u>).

When somebody does not recognize an undesirable motive in himself but accuses others of having it, this is called <u>projection</u>. Our text gives a very clear example of this mechanism.

> 4. The monks reprove a fellow monk for some offense, and he, when reproved by them, evades the question through another, turns the issue aside and shows anger, hatred and sulkiness (<u>... aññen' aññam paticarati, bahiddhā katham apanāmeti, kopañ ca dosañ ca appaccayañ ca pātukaroti</u>).

This man evidently finds no intelligent defense but reverts to a rather childish and disorganized behavior. This is what the psychoanalysts call <u>regression</u>, although there are also aggressive elements.

> 5. The monks reprove a fellow monk for some offense, and he, when reproved by them, speaks in the assembly of monks with much gesticulation (<u>... sanghamajjhe bāhāvikkhepam bhanati</u>).

It is not mentioned what this monk had to say, so the Buddha probably just wanted to draw the attention to his performance. Probably the monk wanted to make a good impression by an imposing performance: in this way he could make his fellow monks forget the real issue, i.e., his offense. The Order of monks admires and has use for a good speaker and can therefore disregard minor offenses. Such an attempt to hide a weakness by a good achievement in a different field is what we call <u>compensation</u>.

> 6. The monks reprove a fellow monk for some offense, and he, disregarding the Order and the reprover, goes on as offender

just as he likes (... anādiyitvā sangham ānadiyitvā codakam
sāpattiko va yenakāmam pakkamati).

This monk seems to refuse to see the problem and try to disregard it
completely and behave as if it did not exist. This means that he
isolates himself from his problem: he uses then another psychoanalytic mechanism of withdrawing from the demands of life by refusing to
see some of his own tendencies.

> 7. The monks reprove a fellow monk for some offense, and
> when reproved by them he says: "I am neither guilty nor con-
> cerned," and he annoys the Order by his silence (... ñevāham
> āpanno ' mhi, na panāham āpanno 'mhī 'ti. So tunhībhāvena
> sangham viheseti).

This would be a case of denial. The monk refuses to see his own offense and may sincerely believe that he is innocent. Evidently an
act of repression is then also involved; this may have created a certain tenseness which makes him silent, and this annoys his fellow
monks. He refuses to discuss the problem, since he dares not even
direct his consciousness to it.

> 8. The monks reprove a fellow monk for some offense, and
> when reproved by them he says: "Reverend sirs, why should you
> worry so much about me since I shall give up the training now
> and return to the lower life?" And when he has given up the
> training and returned to the lower life, he says: "Now,
> reverend sirs, be satisfied!" (... evam āha: 'kim nu kho tumhe
> āyasmanto atibālham mayi vyāvatā yāva idānāham sikkham
> paccakkhāya hīnāyāvattissāmī ⌐ti. So sikkham paccakkhāya
> hīnāyāvattitvā evam āha: 'idāni kho tumbe āyasmanto attamanā
> hothā 'ti).

This monk evidently was conscious of his offense, but his self-image
would not permit him to repent and make amends. Therefore he with-
draws from the whole situation. This can be understood as another
case of isolation or restriction of the ego. In this case, the self-
image is saved by a physical escape from the problem and in the case
mentioned earlier, by a psychological screening-off.

We see, then, that nearly all of the defense mechanisms discussed
by psychoanalytic writers have actually been discovered and described, although not explained and named, in this passage. They are
called attha purisakhalunkā attha ca purisadosā, "eight recalcitrant
men and their eight defects" (the literal meaning of khalunka is
"shaker"), but this is meant as a joke, since the eight types of
monks are compared to eight types of recalcitrant horses who behave
in different ways when "told to go on, being beaten and urged by the
driver": one "backs and twists the carriage round with his hind-
quarters," another "jumps back, batters against the carriage railing
and breaks the triple bar," etc. The word for defect, dosa, is not
commonly used in the Nikāya literature. So we have only descriptions
of external reactions, but no explanation why the different monks behave in these ways. Still, the text is remarkable enough. The Buddha seems to have been a keen observer of human nature and liked to

classify and describe what he saw. We find many similar passages in
the Nikāyas, although the quoted text is the only one in which several types of defense reactions are collected. Separate descriptions
can be found scattered all over the literature. Let us collect a few
more instances.

A case of rationalization is mentioned[17] describing how a lazy
man avoids work by saying things like: "it is too cold," "it is too
hot," "it is too early," "it is too late," "I am too hungry," "I am
too full." By rationalizing, one tries to find a convincing argument
for not doing what one hates to do but ought to do.

The tendency to avoid frustrations and hard work while trying to
keep one's self-respect was found even among the Buddhist monks. All
religions have problems with people who want to reap the fruits prom-
ised by its preachers but do not have the ability or the energy required for achieving the personality transformation, which is the
essential thing. The Buddha often criticized monks who wanted to
have a feeling of being successful and useful without being really
engaged personally. In one of the Nikāya texts, four ways of
avoiding "living by the doctrine" (dhammavihārī) are enumerated.[18] A
monk may learn all the Buddhist texts by heart. He may teach others
the doctrine. He repeats and recites the Buddhist texts. Or he
spends his day in thinking about the doctrine. These activities are
quite similar psychologically and can be referred to the type of
compensation sometimes called intellectualization. If the early
experiences of meditation and other forms of training have proved
frustrating, the self-image of a successful monk can be kept by doing something useful but less strenuous. In this way theologies and
philosophies are born.

Another passage describes a similar situation: some "foolish
people" (moghapurisā) learn all the texts by heart.[19] But they do
not investigate their meaning by understanding (paññā); therefore,
they will not comprehend what they have learned. "They learn the
doctrine in order to reproach others and pour out gossip" (te
upārambhānisamsā c' eva dhammam pariyāpunanti itivādappamokkhānisamsā
ca). Here the compensative achievement is used in the continued process of aggressive self-assertion. "I know this better than you and
you should learn," or he spends his time talking loosely about the
doctrine and related topics in order to impose on fellow monks. A
monk like this, wanting to "show off and boast about his achievements" (katthī hoti vikatthī adhigamesu)[20] may, for instance, pre-
tend that he has attained one or another of the higher levels of
samādhi and talk boastingly about this. This may be a case of either
compensation or denial in fantasy: the failure is denied and the
level of one's achievements greatly exaggerated in imagination.

Situations in which regressive behavior often had been observed
are described in one of the Nikāya texts.[21] "To a person without
faith talk about faith is unpleasant talk," and in the same way, immoral people dislike to hear about morality, people with little
learning dislike to hear about great learning, stingy people dislike
to hear about generosity, and unwise people dislike to hear about
wisdom. So, exposed to the type of talk they dislike, they "will be
upset, angered, troubled and will resist; they will show temper,
hatred and sulkiness" (abhisajjati kuppati vyāpajjati patitthīyati
kopañ ca dosañ ca appaccayañ ca pātukaroti). And it is explained

that talk of these types gives them no pleasure, since they have not been successful in that field. It will disturb their self-image, and defense becomes necessary. Aggressive and regressive behavior will be resorted to, although one could also expect others, not mentioned here, for instance isolation, withdrawal, and rationalization.

In the great discussion between prince Pāyāsi and Kassapa, one of the Buddha's disciples,[22] the former is conquered and admonished to renounce his wrong opinion. But he replies:

> Even though Master Kassapa says this, I still cannot bring myself to renounce this evil set of views. King Pasenadi the Kosalan knows me, and so do foreign kings, as holding to the creed and the opinion that there is neither another world nor rebirth other than of parents, nor fruit or result of good and bad actions. If I renounce these opinions, people will say of me: "How silly is prince Pāyāsi, how unintelligent, and how badly he grasps anything." In anger I will stick to it. Secretly and in spite I will stick to it.

To be conquered in a discussion is of course a frustration, and Pāyāsi could not give up his view, since his self-image would then be destroyed. The psychological process involved is very clearly described. His defense is aggression and isolation: he shows anger and spite externally and builds a wall of unconcernedness around his internal conviction.

Is the Ego Defense an Āsava?

I have quoted some of the more spectacular descriptions of defense reactions in the Pali Nikāyas. They are called "defects" (dosa)[23]--and so far there is agreement with psychoanalysis which also considers these reactions undesirable, at least in their neurotic forms--but otherwise no explanation is provided. My hypothesis is that they are closely related to and could be called a type of āsava.

Āsava literally means "influx" and refers to a number of undesirable psychological states which must be eradicated if nirvāna is to be attained. Their disappearance is actually described as the final and most difficult achievement in the attempt to reach nirvāna. As the word indicates, they "flow in" (anusavanti)[24] and are therefore to be understood as secondary processes, not as original traits in the personality. Actually, they are said to flow in through the sensory channels as long as they are admitted through "improper attention" (ayoniso manasikāra).[25]

There are four main types of influxes, related to ignorance, love, growth, and speculation (avijjā, kāma, bhava, ditthi). At least the last two types, and perhaps all, seem to have some relation to the ego functions of the person in question.

We have seen that the psychoanalysts distinguish between two types of conscious centers in the personality. There is the ego, which is the collective name of the conscious, will-determined, realistic processes, and the self-image, which is the individual's partly realistic, partly idealized image of himself. Buddhist psychology

makes a similar distinction. Citta, here translated by "the mind,"
is the empirical, will-determined ego, constituted by conscious processes. In addition there is atta, which is a very special type of
self-image, the self as an idealized, immortal essence. This self
was considered an illusion, and one of the aims of the Buddhist
training was to eradicate the belief in it.

The influxes are processes of citta[26] and have many relations to
atta and to the ego experience generally. Pride (mana) is an influx
according to one of the Nikaya texts[27] just as all types of vanity:
to use clothes for their beauty or as sign of importance, or lodgings
for other purposes than warding off cold or heat or dangerous animals.[28] Pride and vanity are of course ego-inspired feelings. Similar ego-related words are found in the following passage, describing
the origin of influxes: "when a monk lives with gain, loss, fame,
obscurity, honor, lack of honor, evil intentions and evil friendship,
which arise, unmastered, there arise the influxes, full of distress
and anguish."[29] Here a monk is described who thinks that his own
self-image is important and probably wants to bolster and defend it;
the influxes are the anxieties created in this process.

Some influxes are said to be "conditioned by individuality"
(sakkayapaccaya asava).[30] This word for individuality (sakkaya) refers to the same unrealistic self-image as atta, as can be seen in a
passage defining the theory about individuality (sakkayaditthi) as
"he regards form (sensation, ideation, the activities, consciousness)
as self" (atta).[31] This means also, that the idea of self is created
through identification (a type of defense mechanism according to the
psychoanalysts): a person can, for example, identify himself with
his conscious processes (viññana) and believe that he as consciousness is a unique being that will never change or end. To identify
one's real nature with something that seems indestructible could
function as a defense against the frustration of death. But if he
understands that his consciousness, just like his other personality
factors and the natural elements, are nothing but processes, then the
influxes will stop flowing.[32] This proves that the ego-illusion is
a type of influx: when the illusion is eradicated, the influx will
end.

The belief in a self and theorizing about the nature of the self
is an influx.[33] Especially the types of influx called bhavasava
(influx of growth) and ditthasava (influx of speculation) are involved here, in the form of concern with the future, fright of death,
speculation about the nature of the self and the possibilities to
survive death, etc. This type of theorizing can be seen as a form of
defense against the prospect of death and is therefore comparable to
the defense mechanism of intellectualizing referred to above. So at
least this mechanism can safely be called an influx, but all kinds of
rationalization would seem closely related to the ditthasava, since
they are all verbal constructs used to make uncomfortable facts acceptable. The word ditthi usually refers to speculative explanations, mainly philosophical but certainly with personal reference
also.[34] Similarly, all kinds of compensatory dreams about a brighter
future for the ego can be called bhavasava.

In one of the Nikaya texts[35] it is pointed out that we have a
"disposition to ignorance" (avijjanusaya); because of this we do not
understand neutral sensations. This probably refers to the well-

known fact that uninteresting parts of the perceptual field remain unconscious.[36] But this type of "ignorance" may affect not only uninteresting but also uncomfortable facts; in that case we have the defense mechanism of repression and although this explanation was not given by the Buddha it could be called a form of avijjāsava to which all kinds of harmful misunderstandings belong.

The Sabbāsavasutta mentions one type of āsava as directly resulting from frustrating experiences like cold, hunger, thirst, unpleasant animals, and abusive words. These influxes "snould be expelled by endurance" (āsavā adhivāsanā pahātabbā),[37] which means that these frustrations should be patiently tolerated and no emotional or defensive reaction be resorted to. Normally we would try to defend ourselves in situations like these by means of aggressive or regressive behavior. The text does not specify the reactions expected, but for our argument it is a crucial fact that āsavā here are derived from frustrations. The regressive behavior just referred to would generally belong to the area of the kāmāsava, the "influx of sensuality and emotionality," and the aggressive defense in one Nikāya text[38] is described as resulting from aggressive and harmful thoughts (byāpādavitakka, vihimsāvitakka): these thoughts should be expelled, and so the influxes are got rid of "by elimination" (vinodanā). These two types of āsava are therefore not without relation to the defensive reactions.

These are the relations I have found between the concepts of defense and āsava. The latter are evidently not basically defense reactions, but they are to a great extent ego-involved attitudes and reactions aiming at asserting and inflating the ego. This ego-relatedness is so characteristic that one might well suggest "inflation" as a possible translation.[39] And the defense mechanisms might be one of the many types of reaction covered by that word.

Notes

1. In this article I shall consider only the teachings of the Pāli Nikāya literature.
2. Anna Freud, The Ego and the Mechanisms of Defense (New York: International University Press, 1936).
3. R.B. Cattell, Personality (New York: McGraw-Hill, 1950).
4. Ibid., p. 229.
5. Ibid., p. 247.
6. Ross Stagner, Psychology of Personality, 2nd ed. (New York: McGraw-Hill, 1948), p. 134.
7. Freud, The Ego.
8. For a fuller exposition see, for example, Rune E.A. Johansson, The Dynamic Psychology of Early Buddhism (London: Curzon Press, 1979), pp. 99-124.
9. Anguttara Nikāya, V, 343. Regarding the Nikāya works, the Pāli editions of the Pāli Text Society, London, have been referred to. The following abbreviations are used for the remainder of this article: A: Anguttara Nikāya, D: Dīgha Nikāya, M: Majjhima Nikāya, and S: Samyutta Nikāya.
10. A, I, 203.
11. Ibid., III, 446.

12. M, III, 285.
13. As in A, II, 149.
14. Johansson, Dynamic Psychology, pp. 158-161.
15. D, II, 305.
16. A, IV, 192-195.
17. D, III, 184.
18. A, III, 86f.
19. M, I, 133.
20. A, V, 157.
21. A, III, 181.
22. D, II, 316-356.
23. A, IV, 192.
24. S, II, 54.
25. M, I, 7.
26. As we see, for instance, in D, I, 84.
27. M, I, 12.
28. M, I, 10.
29. A, IV, 161.
30. D, III, 240.
31. M, I, 300.
32. S, III, 152; M, III, 31.
33. M, I, 8.
34. See Padmasiri de Silva, An Introduction to Buddhist Psychology (London: Macmillan, 1979), p. 96.
35. M, III, 285.
36. See discussion in Johansson, Dynamic Psychology, pp. 115ff.
37. M, I, 10.
38. M, I, 11.
39. See Johansson, Dynamic Psychology, p. 181.

PYSCHOLOGICAL OBSERVATIONS ON THE "LIFE OF GAUTAMA BUDDHA"

George R. Elder

Introduction

Toward the beginning of his long and important Histoire du
Bouddhisme Indien, Étienne Lamotte remarks: "Buddhism would be inex-
plicable if we did not place at its foundation a personality sufficiently powerful to have given it its impetus and to have stamped it
with those essential traits which have persisted through history."[1]
He means, of course, the "personality" of Siddhartha Gautama; and his
statement signifies the premier place that the study of this personality—properly speaking, a "psychology"—should have within the
field of Buddhist studies. It is a fact, however, that the psychological study of Gautama Buddha is virtually nonexistent; and studies
of the "Life" from whatever perspective are generally less common
than treatments of what the Buddha taught. Lamotte frankly admits
that it is "discouraging" to take up the study of the "Life."[2] E.J.
Thomas—credited with a classic in this area, The Life of Buddha as
Legend and History—tells us also that in the "Triple Jewel the great
problem has always been the person of Buddha."[3] For both of these
scholars, and for others as well, the problem is named in the full
title of Thomas's work: it is the problem of "legend and history."
What this means can be observed by way of an example from the
Mahāvastu. Its "history" informs us, it would seem, that Gautama re-
turned to Kapilavastu to visit his family sometime after the Enlightenment; but the likelihood of this event is embedded in a story of
much less likely proportions. The "legend" tells us that Gautama was
accompanied by roughly 20,000 disciples, one of whom flew on ahead to
reassure the family. Gautama himself, upon arriving, is said to have
taken a walk in the air at the height of a man, then to have risen to
the height of a tree in order to cause fire to issue from the top
half of his body and water to flow from his lower half—followed by
fire from the right side of his body and water from his left, through
twenty-two combinations![4] What is a scholar to make of such materials? He or she can say, as H.H. Wilson did in the nineteenth century, that it is "not impossible, after all, that Sakya Muni is an
unreal being, and that all that is related of him is as much a fiction as is that of his preceding migrations."[5] This is a conclusion
interestingly akin to that of the Mahāsaṅghika Buddhists at the
Second Council.[6] Generally, however, scholars today have concluded
that there really is an historical personality reflected in the
sources; but the facts of that history, obscured as they are by

legend, are largely inaccessible. As a result, the scholarly statements in this area of research are usually confined to a curious
amalgam: the history of the legend, or the likely development of unlikely events.

Here, I think, we can begin to see the usefulness of a psychological approach to the "Life." It is not that this approach has special access to historical facts which are, no doubt, gone. Rather,
psychology states that what remains—what all scholars refer to as
"imaginary"—is itself a kind of fact of the imagination and, with
the proper attitude, can reveal to our view the nature of the pysche.
If we notice that Buddhist legends were in the past popularly understood to refer to miraculous external events while we today see them
clearly as mental, then we can conclude that the less likely stories
of religion reflect a less conscious level of psychological development, i.e., unconscious contents. Further, if we accept the hypothesis—advanced by Carl Jung and analogous to the hypothesis of the
biological development of the body—that what has gone before us
psychologically is somehow preserved today within the deeper structure of our own psyches, then we arrive at the most significant conclusion of all: namely, that the imaginary material of the "Life of
Gautama Buddha" is not so much discouraging as it really encourages
us to explore its mysteries to gain insight into the nature of our
own unconscious selves.[7] Obviously, what I am calling the psychological approach is in some respects just the opposite of conventional
scholarship in the field of Buddhism; but it should be obvious, too,
that this way of working can compensate for the field's inability to
deal seriously with those materials in religion which religion itself
considers most important. Finally, I think it can be added that Buddhism might applaud our efforts: we will, after all—as the Platform
Sutra advises—be looking into ourselves to "know the mind and see
its true nature."[8]

The texts on the "Life of Gautama" are so rich and of such a var-
iety, however, that we had best focus upon a single one: the
Nidānakathā or Statement of Introduction (to a commentary on the
Jātaka), a fifth century, C.E., Singhalese compilation.[9] I will be
looking only at the second section of this text, the avidurenidāna or
"Introduction to Less Distant Events," which covers the life of
Siddhārtha from the time that he was said to have been in Tuṣita
Heaven up to the time of his Enlightenment. Indeed, for the purpose
of this article, there will be room to consider only some of the
issues within this section. There are, I think, advantages to our
choice of data. For one thing, Lamotte informs us that the text does
reflect its late date yet also preserves early Indian fragments; further, he tells us that the stories are not particularly full of
"exaggerations" and are, therefore, not biased in favor of our
psychological approach.[10] In addition, the text is readily available
to the reader in H.C. Warren's English translation prepared from V.
Fausboll's edition in Pāli.[11] Although the edition and translation
are dated, they are accurate enough for our purposes and will be used
without citation in what follows. Other philological materials will
be consulted where necessary; and, for the most part, Sanskrit forms
will be used.[12]

The Coming into Existence

According to the Ratnagotravibhāga, there are three significant
events which surround the Birth of Gautama: his "Descent from Tusita
Heaven," "Entrance into the Womb," and the "Rebirth" itself.[13] These
are the first three of "twelve acts" which must be performed by every
Buddha in his last, and human, lifetime. Thus, we are being told by
this Mahāyāna scheme--which does have Hīnayāna antecedents--that
there exists a paradigm or a model for becoming Buddha. Since becoming buddha means to become "awake"--a term recognized within Buddhism itself as a symbol for the psychological event of becoming
"conscious"--we can say that the "Last Life of a Buddha" is something
of a model for becoming a more conscious human being. But our section of the Nidānakathā opens with a view of a very strange world:
we find ourselves not on earth but in a heaven called "Tusita;" and
"Gautama" is not yet Gautama but a god. Much, of course, is being
assumed. Not only has the durenidāna already been told--those
distant events from the time that "Gautama" was "Sumedha" more than a
hundred thousand kalpas earlier--but also there is assumed the ancient Indian cosmology of a three-storied universe (of heavens,
earth, and hells) filled with sentient beings of five kinds (including gods and humans) whose "destinies" (gati) are determined by the
twin laws of karmic retribution and transmigration. While each of
these elements deserves particular psychological comment we cannot
give here, let it suffice to say that these cosmological details dif-
fer so much from what we know of our external universe--since the
time of Galileo--that they necessarily reveal to our view the mind
itself as a kind of "universe" filled with "living beings" and determined by "laws." Within that psychological universe, the Hero of the
story of consciousness is not yet conscious, not yet "born" as a "human here on earth." And so we are being told that there exists beyond our conscious lives and within the region of the unconscious
itself a divine potential for consciousness; it is what Jung has
called the archetype of the Self and what I think Buddhists themselves refer to as the "embryo of the Tathāgata" innate within us
all.[14]
    There is so much activity within this heaven! A "Buddha Uproar"
has gone up to announce the future birth of one who will become
"awake;" and the "gods of all ten thousand worlds come together into
one place" to ascertain who it is that will become a Buddha and to
"beseech him to become one." This is an extraordinary view of ourselves. It means that we are "called" to our vocation for psychological development by the "gods" and that we are called first of all
beyond our awareness within the depths of the unconscious psyche.
Further, an impending development of consciousness is obviously no
small event for the psyche: it has the support of all the forces of
libido which "come together," are constellated. Something of what it
actually means to be conscious is anticipated by "Gautama's" perform-
ing in Tusita the "Five Great Observations": He discriminates. With
each discrimination, however, there is imagery of the "middle" or of
"union" or of the "fourth of four;" and this imagery points to the
psychological wholeness--the conscious integrating of previously unconscious contents--that realization of the Self brings. For example, the "country" chosen is the "Middle Country" which probably is

located historically in the foothills of the Himālayas in northeast
India but where—says our text—are "born" all Buddhas, all Pratyeka-
buddhas, all Arhats, Cakravartins, and higher classes, i.e., all
those who are perceived to possess a superior development of consciousness.

The most significant discriminations have to do with the future
family. "Gautama" chooses the high ksatriya class and a father named
"Suddhodana" who is said to be a "king." While historically it is
likely that Siddhartha Gautama was of the warrior class and that his
father's name was Suddhodana, it is not very likely that the father
was actually a "king."[15] Here, then, a psychological element intrudes perhaps merely to show the extraodinary power and value of one
who is to become "awake;" and we are struck by the symbolic contrast
with the Christian legend of Jesus Christ who is also associated with
consciousness as "Light of the world" but whose value is initially
obscured in a manger. It should be said, however, that Gautama's
father as "king" is an image which also introduces the profound ambiguity of Cakravartin or Universal Monarch psychology yet to emerge
in the story. The choice of mother is also colored by the psyche.
Her name is "Māyā," a name Buddhists themselves make nothing of and
which, therefore, is quite likely an historical fact. But Māyā means
"Illusion," a fact that has caused some stir among scholars, but to
no great consequence.[16] From a psychological point of view, however,
she could not be better named: this "Mother" sits very close to the
nonrational realities of the unconscious which, of course, is capable
of being projected as our own "illusions." And She is present
throughout the "Life," I suggest, in her symbolical fertile form as
"tree," as "earth," as the "full moon."[17]

A personal note may be signaled by the fact that the mother is
said to "die" only seven days after the birth of Siddhārtha; the
child then is raised by Māyā's sister, Prajāpatī, who was also a member of Suddhodana's harem. E.F. Edinger, a Jungian analyst, has
written about the psychology of the "lost parent" in relationship to
the uncertain presence of the father in the "Life of Christ":

> When the personal father is missing and, more particularly,
> when he is completely unknown, as may happen with an ille-
> gitimate child, there is no layer of personal experience to
> mediate between the ego and the numinous image of the arche-
> typal father. A kind of hole is left in the psyche through
> which emerge the powerful archetypal contents of the collec-
> tive unconscious . . . . If, however, the ego can survive
> this danger, the "hole in the psyche" becomes a window pro-
> viding insights into the depths of being.[18]

For us, this means that the "death" of Gautama's mother may indeed be
an historical fact that leads to a certain psychological understanding. It gives meaning to the inordinate influence of the father over
the son in the story; but, most important, it provides an understanding of Gautama's peculiar quest. Missing that connection to the
"feminine," which only the personal mother can provide, Siddhārtha
Gautama will be forced to seek for Her—and eventually find that
transpersonal Mother beneath the "Tree of Enlightenment" through an
"earth-shaking" religious experience, at "full moon."

It must be said, however, that Jung has noticed this feature of "death" in the "Life of Gautama" and suggests that it refers to the archetype of the "dual mother," i.e., the psychological pattern that the unconscious connection to the personal mother must in fact "die" if we are to do discover the "other mother" within the creative depths of the soul.[19] In this view, Prajāpatī as "stepmother" provides us with the symbol of the Mother within. Since we are dealing with the pyschology of religious materials, I think it is no contradiction to say that both Jung's interpretation and what we have said above fit the meaning of the "Life"; together, they reveal the richness of Buddhist legend and the fact that personal and transpersonal levels of meaning coexist. We can even add a possible cultural significance. It could be said that India itself suffered a "loss" of "feminine" values with the coming of the Āryans a thousand years before the time of Buddha: those broad-hipped fertility goddesses made of clay (surviving among the archaeological finds of the Indus Valley) were no doubt crushed by those powerful invaders who prayed chiefly to a male god Indra for the "masculine" virtues of war. In this way, we can say that Gautama's personal problem is symbolic of the collective problem of his people. His solution, then, will be a solution for his people; and they will revere him.

The Youth

Since we are working in a limited way, I would like next to consider some of the events surrounding the youth of Gautama: in the Ratnagotravibhāga, they are expressed in the "acts" called "Skill in Worldly Arts" and "Enjoyment of the Women." In the first of these, Gautama is sixteen years of age and is called upon by his people to demonstrate his capacities in the "manly art" of war. The Prince responds without the need of training by exhibiting what the Nidānakathā refers to as a "twelvefold skill" in the art of archery; other versions of the "Life" inform us that Gautama's skill includes such things as being able alone to string a bow that would otherwise take the strength of a thousand men.[20] Obviously, we are in the arena of legend here and are being told a story of the strength and readiness of the Self as it is actualized on "earth." But we are also being treated to a view of what is necessary for the development of consciousness: one must develop the skills that are associated with one's station in life. There is no premature "religious" attitude here, no monastic introversion in youth which would sap the development of the ego. Instead, we are being told that the divine "vocation" of the psyche includes the establishment of a confident ego capable of engaging even in an extroverted way the "worldly" reality which challenges it.

These conclusions follow, of course, from the fact that we are observing a paradigm or an archetypal portrait of what is required for psychological development. And what we have said with regard to the "Skill in Worldly Arts" must apply to the "Enjoyment of the Women." The scene in the Nidānakathā is one of sybaritic luxury:

And the king built three palaces for the Future Buddha, suited to the three seasons,--one of nine stories, another of seven

> stories, and another of five stories. And he provided him with forty thousand dancing girls.

Other versions have Gautama claim:

> I used no sandalwood that was not of Benares, my dress was of Benares cloth, my tunic, my under-robe, and cloak. Night and day a white parasol was held over me so that I should not be touched by cold or heat, by dust or weeds or dew.[21]

Put simply, these materials are telling us that unless one develops the capacity to enjoy the sensual life--the wine, women, and song most appropriately enjoyed in one's youth--there will be no Buddha-hood. What remarkable stories these must be for a Westerner to hear! One imagines the Christian youth looking to the "Life of Christ" for insight into how to lead the proper kind of adolescence and young adulthood only to find that the guiding Hero is already thirty years old and, seemingly, without a youth at all. Should this young Christian search the scriptures and find that single story of a twelve-year-old Jesus who rebelled against his parents to teach a day in the temple, he will find here no adequate image around which to express burgeoning young life. Thus, we can begin to see the usefulness of a comparative psychology of religion; for such investigations as this provide a sharper sense of what is valued in each tradition, what the gaps are, where the biases lie. But it has to be admitted that what we have just analyzed from assumptions that are Buddhist is not what one hears from Buddhists themselves who tend to be adult monastics teaching indiscriminately the adult psychology of monasticism. Daisaku Ikeda, although a lay Buddhist leader in Japan today, sees fit to remark about these matters only that they give "some indica-tion of the care and lavishness with which the young prince was brought up."[22] It may be, however, that what orthodox Buddhism tends to ignore in the paradigm of the "Life of Buddha" is compensated within the religion itself by the unorthodox "sensual" traditions of Buddhist Tantra.[23]

At the same time, there is a profound ambiguity in all of this. Gautama's youth is full of pleasure--indeed, it is "too full." His skills come too easily, without the need to train; three palaces are more than enough and forty thousand dancing girls are really too many for one man. After all, the people had demanded that the Prince demonstrate his skill in archery because they were worried that "Siddhattha is wholly given over to pleasure" and would not be able to respond realistically in time of war. In the Aṅguttaranikāya, the Buddha tells his congregation, as Thomas translates: "I was deli-cate, O monks, extremely delicate, excessively delicate."[24] A more literal translation might read: "I was refined (sukhumālo) . . . most refined (paramasukhumālo), extremely refined (accantasukhumālo)."[25] But in either case, the meaning is clear: young Gautama's life is "excessive," he has been necessarily caught in an "extreme." Edinger helps us to understand that what we are ob-serving is the psychology of inflation. He writes:

> I use the term inflation to describe the attitude and the state which accompanies the identification of the ego with

the Self. It is a state in which something small (the ego)
has arrogated to itself the qualities of something larger
(the Self) and hence is blown up beyond the limits of its
proper size.[26]

Yet this analyst goes on to explain--in a manner consistent with the
meaning of our Buddhist model--that the act of inflation is a kind of
"necessary crime" that prompts the ego to develop fully to prepare it
for the drama of what has yet to unfold.

    Behind the inflation in the "Life of Gautama" is the driving
force of the father. He has heard from prophecy that his son actually has the potential to become one of two kinds of men: a Buddha
or a Cakravartin. This latter term means literally "Wheel Turner"
and may be rendered more loosely perhaps as "One who rules over the
sphere of his power"; Warren translates in an interpretive way, "Universal Monarch."[27] To become cakravartin is to become a king who
rules everywhere; and he is a figure supported by the story that such
a one possesses a "divine wheel" which rolls in each of the four directions conquering all in its path even to the surrounding sea.[28]
Hearing of the two possibilities for his son, the father knows exactly what he himself wants:

    It will never do for my son to become a Buddha. What I
    would wish to see is my son exercising sovereign rule and
    authority over the four great continents and the two
    thousand attendant isles, and walking through the heavens
    surrounded by a retinue thirty-six leagues in circumference.

Suddhodhana's inflated attitude is obvious; he is caught in what Buddhist doctrine calls the problem of "I and mine." While this sort of
father may have been experienced personally by Siddhārtha--if the
"loss" of his mother's influence is a personal loss--this "father" is
surely also the archetypal image of obstructing authority. Without
reflection, Suddhodana simply knows what is "best" for his son: if
Siddhārtha has the opportunity to perpetuate to a higher degree what
the father, as king, has accomplished in part, then that is the proper course. But what an extraordinary expectation this is: for the
father, in wanting what is "best" for his son, is also willing to
sacrifice his son's potential for Buddhahood, i.e., he is willing to
sacrifice his son's own consciousness! Hearing further from prophecy
that Siddhārtha's Buddhahood is inevitable should he see "four
sights"--an old man, a sick man, a dead man, and a monk--Suddhodana
sets a guard and proclaims: "From this time forth . . . let no such
persons be allowed to come near my son." And so it is in this context that we view the Prince with his palaces, his fine clothes, the
women--the image of an over-protected son who is shielded from reality, and who arrogates to himself more than belongs to a mere human
being.

    The reader may have noticed, however, a secret connection between
the opposites, "Buddha or Cakravartin." Both are surrounded by the
imagery of psychological wholeness: Buddha, as we have observed, by
the imagery of the "fourth" and the "middle"; the Cakravartin by the
imagery of the "four directions" and the wheel as "circle." Further,
there exists an ancient tradition in India which states that the body

of a Great Being (mahāsattva) possesses "thirty-two characteristics and eighty minor marks": e.g., a protuberance on the crown of the head called usnīsa, a tuft or "treasure of hair" (ūrnākośa) at the middle of the forehead, the upper part of his body "leonine," the mark of a "wheel rim" on hands and feet.[29] Both the Buddha and universal king possess these marks; and their peculiarities are what one sees in the iconography of Buddhist art. But there remains a critical difference between these two figures: the Buddha is "awake" by definition--which means that his opposite, the Cakravartin, is not. Thus, we are shown in most striking fashion that the inflated state does arrogate to itself and imitate the wholeness of the Self; that is the secret of its attraction and power. But the inflated one is also unconscious and does not really know what he is doing. Finally, with regard to this imagery, we think again of a cultural significance. That "wheel" of the "Wheel Turner" is no doubt associated with the coming of Āryan chariots; and it may be that we are observing in the "Life" at this point a crisis of libido within Indian culture generally or, at least, within the ksatriya class. Indigenous "feminine" India has been conquered in fact by the time of Gautama: but where will the libido, freed from this historical task, flow now? Will it be channeled through the symbol of the "Cakravartin" and contine to conquer even to the "ends of the earth?" Or will the psychological energy be influenced by the image of "Buddha" and turn back, introvert, and conquer instead an inner world of ignorance? The Buddhist story, of course, turns finally in the direction of developing consciousness but also, as we shall see, turns back to recover consciously the once-conquered "feminine."

The Breakthrough

A state of inflation cannot really last and, like a balloon, must sooner or later burst against the demands of reality. For Siddhārtha, this reality is expressed by the imagery of the "four sights"-- the old man, the sick man, the dead man, and the monk--which the future Buddha did see despite his father's best efforts. Objectively these sights are not extraordinary; but they have an extraordinary effect upon an "extremely refined" Prince. Our text says that Gautama was "agitated in heart"; the Aṅguttaranikāya has him say, "As I reflected on it, all the elation in youth (yobbanamado, literally, "intoxication of youth") utterly disappeared."[30] Inflation turns to deflation; or, as Jung would put it--borrowing a term from Heraclitus--Siddhārtha Gautama experiences an enantiodromia. Jung explains:

> I use the term enantiodromia for the emergence of the unconscious opposite in the course of time. This characteristic phenomenon practically always occurs when an extreme, onesided tendency dominates conscious life; in time an equally powerful counter-position is built up, which first inhibits the conscious performance and subsequently breaks through the conscious control.[31]

What this means for our story is that Gautama's "extremity of pleasure" gives way to an "extremity of pain." It is an event in the

"Life" expressed in Buddhist doctrine as the "pleasure" (sukha),
first of the Four Delusions, which must give way to "pain" (duhkha),
first of the Four Noble Truths. Indeed, in my opinion, it is only in
the light of the psychology of Gautama's "Life" that the extremity of
the first Noble Truth—that "all is pain"—makes sense. But the pain
is paradigmatic. Without it, Gautama would not discover the two
sides of life and deserve his title of being "awake." Without the
experience of both pleasure and pain, he would not be able to grasp
something of the nature of the "opposites" which shape our experience. Nor, without duhkha, would this overprotected Prince feel the
sting that will drive him away from the authority of his father—to
seek that Mother who is truly "lost" in the midst of all this Cakravartin psychology.

At the age of twenty-nine, Gautama leaves the "household life"
and—after six long and difficult years—finally becomes "awake" at
the "dawning of the sun." Timing is critical, says our text: it is
the lush spring season, the same season as Gautama's birth; it is the
time of full moon, as it was at the birth but also at the conception.
In other words, it is the time of the fertile Mother who creates in
her natural way—not as we have planned but . . . when it is time.[32]
It is also "evening" (sayanha) when, symbolically but also literally,
the sharpness of consciousness is dulled and the unconscious begins
to act without obstruction. Gautama rises up like a "lion"—for
ancient India, an animal of strength and courage—and proceeds to the
"Tree" of his Enlightenment. It would seem that this Tree is assimi-
lated by the cosmological symbolism of Mt. Meru, which traditionally
is said to stand at the center of a flat, round earth.[33] For, around
this special Tree, lies the "broad earth" like a "huge cart-wheel
lying on its hub." What a wonderful way to inform us that Siddhartha's breakthrough will require his wholeness but also his facing the
psychology of a "Wheel Turner"! Yet it is also here that the youth-
ful development of a strong ego will begin to pay off; the work ahead
will not be easy. When Gautama stood on the southern side of that
earth, "Instantly the southern half of the world sank, until it
seemed to touch the Avīci hell, while the northern half rose to the
highest of the heavens." He walked around to each of the four directions only to find that the same upsetting event recurred. Where,
the text is asking, is that "immovable spot" on which all the Buddhas
find security? And the answer comes: it is at the center, sitting
down cross-legged on the earth with one's back to the tree, facing
the East. In other words, in the midst of an individuation crisis,
we must make every effort to find the place of the Self which values
both conscious and unconscious processes, to stay in touch with the
"feminine" or feeling reality of the psyche, to anticipate our destiny with confidence. Gautama is perhaps too confident; he resolves:

Let my skin, and sinews, and bones become dry, and welcome!
and let all the flesh and blood in my body dry up! but never
from this seat will I stir, until I have attained the supreme
and absolute wisdom!

And at precisely that moment, Māra appeared.

"Māra"—a term which literally means "killing"—is the name of a
deity sometimes referred to as "Lord of this world." The epithet is

derived from the fact that this male god's heaven is said to be located at the top of the Realm of Desire. Gods there are generally referred to as paranirmitavaśavartin because they enjoy "having power over what has been created by others."[34] And so we can see that Māra is a greedy, powerful god willing to kill for what he wants. What he wants now is that Gautama not become Enlightened. He exclaims:

> "Prince Siddhattha is desirous of passing beyond my control, but I will never allow it!" [He] went and announced the news to his army, and sounding the Māra war-cry, drew out for battle . . . [and] the host swept on like a flood to overwhelm the Great Being (mahāsatta).

It is significant that here Gautama is called a "Great Being," for that reminds us that mahāsattva is an epithet common to Buddha and Cakravartin. It is significant because Māra is a perfect portrait of a "divine" Cakravartin, the warrior who conquers all in his path. In this way, we begin to see a secret connection between Gautama and the divine adversary just as we have seen a secret connection between Gautama and the Wheel Turner. But there are direct hints of this relationship if one considers the data psychologically. Māra first appeared in the Nidānakathā as Gautama departed from his home; the text reads: "'I shall catch you,' thought Māra, 'the very first time you have a lustful, malicious, or unkind thought.' And, like an every-present shadow, he followed after, ever on the watch for some slip." This god represents the "shadowy" unconscious side of the Prince: Siddhartha Gautama's lust or greed (kāma), his malice (vyāpāda), and cruelty (vihimsa)—aspects of the power complex which caused his inflation and which brought about his painful fall.[35] The same psychological point is made when Māra advised his army not to try to conquer Gautama from "in front": "We will attack him from behind"—i.e., from the side of this man's psyche that is not yet conscious.

Of course, Gautama at this point in the story does not really know what is happening to him; that is his problem. He is not yet "enlightened" about the reality of the Shadow and does not yet grasp the meaning of his pain. Thus, he must go on "fighting"—we have two Cakravartins here!—with an adversary he thinks is outside himself. Were he to see that Māra is also Gautama, there would be no conflict; a dangerous god would become a content of consciousness—and an aspect of the Self would be realized. At the same time, this ancient Indian would discover something about the nature of "deity" as an external manifestation of one's own unconscious; as the tantric Buddhists put it, the "gods do not exist" apart from the Mind of Enlightenment.[36] Finally, he would know that a collective unconscious force lay behind his people's attitude toward life and behind the specific obstructions of his father.[37]

It remains to be seen if the imagery of our story supports in any way our analysis along the lines of a pyschology of integration as opposed to a psychology of repression. We are told that when Māra's "nine storms" are unsuccessful at driving Gautama away from his "immovable spot," the deity "drew near"—the experience deepened in its intensity. But at the same time the experience opened up into a curious dialogue which announces relationship and the beginning of an integration process. Reminiscent in particular of Job's dialogue

with the Old Testament YHVH, a sort of legal debate takes place.
Here, the god claims Siddhārtha's spot: "Siddhattha arise from this
seat! It does not belong to you, but to me." Gautama answers in
kind, "This seat does not belong to you, but to me." Gautama then
goes on to ask if Māra has any "witness" (Sanskrit, sākṣī) to his
having done good deeds as support for his claim—whereupon Māra turns
to his army which eagerly perjures itself, "I am his witness! I am
his witness!" There is in this event, and in the story of Job as
well, a sober message about ourselves: we naively assume that archetypal forces of the psyche will respond to logic and that they are
subject to the reasonable constraints of conventional law. But
Gautama's naivete is necessary; it creates a dilemma for him that
leads to unexpected consequences. Very cleverly now, Māra simply
turns the question back at his opponent: "Siddhattha, who is witness
to your having given donations?" Siddhārtha, of course, is alone:
he has left his family, and his small band of followers called the
"Band of Five" have left him. All that remains is his resolve. But
it must be obvious that Gautama's vigorous "will" to Enlightenment is
precisely what evoked—almost like a prayer—the "will" of Māra to
oppose him. It had happened before as the Prince left home: faced
with a heavy gate, he had claimed "I will" leap over the wall, his
courtier claimed "I will," his horse claimed "I will"—and, then,
there stood Māra.

From all of this, perhaps we can venture some conclusions about
the mysterious operations of the power complex especially when there
is the psychological demand for its conscious integration. As long
as the ego is simply identified with the complex, there is no apparent problem. But as soon as it moves toward becoming conscious of
this reality, the complex seems to move away from the ego and confronts it in projection: paradoxically, one begins to see outside
one's self the unconscious content with which one is unconsciously
identified. A "battle of wills" ensues and, locked in contention
with one's own self, one falls into a kind of psychological paraly-
sis—the sort of standoff depicted by our story. At this point, however, Gautama is forced to do something that no Cakravartin would be
expected to do:

> And drawing forth his right hand from beneath his priestly
> robe, he stretched it out towards the mighty earth, and
> said, "Are you witness, or are you not, to my having given
> a great seven-hundred-fold donation in my Vessantara exis-
> tence?"

This is that scene which became a favorite source for Buddhist sculp-
ture—the Great Being with his golden skin sitting cross-legged and
reaching out over his right knee for help. Gautama reached out beyond the conflict for grace from a "feminine" reality; and some versions say he "touched" Her.[38]

> And the mighty earth thundered, "I bear you witness!" with
> a hundred, a thousand, a hundred thousand roars, as if to
> overwhelm the army of Māra. . . . And the followers of Māra
> fled away in all directions.

The "earth," Pṛthivī, is a goddess in her own right within Indian religion; but here she symbolizes one man's giving up of "will" and becoming disidentified from compulsive "masculine" power—and Māra and his army flee. The withdrawal of the "army" outside Gautama would symbolize the withdrawal of a projection; but, just as our story suggests, projections are withdrawn only when the conscious position is relativized and one gets in "touch" with the unconscious Source of "illusions." That She should be a supporting "witness" may allude to an archetypal expression for the gaining of insight. There is, after all, in the Christian Gospel of John the forensic figure of the Paraclete, the saving "witness" within us—a "spirit of truth," "comforter"—rooted in the feminine figure of Wisdom in the Book of Proverbs.[39] And so, in closing, we seem to have come upon what might be called the Soul of Buddhism: She is that prajñā, "Insight" or "Wisdom," whom the late Tantrics say we must embrace, whom the Mahāyānists generally say we should worship as Prajñāpāramitā, and who—says the Hīnayāna "Life of Siddhārtha Gautama"—is the Mother of all Buddhas.

NOTES

1. Étienne Lamotte, Histoire du Bouddhisme Indien (Louvain: Institut Orientaliste, 1958), p. 16.

2. Ibid.

3. Edward J. Thomas, The Life of Buddha, 3rd ed. (London: Routledge and Kegan Paul, 1949), p. 211.

4. Ibid., pp. 98–99. The Mahāvastu, trans. J. J. Jones (London: Luzac and Co., Ltd., 1956), vol. 3, pp. 93ff.

5. Thomas, The Life, p. xvi.

6. Nalinaksha Dutt, Buddhist Sects in India (Calcutta: K. L. Mukhopadhyay, 1970), pp. 75ff.

7. Consider the following comment by C. G. Jung, The Collected Works, eds. Sir Herbert Read et al., vol. 11: Psychology and Religion: West and East (Princeton: Princeton University, 1969), par. 228:

> Naturally, it never occurs to these critics that their way of approach is incommensurable with their object. They think they have to do with rational facts, whereas it entirely escapes them that it is and always has been primarily a question of irrational psychic phenomena. That this is so can be seen plainly enough from the unhistorical character of the gospels, whose only concern was to represent the miraculous figure of Christ as graphically and impressively as possible. . . . At a very early stage, therefore, the real Christ vanished behind the emotions and projections that swarmed about him from far and near; immediately and almost without trace he was absorbed into the surrounding religious systems and moulded into their archetypal exponent. He became the collective figure whom the unconscious of his contemporaries expected to appear, and for this reason it is pointless to ask who he "really" is.

8. The Platform Sutra of the Sixth Patriarch, trans. P. B.

Yampolsky (New York: Columbia University, 1967), pp. 128, 132.

9. Lamotte, Histoire, 731ff.

10. Ibid.

11. Buddhism in Translations, trans. H. C. Warren (Cambridge: Harvard University, 1896; reprint ed., New York: Atheneum, 1970), pp. 38-83. V. Fausboll, ed., The Jātaka (London: Trubner and Co., 1877), pp. 47-77.

12. The following dictionaries have been consulted: T. W. Rhys-Davids, et al., eds., The Pāli Text Society's Pāli-English Dictionary (1921-1925) and Monier Monier-Williams, A Sanskrit-English Dictionary (1899).

13. Alex Wayman, "Buddhism" in Historia Religionum, eds. C. J. Bleeker and G. Widengren (Leiden: E. J. Brill, 1971), vol. 2, p. 393.

14. See Jung, Collected Works, vol. 17: The Development of Personality, par. 284-323. The Lion's Roar of Queen Śrīmālā, trans. A. Wayman and H. Wayman (New York: Columbia University, 1974), pp. 42ff.

15. Thomas, The Life, pp. 20, 228.

16. Ibid., p. 25n.

17. See Erich Neumann, The Great Mother (Princeton: Princeton University Press, 1963).

18. Edward F. Edinger, Ego and Archetype (Baltimore: Penguin Books, 1972), p. 132.

19. Jung, Collected Works, vol. 5: Symbols of Transformation, par. 494-497.

20. Thomas, The Life, p. 48.

21. Ibid., p. 47.

22. Daisaku Ikeda, The Living Buddha, trans. B. Watson (New York: Weatherhill, 1976), p. 13. This work is called an "Interpretive Biography" and is significant for attempting to go behind traditional Buddhist imagery; but, as our example shows, it does not go very far.

23. See George Elder, "Problems of Language in Buddhist Tantra," History of Religions 15, no. 3 (February, 1976): 231-250. See also my discussion of Buddhist Tantra in "The Significance of Jung's Psychology for the Study of Eastern Religions" in Jung and Eastern Religions, ed. G. Williams (forthcoming).

24. Thomas, The Life, p. 47.

25. R. Morris, ed., Aṅguttara-nikāya (London: Pāli Text Society, 1885), part 1, p. 145.

26. Edinger, Ego and Archetype, p. 7.

27. See Thomas, The Life, p. 219.

28. Ibid.

29. Wayman, "Buddhism," pp. 393-394.

30. Thomas, The Life, p. 51; Aṅguttara-nikāya, p. 145.

31. Jung, Collected Works, vol. 6: Psychological Types, par. 709.

32. See Erich Neumann, "The Moon and Matriarchal Consciousness" in Fathers and Mothers, ed. P. Berry (Zurich: Spring Publications, 1973), pp. 40-63.

33. See A. L. Basham, The Wonder that was India (New York: Grove Press, 1954), pp. 488-489.

34. Lamotte, Histoire, p. 761.

35. For discussion of the "power problem" with some references to

Buddhism, see M. Esther Harding, Psychic Energy (Princeton: Princeton University, 1963), pp. 196-237.

36. Consider the following verse translated by A. Wayman from what he calls the "Guhyasamāja-nidāna-kārikā" in Yoga of the Guhyasamājatantra (Delhi: Motilal Banarsidass, 1977), p. 11: "Of the different gods and goddesses generated by him and his family, neither the gods nor goddesses exist, but are displayed for the sake of sentient beings." This means that all deities are "generated" as aspects of the Lord or as aspects of bodhicitta, Mind of Enlightenment; see also pp. 246-251.

37. Jung says the following in his Collected Works, vol. 17: The Development of Personality, par. 309:

> The story of the Temptation clearly reveals the nature of the psychic power with which Jesus came into collision; it was the power-intoxicated devil of the prevailing Caesarean psychology that led him into dire temptation in the wilderness. This devil was the objective psyche that held all the peoples of the Roman Empire under its sway, and that is why it promised Jesus all the kingdoms of the earth, as if it were trying to make a Caesar of him. Obeying the inner call of his vocation, Jesus voluntarily exposed himself to the assaults of the imperialistic madness that filled everyone, conqueror and conquered alike. In this way he recognized the nature of the objective psyche which had plunged the whole world into misery and had begotten a yearning for salvation that found expression even in the pagan poets. Far from suppressing or allowing himself to be suppressed by this psychic onslaught, he let it act on him consciously, and assimilated it.

See also par. 319 for a specific parallel between Christ's Temptation and the Māra episode.

38. The Mahāvastu, vol. 2, p. 264:

> Then, monks, the Bodhisattva, fearless, undismayed, without fear and terror drew out his golden arm from beneath his robe, and with his webbed and jewel-like right hand, which had copper-coloured nails and a bright streak, and which was the colour of lac, was soft like cotton to the touch, and endowed with the root of virtue acquired in several kotis of kalpas, he thrice stroked his head; thrice he stroked his couch and thrice he stroked the ground.

See George Elder, "'Grace' in Martin Luther and Tantric Buddhism" in Cross and Lotus, ed. G. W. Houston (forthcoming).

39. "The Gospel According to John," trans. R. Brown in The Anchor Bible vol. 29a (Garden City: Doubleday, 1970), pp. 1135ff.

THE CONCEPT OF CITTA IN SOME EARLY BUDDHIST TEXTS AND JUNG'S ANALYTICAL PSYCHOLOGY

Jan T. Ergardt

Introduction

The aim of this article is twofold. First, it is to describe and explain human processes in the religious life by using contexts containing the word citta, mind. The presupposition is that its contexts may give some information about its processes. This use of citta should not be understood as a depreciation of the precise analyses in commentarial literature and onward. Rather, it is assumed that contexts within the chosen sources give enough basis for the study of human beings on the way from ego to nibbāna, that is, for the study of human processes in religious life, not for the study of the full and exact meaning of doctrinal concepts.

Secondly, I intend to apply Jungian categories in descriptions and explanations of Buddhist religious life as presented in ancient Buddhist texts. Those who have experienced the difficulties of teaching Buddhism to Western students in a Christian culture may realize that analytical psychology, through studies of the mental life in categories of processes, can contribute to our understanding of this great religion based on a philosophy that gives room for psychology. Within this religion we find a unique solution for the great problem of man and his destiny.

> In the comparative study of religion the subcontinent of India has the distinction of being the place of origin and the continuing homeland of an estimate of human nature and destiny which differs fundamentally from the interpretations current in other lands.[1]

Human nature and thoughts of destiny are correlated as is the view of the religious goal.[2] Within this frame of man's religious capacity built upon his own experience of the interdependence of human nature and human destiny, we have chosen to focus on the function of mind through the concept of citta. This leads to a meeting point between cosmic and individual levels and brings the perspective of macrocosmos-microcosmos to the foreground.

The Choice of citta

In our main source, the Majjhima-Nikāya, the word citta itself or in compounds occurs in around 1,500 contexts, which can be reduced to

some basic coherent patterns. The important coherence within the
Majjhima-Nikāya can be illustrated by its Sutta 148. Thirty-six processes, constituting human beings, are mentioned. Among them are
mano, mind and/or thought, and viññāna, mind and/or consciousness.
It is said about either of them that they are not-self (anattā).
Citta, however, is not mentioned, whereas the idea of this very sermon by the Buddha becomes clear at the end through the often recurring phrase, "the minds (cittāni) of as many as sixty monks were
released from influxes with no grasping (remaining)."[3] Citta expresses the experince of nibbāna-release.[4] The "I" which is referred
to in the vimutti-process as it is given through arahant-formula A
and its contexts brings into focus citta as being released. Within
the Majjhima-Nikāya this is the case in twenty-one of the Suttas.[5]
It reinforces the view held by Johansson who looks upon citta as "the
core of our personality around which all personal processes re-
volve."[6] Further he says:

> Citta is one of the important words in early Buddhist psychology
> and usually translated by "mind." The meaning is, however, some-
> what unclear, and the concept seems sometimes imperfectly inte-
> grated in the Buddhist system.[7]

It should be added that throughout this article we will use only
the word "mind" as a hypothetical translation. This will not overshadow the ambiguity of the meaning but keep us close to the aim of
this study: the processes toward the holistic view of human beings
and their capacity for release, the experience of such a release, and
the effects thereof. While other concepts are fairly well defined,
citta is vague and many-sided, just like human beings. Therefore it
is supposed that citta can lead us to a certain understanding of man,
functioning within a given, eternal frame of reference. It may also
be intimated that this frame of reference for the Buddhist is dhamma,
that which holds, supports—"dhāretī ti dhamma."[8] Before we look at
the vimutti-process in the Majjhima-Nikāya, we will briefly meet,
with the help of Pannasanipata of the Theragāthā,[9] a conflicted man
in a dialogue between "I" and citta.

A Dialogue Between "I" and citta

The group of fifty verses is ascribed to Tālaputa. They show
both his "I-activity"[10] and an outspoken dialogue between him and his
citta.[11] In the "I-activity" we meet a man who, obviously, has made
his choice; he has gone from "home to homelessness." Consequently
there are outward signs of the life of a bhikkhu. Being included in
Theragāthā he cannot be a below average bhikkhu. Still within these
verses the great problem is the lack of correspondence between the
outward expressions of his chosen way of life and his inward processes of spiritual life. The outward and inward are contrasted in
at least six verses. The inward problems are all-pervading. The
ideal state is only to be dreamt about. Such is the problem for this
very "I."
He should see all existence as impermanent.[12] He is a muni who
knows that he is attaining perfection but who has not removed

(hantvā) craving, anger, and bewilderment, and who, therefore, is not yet living happily (sukhin).[13] The goal is still lying ahead. Expected experience is intimated by phrases connected through the word sahasā, meaning forcibly or suddenly. It is connected to "I shall destroy Māra and his army."[14] That will happen when he, also suddenly, "has grasped the seer's weapon, which is made by knowledge."[15] Then, he believes, he will suddenly be transformed by knowledge.[16] This is equal to sitting among the good ones, who pursue dhamma (dhammagaru).[17] They are at one with dhamma, while he is still only trying to adjust, and this is the conflict reflected in his innermost experience. When will he see the dhammas as burning things (dhamme ādittato) in the light of knowledge?[18] The things, factors, dhammas without measure (amite dhamme), whether internal or external, should be seen as they really are.[19]

This is the situation: our friend, a bhikkhu named Tālaputa, is walking the path trodden by seers, looking forward to the moment when his mind will be centered around the attainment of "the undying" (amatassa pattiyā samcintaye); so too, when his extraordinary psychic powers will be unimpeded, and outward things, signs, and causes, centered around an illusory ego, will appear irrelevant to him in comparison to the greatest inner freedom. To sum up, Tālaputa looks forward to the moment when he will acquire the great seer's teaching and with it the experience of satisfaction.[20] At this point in time dialogue between the man and his mind becomes even more intense. Mind has begged him (yācati) to give up worldly life, to be a pabbajita, and he has followed its intention and tasted the meditational life.[21] "Even then you are not satisfied with me, mind."[22] There is disturbance within the process. In eight verses with the phrase "so you used to beg me, mind," we can see what mind looked for.[23] It begged of him all the good activities including good processes, outwardly of course but, more important, inwardly. For example, the development (bhāvehi) of human capacities, culminating in threefold knowledge[24] in the Buddha's teaching (tisso vijjā phusa buddhasāsane), of which the final process is release from influxes (āsava), must be regarded as equivalent to nibbāna, or development (bhāvehi) of obtaining the deathless (state).[25] Mind has begged of him a close observation of the factors as originally suffering. He should be devoid of their causes.[26] It begs of him to stop mind's (ceto) preoccupation with thinking (mano) by way of insight and to understand the impermanent as suffering, the emptiness as not-self, the pain as destruction.[27] In all prescribed circumstances of life, mind begs of him the well-controlled self (susamvutatta).[28]

Now we meet man in conflict. Mind is tempting him toward the impermanent (anicca) and transient, called "cala," whereas "acala" is often an attribute of nibbāna. In fact, mind is obstructing man from reaching his goal.[29] This process within a state of conflict must be calmed down. The mind, which is formless, far going, wandering alone (arūpa duramgama ekacāri), must be guided by the thinking of (abhimana) nibbāna.[30] He has chosen his way of life in obedience with his citta, and now that same citta begs him to go back to the old way of life.[31] In a good sense he has done what citta asked of him throughout many births (bahūsu jātisu), knowing that samsāra's suffering is caused by mind, whether we reach human existences, deva-like existence, or we reach downward existences.[32] It is all very frustrating and man accuses his mind of playing with him as with one who is out of his mind (ummattaka), blaming mind with the question, "And yet, how have I ever failed you, mind?"[33]

But all this belongs to the past. Now it is time for man to make a summary statement: "I shall control it."[34] He has learned by experience. The teacher has made him see things in the world as they are; "mind, make me take to the victor's teaching."[35] This is something new for the process of citta; it is governed, under the control (vasa) of the great seer's teaching (mahesino sāsana).[36] The "I," included in citta, is within the teaching. The impermanence of the objects dissolves citta as subject, and only in the inmost of the "I"-process is there room for delight. Such a citta-process goes on inside man meditating in the forest, the one who is looked upon with delight by all other creatures.[37]

We still meet a man who dreams about "soft" (mudu) existence, with himself as the master (issara), content with whatever is obtained.[38] His dream is based upon the possibility of making mind well tamed and standing firmly, whereby he will be able to go the fortunate way and pursue it (nisevati) by means of guarding the mind. Then the mind will be well guarded and developed (subhāvita), without support in any existence (anissita sabbabhavesu).[39] The guide is that knowledge (paññā) which makes man see the passing away and coming into existence of the origin (samudayaṃ vibhavañ ca sambhavaṃ).[40] In the last three verses we hear the last fading echo of the conflict between man and his citta, because citta has led him around instead of living with (the teaching of) the compassionate great seer.[41] The echo of the conflict is fading away within a firm belief of a conflict-solving prosperous future expressed in the words asaṃsayaṃ citta parābhavissasi: "you, mind, will certainly perish." As it is a much disputed sentence, one might suggest the translation "you, mind, will certainly suffer defeat."[42] The text tells us that man can delight in his own life with a "perished" or "defeated" citta, but also that the experience of happiness is misleading for men and women who are under citta's control and whose problems are that they are foolish in the sense of not knowing (aviddasu) their whole way of life. They are governed only by citta, or they are "your servant, citta."[43]

Some Concepts Associated with "I"

We have met a conflict within a man who talks as "I" although he belongs to a religion which stresses the doctrinal view upon man as "not-I" or "non-ego," which will always cause trouble to our language games:

> A buddhist once said
> To deny
> That this "I" is an "I" is a lie,
> For if it is not
> I should like to know what
> Is the thing which says: "I am not I".[44]

The "I" of the text is an ego perceiving his mind (citta). In

Jungian terms we may understand "I" or "ego" as "a complex of ideas
which constitutes the center of my field of consciousness and appears
to possess a high degree of continuity and identity. Hence I also
speak of an ego-complex."[45] Furthermore Jung distinguishes between
ego and the self, which means that "the self would be an ideal entity
which embraces the ego,"[46] introduced above as the well-controlled
self.[47] This is a complex concept because it is the unity of the
personality as a whole.

> But in so far as the total personality, on account of its un-
> conscious component, can be only in part conscious, the concept
> of the self is, in part, only potentially empirical and is to
> that extent a postulate. In other words, it encompasses both
> the experienceable and the inexperienceable (or the not yet ex-
> perienced).[48]

Herein lies the possibility of a human conflict of the kind shown by
our text. The Jungian interpretative model offers a further chance
of understanding. Self, representing a totality of the psychological
process, involves a transcendent function,[49] which we meet in
Tālaputa's conflict. Searching for his psychologically true Self, he
must realize not only the nonego but also the not-self of all empty
things,[50] if by means of development and knowledge he is to reach
the transcendental processes of, for example, the undying, release,
deathless state, nibbāna,[51] or in Jungian terms: "In this way it
becomes a new content that governs the whole attitude, putting an end
to the division and forcing the energy of the opposites into a common
channel."[52]

Our next step toward an understanding of these psychological processes must be to focus upon the role of citta. Can it be understood
by itself or does it point to a wider context? The immediate response to this problem would be to show the close connection between
citta and dhamma, which will be done below. But before that one must
discuss citta and the Jungian term "mind." First we must compare the
following German text with the English translation:[53]

Aber ich bin keineswegs	But I am not at all
davon überzeugt, dass	certain whether
das Unbewusste tatsächlich	the unconscious mind
nur meine Psyche ist,	is merely my mind,
denn der Begriff "Unbewusstes"	because the term "unconscious"
bedeutet, dass ich seiner nicht	means that I am not even
einmal bewusst bin...	conscious of it....
Unter solchen Bedingungen	Under such conditions
wäre es vermessen, den Faktor,	it would be presumptuous to call
der die Stimme hervorbringt,	the factor which produces
als mein Unbewusstes oder als	the voice my mind.[54] This
meinen Geist zu bezeichnen.	would not be accurate.
Es wäre mindestens nicht genau.	

We see the word "mind" involves "Unbewusstes," "Psyche" and "Geist."
As noted above the meaning of citta is vague and manysided, and so is
the meaning of mind. In this context, however, we must refer both
"Unbewusstes" and "Psyche" to the self "while the self is the subject

of my total psyche, which also includes the unconscious,"[55] an exclusively psychological concept that covers processes which are perceptibly related to the self, but not to the ego.[56] This self, "the unity of the personality as a whole," has been said above to be in part a postulate; it is that postulate which contains self as "Geist," also included in the English concept "mind." Jung's commentary to The Tibetan Book of the Great Liberation indicates that "Geist," translated as "mind" is part of the self.[57] Summing up this part we may say that citta-mind expresses the processes of the personality as a whole, of the self. However the unconscious is part of its influence, and therefore citta-mind encompasses "Psyche."

For Tālaputa there is a conflict between conscious and unconscious. Concurrently within him there is a guiding idea that, in essence but not always in formulation, "is a psychological determinant having an a priori existence" ("eine a priori existierende und bedingende psychologische Grosse").[58] The psychological determinant is met with in words like "the seer's weapon" which is made by knowledge (paññā) and is represented by the good ones, those who pursue dhamma, who see things as they really are, whose minds are collected around "the undying," and so forth. The guiding idea is the threefold knowledge in the Buddha's teaching, the victor's teaching, the great seer's teaching. That teaching includes the development of human capacities. His development is his individuation. "Individuation means becoming a single, homogenous being, and, in so far as 'individuality' embraces our innermost, last, and incomparable uniqueness, it also implies becoming one's own self."[59]

This "self" is developing toward an awareness of the final release or nibbāna. Personality is taught that it is not-self (anattā), that his citta will be defeated, and that the experience of this is worth anticipating. This gives us reason later to focus upon the citta-dhamma complex within the process of release (vimutti). It is the context in which citta may be understood.

Conflict-Processes Around Some citta-Compounds Within the Majjhima-Nikāya

By far the most frequent conflict-process is around byāpanna-citta,[60] which can be understood as "a malevolent or corrupted mind." The psychological description shows how unhealthy fear and terror are experienced as effects of a malevolent mind, a bad thinking, a defiled intention (byāpannacittapadutthamana-saṅkappa-sandosahetu). Psychological description ends there. On the other hand, according to the Buddha's own experience, the efficient remedy against this state of the ego is a benevolent mind (mettacitta),[61] in our texts frequently met with and part of a noble mind (ariyacitta). The corrupted mind is an experienced symptom; other people may develop it, we do not.[62] On the contrary, this and other unskilled processes are something of which to be rid (pajahati).[63] There is no detailed psychological answer to the question "how?" There are, however, statements about the goal. He experiences himself as cleansed from these evil, unskilled processes (imehi papakehi akusalehi dhammehi) and thereby sees himself as released (vimuttam-attānam).[64] Thus one might develop benevolence, compassion, sympathetic joy, and equanimity, thereby experiencing calm, relief.[65]

There are other nuances in the corrupted mind which appear when contexts force us to look upon it against the background of dhamma and its applications.[66] In a bad life with the symptom of the malevolent mind people create suffering now and in the future. The explanation is connected with cognitive words meaning "living ignorantly, not knowing it as it is, because he has not come to knowledge."[67] No further psychological explanation is given. We are free to live applying dhamma or not, in accordance with our experience of it or not. Whether we do or not the symptom of the processes is clear.

In a discussion between Kaccāna and the king of Madhurā on the four castes, one crucial point is the corrupted mind and the wrong view as contrasted to the uncorrupted mind and the right view (sammāditthī), which is the first part of the eightfold path.[68]

The young brāhmana Assalāyana touches on the same problem in a conversation with the Buddha. Here too the importance of an uncorrupted mind and right view is decisive, irrespective of caste.[69] The question is whether we are capable of developing a benevolent mind (mettacittaṃ bhāvetuṃ). Assalāyana agrees that, if this is the important point, then the four castes are alike; they are all capable of developing metta.[70]

"Corrupted mind" and "wrong view" are also processes within the Buddha's great analysis of kamma, given to Ānanda. This analysis when heard by the monks will be carried in their minds (Bhagavato sutaṃ bhikkhū dhāressanti).[71] The analysis is given in conclusive statements built upon the Buddha's knowledge and experience of kamma.[72]

It has been said that the benevolent mind is a remedy. The Buddha said, "I, brāhmana, seeing within myself this mettacitta, got into greater confidence for living in the forest."[73] In his further development, the Buddha met with the process of the calmed mind (vūpasantacitta)[74] which had the effect of confidence within himself. This is a diminishing of unhealthy fear and terror (bhayabherava).[75] In a further development we also meet the confused mind (vibhantacitta).[76] The whole text shows that the main motivation for spiritual striving is to get rid of that fear and terror which obstruct the mind from reaching the goal.[77]

Obviously the benevolent mind is a very important part of good experiences. In Sutta 21 it is connected to "thus you must train yourself." The important thing is to live with a benevolent mind and without hate "in the heart" (dosantara).[78] Thus man may meet with increase, growth, and full development in dhamma and discipline.[79] The Buddha realizes that inward anger seeks outward expression as an answer to external situations. The remedy to the process of anger is to live honoring, pursuing, and respecting dhamma. This means that even one's way of speaking is connected with the goal (atthasaṃhita) and, most importantly, that one lives with a benevolent mind and without hate in his heart.[80] This is how benevolence is made efficient within our fellowman as well as in the world. Mettacitta is the symptom of our capacity to meet with life situations; it is part of living according to the Buddha's teaching.[81]

In another situation like this the Buddha is said to be a dhammavādin: "speaker of dhamma."[82] The foundation may be seen in these words: "Now I, brāhmana, recognize (make known) that man's property is the ariyan, beyond this world extending dhamma."83 Simultaneously it is, in this world dhammavinaya, the dhamma and discipline made known by the Buddha.84

There are good reasons to talk about citta as process or function. The compound for it is cittasankhāra,85 which in Sutta 9 is presented under "process of body, process of speech, process of mind."86 The whole Sutta is an answer to the question about how to achieve the true dhamma (saddhammam).87 The context of the sankhāras shows that taking them as facts is due to not knowing and that the opposite possibility is sammāditthī, right view as part of the true dhamma.88 These three processes are bound to have been ceased and calmed in a person who has achieved release of the mind (cetovimutti).89 This is known by one who has a developed citta, and he also realizes that citta-processes include activities of perception and feeling, belonging to "mental things." These are dhammas depending upon mind (ete dhammā cittapatibaddha).90 So too processes of mind can be experienced and calmed down as part of a whole training of the mind toward the goal of making it, while still studied, into a released mind (vimoceti).91

We have touched upon the problem of fear and terror. One of its opposites is pasannacitta, the pious and pleased mind, which indicates an attitude of belief. The effect of this intellectual, volitional, and emotional attitude is not limited to one who experiences it. A family saw three sons go from home to homelessness, and their capacity of reaching the utmost goal through the Buddha's talk on dhamma was realized.92 If that family envisions these three sons piously and with a pleased state of mind, the effect is one of goodness and happiness for that family indefinitely.93 The effects go even further; a pious and pleased mind remembering these three dhamma-men, will result in universal experiences of good and happiness because they live for the piety of devas and men.94 No doubt we may see a connection here between pasanna and dhamma, expressed in a process of citta. This connection is beautifully expressed in another context:

> When the Bhagavant knew that the mind of the householder
> Upali was ready, tender, without hindrances, exalted,
> pleased, then he made known to him that teaching of dhamma
> which is vivified by the buddhas: dukkha, its rise, its
> stopping, the way.95

This is the prosperous cofunction of citta and dhamma, a process that is included in the latter, as it is a process developing from the facts of dukkha to release. This view is strengthened by the wider context, which shows insight into dhamma (dhammacakkhum udapādi) expressed thus: "All that is of the dhamma to rise is also of the dhamma to stop." In this very situation Upali anticipated perfection. He is one who has seen, attained, known, and penetrated dhamma; he is one who, not depending on others, has attained full confidence in the teacher's instruction.96 Such a dhamma has the effect of good and happiness for the totality of the world with its men of different castes and devas.97 Upali has become the disciple of the Bhagavant with the brilliant dhamma (ruciradhamma).98

The process of development from the facts of dukkha to release is shown in a convincing way in the contexts above. It cannot be explained without studying the citta-process under the influence of that dhamma which was recognized by the Buddha. Sutta 56 is an important source but the context of citta-dhamma in a release-process is to be found elsewhere as well.[99] It is obvious that human experiences lead toward the goal of release which is experienced by happiness, readiness, tenderness, freedom from hindrances, exaltedness; men who possess such traits are worthy of the epithet bestowed by their teacher of wise and/or skilled (pandita).[100] To be wise implies decisiveness of the mind (āraddhacitta), which is shown by the individual who wants to take the necessary steps toward the goal.[101] The release-experience, expressed by arahant-formula A, is within the range of attainment.[102]

So we face the fact of mind released being a process that goes on in a released mind, and this process is anattā but within dhamma. A person thus released is tathāgata, in other words, he has gone through all speculations, including those about a static reality behind the ego. We can say nothing about the future of a monk whose mind is thus released (evaṃ vimuttacitta).[103] In this citta is like dhamma: "this dhamma is deep, difficult to be seen, difficult to be recognized, peaceful, excellent, undisputable, abstruse, to be known by the clever and/or skilled."[104] It has been guiding the paccekabuddhas during the days before the Buddha and he gives them praise. Fully perfected in final nibbāna (parinibbuta),[105] they were well released in their minds (suvimuttacitta). Man's capacity to reach the goal is demonstrated through citta. The process goes on in the released mind, and this is the dhamma-process which involves release. This ends the conflict. It is the transformed life, or life within the release-process, which will be the focus of the next portion of this study. What we have seen above cannot be described in terms of psychology. Jung says, "It is perhaps not superfluous to mention that the East has produced nothing equivalent to what we call psychology, but rather philosophy or metaphysics."[106] The tendency within our texts can be observed, for we are dealing with processes within a frame of philosophy. This philosophy is acquainted with processes within the macrocosmos and microcosmos as shown in the perspective of dhamma-citta. Many of our texts expose the fact that matter and energy are two sides of the same thing without allowing us to "create: abiding attributes which are manifest in things. Jung says:

> Critical philosophy, the mother of modern psychology, is as foreign to the East as to medieval Europe. Thus the word "mind," as used in the East, has the connotation of something metaphysical.[107]

These words may be seen as a challenge. Psychology must be met with references to that theory of knowledge behind all cognitive words, summed up in a concept of understanding which is tied to human experience. Bringing this a bit further we may come to the meeting point between Buddhist analysis, where man analyzes himself and the processes within himself, and Jungian analytical psychology. They both have use for terms which Westerners call psychology. Citta points to dhamma. The ego points to the vast field of processes which are hidden within what we call the unconscious. In other words, the ego experiences dhamma by means of citta the ego experiencing the unconscious by means of "self." Is there any room for metaphysics?

Citta in the Process of Release

It is convenient to start this section with a quote from Jung's The Synthetic or Constructive Method:[108]

> The process of coming to terms with the unconscious is a true labor, a work which involves both action and suffering. It has been named the "transcendent function" because it represents a function based on real and "imaginary," or rational and irrational, data, thus bridging the yawning gulf between conscious and unconscious.

In Buddhism there is nibbāna, when for example man is released, and this utmost goal is experienced within a so-called citta, which can be known; so too cittaṃ jānāti, "he knows the mind," and other forms thereof.

In Sutta 112 it is stated six times that on the basis of dhamma (anudhammo) it is possible to say, vimuttaṃ me cittan ti pajānāmi: "I know that my mind is released." The mind is released from influxes by way of knowing and seeing things as they really are (evaṃ me jānato evaṃ passato).[109] Behind something "known" there is a process as, for example, in Sutta 6. If a monk wishes to know a mind that is with or without passion, he must lead the religious life. The text enumerates seven symptoms showing mind as undeveloped up to the level of it released or unreleased.[110]

One might ask, "By what means do I know the mind to be equipped or unequipped?" Suttas numbers 12, 73, 77, 108, and 119 give a hint of an answer connected with the word dhammanvayo, "in conformity with dhamma."[111] He who is in conformity with dhamma looks upon the Lord as one who knows the mind of other beings, and is himself in the process of becoming such. Citta is thus an object of knowledge. This is, in general, understandable up to a certain point as citta implies processes. However, on the level of mind released from influxes (āsavehi vimuttaṃ cittaṃ), it is also possible to know and experience the mind, such as the mind without influxes. The importance of the mind's knowledge and experience in the process from unreleased to released is shown in a speech given by Ananda to the householder Dasama. The contexts are given with the words avimuttaṃ cittaṃ vimuccati, "the mind, not released, is released." It is of great interest here to see how close this process is to dhamma and to knowledge and experience. The precondition for the development is one dhamma told or shown (eka-dhammo akkhāto) by the Buddha.[112] By means of that dhamma his development is governed by an experience of everything constructed. What is constructed is impermanent; this impermanence, he knows, has the nature of ceasing (tad aniccaṃ nirodhadhamman-ti pajānāti).[113] Through wishing for dhamma and satisfaction with dhamma (dhammarāgena, dhammanandiyā) one continually reaches more perfected levels of mind release. The goal is complete

destruction of influxes, and yet there is experience.[114]
     This is also the case when one "lives looking at mind in the
mind" (citte cittānupassī viharati), which is closely connected to
"he lives looking at dhamma within the dhammas" (dhammesu dhammānupassī viharati). After "looking upon" there is a process of knowledge; one knows (pajānāti).[115] To know by experience is also to be
able to do something. Citta is the object of our human activity.
Sariputta uses the words cittaṃ virājeti: "he purifies the mind."
Man purifies the mind from elements of earth, water, fire, and wind
both as external and internal elements. How does he release his
mind? The answer is:

> He shall see it as it really is by means of right knowledge
> thus: "this is not mine, this am I not, this is not my self."
> After he has seen it thus, as it really is, by means of right
> knowledge, he turns away from the element "of earth," he puri-
> fies his mind from the element "of earth."[116]

The same goes for the next three elements. It seems very important
here to observe citta in the context of having seen, as it really is,
through right knowledge. Sāriputta refers to the Buddha with the
words, "Thus it was said by the Lord: 'Whoever sees dependent origination, he sees dhamma, whoever sees dhamma, sees dependent origination.'"[117] The purifying activity is also expressed through the
words "he cleanses his mind" (cittaṃ pativāpeti). They are from
those dhammas (tehi dhammehi), which originate in the five personality factors, and thereupon Sariputta concentrates his mind on the
deathless element.[118] The precondition is that one leaves the wrong
view of "one's own body" or "one's own personality" (sakkāya-
ditthi).[119]
     In this Sutta we also learn that the strong man is one whose mind
rejoices, is reconciled, composed, and released when dhamma is
taught.[120]
     When the Buddha told the monks about his own way to perfection of
religious life he could use the form cittaṃ parisodhesim, "I purified
my mind" from greed, ill will, sloth and torpor, restlessness, worry,
and doubt.[121] These five hindrances are impurities to the mind,
weakening knowledge, and are regarded as unskilled dhammas.[122] These
so-called impurities include intellectual, volitional, and emotional
processes. To remove them is a precondition for right meditational
activity. The result may be regarded as freedom from debt, health,
release from bonds, liberation, and a secure place.[123] In Sutta 125
the process of giving up five hindrances is connected with fulfilling
skilled dhammas. The consequence is that one attains the truth
("right path") and realization of nibbāna (ñāyassa adhigamāya
nibbānassa sacchikiriyāya).[124]
     A few more preconditions must be mentioned. They are connected
with the mind as composed, collected (samāhitaṃ cittaṃ ekaggaṃ), meditational or analyzing activities, and with evaṃ samāhite citte
parisuddhe: "thus he (I) with his (my) mind composed, quite purified...."[125] Usually this phrase is connected with citta in an object function, cittaṃ abhininnāmeti, "he directs his mind (to)," or
other forms thereof. In Suttas numbers 4, 19, 36, and 112 the Buddha
says that he directed his mind toward ñāna, "knowledge." Three of

our texts say directed toward "knowledge and remembrance of former
livings," "knowledge of disappearance and reappearance of living beings," and "knowledge of the extinction of influxes;" this third
phrase is the only one mentioned in Sutta 112,[126] which indicates
that this knowledge is all-important. The extinction of influxes implies that one knows (abhijānāti) four truths about dukkha well
which, in turn, implies that one knows four truths about influxes
(āsava) well.[127] This expresses the goal of the religious process.
It is preceded by four meditations (jhāna). As a comparison one
might look at Sutta 119. After four jhānas the text mentions "the
skilled dhammas which are connected with knowledge."[128] This leads
to abhininnāmeti, "he directs," in a new context which might serve as
a commentary to the earlier function of the verb. This context is
repeated four times:

> and it is thus, monks: anyone, in whom mindfulness within the
> body is developed and practiced, directs his mind to realiza-
> tion through knowledge of this or that dhamma, that can be
> realized through knowledge, and he attains status as witness,
> now here, now there, on any level whatsoever.[129]

The interpretations given in the context strengthen the meaning of
this text. The lives of human beings are generally governed by the
possibility of release in and through dhamma, in and through citta.
Then, of course, we know our minds as being released from unskilled
impurities[130] up to the level where one can say:

> he, through the destruction of influxes, after having, by him-
> self, realised here and now, through his own knowledge, the
> release of mind and the release through knowledge that are
> without influxes, after having attained that, lives therein.[131]

Although learned philologists may consider it speculative to
state that the function of citta, hitherto, is adhicitta in cofunction with abhidhamma, it seems convenient to do so in a dialogue
between early Buddhism and analytical psychology. Adhicitta is mentioned only three times in these texts. Adhicitte yuttam, "applied
to the essential citta," is a precondition for dhamma-life leading to
abhidhamma, "the essential dhamma."[132] Adhicittam-anuyuttena
bhikkhunā, "the monk who is intent upon (or following) the essential
citta, should make up his mind from time to time as to the five characteristics. . . ."[133] Thus follows the development from unskilled
to skilled by means of dhamma-life, and one restrains mind with the
mind (cetasā cittam).[134]
    In numerous texts of the Majjhima-Nikāya[135] we read about the
mind in the process of being released. One group has the reading
cittam vimuccittha, "mind was released," preceded by the realization
of four truths: "....for me knowing thus, seeing thus, my mind was
released from the influxes of sense pleasures....from the influxes of
existence....from the influxes of not knowing, and in the release my
knowledge came to be 'it (citta) is released....'"[136]
    Seeing reality as it is (yathābhūtam), the human mind is released
from influxes. Through the word āsava, influx, and its connection
with dukkha we may see this threefold release as a departure from ex-

istential suffering in any form; we may also see the culmination in
knowledge built upon the actual experience of release. This is the
highly important knowledge in these texts.

That which is said here by the Buddha recurs in different Suttas
as an important part of the teaching in general, which brings us to a
second group of texts. The above texts' words are taken to heart,
symbolically presented in the third person singular: "for one knowing thus, seeing thus."[137] In ten of the texts we also encounter interpretation of four truths about dukkha in terms of four truths
about influxes (āsava). The words that express the essence of the
process may be preceded by: "He knows: 'there is this, there is
that which is inferior, there is the excellent, there is a further
escape from this perceptible (world).'"[138]

There is also release from every form of negative processes
(pāpakā akusalā dhammā) and thus a monk is perfected (arahaṃ
hoti).[139] The release process can also be explained as making man
into one who "is here and now satisfied, cooled, tranquilized, experiencing happiness, and who lives with self brahma(n)-become."[140] For
example in Sutta 18, one of the few texts without citta, we may get
the explanation of brahmabhūta in the following phrase met with
twice, "the Bhagavant knows when he really knows, sees when he really
sees, he has become sight, he has become knowledge, he has become
dhamma, he has become brahman."[141]

There is no inherent danger in equating brahmabhūta with dhamma-
bhūta as is done by most interpreters, and this interpretation is
also in line with the tendency of this study.[142] In a speech to
Sandaka Ānanda one sees the release of mind as attaining "the 'right
path,' to dhamma, to what is skilled" (ñāyaṃ dhammaṃ kusalaṃ).[143] In
the epilogue we read: "and there will be no extolling of one's own
dhamma, no spite towards other's dhamma, but both the teaching of
dhamma in its full meaning, and also so many great leaders can be
known."[144]

Citta's release can also be within the frame of dhamma, which is
the higher and more applied dhamma.[145] To this singular function of
dhamma the text also adds its plural function: "These, Udayin, are
both the higher and the more applied dhammas and for the sake of
realizing them monks lead the religious life under me."[146] Thus we
find dhammo and dhammā in the same contextual function, which gives,
no doubt, an intentional meaning within the range of citta, dhammo,
and dhammā.

In Sutta 125 the release process of citta follows after an imperative from the Tathāgata, which results in "live looking at mind in
the mind but do not reflect upon a fixed thought connected with mind,
live looking at dhammas in the dhammas but do not reflect upon a
fixed thought connected with dhammas!"[147] This is followed by four
meditations and release.

In this group of texts there is a thorough treatment of kamma as
part of spiritual development.[148] As kamma is truly part of the
dhamma-complex these Suttas strengthen the main argument about the
close connection between citta and dhamma. Kamma, within these contexts, operates as an existential experience of whether true or false
dhamma is being taught. Experience makes kamma within these Suttas
a nonmetaphysical process and meeting point between citta and
dhamma.[149]

Another group of texts is brought together because they obtain the words "the mind released from influxes without any remaining clinging" (anupādāya āsavehi cittaṃ vimuttaṃ). They are subordinated to pajānāti, "he knows," or they form a statement about an actual, specific religious experience. One version is met with in Sutta 112. Knowledge, recognition is identified with arahant-formula A[150] and the whole process forms the point of departure for a speech by the Buddha on cleansing. The speech is guided by a theory of cognition included in a sequence of cognitive words—see, hear, perceive, think—which are the same found in, for example, Bṛhad-Āraṇyaka-Upaniṣad.[151] The silent question from the reader/listener is, of course, "How do we reach the experience of mind released from influxes wihout any remaining clinging?" The necessary condition is that one knows (pajānāti) and sees (passati), and that his activity is in accordance with dhamma (anudhammo).[152] The fact that the Buddha knows by experience that his mind is released gives strength to his educating statement: "Friends, for me knowing thus, seeing thus within these six internal-external sensefields, my mind was released from influxes without...."[153] Then we find connected "released through right knowledge," "according to dhamma" (sammādaññāvimutta, anudhamma), and the Buddha's teaching (dhammaṃ desesi).[154]

Four texts[155] focus upon the actual, specific religious experience. The Buddha is teaching Dīghanakha about the development toward the state of mind released (vimuttacitta).[156] In the end the venerable Sāriputta appears as a listener to the speech "and indeed, while the venerable Sāriputta was reflecting (on) this, his mind was released...." The immediate context shows how he attains the necessary understanding: "Surely, the Bhagavant speaks to us about giving up by means of knowledge these and those dhammas, the Sugata speaks to us about forsaking by means of knowledge these and those dhammas."[157] Thus the connection between citta and dhamma is strong enough to support the main thesis. Dīghanakha's process went through a view of dhamma (diṭṭhadhammo), attaining dhamma (pattadhammo), getting to know dhamma (viditadhammo), and penetrating dhamma (pariyogālhadhammo). Thus dhamma was made known (dhammo pakāsito) by the good Gotama to the effect that Dīghanakha took refuge in Gotama, in dhamma, and in saṅgha.[158]

The wider context, leading up to the intense experiences, also includes dhamma. Kāyo, our personality, is of certain dhamma which means that it is in the condition of, for example, impermanence, suffering, emptiness, and of being without self (aniccato, dukkhato, suññato, anattato). The same goes for our feelings (vedanā). They are of dependent origination (paticcasamupannā) and as such they are of the dhamma to pass away, decay, fade away, and cease or stop (khaya, vaya, virāga, nirodha). Thus things must be understood.[159] Once sixty monks understood and thereby won distance to "things" (nibbindati). They were delighted with the Buddha's teaching and "their minds were released (cittāni vimuccimsu) from influxes without any remaining clinging."[160]

The monks had received teaching about the five factors (khandha) as a point of departure. The importance of the right view for each factor had been stressed. On the basis of the dhamma of learned people one must realize that they are all impermanent, suffering, and subject to change (viparināmadhamma).[161] By way of existential experience we can also understand the third sign of existence. "Is it clever (or healthy) to regard that which is impermanent, suffering, and under the dhamma of changing as 'this is mine, this am I, this is my self?'"162 Of course, the answer is "no!" With that negative response man indicates that he sees things as they really are by means of right knowledge (yathābhūtaṃ sammappaññāya datthabbaṃ).163

The above thoughts are found again in Sutta 147, in which Rāhula is the one whose mind was released. This time the Buddha follows the structure of our six senses. He regards Rāhula as prepared for further learning. "Developed are now the 'release-perfecting dhammas' of Rāhula."164 As above, the sequence of anicca, dukkha, vipariṇā-madhamma, and existential experience of anattā provides the structure of the Sutta. The whole process of teaching and release was witnessed by thousands of devas who experienced the dhamma (dhamma-cakkhuṃ udapādi). Immediately connected with their insight into dhamma is its meaning and comprehension: "All that is of the dhamma to arise, is also of the dhamma to stop."165

The last text in this group presents a most detailed analysis of the smallest processes in the function of a human being.166 All units in the process of what we call "a self" are analyzed under the leading principle of not-self (anattā), which is also a quality within the processes called dhamma, and produced by our faculty of thinking (mano). This doctrine is the very core of the Buddha's teaching. It is indicated by the introductory words Dhammaṃ vo, bhikkhave, desissāmi: "Monks, I will teach you dhamma."167 In the introduction, and only once, dhamma appears in this sense. Only once, and in the epilogue, does the word citta appear: "While this exposition was being given the minds of as many as sixty monks were released from influxes without any remaining clinging."168 This direct statement creates a close connection between dhamma and citta.

The Citta-Dhamma Complex and Jung's Ātman-Brahman Interpretation

It has been said that Jung followed the rule of facts first and theories later; in other words, he was an empiricist. The theories from which he arrived were then applied to concepts from Eastern thinking. The intent of this article is to use Jung's analytical psychology as an interpretative model for understanding early Buddhism. This is possible if it may be shown that, psychologically, his view upon the ātman-brahman complex may be connected to that citta-dhamma complex, which was shown in the above statements based on chosen texts. If it can be demonstrated that the two complexes are psychologically alike, then we will focus upon individuation as the most central notion of Jung's psychological system and therapy.169 A study of individuation will involve observations of the transcendent function.

In general, Buddhist texts are not used by Jung as references for his statements about Eastern or Indian thinking. If we want to grasp his presentation in Psychological Types we can follow the long sequence that starts with his thesis that, in India, introversion into the unconscious is expressed through the brahman-ātman complex.170 This complex is a state of identity between what is inside and outside man.171 It also encompasses the very old concept ṛta as "Weltwesen" and "Weltgrunde."[172] Rta as well as tao is psychologically a course between pairs of opposites; it can be studied in Indian, Chinese, and Buddhist religions. The references for ideas like the ones above are ten quotations from texts connected only with Hinduism.[173] The meaning of the Indian intention is obvious to Jung. The intention is to give release from those conflicting processes which are part of human nature and thus offer new life in Brahman. Brahman is therefore the irrational unification of opposites and, in this way, they are finally overcome.[174]

For this reason Jung gives about twenty quotations from the Indian history of religion as evidence to support his general view. This time, too, he uses non-Buddhist texts. He sees Brahman as a specific psychological state and, through a certain philological interpretation, the concept is taken to indicate "eine spezifische Konzentration der Libido."[175] As such it is also connected to rta as the Indian sources identify Brahman with rta.[176] After a sequence of examples from the texts we hear Jung's opinion:

> There is no need, I think, of further examples to show that the concept of rta is a libido-symbol like sun, wind, etc. Only, rta is less concretistic and contains the abstract element of fixed direction and regularity, the idea of a predetermined, ordered path or process. It is, therefore, a kind of philosophical libido symbol that can be directly compared with the Stoic concept of heimarmene.[177]

It is important to remember that these statements are psychological statements on the basis of libido which, for Jung, means psychic energy as it expresses itself not as psychic strength or power, but as intensities or values.[178] Obviously this psychology emphasizes cooperation of what is rather carelessly called subjective and objective. The holistic view may also be applied to the Chinese Tao and sees its affinity to Brahman.[179] The important part of interpretation is that these Eastern concepts are symbols which unite contradictory processes of cosmos. Focusing upon man we learn that he is a microcosmos who corresponds to these irrational symbols.[180] This results in a differentiation within man and within man's experience of himself. The "I" may be experienced both as individual and universal. The above examples of Jung's thinking, based on the ātman-brahman complex, intimate that the ordinary "I," ego, is something less than the "self." This may give room for statements about a "nonego," if we follow Jung's psychological interpretation further. Obviously Jung has not used the citta-dhamma complex as an argument for his statements. The ātman-brahman complex is, clearly, not to be found in Buddhist texts. The heart of the matter is whether we can find that "nonego" which provides a meeting point between Buddhist texts and Jung's "Indian" texts. If so, the interpretative model from the ātman-brahman complex can be also used in a psychological interpretation of the citta-dhamma complex.

Concerning this we find that there are some examples of nonego. The phenomenon is touched upon in a 1932 essay entitled "The Development of Personality."[181] Jung writes: "It (development) also means fidelity to the law of one's own being." This is a general statement which may apply to our friend Tālaputa and is exemplified in the whole complex of cittabhāvana, mind-development.[182] The concept of nonego is examined in a psychological statement from another source other than Buddhism.

> To the extent that man is untrue to the law of his being and does not rise to personality, he has failed to realize his life's meaning....Primitive people have a far greater capacity in this respect; at least the medicine men are able, as part of their professional equipment, to talk with spirits, trees, and animals, these being the forms in which they encounter the objective psyche or psychic non-ego.[183]

From this objective psyche or psychic nonego, one may hear the inner voice necessary for development. The final reference to this "interior way" is made to the Chinese tao. "To rest in Tao means fulfillment, wholeness, one's mission done; the beginning, end, and perfect realization of the meaning of existence innate in all things. Personality is Tao."[184] In connection with arahant-formula A, the Buddha said: "When he was released there was the knowledge 'it (citta) is released' and I knew: 'Exhausted is birth, completed is religious life, fulfilled is that which was to be fulfilled, nothing more is left for this (sort of) existence.'"[185] Thus there is fulfillment within the objective psyche or psychic nonego. The agreements between these two descriptions are, from a psychological point of view, noteworthy.

It is possible to find even more precise views about nonego. Jung's holistic view is obvious in his 1944 study "The Holy Men of India."[186]

> This melody is built up on the one great theme, which, veiling its monotony under a thousand colorful reflections, tirelessly and everlastingly rejuvenates itself in the Indian spirit.... It is the drama of ahamkāra, the "I-maker" or ego-consciousness, in opposition and indissoluble bondage to the atman, the self or non-ego.[187]

Although this melody is recognizable to Jung and is sufficient for him to "read an Upanishad or any discourse of the Buddha"[188] to recognize the psychology within these views, we must reach a better understanding of this nonego.

In a foreword to Suzuki's Introduction to Zen Buddhism, edited in 1949, Jung makes the following statement:

> However one may define the self, it is always something other than the ego, and inasmuch as a higher insight of the ego leads over to the self, the self is a more comprehensive thing which includes the experience of the ego and therefore transcends it. Just as the ego is a certain experience I have of myself, so is the self an experience of my ego. It is, however, no longer experienced in the form of a broader or higher ego, but in the form of a non-ego.[189]

The meaning of this part is ambiguous both in English and German, but the psychologically important thing seems clear enough: the experi-

ence is no longer seen in terms of a broader or higher ego, but in
terms of a nonego. Indeed, the experience forces us once more to focus on "psyche."

We now have a basis for concern about the Buddhist anattā-
doctrine and the experience of nonego. First, in both cases it is
primarily a question of experience. In this context the doctrine is
not interesting as a static fact as some learned scholars in the West
tend to think. The mere existence of a doctrine points to deeper
layers of psychological experience. Furthermore, the anattā-doctrine
creates problems as can be shown, for example, by pointing to review
essays among Western Buddhists.[190] Although the Buddha taught in opposition to the instruction of his time, as the anātman-anattā-
doctrine indicates, the psychological structure remained. This is
Jung's theory and it is a possible interpretation of Buddhist texts
without adhering to a Vedantic interpretation. Jung's structure can
be summed up thus:

> ego - self; experience in terms of the complex of
> "brahman-ātman," objective psyche, psychic nonego.

The Buddhist texts give us the impression of:

> ego - mind; experience in terms of the complex of "citta-
> dhamma," objective psyche, psychic nonego, and
> doctrinal anattā.

By following Jung's important 1939 study based on Eastern and Buddhist material entitled "Pyschological Commentary on The Tibetan Book
of the Great Liberation,"[191] let us also assume that the psychological structures are alike.

The psychological structure must be understood as something real.
In a commentary on the difficult terms "psychic reality," "psyche,"
and "mind," Jung states that only psychic existence is immediately
verifiable.[192] "In the East, mind is a cosmic factor, the very essence of existence";[193] understanding this psychic reality and cosmic
factor is an activity performed by the introverted mind.[194] In this
context our confrontation between citta and dhamma seems psychologically reasonable: "The psyche is therefore all-important; it is the
all-pervading breath, the Buddha-essence; it is the Buddha-Mind, the
One, the Dharmakāya. All existence emanates from it, and all separate forms dissolve back into it."[195]

In the experience of the psyche there are important values which
must be looked for from within, in the unconscious.

> We shall then discover how great is our fear of the uncon-
> scious ˆnd how formidable are our resistances. Because of
> these resistances we doubt the very thing that seems so
> obvious to the East, namely, the self-liberating power of
> the introverted mind.[196]

It must be quite apparent that from the above descriptions, students of Buddhism recognize the piety demonstrated by the Buddha and
his disciples. The psychological approach brings us close to human
beings of this great religious tradition. Although the careful phil-

ologist may have his objections, nevertheless, the Jungian interpretative model gives dynamic life to our studies. In support of the value judgment above, it seems necessary to offer a long section from Jung's psychological commentary.

It is safe to assume that what the East calls "mind" has more to do with our "unconscious" than with mind as we understand it, which is more or less identical with consciousness. To us, consciousness is inconceivable without an ego[197]....The Eastern mind, however, has no difficulty in conceiving of a consciousness without an ego ("Dem östlichen Geist hingegen fällt es nicht schwer, sich ein Bewusstsein ohne Ich zu denken"). Consciousness is deemed capable of transcending its ego condition; indeed, in its "higher" forms, the ego disappears altogether.[198]

In descriptions like this we recognize the processes of Tālaputa's citta and the constantly intensified development of citta within dhamma on its way to release, such as we have shown the process in our texts. In the following, this citta, which is close in meaning to psyche, is brought into connection with dhamma in Jungian terms:

The psyche is not a nonentity devoid of all quality; it is a definite system made up of definite conditions and it reacts in a specific way. Every new representation, be it perception or a spontaneous thought, arises associations which derive from the storehouse of memory. These leap immediately into consciousness (Bewusstsein), producing the complex picture of an "impression," though this is already a sort of interpretation. The unconscious disposition upon which the quality of the impression depends is what I call the "subjective factor." It deserves the qualification "subjective" because objectivity is hardly ever conferred by a first impression. Usually a rather laborious process of verification, comparison, and analysis is needed to modify and adapt the immediate reactions of the subjective factor.[199]

In the Buddhist texts we have seen symptoms of the "laborious process" within citta, touched by dhamma. Jungian terminology would call this process the transcendent function, which is both process and method psychologically manifest in one as dhamma.[200] It activates in us the unconscious process including the Universal Mind. "Since we cannot attribute any particular form to the unconscious, the Eastern assertion that the Universal Mind is without form, the arupaloka, yet is the source of all forms, seems to be psychologically justified."[201]

Within dhamma as the transcendent function we are supposed not only to gain access to the "One Mind" but also understand "why the East believes in the possibility of self-liberation"; this is the same as transforming one's mental condition and arriving at a solution of painful conflicts. Done when our psyche uses the processes of unconscious compensations, man, however, cannot achieve this at will.[202] As we have seen in the case of Tālaputa and in the citta-

dhamma complex of the Majjhima-Nikāya, unconscious processes are made
conscious initiated by dhamma as a remedy for people who experience
suffering and dissatisfaction (dukkha). In our texts this is explained in psychological terms as āsava, influxes, processes that
disturb one's expected development as well as existential life experience.

So far we have been able to apply Jung's interpretative model to
citta-dhamma. In Talaputa's case we have vaguely seen a process of
individuation and, according to Majjhima-Nikāya that process is shown
in the life of the Buddha and his teaching. The individuation process is brought to fulfillment within the transcendent function. In
terms of our Buddhist texts it is all within citta-dhamma-nibbāna
release, and in this complex dhamma is the connecting word. It is
natural to end this section by quoting Jung's words about the Eastern
goal, applying it to nibbāna-release.

> In the East, there is the wisdom, peace, detachment, and
> inertia of a psyche that has returned to its dim origins,
> having left behind all the sorrow and joy of existence as
> it is and, presumably, ought to be.[203]

If we look for terms which constitute a compromise between English
and German defining the four words above we may look at the Pali
nouns paññā, santi, nibbidā, and the adjective acala. These are
words that connect with the citta in the process of release and are
all closely connected with nibbāna.[204]

Thus, on the basis of our Buddhist texts and Jung's analytical
psychology, we may formulate as a psychological statement that the
more dhamma dominates the personality the more citta disappears in a
process and/or state of release, that is to say, nibbāna.

Individuation and Transcendent Function in the Case of Tālaputa and
in the Majjhima-Nikāya

We have observed the rather modest expressions of conflict within
Tālaputa. His conflict touches both conscious and unconscious. De-
ficiencies of his persona, the role with which he has identified himself, has become obvious. Values have disappeared and new ones have
been produced in his mind. "The unconscious" which produces new
energic values to solve his conflict seems "exclusively psychological."[205] He is in need of individuation, at the point of departure
which is the dissatisfaction of the persona, and wants to go back to
its own wholeness,[206] to a point where ego and self are united in the
process of the mind. At least we left Tālaputa in a situation where
he had a firm belief that conflict would be solved when his mind's
development of knowledge was no longer a "you" against a "me."[207]
This is the point where the psyche is a psychological expression of
the inexpressible.

Individuation, which we have examined so far in terms of development of the self,[208] is a process which, once started, must be
brought to fulfillment or else there will be an artificial crippling
(eine künstliche Verkrüppelung) of the individual.[209] "The aim of
individuation is nothing less than to divest the self of the false

wrappings of the persona on the one hand, and the suggestive power of primordial images on the other."[210] The primordial image covers psychic energy in the form of intensity and value coming to us from the collective unconscious.[211] At least that is the impression given in Talaputa's dialogue. Concerning the nature of the unconscious processes Jung teaches us that "we never succeed in getting further than the hypothetical 'as if.'"[212] It is known from experience that unconscious processes look as if they intended to compensate the conscious mind so that together they form a totality which constitutes the self.[213] In this totality the self is superior, which, in the case of Tālaputa, means that the mind is superior.[214]

In a later discourse Jung writes:

> The self could be characterized as a kind of compensation for the conflict between inside and outside. This formulation would not be unfitting, since the self has somewhat the character of a result, of a goal attained, something that has come to pass very gradually and is experienced with much travail.[215]

The conflict present in teaching from the Majjhima-Nikāya forces man into the process of individuation seeking his goal in "attan," understood in a reflexive function and thereby experiencing nonego as part of the dhamma-experience. We have shown conflicting processes between the malevolent mind involving fear and terror as contrasted with the benevolent mind. So too we have seen the mind observing the healthy processes (dhammā) dreaming about release (vimutta) of the reflexive self (attan).[216] The calmed mind is contrasted with fear and terror and the confused mind.[217] Again and again the texts show nearness to dhamma, even to the true dhamma (saddhamma).[218] If one believes that there must be a basically common content within the concept of dhamma, it is of interest to see conflicting elements within dhamma in its plural function.[219] In this life the guard against fear and terror is confidence in dhamma; confidence in dhamma means belief in the possibility of vimuttacitta, the released mind.[220] Pursuing the goal is filled with moments in which man says to "himself," "This is not mine, this am I not, this is not my self."[221] Vimuttacitta is the main topic dealt with in the above section on Citta in the Process of Release. The mind has been released, dhamma is fulfilled and citta defeated. Knowledge is the last word. The Buddha knew the moment of nibbāna.[222] This is individuation—psychologically.

The Transcendent Function

The transcendent function is within dhamma. Furthermore, the transcendent function is dhamma, in this case part of the individuation process.[223] In a study of a human citta, we have been forced to focus upon dhamma as part of the psychological development. Conceptual occurrences led to the assertion of a connection between the essential mind (adhicitta) and essential dhamma (abhidhamma).[224] We even saw how life in the transcendent function of dhamma can be, within our texts, expressed in words illustrative of the main idea in Jung's thinking. The texts talk about man in the release process "who lives with self brahman-become" (brahma-bhūtena attanā).[225] It

is obvious that this can be interpreted psychologically, which may be
illustrated in Jungian terms thus:

> Diese Tatsache ist es, die auch die Aussage ermöglicht, dass
> wer an Christus glaubt, nicht nur in ihm enthalten ist,
> sondern Christus wohnt dann auch im Gläubigen als der
> gottebenbildliche, vollkommene Mensch, der Adam secundus. Es
> handelt sich dabei psychologisch um sasselbe Verhältnis,
> welches in der indischen Anschauung die Beziehung von Purusha-
> Altman zum menschlichen Ichbewusstsein darstellt.[226]

It is this fact which also make it possible to say that whoever believes in Christ is not only contained in him, but that Christ then
dwells in the believer as the perfect man formed in the image of God,
the second Adam. Psychologically, it is the same relationship as
that in Indian philosophy between man's ego-consciousness and purusa
or ātman. The Buddhist setting becomes clear in the connection between dhamma-bhūta and brahmabhūta; he has become dhamma, he has become brahman.[227] The transcendent function of dhamma can also be
elucidated by the following quotation from Psychological Types:

> In this way it becomes a new content that governs the whole
> attitude, putting an end to the division and forcing the en-
> ergy of the opposites into a common channel. The standstill
> is overcome and life can flow on with renewed power towards
> new goals.
>   I have called this process in its totality the transcen-
> dent function, "function" here being understood not as a basic
> function but as a complex...activity made up of other func-
> tions...."Transcendent" is not...denoting a metaphysical qual-
> ity but merely the fact that this function facilitates a
> transition from one attitude to another. The raw material
> shaped by thesis and antithesis and in...which...opposites are
> united, is the living symbol. Its profundity of meaning is
> inherent in the raw material itself, the very stuff of the
> psyche, transcending time and dissolution....; its configura-
> tion by the opposites ensures...sovereign power over all the
> psychic functions.[228]

We will now see the transcendent function of dhamma in six situations from the study of our texts.

1. Dhamma can be seen as dependent origination. By realizing
this aspect of dhamma we may gain access to the process of release.[229]

2. Kamma as action-reaction or cause-effect is part of the
dhamma-complex and a nonmetaphysical meeting point between citta and
dhamma; it is existentially experienced. We must remember that the
foundation of knowledge is that we see, hear, perceive, and think,
behind which there is a latent theory of knowledge built on experience.[230] Jung does not seem absolutely sure of the function of kamma
as part of dhamma. In "Concerning Rebirth" he says:

> Even in Buddhism, where this doctrine is of particular im-
> portance--the Buddha himself experienced a very long sequence

of such rebirths--it is by no means certain whether continuity
of personality is guaranteed or not: there may be only a
continuity of karma.[231]

The "continuity of karma" is the Buddhist view. Nevertheless, kamma
is a philosophical problem. There is the risk of making causal connection into a law which is a third unobservable existence of something.[232] Some observations concerning this problem are to be found.
In his 1955 study, "Synchronicity: An Acausal Connecting Principle,"
Jung contrasts the causality and synchronicity principles.

> The causality principle asserts that the connection between
> cause and effect is a necessary one. The synchronicity prin-
> ciple asserts that the terms of a meaningful coincidence are
> connected by simultaneity and meaning.[233]

It is preferable that in this context we interpret kamma-dhamma in
psychological terms, as a synchronicity principle, although our texts
do not exclude the possibility of the causality principle. "Synchronicity is not a philosohical view but an empirical concept which postulates an intellectually necessary principle. This cannot be called
either materialism or metaphysics."[234]
     3. Dīghanakha shows a process culminating in the penetration of
dhamma as an effect of dhamma teaching from the Buddha. The penetra-
tion led to insight into the very nature of things as impermanent,
suffering, empty, and without self; they are of dependent origination. It is a precondition for the release of the mind to realize
this. The transcendent function of the Buddha's teaching is expressly stated in another such context.[235]
     4. Dhamma means that everything is impermanent, suffering, and
subject to change, consequently it should be looked upon in these
terms: "tnis is not mine, this am I not, this is not my self." By
means of knowledge we can see things as they really are.[236]
     5. An insight into or knowledge of dhamma, the nature of
"tnings," arises: "All that is of the dhamma to arise, is also of
the dhamma to stop." This happened to the thousands of devas that
witnessed the release process of Rahula.[237]
     6. Dhammaṃ vo desissāmi--the Buddha wants to teach "the Dhamma."
Within the teaching we learn that all processes (dhamma) are not-self
(anattā). "Wnile this exposition was being given the minds of as
many as sixty monks were released from influxes without any remaining
clinging."[238] The sequence of Dhammaṃ--dhammā--citta ends when the
minds are released or, in other words, reach nibbāna. In this study
it seems obvious that "the dhamma" as the teaching and part of Buddha, Dhamma, Saṅgha, proves to be the first function of that difficult concept. It is the symbol which is the transcendent function.
     In a 1916 essay on that subject, reviewed and published in 1958,
Jung presents the transcendent function as an answer to the question,
"How does one come to terms in practice with the unconscious?"[239]
There is the possibility of a union between conscious and unconscious
contents of the mind. The transcendent function "is a way of attaining liberation by one's own efforts and of finding the courage to be
oneself."[240] As the symbol, transcendent function is "the dhamma."
     Secondly dhamma expresses the law of the universe which, in addi-

62

tion, if not understood provides room for bad processes (akuṣalā dhammā). If rightfully understood it provides room for good processes (kusalā dhammā), ending in perfected release, the supreme dhamma, which is nibbana. Psychologically the mind, citta, has been defeated, released, and only knowledge exists. Such is the paradox.

NOTES

1. S.G.F. Brandon, Man and his Destiny in the Great Religions (Manchester: The University Press, 1962), p. 301.
2. Jan T. Ergardt, Faith and Knowledge in Early Buddhism, Studies in the History of Religions (Supplements to Numen), XXXVII (Leiden: E.J. Brill, 1977), p. 2.
3. V. Trenckner and R. Chalmers, eds., Majjhima-Nikāya vol. 3 (London: Pts., 1888-1889 and 1960-1964), p. 287.
4. Ergardt, Faith and Knowledge, pp. 48-49.
5. Ibid. See this work for a full elaboration of "arahant formula A."
6. R.E.A. Johansson, The Dynamic Psychology of Early Buddhism (London: Curzon Press, 1979), p. 142.
7. Johansson, Dynamic Psychology, p. 157.
8. J.R. Carter, Dhamma: Western Academic and Sinhalese Buddhist Interpretations, A Study of a Religious Concept (Tokyo: The Hokuseido Press, 1978), p. 179.
9. H. Oldenberg and R. Pischel, eds., Thera-gāthā (1883), 2nd ed., with Appendix by K.R. Norman (London: Pts., 1966). Future references will be made to Thag. and number of verse.
10. Thag. 1091-1106, 1110, 1125, 1137-1139.
11. Thag. 1107-1109, 1113-1121, 1122-1124, 1126-1129, 1131-1136, 1140-1141, 1143, 1145.
12. Thag. 1091.
13. Thag. 1092.
14. Māram sasenam bhañjissam.
15. paññāmayam sattham isīnam ādiyitvā.
16. Thag. 1095.
17. Thag. 1096.
18. Thag. 1099.
19. Thag. 1101.
20. Thag. 1102-1106, 1110, 1125.
21. Thag. 1107-1109.
22. Thag. 1109.
23. Thag. 1113-1120.
24. For example knowledge of earlier lives, of seeing with the heavenly eye, of release from influxes, i.e., nibbāna.
25. Thag. 1114-1115.
26. Thag. 1116.
27. Thag. 1117.
28. Thag. 1119.
29. Thag. 1121.
30. Thag. 1122.
31. Thag. 1123-1124.
32. Thag. 1126-1128.
33. Thag. 1129.

34. Thag. 1130.
35. Thag. 1131.
36. Thag. 1132.
37. Thag. 1133-1136.
38. Thag. 1137-1139.
39. Thag. 1140-1141.
40. Thag. 1142.
41. Thag. 1143.
42. Thag. 1144.
43. Thag. 1144-1145.
44. Buddhist Lodge, ed., Buddhism in England (London, 1926-1943), p. 10.
45. C.G. Jung, Psychological Types from The Collected Works of C.G. Jung, vol. 6, (Princeton: Princeton University Press, 1971), p. 425.
46. Ibid.
47. susamvutatta.
48. Jung, Collected Works, vol. 6, p. 460.
49. Ibid., pp. 460, 480.
50. suññam anattā.
51. Jung, Collected Works, vol. 6, pp. 4-5.
52. Ibid., p. 480.
53. C.G. Jung, Psychologie und Religion, Die Terry Lectures 1937 (Zürich and Leipzig: Rascher Verlag, 1942), p. 73; and C.G. Jung, Psychology and Religion (New Haven: Yale University Press, 1938), pp. 46ff.
54. C.G. Jung, Psychology and Religion: West and East from Collected Works, vol. 11, p. 40: "Under such conditions it would be presumptuous to refer to the factor that produces the voice as my unconscious or my mind."
55. Jung, Collected Works, vol. 6, p. 425.
56. Ibid., p. 483.
57. C.G. Jung, Zur Psychologie Westlicher und Ostlicher Religion (Zürich and Stuttgart: Rascher Verlag, 1963); cf. Jung, Collected Works, vol. 11, pp. 475, 511.
58. Jung, Collected Works, vol. 6, pp. 437ff.; and C.G. Jung, Psychologische Typen (Zürich and Leipzig: Rascher Verlag, 1937), p. 631.
59. C.G. Jung, Two Essays on Analytical Psychology (New York: Meridian Books, 1956), p. 182.
60. See M.: Suttas nos. 4, 8, 27, 38, 40, 41, 42, 46, 51, 76, 84, 93, 94, 96, 101, 107, 114, 136.
61. M I: 18.
62. M I: 42-46.
63. M I: 281-283.
64. M I: 283.
65. M I: 284.
66. M I: 311.
67. M I: 311.
68. M II: 86f.
69. M II: 149f.
70. M II: 151.
71. M III: 209f.
72. M III: 215.

64

73. M I: 18.
74. See also Suttas nos. 27, 39, 75, 101, 107, 125, 150.
75. M I: 18.
76. M I: 20, also in Suttas nos. 5, 29, 30, 107.
77. M I: 21.
78. M I: 123ff.
79. M I: 124f.
80. M I: 125ff.
81. M I: 129.
82. M II: 148.
83. M II: 181.
84. M II: 182-184.
85. See for example Suttas nos. 9, 43, 44, 57, 118.
86. M I: 54.
87. M I: 46ff.
88. M I: 54.
89. M I: 296.
90. M I: 301f.
91. M III: 83f.
92. M I: 209f.
93. M I: 210.
94. M I: 211.
95. M I: 379f.; Yadā Bhagavā aññāsi Upālim gahapatim kallacittam muducittam vinīvaranacittam udaggacittam pasannacittam atha vā buddhānam sāmukkamsikā dhammadesanā tam pakāsesi: dukkham samudayam nirodham maogam. See also M II: 145.
96. M I: 380; ditthadhammo, pattadhammor viditadhammo, pariyogālhadhammo, vesārajjappatto aparappaccayo satthusāsane.
97. M I: 383f.
98. M I: 386.
99. See cf. M I: 500f., M II: 145, M III: 280f.
100. M II: 145f.
101. M I: 391, 494, 512.
102. M I: 392, 496, 513.
103. M I: 486.
104. M I: 487; gambhīro h 'ayam dhammo duddaso duranubodho santo panīto atakkāvacaro nipuno panditavedaniyo.
105. M III: 113.
106. Jung, Collected Works, vol. 11, p. 475.
107. Ibid.
108. Jung, Analytical Psychology, p. 90; and C.G. Jung, Die Psychologie der Unbewussten Prozesse (Zürich: Rascher & Cie Verlag, 1918), p. 106.
109. M III: 30ff.
110. M I: 34f.
111. For example, M I: 69.
112. M I: 349ff.
113. M I: 350ff.
114. M I: 352.
115. M I: 56f., M III: 84, 136, 252.
116. M I: 185; Tam: n 'etam mama, n 'eso 'ham-asmi, na meso attā ti evam-etam yathābhūtam sammappaññāya datthabbam. Evam-etam yathābhūtam sammappaññāya disvā pathavīdhātuya nibbindati, pathavīdhātuyā cittam virājeti.

117. M I: 190f.; Yo paticcasamuppādaṃ passati so dhammaṃ passati, yo dhammaṃ passati so paticcasamuppādaṃ passatīti.

118. M I: 435f.

119. M I: 433f.

120. M I: 435.

121. M III: 35.

122. M III: 36.

123. M I: 276.

124. M III: 136.

125. M I: 22, and in, for example, Suttas nos. 19, 36, 39, 51, 60, 65, 76, 79, 85, 94, 100, 101, 125.

126. M I: 22f., 117, 248f., M III: 36.

127. In the teaching we find the verb in 3rd sg. and sometimes with the alternative pajānāti in, for example, Suttas nos. 27, 39, 51, 60, 65, 76, 79, 94, 125.

128. M III: 94; kusalā dhammā ye keci vijjābhāgiyā.

129. M III: 96f.; evam eva kho, bhikkhave, yassa kassaci kāyagatā sati bhāvitā bahulīkatā so yassa yassa abhiññāsacchikaraṇī-yassa dhammassa cittaṃ abhiniññāmeti abhinnāsacchikiriyāya, tatra tatr' eva sakkhibhavyataṃ pāpuṇāti sati sati āyatane.

130. M III: 98.

131. M III: 99; āsavānaṃ khayā anāsavaṃ cetovimuttiṃ paññāvimut-tiṃ ditthe va dhamme sayaṃ abhiññā sacchikatvā upasampajja viharati.

132. M I: 451f.

133. M I: 119.

134. M I: 121.

135. M I: 23, 117, 249, M II: 93, 212, M III: 36.

136. tassa me evaṃ jānato evaṃ passato kāmāsavā pi cittaṃ vim-mucittha, bhavāsavā pi cittaṃ vimuccittha, avijjāsavā pi cittaṃ vim-uccittha, vimuttasmiṃ vimuttam-iti ñāṇaṃ ahosi; cf. Ergardt, Faith and Knowledge, pp. 48ff.

137. Suttas nos. 7, 27, 39, 51, 60, 65, 76, 79, 94, 101, 121, 125.

138. M I: 38.

139. M I: 280.

140. M I: 349; ditthe va dhamme nicchāto nibbuto sītibhūto sukha patisaṃvedī brahma bhūtena attanā viharatīti.

141. M I: 111; Bhagavā jānaṃ jānāti passaṃ passati, cakkhubhūto ñānabhūto dhammabhūto brahmabhūto. See also M III: 195, 224.

142. Cf. Ergardt, Faith and Knowledge, p. 97.

143. M I: 522.

144. M I: 523f.; na ca nāma sadhammokkaṃsanā bhavissati na paradhammavambhanā, āyatane ca dhammadesanā tāva bahukā ca niyyātāro paññāyissanti.

145. M II: 38f.; ayaṃ...dhammo uttaritaro ca panītataro ca.

146. M II: 39; Ime kho, Udāyi, dhammā uttaritarā ca panitatarā ca, yesaṃ sacchikiriyāhetu bhikkhū mayi brahmacariyaṃ carantīti.

147. M III: 136; citte cittānupassī viharāhi mā ca cittūpasaṃ-hitaṃ vitakkaṃ vitakkesi, dhammesu dhammānupassī viharāhi mā ca chammūpasaṃhitaṃ vitakkaṃ vitakkesīti.

148. Suttas nos. 60, 76, 121.

149. Cf. Ergardt, Faith and Knowledge, pp. 93-113.

150. Sutta no. 5.

151. M III: 29f., and cf. Ergardt, 1977, p. 18.

152. M III: 30-32.
153. M III: 32.
154. M III: 33.
155. Suttas nos. 74, 109, 147, 148.
156. M I: 500.
157. M I: 501.
158. M I: 501.
159. M I: 500.
160. M III: 20.
161. M III: 18f.
162. M III: 19f.; Yam panāniccaṃ dukkhaṃ viparināmadhammaṃ kallan nu taṃ samanupassituṃ: Etaṃ mama, eso 'ham asmi, eso me attā ti.
163. M III: 20.
164. M III: 277; Paripakkā kho Rāhulassa vimuttiparipācaniyā dhamma.
165. M III: 280; Yaṃ kiñci samudayadhammaṃ, sabban taṃ nirodhadhamman ti.
166. A synopsis is given in Ergardt, Faith and Knowledge, pp. 60-63.
167. M III: 280ff.
168. M III: 287; Imasmiṃ kho pana veyyākaranasmim bhaññamane satthimattānaṃ bhikkhūnam anupādāya āsavehi cittāni vimuccimsūti.
169. H.F. Ellenberger, The Discovery of the Unconscious (New York: Basic Books, Inc., 1970), p. 710.
170. Jung, Psychologische Typen, pp. 164-165.
171. Ibid., p. 166.
172. Ibid., p. 168.
173. Ibid., pp. 276-279.
174. Ibid., p. 280: "Der Sinn der indischen Absicht ist daher klar: sie will von den Gegensätzen der menschlichen Natur überheupt befreien, und zwar zu einem neuen Leben in Brahman, dem Erlösumgszustand und Gott zugleich. Brahman muss also die irrationale Vereinigung der Gegensätze und somit ihre endgültige uberwindung bedeuten."
175. Ibid., pp. 280-286.
176. Ibid., p. 295.
177. Ibid., pp. 299ff.; also Jung, Collected Works, vol. 6, p. 211.
178. Jung, Psychologische Typen, p. 645.
179. Ibid., p. 304: "....und das urtümliche Bild, das dem rita-Brahman-Atman und Taobegriff zugrunde liegt, ist allgemein menschlich und findet sich als primitiver Energiebegriff, als 'Seelenkraft' oder wie es sonst bezeichnet werden mag, überall wieder."
180. Ibid., p. 306: "Der Mensch als ein die Weltgegensätze in sich vereinigender Mikrokosmos entspricht also dem irrationalen Symbol, das psychologische Gegensätze vereinight."
181. Jung, Collected Works, vol. 17, pp. 167-186.
182. See, for example, the section on Citta in the Process of Release, above.
183. Jung, Collected Works, vol. 17, p. 183.
184. Ibid., p. 186.
185. See for example M I: 23, 249, M III: 36. For variations in translations see Ergardt, Faith and Knowledge, pp. 48-49.

186. Jung, Collected Works, vol. 11, pp. 576-586.

187. Ibid., p. 579; also p. 625: "....in seinem Widerspruch zum und in seiner unaufloslichen Gebundenheit an den Ātman (das Selbst oder Non-ego)."

188. Ibid., pp. 577ff.

189. Ibid., p. 542, and Jung, Psychologie Westlicher, vol. 11, p. 586: "Gleich wie das Ich eine gewisse Erfahrung meiner selbst ist, so ist das Selbst eine Erfahrung meines Ich, welche aber nicht mehr in Form eines erweiterten oder höheren Ich, sondern in Form eines Nicht-Ich erlebt wird."

190. In my investigation of the leading English Buddhist Periodicals from 1909-1967 I have shown that the anattā-doctrine is one of the most frequently treated problems for the Buddhists. (J. Ergardt, Buddhismen i Vasterlandet, Undersokning av engelsk buddhism under 1900-talet (Lund, 1970).

191. Jung, Collected Works, vol. 11, pp. 475-508; Jung, Psychologie Westlicher, vol. 11, pp. 511-549.

192. Jung, Collected Works, vol. 11, p. 480.

193. Ibid.

194. Ibid., p. 481.

195. Ibid., p. 482.

196. Ibid., p. 484.

197. Jung, Psychologie Westlicher, vol. 11, p. 521: "Wir können ruhig annehmen, dass der östliche Ausdruck, der dem Begriff 'mind' entspricht, sich unserem 'Unbewussten' annähert, während unser Begriff 'Geist' mehr oder weniger identisch ist mit Bewusstheit. Für uns ist Bewusstheit undenkbar ohne ein Ich." Thus we may say that "Geist," "Bewusstheit" is near the pāli word "sati," usually translated with "mindfulness."

198. Jung, Collected Works, vol. 11, p. 484.

199. Ibid., p. 486.

200. Ibid., p. 489.

201. Ibid., p. 490.

202. Ibid., p. 491.

203. Ibid., p. 493, and cf. Jung, Psychologie Westlicher, vol. 11, p. 531: "Im Osten sind es Weisheit, Friede, Losgelöstheit und Unbewegtheit einer Psyche,..."

204. Cf. R. Johansson, The Psychology of Nirvana (London: George Allen and Unwin, 1969), pp. 112-115.

205. Cf. Jung, Psychologische Typen, pp. 687ff.

206. See above section on The Choice of Citta.

207. See above section on A Dialogue Between "I" and Citta.

208. See above section on Some Concepts Associated with "I."

209. Jung, Psychologische Typen, p. 637.

210. Jung, Analytical Psychology, p. 183.

211. See above section on The Citta-Dharma Complex and Jung's Ātman-Brahman Complex.

212. Jung, Analytical Psychology, p. 186.

213. Ibid.

214. See above section on The Citta-Dharma Complex.

215. Jung, Analytical Psychology, p. 252.

216. See above section on Some Concepts Associated with "I."

217. Ibid.

218. Ibid.

219. Ibid.

220. See section on _Citta_ and the Process of Release.

221. Ibid.

222. Ibid.

223. Jung, _Psychologische Typen_, p. 637.

224. See section on _Citta_ and the Process of Release.

225. Ibid.

226. C.G. Jung, _Antwort auf Hiob_ (Zürich: Rascher Verlag, 1952), p. 126, and also the connection with the Buddha on p. 96f.

227. See section on _Citta_ and the Process of Release.

228. Jung, _Collected Works_, vol. 6, p. 480; Jung, _Psychologische Typen_, p. 684.

229. See section on _Citta_ and the Process of Release.

230. Ibid., and following.

231. C.G. Jung, _The Archetypes and the Collective Unconscious_ from _Collected Works_, vol. 9, part 1 (New York: Pantheon Books, 1959), p. 113.

232. Cf. G. Ryle, _The Concept of Mind_ (Middlesex: Penguin Books, 1976), pp. 117ff.

233. C.G. Jung, _The Structure and Dynamics of the Psyche_ from _Collected Works_, vol. 8 (New York: Pantheon Books, 1960), p. 485.

234. Ibid., p. 512.

235. See section on _Citta_ and the Process of Release.

236. Ibid., and following.

237. Ibid.

238. Ibid.

239. Jung, _Collected Works_, vol. 8, p. 67.

240. Ibid., p. 91.

MIND/COSMOS MAPS IN THE PĀLI NIKĀYAS

Peter Masefield

According to the Bṛhadāraṇyaka Upaniṣad two quite separate forms of Brahman are to be distinguished, those forms that are:

(a) gross, mortal, immobile and of finite[1] existence; and

(b) subtle, nonmortal, mobile and not subject to decay.[2]

This distinction might be represented diagrammatically in either of two ways:

FIGURE 1

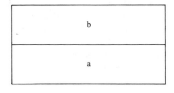
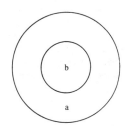

The verses immediately following[3] go on to assert that a similar distinction pertains also in the case of the Ātman—that there are forms of the Ātman that are:

(c) gross, mortal, immobile, of finite[1] existence, other than the breath, other than the space within the Ātman, its essence being the eye; and another that is:

(d) subtle, nonmortal, mobile, not subject to decay, that is the space within the Ātman, its essence being the person in the right eye, and likened to, amongst other things, a flash of lightning or a fire's flame.

This distinction could, in accordance with the above model, be represented as follows:

FIGURE 2

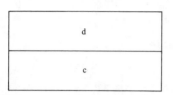

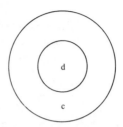

But as everyone knows a recurring theme of many an Upaniṣad is the assertion of the identity of Brahman and Ātman. This should not, of course, be taken as stating that Ātman, the innermost essence of man, enjoys—or can be made to enjoy—unity with Brahman, the innermost essence of the cosmos. Rather it is simply a case of the innermost essence of man being none other than the innermost essence of the cosmos. Ātman simply is Brahman. Or put another way, Ātman and Brahman are two quite separate, but equally legitimate, ways of denoting the same thing, just as the expressions "the morning star" and "the evening star" can both be used to denote the same astral body, Venus. For just as the expression "the morning star" is used to denote the planet Venus from the point of view of the last star to remain visible in the morning, and the expression "the evening star" the planet Venus from the point of view of the first star to become visible in the evening, so do the terms Brahman and Ātman denote the same "something" from first the cosmic standpoint and then the individual person's standpoint. And for this reason such a teaching has, on occasion, come to be called advaita, or, literally, without-a-second. However, continuing the comparison we may also say that just as the expressions "the morning star" and "the evening star" are used to denote what is not, strictly speaking, a star at all, but a planet of this solar system, so too are the terms Brahman and Ātman used to denote an elusive "something" which is, in truth, neither exclusively cosmic nor exclusively individual. And as the above passage makes abundantly clear, this "something"—let us call it reality—when viewed from the cosmic perspective (adhidaivatam) is Brahman, but Ātman when viewed from the perspective of the individual person (adhyātman).[4] And this, it will be noted, is true whether it be the gross or subtle form of either that is in question, although it would seem that the equally important identity pertaining between the gross forms of Brahman and Ātman has not apparently captured the imagination of scholars to the same extent that the identity that pertains between their subtle forms has, despite—or perhaps for reason of—the perturbing challenge that is presented to our intellect by the claim that to talk about the cosmos and to talk about the individual human being are, even at the gross level, but two different ways of talking about the same thing:

FIGURE 3

| Brahman (b) = Ātman (d) |
| Brahman (a) = Ātman (c) |

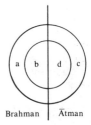

Brahman | Ātman

But we can go even further. For it will be clear that neither talking adhidaivatam nor adhyātman entirely exhaust the various perspectives from which reality can be viewed. Neither cosmic nor
anthropocentric talk can succeed in accommodating the vast variety of
nonhuman furniture about us: tables, trees, cabbages, speech, and so
forth. The Upanisads, not unaware of this, thus introduce us to yet
a third perspective from which reality may be viewed: that from the
perspective of such objects (adhibhūtam).[5] And although this third
perspective does not find mention in the above mentioned
Brhadaranyaka passage, we may, I think, suppose that had it appeared
it too would have been differentiated into a gross and subtle form--
with the result that these forms would, in turn, have to be seen as
similarly identical at the appropriate level with Brahman and Ātman,
such that the true picture would be as follows:

FIGURE 4

| Brahman (b) = Ātman (d) = Objects (f) |
| Brahman (a) = Ātman (c) = Objects (e) |

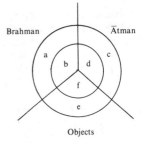

Brahman ... Ātman

Objects

Adhidaivatam, adhyātman, and adhibhūtam are thus three different and
equally relative means of referring to the same neutral "something"
that is reality. All three perspectives on reality admit of differentiation into gross and subtle forms and it is perhaps the relationship pertaining between these two forms within any given perspec-
tive--rather than the identity of each of the three perspectives at a
given level--that has given rise to the more acute philosophical
problems.[6] To assent to the view that one's innermost essence is
ultimately identical with the innermost essence of the cosmc⁻ seems
an easy step when set beside the difficulty of providing a coherent
account of what is meant by the subtle form of a table or of speech.
   To begin to come to an understanding of what these might be one
has to turn to the admittedly somewhat hazy notion of the creation
event alluded to in a few Vedic hymns in which an original and inde-

finable state of cosmic potential in which being born and dying—and indeed time itself—were unknown gave birth from itself, for reasons unknown and in a manner variously hinted at, to a manifest realm in the form of the phenomenal world whose subjects have but finite existence, being firmly under the sway of decay and death. But in the process the original state of potential did not entirely disappear; instead it remained as a hidden three-quarters beyond its one manifest quarter. On occasion the whole was conceived of in the form of a man:

> The Man, indeed, is this All, what has been and what is to be the lord of the immortal[7] spheres which he surpasses by consuming food. Such is the measure of his might, and greater still than this is Man. All beings are a fourth of him, three-fourths are the immortal[7] in heaven. Three-fourths of Man ascended high, one-fourth took birth again down here. From this he spread in all directions into animate and inanimate things.[8]

From this it is clear that the whole of the phenomenal world together with its human inhabitants, its animate and inanimate objects—that is to say, whether looked at adhidaivatam, adhyātman, or adhibhūtam— was considered to be simply a manifest quarter of all that is, being transcended by a further hidden, and unmanifest, three-quarters where death does not pertain:

> Knowing eternity, may the gandharva declare to us that highest secret station. Three-quarters thereof lie hidden in the darkness . . . .[9]

Moreover, since each constituent of the phenomenal world is none other than a "spreading" of the manifest quarter of the Man, and since a further three-quarters of that Man remain unmanifest on high, each constituent must be thought to have, in some sense, as part of its being a further unmanifest aspect, a hidden three-quarters on high. Such was, at least, believed to hold in the case of speech:

> Speech is measured in four quarters. Brāhmaṇas who possess insight know these four divisions. Three-quarters, concealed in secret, cause no movement. The fourth is the quarter that is spoken by men.[10]

And if this be true of speech—itself but one element of the "spreading"—it seems reasonable to suppose, in light of the foregoing considerations, that this might also be true of all such elements, including tables.

Thus it would appear that each and every constituent of the phenomenal world was thought simply the manifest (or gross), mortal form of something whose total nature included a further unmanifest (or subtle), nonmortal form by means of which it was rooted in the nonmortal transcendent three-quarters; and that this is true, moreover, whether reality be looked upon adhidaivatam, adhyātman, or adhibhūtam.

Figure 5

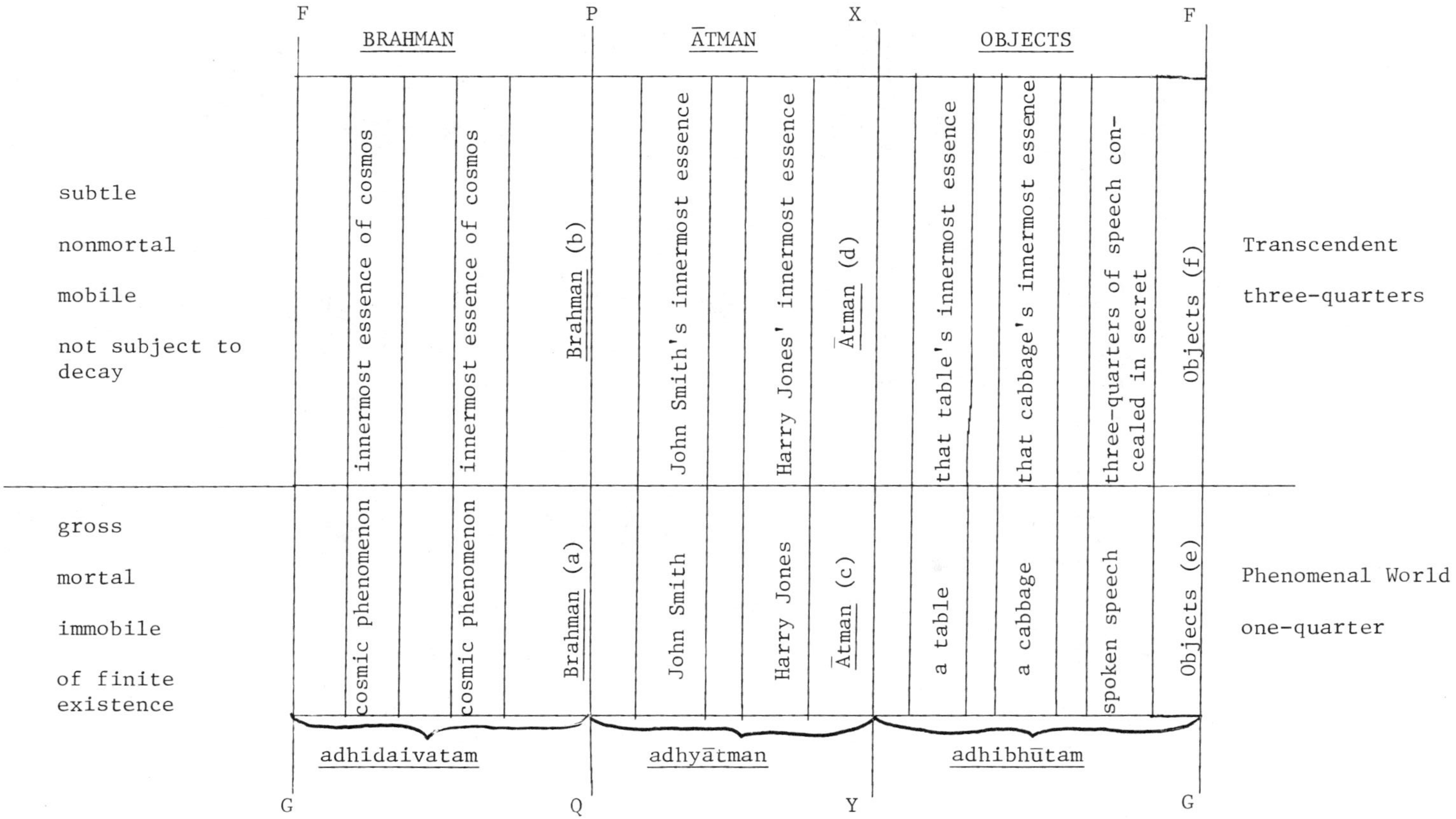

	gross / mortal / immobile / of finite existence	subtle / nonmortal / mobile / not subject to decay
BRAHMAN (adhidaivatam)	cosmic phenomenon	innermost essence of cosmos
	cosmic phenomenon	innermost essence of cosmos
	Brahman (a)	Brahman (b)
ĀTMAN (adhyātman)	John Smith	John Smith's innermost essence
	Harry Jones	Harry Jones' innermost essence
	Ātman (c)	Ātman (d)
OBJECTS (adhibhūtam)	a table	that table's innermost essence
	a cabbage	that cabbage's innermost essence
	spoken speech	three-quarters of speech concealed in secret
	Objects (e)	Objects (f)
	one-quarter Phenomenal World	three-quarters Transcendent

74

FIGURE 6

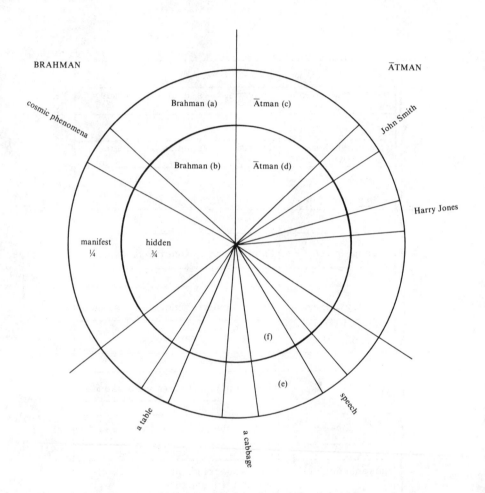

OBJECTS

In addition, we can see at a glance from Figure 5 precisely what is meant by the frequently recurring Upanisadic assertion of the identity of Brahman and Ātman (and, presumably of objects too): all we have to do is imagine the figure folded along the lines PQ and XY to form a triangular tube. Or better still we might conceive the whole as an inverted three-faced pyramid:

Figure 7

OBJECTS

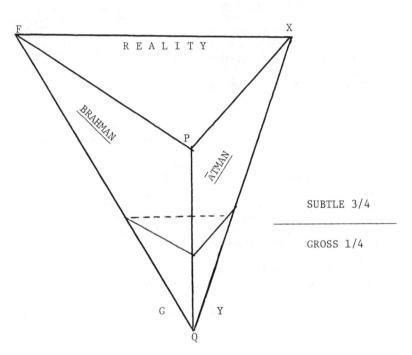

REALITY

BRAHMAN

P

ĀTMAN

SUBTLE 3/4

GROSS 1/4

G   Y

Q

Reality is Brahman when viewed adhidaivatam, Ātman when viewed adhyātman and objects when viewed adhibhūtam—and this is true whether it be the subtle or the gross form of that reality that is under discussion. It should also be noted, however, that such an assertion of identity by no means implies any further identity between these subtle and gross forms—these remain, rather, quite distinct, as indeed the Brhadaranyaka passage above makes quite clear.

Thus we may say, by way of summary, that the Vedic-Upanisadic tradition culminated in the view that to talk in terms of cosmic phenomena (adhidaivatam) and to talk in terms of individual persons (adhyātman) was, ultimately, simply to employ different modes of expression to denote one and the same thing, namely reality; but at the same time that reality nonetheless admitted of two aspects, or forms, namely the gross, the phenomenal world of becoming characterized by the presence of being born and dying, and the subtle, the hidden three-quarters transcending that world where such being born and dying were unknown.

To draw attention to these points may be felt, by some, not to
say anything very new. But I have felt the need to labor these
points since I feel that it has not been generally appreciated, or at
least ever taken into serious account, that very much the same world
view is presupposed in the teachings of the Pāli Nikāyas.[11] That is
to say, it is simply taken for granted in these texts (and assumed
that those to whom their teachings are addressed already are fully
aware) that to talk in terms of the cosmos and to talk in terms of
the individual--or better in terms of an individual's various levels
of consciousness--are simply two alternative, and equally valid,
means of denoting the same thing, some neutral, though elusive,
ground lying amidst the two. And as with the Upaniṣads neither is in
any sense prior nor, by the same token, is either reducible to the
other. It is simply not true that to talk adhidaivatam is merely a
figurative means of alluding to what is in fact purely a state of
mind. Regrettably such a view has, however, tended to become
fashionable among Western scholars of Buddhism (and among those in
the East aping the bad habits of the West)--and particularly so in
the case of nibbāna, despite the fact that in the Nikāyas nibbāna is
spoken of, if anything, as a place as often as it is a state of mind.
Some blame in this regard must be levelled against the Pāli Text
Society's Pāli-English Dictionary which, while citing many of the
adhidaivatam epithets for nibbāna, nonetheless prefaces the entry
with the statement that "Nibbāna is purely and solely an ethical
state, to be reached in this birth by ethical practices, contemplation and insight. It is therefore not transcendental." That such a
view is out of keeping with the teachings of the Nikāyas can be seen
from an examination of Buddhist cosmography and it is to this that
we, keeping in mind the above Upaniṣadic models, must now turn our
attention.

It may be said to begin with that Buddhist cosmography differentiated a subtle level of reality, or nibbāna, from the gross level,
the phenomenal world of becoming, or saṃsāra, which it transcended.
The latter it then subdivided into the Brahmaloka and the kāmaloka:[12]

FIGURE 8

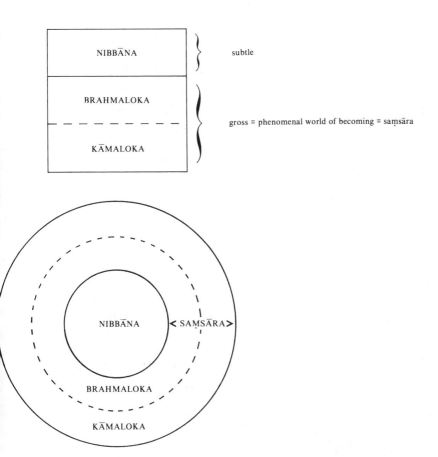

Each of these subdivisions is, in turn, further differentiated, adhidaivatam, into a number of cosmic regions arranged hierarchically in vertical succession (e.g., M,i,289; iii,99ff.). At the same time, however, these two subdivisions were also regarded, adhyātman, as the sphere—or part thereof—of human consciousness and internally stratified in accordance with the various levels of such consciousness differentiated by the Buddhists. And most importantly, perhaps, the various cosmic regions seem to have been regarded as the adhidaivatam counterparts of these different levels of consciousness—or rather reality, at any given level, seems to have been considered, adhidaivatam, as this or that cosmic region and at the same time, adhyātman, as this or that level of consciousness. In particular, the kāmaloka was understood, adhidaivatam, generally as consisting of six heavenly worlds[13] but, adhyātman, as the five (or six) types of sensory consciousness, while the Brahmaloka was similarly understood, adhidaivatam, as a variety of cosmic regions but, adhyātman, as the four jhānas or the four jhāna-associated Brahmavihāras.[14]

Figure 9

	Adhidaivatam	Adhyātman
NIBBĀNA	Place	State of mind
BRAHMALOKA	Akanittha Sudassī Sudassa Atappa } Pure Aviha } Abodes Asaññasatta Vehapphala	4th jhāna
	Subhakinha Appamānasubha Parittasubha	3rd jhāna
	Ābhassara Appamānābha Parittābha	2nd jhāna
	Mahābrahmās Brahmapurohitas } Brahmakāyika Brahmaparisajjas } devas	1st jhāna
KĀMALOKA	Paranimmitavasavatti Nimmānarati Tusita Yāma Tāvatimsa Cātummahārājika devas (Earth)	Six types of sensory consciousness

While there is, to my knowledge, no complete and detailed account of these correlations in the Nikāyas, they nonetheless seem frequently taken for granted as, for instance, in the belief that rebirth in this or that region of the cosmos was dependent upon the appropriate modification of an individual's consciousness prior to dying (M,iii, 99ff.), especially in the case of rebirth in the Brahmaloka for which prior cultivation of the appropraite jhāna or Brahmavihāra was essential.[15] That is to say, it seems assumed that one could not hope to attain, adhidaivatam, any world without prior experience of its adhyātman counterpart—and since attainment, adhidaivatam, of the Brahmaloka requires that all six heavens of the kāmaloka be transcended, so too would such attainment be open only to those who had, at some point hitherto, similarly transcended that kāmaloka adhyātman, as one indeed does when separating oneself from all sensory consciousness as a preliminary to the attainment of jhāna.[16] By the time of the Abhidhamma literature and the commentaries, however, such views begin to be stated more explicitly[17] and at Dhs,160ff., for instance, we find it stipulated that jhāna is the means of attaining the Brahmaloka.[18] Similarly at Asl,388 we find the bold assertion that the nethermost region of the Brahmaloka is "the 'place of Brahma-(devas)' called the plane of First Jhāna,"[19] a statement having fascinating implications. For it must, by now, be apparent that since we all, for most of the time, inhabit the kāmaloka both adhyātman and adhidaivatam in the sense that sensory consciousness is operative within us and we are, simultaneously, moving about one or other cosmic region of the kāmaloka, so too does it follow that anyone who attains the Brahmaloka adhyātman through entry into one or another jhāna must simultaneously, so long as that jhāna persists, in some sense participate adhidaivatam in the corresponding region of the Brahmaloka. Certainly it has become the traditional belief that it is possible to make contact with the devas of a particular region of the Brahmaloka through entering into the appropriate jhāna,[20] and this belief finds support at M,ii,37 (cf. D,i,215ff.) where a monk is said to attain the fourth jhāna and then to remain talking and carrying on conversation with all the devatās that have arisen in that world, and even more vividly at A,i,182ff. where the Buddha states that at such times as he enters upon the jhānas or Brahmavihāras, his walking up and down, his standing, his sitting and lying down is, respectively, dibbam or brahmam.[21]

Now it will no doubt have already been noticed that the analysis in Figure 9 fails to accommodate the so-called arūpa-jhānas and the nirodha-samāpatti to which these pave the way. But this is no accident, for it is only in the later literature that the four arūpāyatanas begin to be spoken of as jhānas. And even when they do, it remains clear that they continued to be looked upon, as they always had been looked upon, not as separate jhānas over and above the four rūpa-jhānas but simply as modifications on the fourth of those rūpa-jhānas due to the persistence in such states of concentration and equanimity, the twin jhāna-factors characterizing the fourth rūpa-jhāna (e.g., Vsm,X,5ff.). This suggests that we should hesitate before assuming that the arūpaloka (or arūpāvacara) was ever thought, either adhidaivatam or adhyātman, to intervene between the rūpaloka and nibbāna. Rather we might suppose that since these four arūpāyatanas were simply modifications of a jhāna whose adhidaivatam

80

counterpart admitted of no less than seven distinct regions—and
since access to the adhidaivatam counterparts of those modifications
should, in principle, be gained from any one of these seven—the true
location[22] of these realms had been understood by the authors of
the Nikāyas as follows.

Figure 10

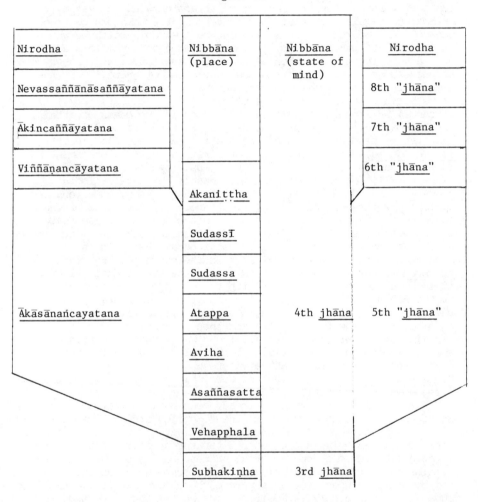

Such an analysis, we may note, finds independent support from the otherwise rather curious statement[23] that the Buddha, at his Parinibbāna, rose progressively through the four rūpa-jhānas, the four arūpayatanas and, according to some accounts,[24] into nirodha-samāpatti, then descended through each of these in reverse order and finally ascended yet again to the fourth rūpa-jhāna from which he passed into nibbāna. For if the presuppositions of Figure 10 are correct, this is precisely what he would have had to do—it was necessary that he return to the fourth rūpa-jhāna in order to pass into nibbāna since no such route exists from any of its arūpāyatana modifications. The fourth rūpa-jhāna alone shares a common border with nibbāna.

Or rather we should say that the border between nibbāna and the phenomenal world of becoming consists, adhyātman, of the fourth jhāna but also, adhidaivatam, of the Akaniṭṭha realm. For just as there is, for any level of consciousness, a cosmic realm that is its counterpart, so too do we find nibbāna spoken of as a place as often as it is a state of mind: it is the island (dīpa), the cave (lena), the shelter (tāṇam), the refuge (saraṇam),[25] the delightful stretch of level ground (S,iii,108f.),[26] that lying beyond (pāram)[27] the world becoming (Dhp,348) into which the path plunges (S,v,41,43,54), the unchanging place in which those who go (yanti) there, having gone (gantvā) do not grieve (Dhp,225). There is, to my mind, no reason why we should not take such expressions quite literally—had the authors of the Nikāyas wished they could, as indeed they do when speaking of the adhyātman attainment of nibbāna, have chosen from a wide range of Pāli terms. But when, as here, the emphasis is instead on its adhidaivatam attainment, it is not at all unusual to find the goal spoken of as a cosmic location—for example, disā (A,iii,164; Dhp,323; cf. Sn,960)—and, as above, the means of getting there expressed by such common verbs for physical motion as yāti and gacchati. Indeed, given the right conditions, nibbāna like all places, was capable also of being both seen and heard:[28] the texts frequently mention those who were seers of the nonmortal (amataddasa—A,ii,451; Vv,I,16[11] [=nibbānadassāvinī, VvA,85]), while as the Buddha, the veil-lifter (D,i,89 = ii, 16 = iii, 142 = Sn,p. 106), himself points out (M,i,509ff.), he, the unsurpassed physician and surgeon (It,101) was able, through teaching Dhamma in such a way that others might see nibbāna (nibbānam passeyyāsi), to restore the sight of a world that had become blind (Vin,i,7 = M,i,171). And this was, in turn, possible since through the Buddha's decision to teach the doors to the nonmortal, or nibbāna, had been flung wide open (Vin,i, 7 = D,ii,39 = M,i,169 = S,i,138; cp. It,80; Mhv,iii,319), causing that nonmortal to become both visible and audible. Thus it was that, shortly after this decision, the Buddha journeyed to Kasi beating the drum that is the nonmortal (amata-dundubhim—Vin,i,8 = M,i,171) for those with ears to hear, those that did so hear, the Buddha's sāvakas,[29] finding themselves as a consequence standing knocking at those same doors (S,ii,43,45,54).

It would be—indeed for most has been—an all too easy step into assuming that this admittedly vivid language is nonetheless simply a figurative means of referring to what is, in fact, only a state of mind. But this is, I feel, a temptation to be avoided: if, as I have tried to show, there is reason to believe that for the authors of the

Pāli Nikāyas to talk adhidaivatam or adhyātman were simply alternative windows on the sensory world of the kāmaloka and supersensory
world of the Brahmaloka, there seems no good reason why they should
not also have held this to be so in the case of nibbāna; and while it
would be foolish to deny that nibbāna, as the Buddhist goal, is frequently depicted as a mental state, such as the destruction of passion, hatred, and delusion (e.g., S,iv,251,261) and so forth, we need
not allow this to overshadow the fact that it is, perhaps equally
often, portrayed, adhidaivatam, as a visible and audible place or
region transcending the phenomenal world of becoming. And when it is
spoken of in this way it sounds extremely reminiscent not only of the
hidden nonmortal three-quarters of the Vedas but also of the subtle
nonmortal form of Brahman encountered here and there in the
Upanisads. For in addition to being styled nonmortal, it is also
frequently said to be unborn (Ud,80f; It,37; cp.M,i,326ff. S,i,
142ff.), undecaying (ajjaram--S,iv,369) and free from fear (abhayā
nāma sā disā--Sn,33; nibbānaṃ akutobhayaṃ--S,i,192; It,122)--and thus
remarkably similar to the following account of the subtle form of
Brahman:

> This is that the great unborn self who is undecaying,
> undying, nonmortal, free from fear, Brahman. Verily,
> Brahman is free from fear. He who knows this becomes
> Brahman who is free from fear (sa vā esa mahān ajātmā
> ajaro amaro 'mrto 'Bhayo brahma; abhayam vai brahma,
> abhayam hi vai brahma bhavati ya evaṃ veda--BU,IV,4,25).

Nor is this all, for at several places in the Upanisads the hidden
three-quarters is also spoken of in the following terms:

> In the highest golden sheath is Brahman, stainless,
> without parts; pure is it, the light of lights. That
> is what the knowers of the self know. The sun shines
> not there, nor the moon and stars, these lightnings
> shine not, where then could this fire be? His shining
> illumines all this world. Brahman, verily, is this
> nonmortal (Mundaka,U,II,2,10-12; cp. SU,VI,14; Katha,U,II,2,15).

This description finds extraordinary parallel at two places in the
Nikāyas:

> Where water, earth, heat, and wind find no footing,
> there no stars gleam, no sun is made visible, there
> shines no moon, there the darkness (tamo = Mara's
> realm) is not found; and when the sage, the brahmin,
> himself in wisdom knows (this place) he is freed from
> the rūpa and the arūpa realms, from happiness and
> dukkha (Ud,9).

Similarly:

> There is, monks, that sphere where there is neither
> earth, water, heat, wind; nor the spheres of
> infinite space, infinite consciousness, nothingness,

neither-consciousness-nor-unconsciousness; nor this
world nor a world beyond nor both together nor sun
and moon. There too, monks, I say there is no
coming to birth nor going to another destiny, no
duration, no falling, no arising. It is without
support, without foundation, without basis whatsoever.
This is indeed the end of dukkha (Ud,80).

I do not believe that we have in such passages, descriptive of
the Buddhist goal, either an ethical state pure and simple or even
such a state referred to merely figuratively. Rather it seems abundantly clear from these and other passages cited elsewhere in this
article that there was envisaged, even witnessed, by the authors of
the Nikāyas a realm lying beyond the phenomenal world of becoming,
beyond this world of conditioned existence, in which the limitations
pertaining in the phenomenal world—such as being born and dying—
were unknown. Moreover it is also abundantly clear that this realm
is often spoken of in terms surprisingly reminiscent of the manner in
which the hidden three-quarters is portrayed in both the Vedas and
the Upanisads; and that, indeed, were it not for the postulation of
such a place, of such a sanctuary, beyond the phenomenal world, it
would be difficult to see how the Buddhists could have avoided the
charge that their description of nibbāna was tantamount to one of
annihiliation. Such a thought, it seems, also occurred to the Buddha
himself:

Monks, there is that which is not subject to being
born, to becoming, to being made, to being conditioned.
Monks, if there were not that which is not subject to
be born, to becoming, to being made, to being conditioned,
there could be made known no escape from that which is
subject to being born, to becoming, to being made, to
being conditioned here.
But since, monks, there is that which is not subject
to being born, to becoming, to being made, to being
conditioned, therefore the escape from that which is
subject to being born, to becoming, to being made, to
being conditioned, is made known (Ud,80f.).

It was precisely because there was a further realm, both adhidaivatam
and adhyātman, beyond the phenomenal world of samsāra that escape
from the latter's conditioned existence was at all possible, such escape being effected by treading the eightfold path to the nonmortal
sanctuary into which it plunged.[30]
Thus I have tried to show that an examination of the various
terms and modes of expression employed by the authors of the Pāli
Nikāyas suggests that they, in all probability, shared a worldview
very similar to that encountered in the Vedic and Upanisadic tradition, a worldview which while differentiating reality into a subtle,
unmanifest form and a gross, manifest form at the same time took for
granted that to talk about the cosmos or to talk about human consciousness were simply two alternative means of denoting one and the
same reality. In Buddhist hands the subtle form of that reality also
came to be spoken of as lokuttara, the gross as lokiya—terms which

in themselves might be thought further evidence for the position I
have been outlining—yet, at the same time, it is here that the Buddhists may have deviated somewhat from the tradition that had gone
before. For as I have suggested elsewhere[31]—and a matter too complex other than simply to hint at here—when the Buddha did bring it
about that some individual experienced nibbāna both visually and
aurally, that person at that same moment underwent a spiritual rebirth, the ariyan birth (M,ii,103; VvA,81,194f), which resulted in a
transformation of his entire being in which he was removed, once and
for all, from the lokiya plane and translated, instead, onto the
lokuttara plane. In the process he was exorcised from Mara's powerful influence,[32] was spared the possibility of any future birth other
than as a man or deva, while of these a maximum of only seven could
intervene before he quit samsāra altogether and, we may presume, re-
sort to his essence in the hidden three-quarters.[33] But the very
fact that some humans and devas might themselves be lokuttara suggests that the lokuttara plane, through their presence,[34] was believed somehow to intervene amidst the lokiya. That is to say, it
seems that in the Buddhist context reality was understood, not so
much in terms of a dichotomy between, on the one hand, its gross and
subtle forms and, on the other, its adhidaivatam and adhyātman aspects, but rather that it was possible to discern within both the adhidaivatam and adhyātman aspects, both a lokuttara and a lokiya
plane. Or put another way, the transcendent was in some sense
dragged down partially into the mundane, such that the true analysis
of the cosmic mind/mental world encountered in the Nikāyas might be
shown as follows.

85

Figure 11

a place =   NIBBĀNA   = state of mind

Nirodha
Nevasaññānāsaññāyatana
Ākincaññāyatana
Viññānañcāyatana

Ākāsānañcāyatana

Nirodha
8th "jhāna"
7th "jhāna"
6th "jhāna"

5th "jhāna"

Lokuttara
plane =
subtle
Brahman/Ātman

ADHIDAIVATAM	NIBBĀNA	ADHYĀTMAN
Akaniṭṭha		
Sudassī		
Sudassa		
Atappa	4th jhāna (lokuttara)	
Aviha		
Asaññasatta	4th jhāna (mundane)	
Vehapphala		
Subhakiṇha		
Appamāṇasubha	3rd jhāna	
Parittasubha		
Ābhassara		
Appamāṇābha	2nd jhāna	
Parittābha		
Mahābrahmās		
Brahmapurohitas	1st jhāna	
Brahmaparisajjas		
Paranimmitavasavatti		
Nimmānarati		
Tusita		
Yāma	sense-consciousness	
Tāvatiṃsa		
Cātummahārājika devas		
Earth		
Vinipāta		

Despite this slight deviation—and who is to say that such a deviation might not also be necessary in the Upaniṣadic model in order to accommodate humans who had similar insight[35]—the basic relationship between the two planes remains: while reality might, adhidaivatam and adhyātman, be ultimately the same thing, the lokuttara and lokiya planes wherever they were to be found remained as mutually exclusive as had the subtle and gross forms of Brahman/Ātman. Nowhere in the nikāyas is there any suggestion that the lokuttara plane of nibbāna and the lokiya plane of saṃsāra are anything but distinct: the additional identification of the lokuttara and lokiya planes had to await Nagarjuna's assertion of there being, ultimately, no differentiation between nirvāṇa and saṃsāra, just as the same identification of the subtle and gross forms of Brahman/Ātman had to await Śankara's similar assertion to the effect that the gross was, in fact, none other than the subtle seen through the distorting influence of māyā. And it may be for this reason above all others that the latter came to be daubed a crypto-Buddhist.

NOTES

1. Or temporal; since it exists in time it is finite.
2. Dve vāva brahmano rūpe, mūrtam caivāmūrtaṃ ca, martyaṃ cāmṛtam ca, sthitam ca, yac ca, sac ca, tyac ca—BU,II,3,1.
3. BU,II,3,4-6.
4. BU,II,3,3-4.
5. Compare the observations of R.C. Zaehner:

adhyātman, adhibhūtam, and adhidaivatam are all common Upanishadic adverbs meaning "with reference to the individual" (=exactly Pāli ajjhattaṃ), "with reference to creatures or contingent beings in general," and "with reference to the gods or external phenomena": see G.A. Jacob's Concordance ad loc.. . . To translate them as if they were independent substantives is quite contrary to Upanishadic usage and therefore inadmissible. Adhyātman is in fact used in the sense indicated thirty-seven times in the classical Upanishads, adhibhūtam four times, and adhidaivatam fourteen times. Adhyātman and adhidaivatam are regularly contrasted (twelve times) while the three terms appear together in BU,3,7,14-15; adhidaivatam referring (as always) to what is outside man (earth, water, sky, sun etc.), adhyātman to what is inside man, while adhibhūtam refers to contingent beings in general.

See The Bhagavad-Gītā (London: 1969), pp. 259f.

6. For some, of course, and somewhat contrary to this Upaniṣadic passage at least, the gross is in fact the subtle distorted by māyā and taken to extremes the introduction of the notion of māyā allows the move to a position of extreme advaita in which the apparent distinction between the gross and subtle forms as well as that between the three different perspectives collapses. The relationship of the gross to the subtle rears in Buddhist circles in the guise of the relationship between saṃsāra and nirvāṇa.

7. Or nonmortal, amṛta-.
8. RV,S,90,2-4.
9. AV,II,1,2.
10. RV,I,164,45.
11. This should not, of course, be taken as implying that the Buddha, whose recorded utterances the Nikāyas are traditionally held to be—or other authors of these texts—were necessarily familiar with Upaniṣads or their teachings, and especially not in the form in which we now have them today. Nor does it necessarily have anything to say on the (to my mind) relatively uninteresting question as to whether the Nikāyas, in whole or in part, either preceded or were subsequent to the Upaniṣads. Indeed, the fact that the Nikāyas seem to assume a world view only rarely made explicit in the Upaniṣads may imply nothing more than that these two bodies of texts took for granted the world view common in the society of their day; or alternatively, and perhaps more charitably, we ought not to be too surprised if windows on reality opened by the enlightened minds of roughly contemporaneous men, reared and nourished in much the same cultural and geographical setting, tend to allow one a remarkably similar vision. As to the objection that the Upaniṣadic assertion of the existence of the Ātman and its apparent denial in the so-called doctrine of anattā in the Nikāyas does much to undermine the parallel, I simply crave the reader's patience to postpone judgment on this issue until the Buddhist position has been more fully reviewed.
12. The meanings of these terms—or at least the way in which they might best be rendered into English so as to retain those meanings—is somewhat unclear. The kāmaloka, which might be rendered "the sense-desire world," seems rather to mean the world in which the sense-desires pertain, whether this be the sense-desires themselves, adhyātman, or the cosmic worlds which correspond, adhidaivatam, to such sense-desires. This should become clearer below. I do not think that the true meaning of the term Brahmaloka has ever attracted the investigation it assuredly deserves. And if caution be advisable to avoid a hasty, and quite probably faulty, interpretation of the term kāmaloka, how much more is this necessary in the case of the term Brahmaloka, especially when we cannot be sure whether the first member of the compound was intended as a reference to Brahman, Brahmā(s) or simply (though I very much doubt it) adjectivally in the sense of "holy" or "pure" and so forth. It may also be mentioned here that the Kāmaloka is often also referred to by means of the term kāmāvacara. In such cases the Brahmaloka is, instead, denoted jointly by the terms rūpāvacara and arūpāvacara, or by the terms rūpaloka and arūpaloka. This further subdivision of the Brahmaloka into its rūpa and arūpa aspects does not affect the points being made here. While one can speak of an arūpaloka as a cosmic counterpart of the arūpa jhānas, it would be fallacious to assume that this "world" intervened between the rūpaloka and nibbāna. Strictly speaking, the arūpa jhānas are not separate jhānas at all but simply modifications upon the fourth jhāna, and thus the arūpaloka as their cosmic counterpart—if talk of an arūpa cosmic region makes any sense whatever—is but itself a side-step within the cosmic counterpart of the fourth jhāna. This too should become clearer below.
13. According to Dhs,1281-7 the kāmaloka extends from the Avīci hell up to the Paranimmitavasavatti deva world which, of course, in-

cludes in passing the earth itself. For this reason it might be argued that the kāmaloka admitted, adhidaivatam, of more than six regions, and this may well be a valid objection. It may, in fact, be simply a coincidence that the kāmaloka had six heavenly regions and six types of sensory consciousness. At the same time, however, it is worth bearing in mind that (1) at times the tradition has tended to conflate the Nimmānarati and Paranimmitavasavatti devalokas (e.g. VvA,79f., on which see the note in my forthcoming translation to be published by the Pāli Text Society, London) allowing the earth, together with its subterranean hells, to form a sixth region; while (2) at others it has appeared to consider the earth—and certainly the peta world (D,iii,197f.)—as part of the region policed by the Cātummahārājika devas whose authority extends from the earth's surface to the summit of Mount Meru, where begins the tāvatimsa realm (see PS,147[132] and the Introduction to the forthcoming translation of VvA). I admit that at first sight a one-to-one correlation may seem unlikely but I am not, at the same time, convinced that the occurrence of a sixfold division adhidaivatam and adhyātman is entirely accidental.

14. It is worth noting in passing that the original connotation of this term may have been simply an abiding (vihāra) in the Brahma (loka) which is, of course, precisely what these four, adhidaivatam, are.

15. In the series of suttas at A,ii,126-30 we find practice of the four jhānas leads respectively to rebirth among the Brahmakāyika, Ābhassara, Subhakinha and Vehapphala devas or alternatively among the devas of the Pure Abodes, the same destiny awaiting those who, instead, had been given to cultivating the four Brahmavihāras; while at A,i,266f. rebirth in the arūpa worlds is similarly dependent upon prior familiarity with the arūpa modifications on the fourth jhāna that are their adhyātman counterparts (see below). Interesting in this connection is Sāriputta's establishment of the dying Dhānañjāni in the Brahmaloka, apparently by way of the Brahmavihāras (M,ii,194f.) as are the other cases of deathbed exhortation recorded in the Nikāyas, which seem to anticipate the practice of postmortem exhortation by way of the Tibetan Book of the Dead. For details, see my doctoral dissertation "Thus They Once Heard: Oral Initiation in the Pāli Nikāyas" (author's Ph.D. dissertation, University of Lancaster, 1980), p. 186f. Upon the question of correlation it must here be added that although as already noted, all the cosmic regions in Figure 9 are attested in the Nikāyas, there is, to my knowledge, no attempt to correlate any of the worlds of the rūpaloka other than those mentioned in A,ii,126-130 with either the four jhānas or the Brahmavihāras. When the later tradition did so, they assumed that each of the first three jhānas were associated with three cosmic regions, the latter being, in the case of each jhāna, the cosmic destiny for those who had previously enjoyed weak, medium, and full experience of that jhāna (e.g. Vbh,424; quoted Vsm,Xi,123, for which a possible forerunner may be found in M,iii,147). But this fails to explain why the adhidaivatam counterpart of the fourth jhāna admits of no less than seven distinct realms. In his Buddhist Dictionary (Colombo: Deva, 1972), Nyanatiloka suggests that the Vehapphala and Asaññasatta realms are for those with experience of the fourth jhāna, while the five Pure Abodes are for anāgāmins. This is, however, not

entirely correct, for while it may certainly be true that the Pure
Abodes do not open their doors to anyone who is not an anāgāmin (cf.
M,i,82), it does not follow that anāgāmins are not to be found elsewhere in the Brahmaloka, such as among the Brahmakāyika devas
(A,ii,126,129; iii,287; iv,59ff.), the Ābhassara, Subhakiṇha, and
Vehapphala devas (A,ii,126-30), and indeed also in the various arūpa
worlds (A,i,267f.; ii,160). One may feel that the uneasiness already
noted in the correlation of the adhidaivataṃ and adhyātman aspects of
the kāmaloka are, if anything, only exacerbated by the correlation of
each jhāna with several distinct cosmic regions and that we have in
the Nikāyas either a cosmography in the making or one inherited, in
whole or in part, from some contemporary or preceding tradition. The
Upaniṣads list, on occasion, numerous heaven worlds in apparent vertical array (e.g. BU,III,6,1; IV,3,33) as do the various texts of the
Jainas though I do not suggest that either was the source upon which
the Buddhists may have drawn—and especially not in the case of the
latter which are, given the relatively recent date of extant Jaina
works, more likely to have themselves been influenced by the Buddhists. But since a multilayered cosmos is encountered in the works
of sects other than Buddhist it may be that while, in the Nikāyas,
the adhidaivataṃ/adhyātman correlation was taken for granted, the
marriage between the Buddhist experiences of jhāna and an inherited
cosmography was not for some time a very happy one.

16. Vivicc' eva kāmehi-stock (e.g., M,i,181). See also A,iv,
410f. and its commentary AA,iv,193f. which both assert, quite explicitly, how the senses are transcended during the attainment of jhāna.

17. That the Brahmavihāras are the means to the Brahmaloka
adhidaivataṃ is, of course, already explicitly asserted at such
places as D,i,250f., M,ii,207f. and so forth. However it is of great
interest to find in these later texts the introduction of the view
that reality was divisible into that which was ajjhattaṃ (=the precise Pāli form of Sanskrit adhyātman) and that which was bāhira/
bahiddha (external). Thus at Dhs,673f. (742ff. 1207ff.) rūpa is
explained ajjhattikaṃ as the five (or six) senses, bāhiraṃ as the
five (or six) kinds of sense objects. In the Buddhist context it
would seem that while ajjhattaṃ at all times closely parallels
Upaniṣadic adhyātman, in the case of the kāmaloka the emphasis of its
opposite, bāhira/bahiddha, tends to fall on the adhibhūtaṃ aspect and
in the case of the Brahmaloka on the adhidaivataṃ aspect.

18. In such literature the view also emerges that the reason
for this is kamma (e.g. Dhs,499ff., quoted Vsm,XVII,123ff.; also
Vsm,VII,17-19) although no further details or elaboration seem provided. I am informed that Vasubandhu states in his Abhidharmakośa
that a unique species of karma is generated in samādhi (called apparently mi gyo ba'i las in Tibetan) and that it is this that results
in the subsequent rebirth in the Brahmaloka. I have been unable to
confirm this since at the time of writing this work was not available
to me.

19. So the rendering at Expositor 496; the Pāli original was
not available to me.

20. I suspect (despite MA,iii,275) that such cases are quite
distinct from the more common phenomenon of individuals visiting
various regions of the cosmos—both in the kāmaloka and the
Brahmaloka—through the power of iddhi based on the fourth jhāna, a

practice in which, if VvA is anything to go by, Mahāmoggallāna was
most adept. This latter allows the Buddha to visit the Brahmaloka
with his own body and not simply in a mind-made body created for the
purpose (S,v,282) and is presumably the means employed at M,i,326ff.

S,i,142ff. when the Buddha visits the Brahmaloka to chastise Baka
Brahma and D,ii,50ff. when he repairs to the Pure Abodes to question
their anāgāmin inhabitants.

21. The precise distinction intended by styling such activities
dibbaṃ (heavenly) if performed after entering into one or another of
the jhānas and brahmaṃ (?) if performed after entering into one or
another of the Brahmavihāras escapes me completely. Whatever its
meaning, the same distinction seems in mind at A,ii,183f. where one
is said to become devappatta when dwelling in any of the four jhānas
and Brahmappatta when dwelling in any of the four Brahmavihāras; and
also at A,iii,224ff. where one is said to become devasama on being
reborn in a sugatiṃ saggaṃ lokaṃ after practice of the four jhānas
and Brahmasama on being reborn in a sugatiṃ Brahmalokaṃ after practice of the four Brahmavihāras. One might suppose that expressions
such as dibbaṃ, devappatta, and devasama—as indeed that of sugatiṃ
saggaṃ lokaṃ—would refer to the various heavenly realms of the
kāmaloka, were it not for the counterevidence against these apparently maverick passages to be found elsewhere in the Nikāyas. The
commentaries are unanimously of no help whatsoever, leaving one to
speculate whether their authors were not themselves at a loss to know
how to deal with these apparent deviations.

22. If the location of an arūpa realm makes any sense.

23. One may wonder as to the basis for such a statement. It is
unlikely that the Buddha himself gave a running commentary on his
last moments; while at the same time it seems dubious, to say the
least, that any of those present were able to witness the events
interior to the Buddha's chain of consciousness. And since the
Nikāyas, of which this passage forms a part, are, as canonical texts,
attributed to the Buddha's own mouth, the true origin of these texts
is itself brought into question.

24. So D,ii,156; S,i,158 omits.

25. S,iv,372.

26. The significance of this epithet can be understood better
when the episode at M,iii,130 is consulted.

27. S,iv,369.

28. See Masefield, "Oral Initiation in the Pāli Nikāyas," pp.
78–93 and passim.

29. See Masefield, "Oral Initiation of the Pāli Nikāyas," which
is a study of the concept of the sāvaka.

30. Once one allows that nibbāna can be seen as a place
existing, to some extent, independently outside of one, rather than
as a state of mind to be cultivated within, Nāgasena's remarks that
although the Lord had pointed out to his sāvakas the path to the
realization of nibbāna, he had not, in so doing, pointed out any
cause for this production of nibbāna are easily understood, as is his
choice of similes to explain the matter in terms of one's reaching
the Himālaya or the further shore of the Great Ocean (Miln, 268ff.).
However, given the identity that pertains between the adhidaivataṃ
and adhyātaman aspects, the claim that nibbāna is any more outside of
one than is, say, the Brahmaloka must ultimately, of course, be dis-

missed—a fact which the Mahāyāna was to make more explicit.

31. In Masefield, "Oral Initiation in the Pāli Nikāyas."

32. See Trevor Ling, Buddhism and the Mythology of Evil (London: Allen & Unwin, 1962), pp. 13ff. and passim. It is worth noting that, contrary to Professor Ling's suggestion that the various portrayal of Mara as, at the one extreme, a cosmic entity and, at the other, psychological forces are simply two poles of a continuum, it is perhaps more likely that the figure of Mara was itself viewed at times from the adhidaivatam perspective and at others from the adhyātman perspective. Hence we find Māra portrayed on the one hand as a being with an elephant for his mount (S,ii,278; A,ii,18; It,50; cf. GS,ii,18[3]), who can take on many shapes (s,i,104ff.), who enters the Brahmaloka and speaks with the Buddha who is himself on a visit there (M,i,326), who, when defeated, sits with drooping shoulders scratching the ground with a stick (S,i,124) or departs dejected, his lute having slipped from his armpit (Sn,449) and who, in one instance, was in fact a former birth of Moggallāna who, as Māra Dūsin subsequently went to hell to atone for his deeds (M,i,332ff.); while on the other as anger (A,iv,97), the khandhas (S,iii,189,195,198), the senses (S,iv,38f.), passion, hatred, and delusion (It,56) and various other psychological motivations (Sn,436ff.).

33. The extent to which the remarks in this article might be thought to go counter to the supposed doctrine of anattā will depend largely on the reader's own understanding thereof. As far as the Nikāyas are concerned it is clear that the existence of an attā, equivalent either to Upaniṣadic Ātman (c) or (d), is simply never discussed. All that the Buddha is recorded as having said—his remarks being addressed at the time, it may be added, to his sāvakas whom he had already caused to witness not only the rise and fall, the impermanence and dukkha, of the khandhas in the phenomenal world but also the sanctuary beyond—is that those khandhas (e.g. Vin,i,13f.), and on occasion the senses and their objects (e.g., S,iv,1ff.), through being both impermanent and a source of dukkha, were to be considered anattā; and that, moreover, he would agree with any of them who said that such were "Not mine, nor am I they nor are they for me any self" (n' etam mama n' eso 'ham asmi na m' eso attā ti). The possibility of there being within each one of them a hidden three-quarters, which being devoid of the defects disallowing any entitlement of the khandhas to be regarded as attā, might be considered attā is neither asserted nor denied—it is simply not discussed. However one may feel that it is often taken for granted, as for instance when the Buddha tells Ānanda that he will speak constantly reproving, constantly cleansing so that that which is the pith will stand fast (yo sāro so thassati—M,iii,118) which becomes intelligible in the light of the passage at M,i,488f., in which Vacchagotta says of his own conversion onto the lokuttara plane (MA,iii,199) that,

> It is like a great sāl tree not far from a village or market town whose branches and foliage might be dissolved because of their impermanence, whose bark and young shoots might be dissolved, whose softwood might be dissolved, so that after a time the branches and foliage gone, the bark and young shoots gone, the softwood gone, clear of them it would be established on

the pith (sāre patitthito).

And the statement at M,iii,80 that the entire lokuttara sāvakasaṅgha is similarly established on the pith. The branches and softwood and so forth are an obvious reference to the khandhas and seeking a self in the khandhas is like searching for pith in the hollow stem of a plantain tree (M,i,233); and one might here recall the inverted cosmic tree of Gītā XV with its branches and twigs samsarically enmeshed in sense-objects and so on. But to what does the pith refer?

34. See for instance A,i,184 where the Buddha claims his walking up and down, standing, sitting, and lying down is Ariyan (=lokuttara, M,i,323f., iii,75,115); also S,iii,120 where the Buddha points out to Vakkali that there is nothing in seeing his putrid body—whoever sees Dhamma sees him and whoever sees him sees Dhamma, Dhamma being here his lokuttara nature as SA,ii,314 confirms, as does Asl,350f. on Dhs,1003 where this episode is quoted. The topic permeates Masefield, "Oral Initiation in the Pāli Nikāyas." On the basis of Figure 7 above we might illustrate the intrusion of the lokuttara plane amidst the mundane as follows:

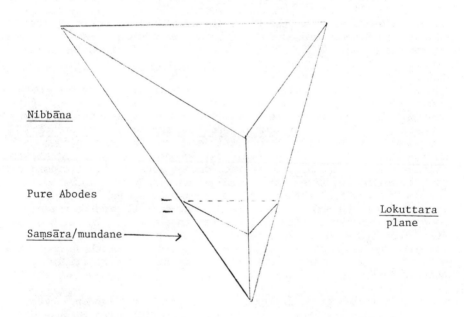

Nibbāna

Pure Abodes

Saṃsāra/mundane ⟶

Lokuttara
plane

The thing that may first strike one about such a representation is the impressive size of the lokuttara plane or indeed of those on it. But just as it is a feature of the various devalokas that each is far greater in size and life span than that immediately beneath it (e.g. A,i,213f., 267f., ii,126-130; also A,i,227f., etc.), so too is enormity of size a common, though without this diagram a somewhat perplexing, predication of lokuttara persons, and especially of the Buddha. Thus we find that the Buddha (M,i,386; Ud,58), Sāriputta and Moggallāna (M,i,32) and arahants in general (M,i,145) are all called nāgas, nāga being a term used by the world to express greatness (A, iii,345f.). Similarly just as nāgas, reared and nurtured in the Himālaya, later travel down the streams and rivers to the mighty ocean where they attain to great size in body, so do those who follow the eightfold path subsequently arrive at greatness (S,v,47-63), nibbāna being like the mighty ocean (SA,iii,135). This may lead one to recall the fact that the tathāgatas are said to be immeasurable (A,i,227)—as are arahants (A,i,266)—and, being set free from reckoning as this and that khandha, are deep, immeasurable and fathomless as is the mighty ocean (S,iov,375ff.), by virtue of which, no doubt, it is no more possible to harm a Tathāgata than it is to soil an ocean with a pot of poison (It,86). Similarly arahants, being unrestricted, with the great self and dwelling in that which is immeasurable (aparitto mahattā appamanavihārī) would be no more likely to be much troubled by some trifling deed than would the Ganges be spoiled by a grain of salt, whereas insignificant men, being restricted, with limited selves and dwelling in the dukkha of that which is limited (paritto app' ātumo appadukkhavihārī), would be as troubled as a cup of water would be spoiled by that salt, the further similes appended similarly illustrating the enormous size of the former compared with the latter (A,i,249f.). It is not altogether clear what exactly was meant here by the terms mahattā and app' ātumo, though the former seems elsewhere to be the goal sought by those treading the Buddhist path (mahattam abhikaṅkhatā—A,ii,21=iv,91). It is tempting to see these as the Buddhist way of referring, respectively, to the subtle and gross forms of Ātman but I leave this for the reader to decide for himself. At the same time, however, I would welcome comments or criticisms on this and any other aspect of this article.

35. The Upanisadic model would surely require some modification if it were to accommodate the jīvanmukti, for so long the bane of Indian philosophy. I admit also that the suggestion that, in the Buddhist context, the notion that a lokuttara individual might yet, through his necessity of enduring a limited number of further rebirths, be thought still to reside within saṃsāra is in need of some explanation, but such explanation seems totally lacking in the Nikāyas.

THE IDEATIONAL CONTENT OF THE BUDDHA'S ENLIGHTENMENT AS SELBSTVERWIRKLICHUNG

Mokusen Miyuki

Buddhism is a pragmatic religion and stresses the lifelong process of Awakening (bodhi) as the basis for a more meaningful life. It has emphasized that one's Awakening (bodhi) is a continual process which is accomplished by the practice of the Threefold Study of sīla or morality, samādhi or concentration, and paññā or widsom.[1] In this world of impermanence (anicca), both the objective conditions and subjective factors change so that one's Awakening also does not remain unaltered. Therefore, one's Awakening is not a completed, or perfected, state but an ever-changing process which forms a continuum with the impermanence of the inner and exterior world of an individual. The concept of Awakening as a process is indicated by the well-known Sino-Japanese definition of the term "Buddha": "The one who wakes up to oneself (tzu-chüeh) and helps others wake up to themselves (chüeh-t'a) so that the Awakening activity (chüeh-hsing) goes on to manifest itself infinitely (ch'iung-man)."[2]

The process of further Awakening is fundamental to an effective confrontration with the "dis-ease", or dukkha, brought about by impermanence. Accordingly, I wish to maintain that Buddhism aims at transformation of the ego so as to overcome the "dis-ease" of the human condition.[3] In this sense, Buddhism contradicts the generally prevailing Western psychological view of Buddhism as aiming at ego-negation or ego-dissolution.

Misconceptions regarding the nature of Buddhism as ego-negating seem to me to have arisen partly because of the efforts to understand Buddhism through the utilization of extant philosophical and religious categories in the West, which are rooted in a weltanschauung that is foreign, if not antithetical, to Buddhism. It is my view that C.G.Jung's analytical psychology has provided the West with the first meaningful psychological perspective to Buddhism and other Asian religious experience.

Jung's perceptive observations and statements concerning Asian religions reveal the depth and richness of the insights afforded him by his empirical and phenomenological methodology. Jung's concept of the individuation process as Selbstverwirklichung, or the Self's urge to realize itself, can be useful in gaining a better psychological understanding of Buddhism: Buddhism aims at transformation of the ego in order to help the individual to overcome the "dis-ease" of life brought about by impermanence.

I. The Dhamma of Interdependent Origination as the Ideational
   Content of the Buddha's Enlightenment

The dhamma (truth/teaching) of Interdependent Origination
(paticcasamupāda) has traditionally been accepted in Buddhism as the
ideational content of the Buddha's Enlightenment.[4] As such, it has
been considered throughout the ages as the teaching which is basic to
all other important doctrines in Buddhism.[5] Certain canons even declare that this dhamma exists independent of the Buddha's discovery
and teaching of it.[6] Also supporting this view are those canons
which, while not specifically stating that Interdependent Origination
is the content of the Buddha's Awakening, indicate it by relating
that this dhamma is "too profound and unfathomable to grasp."[7] However, there are also various canons which give other major teachings
of the Buddha, such as the Four Noble Truths, the Noble Eightfold
Way, or the Middle Path—all of which constitute the essential doctrine promulgated by the Buddha in his First Sermon—as the content
of the Buddha's Awakening.[8]

Major Teachings in Buddhism as Expressions, or Amplifications, or an
Ineffable Experience

Inconsistencies concerning the content of the Buddha's Enlightenment could be historically accounted for, in part, as the product of
various sectarian traditions; but, for the following reason, this issue can also be considered from a psychological standpoint. Namely,
all human experience is essentially psychological in the sense that
immediate "reality" is perceived and apprehended in and through the
psyche. To quote Jung, "the psyche and its contents are the only
reality which is given to us without a medium."[9] Hence, the dhamma
realized by the Buddha in samādhi-meditation, though characterized as
"too profound and unfathomable to grasp" was expressed and apprehended by the Buddha's psyche in terms of the various teachings mentioned above. Viewed thus, the major doctrines of the Buddha can
also be considered as a consequence of his efforts to convey the content of his Awakening experience which is essentially indescribable
from a rational and intellectual standpoint. In this sense, they are
to be regarded not as distinct doctrines but, rather, as mutual amplifications of an ineffable experience. As such, the essential
teachings of Buddhism can validly be subjected to a phenomenological
analysis through the use of the methodology and structure of Jung's
psychology.

II. Jung's Interest in the Psychological Aspects of the "Numinous
    Experience"

A. Jung's View of Religion

As a psychologist, Jung regards religion as based on an experience of the numinous. He states:

...Religion, as the Latin word denotes, is a careful
and scrupulous observation of what Rudolf Otto aptly

termed the numinosum, that is, a dynamic agency or
effect not caused by an arbitrary act of will. On the
contrary, it seizes and controls the human subject,
who is always rather its victim than its creator.
The numinosum--whatever its cause may be--is an
experience of the subject independent of his will. . . .
The numinosum is either a quality belonging to a
visible object or the influence of an invisible presence that causes a peculiar alteration of consciousness.[10]

The key word in this quotation is "dynamic": it refers to the
energy or power of the numinosum which causes, independent of the
will of the subject who experiences it, "a peculiar alteration of
consciousness." This altered consciousness creates a new ego attitude congenial to it and a transformation of personality occurs.[11]
The Awakening of the Buddha is a clear example of an experince of the
numinosum which transformed Gautama the man into Gautama the Buddha.

B. Samādhi Practice as Aiming at Creating Numinous Experience

Jung maintains that religious practice or ritual such as invoca-
tion, incantation, or meditation, is "carried out for the sole purpose of producing at will the effect of the numinosum."[12] As an
empiricist and phenomenologist, Jung is concerned with the observation and description of the psychological aspects, not the metaphysical cause, of such numinous experience as those produced by the
Buddha's samādhi practice. Samādhi concentration can be understood
as a practice or means for creating an experience of the numinosum,
and the Buddha's Enlightenment is said to have occurred as he sat in
samādhi.

III. The Importance of an Appropriate Method for Understanding the
      Numinous Experience

A.   Impossibility of Intellectually Communicating the Numinous
      Experience

Unconscious materials, such as the contents of a numinous experience, have no conscious language adequate for clarifying their meaning. Thus, a numinous experience cannot be conceptually formulated
or intellectually understood and a person who wished to share it with
another is at a loss for a means of logical communication. One who
has had the experience, such as a Zen master, may make an effort to
convey or impart the experience by using gestures, a specific tone of
voice, or even by resorting to physical violence. Also, he may cite
familiar materials which appeal to intuition or feeling, but he will
not be able to explain the experience intellectually.

B.   Jung's Methodology of "Amplification"

This lack of an appropriate language occurs because unconscious
materials are a psychological phenomenon alien to the conscious mind
through which they are communicated. Jung has observed that uncon-

scious contents, because their nature is unknown, have a tendency to self-amplification, that is to say, "they form the nuclei for an aggregation of synonyms."[13] He states: "When something is little known, or ambiguous, it can be envisaged from different angles, and then a multiplicity of names is needed to express its peculiar nature."[14] These synonyms are images which are unmistakably mythological in their character, and Jung regards them as the expression of "the inborn language of the psyche and its structure,"[15] or "the language of the unconscious which lacks the intentional clarity of conscious language."[16] This archaic, nonrational language of the pysche is universally found in such unconscious materials as dreams, fantasies, psychotic episodes, fairy tales, mythology, or religious literature, such as the various accounts of the Buddha's experience of the numinosum.

Speaking of an appropriate method to examine unconscious materials, Jung states, "we are . . . obliged to adopt the method we would use in deciphering a fragmentary text or one containing unknown words: We examine the context."[17] Jung has termed his method of dealing with unconscious materials "amplification." He maintains that "amplification is always appropriate when dealing with some dark experience which is so vaguely adumbrated that it must be enlarged and expanded by being set in a psychological context in order to be understood at all."[18] The method of amplification, accordingly, attempts to place such unconscious materials as the Buddha's Enlightenment in a wider and more appropriate psychological context while it holds in check the appropriating intellect which tends to make irrelevant, if not jeopardizing judgments.

Jung's method of amplification, thus, can be understood as aiming at activation of an "insight" into the nature and essence of the psychic process. This insight is accomplished by examining the images or ideas produced by a psychological situation with the help of associated materials drawn from parallels found in other unconscious materials. The images thus amplified, which are otherwise obscure and confusing, can become clearer and more intelligible by being permitted, in a sense, to speak for themselves. The method of amplification cannot attempt to establish or designate the specific content of a numinous experience; it can, however, approximately reveal the essential nature of the experience. As mentioned above, in Buddhism, an example of amplification is found in the Buddha's First Sermon in which he expounds his major teachings as an inseparable continuum; he uses each of the doctrines to amplify the other, and employs all of them as expressions of the numinous experience, or his "profound Awakening."[19]

IV. The Individuation Process as the Basic Hypothesis of Jung's
     Psychology

A. The Collective Unconscious

It is generally accepted by Jungians that Jung's basic discoveries, or his great contribution to the knowledge of the psyche, are those concepts of the individuation process and the collective unconscious.[20]

Jung uses the term "collective unconscious" to designate that part of the unconscious which is transpersonal and common to all humanity. Speaking of the relationship between consciousness and the unconscious, Jung states:

> Consciousness, no matter how extensive it may be, must always remain the smaller circle within the greater circle of the unconscious, an island surrounded by the sea; and like the sea itself, the unconscious yields an endless and self-replenishing abundance of living creatures, a wealth beyond our fathoming.[21]

Jung regards the unconscious as the creative matrix of life. In contrast to the "personal unconscious" which is made up of forgotten or repressed feelings, thoughts, and images, or those psychic contents which are unique to the individual, the collective unconscious consists of instinct and archetypes, or the psychic contents which are universal. Viewed thus, the psyche is a dynamic process in which consciousness is constantly regenerated and replenished by the unconscious as the source of life. What Jung refers to in his definition of religion by the word numinosum, or "a dynamic agency or effect," can be understood as an activation of the creative unconscious.[22] Thus, religious practices or rituals such as samādhi, which is "carried out for the sole purpose of producing at will the effect of the numinosum,"[23] is a creative act of the ego relating itself to the unconscious.

B. The Numinous Experience as a Confrontation with the Archetype of the Self

The experience of the numinosum, which creates a transformation of personality, can be regarded from a Jungian viewpoint as the ego's confrontation with the archetype of the Self. Archetypes are "a formative principle of instinctual power,"[24] which universally condition human behavior and perception. As part of the collective or transpersonal psyche, they consist of forms that can never be made wholly conscious although they are approximately represented by mythologems, or recurring themes, consisting of images and symbols expressed in such unconscious materials as myths, dreams, folklore, and religious experience. It should be noted here that, as in the case of the numinosum, Jung is concerned with the observable phenomena of the archetypes, not the archetype per se in the metaphysical sense, which are determining factors in the psychological life of an individual.
Central to the total dynamic process of the psyche is the archetype of the Self. Jung defines the Self as follows: "The Self is not only the center but also the whole circumference which embraces both conscious and unconscious; it is the center of the totality, just as the ego is the center of the conscious mind."[25] Presumably the ego, the center of consciousness, is closely and dynamically connected with the Self—the paradoxical totality being both the whole circumference and the center of the entire psyche embracing conscious and unconscious.

C. The Individuation Process as <u>Selbstverwirklichung</u>

    1. <u>Selbstverwirklichung</u> as the Self's Innate Urge to Realize
       Itself

Jung uses the term individuation "to denote the process by which
a person becomes a psychological 'in-dividual,' that is, a separate,
indivisible unity or 'whole.'"[26] Jung also uses the term <u>selbstver-</u>
<u>wirklichung</u> to designate the individuation process. He states:

> Individuation means becoming a single, homogeneous being,
> and, in so far as "individuality" embraces our innermost,
> last, and incomparable uniqueness, it also implies becoming
> one's own self. We could therefore translate individuation
> as "coming to selfhood" (<u>zum eignen Selbst werden</u>) or "Self-
> realization" (<u>Selbstverwirklichung</u>).[27]

The German term <u>Selbstverwirklichung</u>, which is translated as
"self-realization" in English, indicates psychologically the Self's
innate urge to realize itself. This point is clarified by E.F.
Edinger when he says:

> Individuation seems to be the innate urge of life to
> realize itself consciously. The transpersonal life
> energy in the process of self-unfolding, uses human
> consciousness, a product of itself, as an instrument
> for its own self-realization.[28]

    2. <u>Selbstverwirklichung</u> as the Process of Integrating of "Evil"

According to Jung, therefore, individuation begins, with the innate urge of the Self for realization, regardless of the conscious
will or external situation. To become "a single, homogeneous being"
is not something the ego can create at will. Being driven by the
Self's urge, it is possible for the ego to evolve. As "the smaller
circle within the greater circle of the unconscious,"[29] the ego is
constantly conditioned by the Self as the determining factor for its
existence and development. Therefore, once <u>Selbstverwirklichung</u>, or
the innate urge of the Self realizing itself, takes place, the activated Self provides the ego with the strength and stability for its
development while it simultaneously imposes on the ego the task of
integrating the dark side of the personality. The Self is the paradoxical totality in which the opposites such as conscious and unconscious, light and darkness, good and evil, are united; and,
consequently, without integration of "evil," there is no realization
of totality, Jung states; "Whenever the archetypes of the self pre-
dominates, the inevitable psychological consequence is a state of
conflict . . . and man must suffer from the opposite of his intention
for the sake of completeness."[30] The struggle and suffering of the
ego in confronting the dark side of the psyche is exemplified by the
legend of the Buddha's battle with the threatening power of Māra, the
king of the desire realm (<u>kāmadhātu</u>), or the personification of the
dark side of the Buddha's personality.[31]

3. Selbstverwirklichung as an Enrichment of the Individual's
   Psychological Life

Selbstverwirklichung, or the encounter with the archetype of the
Self by the ego, is not a neutral experience. It is an experience of
the numinosum which exercises a powerful influence on the shaping, or
reshaping, of conscious orientation by regulating, modifying, and mo-
tivating the ego. Jung states:

> . . . . the archetypes have, when they appear, a distinctly
> numinous character which can only be described as "spiritual,"
> if "magical" is too strong a word. Consequently this phenom-
> enon is of the utmost significance for the psychology of
> religion. In its effects it is anything but unambiguous.
> It can be healing or destructive, but never indifferent,
> provided of course that it has attained a certain degree
> of clarity.[32]

E.F. Edinger characterizes the development of the ego in its confrontation with the archetype of the Self as a circular process of
alternating ego-Self separation and ego-Self union. He notes: "indeed, this cyclic (or better, spiral) formula seems to express the
basic process of psychological development from birth to death."[33]
In this manner, the progressive differentiation of the consciousness
takes place continually throughout life as the result of conscious
assimilation of the unconscious contents, or the enrichment of consciousness by the integration of the unconscious. The psychological
phenomena of the progressive enrichment of the conscious life is
depicted in the legendary story of the life of the Buddha in which he
continually confronts Māra.[34]

4. Selbstverwirklichung Viewed Psychodynamically

Selbstverwirklichung, or the ego's confrontation with the archetype of the Self manifesting itself, is not only mysterious and
powerful but also incomprehensible and dangerous to the conscious
personality which is ego-bound and thing-bound. Such an experience
produces a state of abaissement du niveau mental, or the lowering of
the threshold of consciousness. Jung describes such a state as a
state which "abolishes the normal checks imposed by the conscious
mind and thus gives unlimited scope to the play of the unconscious
'dominants.'"[35] According to Jung, this description indicates also
the essential characteristic of mental illness.[36] The menacing power
of the unconscious which may cause the disintegration of the ego is
symbolized by Māra's powerful attack on the Buddha seated at the root
of the Bodhi tree. Therefore, it is of vital importance for the ego
to have the strength and stability to maintain its function and
integrity in encountering the numinosum of the unconscious.
   Psychodynamically viewed, the state of mind thus created in confronting the unconscious can be regarded as a state of introversion
in which "a withdrawal of the center of psychic gravity from ego consciousness" occurs; and the energy thus invested in the unconscious
stimulates the activation of the contents of the unconscious.[37] The
psychic condition thus produced can result in a creation of a new

pattern of psychic functioning, which is no longer centered around ego consciousness. This psychodynamic interpretation regarding the state of introversion is applicable to that produced by the religious practice of samādhi, which Jung refers to as "an ego-less mental condition" (ein Ich-loser geistiger Zustand), or "a consciousness without an ego" (ein Bewusstsein ohne Ich).[38]

This "ego-less mental/spiritual [geistiger] condition," which is created through the religious practice of samādhi, is also to be designated by what Jung calls the state of "an empty consciousness" (ein leeres Bewusstsein) which "stands open to another influence." He states:

> This new state of consciousness born of religious practice is distinguished by the fact that . . . an empty consciousness stands open to another influence. This "other" influence is no longer felt as one's own activity, but as that of a non-ego (die Wirkung eines Nicht-Ich) which has the conscious mind as its object. It is as if the subject-character of the ego had been overrun, or taken over, by another subject which appears in place of the ego. This is a well-known religious experience, already formulated by St. Paul. Undoubtedly a new state of consciousness (eine neue Bewusstseinslage, "a new situation/condition of consciousness") is described here, separated from the earlier state (vom fruheren Bewusstseinszustand, "from the previous condition/situation of consciousness") by an incisive process of religious transformation (ein tief eingreifenden religiösen Wandlungsprozess, a profound overwhelming religious transformation process).[39]

Jung's idea expressed in this quotation--which I have translated in parentheses somewhat differently from the accepted English translation--can be taken as clarifying the function of the ego in "a profound overwhelming religious transformation process" which results in the birth of a new ego orientation. The new psychic condition of "empty" consciousness makes the ego also "empty," which can be understood as "being free from conscious assumptions," so that the ego stands "open to another influence" of the unconscious, or the Self. In this sense, what Jung terms "ego-less mental/spiritual condition" refers to "a new condition of consciousness" freed from its previous condition, which is ego-bound and thing-bound. Thus, this new psychic situation provides the ego with a new orientation in which the ego can function in the service of the Self. What is dissolved is the former manner of the ego's functioning, which is ego-bound and thing-bound, or "egocentric." In contrast to the previous "egocentric" attitude of the ego, the new way in which the ego functions can be termed as "Self-centric," meaning that it functions in the service of the Self.[40]

5. The Ego/Self Axis

This basic dynamic interaction of the ego/Self, which I designate as "Self-centric," is also a crucial factor in the psychological development of the individual. Speaking of the close connection between ego and Self, Jung states:

> The term "self" seemed to me a suitable one (eine passende bezeichung, "an appropriate characterization") for this unconscious substrate (diesen unbewussten Hintergrund, "this unconscious background"), whose actual (jeweiliger, "respective" or "occasional") exponent in consciousness is the ego. The ego stands to the self as the moved to the mover, or as object to subject, because the determining factors which radiate out from the self surround the ego on all sides and are therefore supraordinate to it. The self, like the unconscious, is an a priori existent (Vorhandene, "that which is at hand") out of which the ego evolves. It is, so to speak, an unconscious prefiguration of the ego. It is not I who create myself, rather I happen to myself. This realization is of fundamental importance for the psychology of religious phenomena.[41]

This quotation indicates the importance of the "Self-centric" function of the psyche for the development of the ego. The ego is not the "master" of the psyche. It is a mere "occasional" exponent of the Self. It is the Self that determines the "occasional" manifestation of the ego as its exponent. This means that the archetype of the Self is a living matrix, which is indicated by the German term Vorhandene, "out of which the ego evolves." In other words, the "ego-centered" life of consciousness can only take place in the dynamic context of the unconscious with the Self as its center. Jung's idea that the Self is "an unconscious prefiguration" designates this creative urge of the Self to realize itself simultaneously as it causes, or prefigures, the "occasional" manifestation of the ego, or its exponent.

The importance of the basic connection of the ego/Self is further emphasized by Erich Neumann in terms of the ego/Self axis. He explains:

> We speak of an ego-self axis because the processes occurring between the systems of consciousness and the unconscious and their corresponding centers seem to show that the two systems and their centers, the ego and the self, move toward and away from each other.[42]

This quotation seems to indicate that the word "axis" is used to designate the dynamic interaction between ego and Self, with the ego on the one end of the pole and the Self on the other end as the determining factor for the development of the ego. This means that the psychological development of an individual is founded on the operation of the ego/Self axis. Edinger maintains that this "vital connecting link between ego and Self . . . ensures the integrity of the ego."[43] He even postulates its "crucial importance for maintaining the function and integrity of the ego."[44]

Jung's hypothesis of the individuation process as Selbstverwirklichung, or the innate urge of the Self to realize itself, is "of fundamental importance for the psychology of religious phenomena."[45] As Jung mentions, the well-known dictum of St. Paul (Gal. 2, 20) is to be taken as a classical expression of the "Self-centric" function of the ego, or the ego's functioning in the service of the Self. The "profound Awakening" of the Buddha in samādhi can also be viewed as the "Self-centric" functioning of the ego. In this "Self-centric" function of the ego, the ego is conscious of being directed by the Self while it can function in a state of harmonious unison with, and in service of, the Self.[46]

V. Mandala Symbolism in Selbstverwirklichung

A. The Mandala as the Symbol of the Self

Jung has observed that in Selbstverwirklichung, or the Self realizing itself, mandala symbolism often emerges in the manifested unconscious materials. A mandala is, according to Jung, a symmetrical structure consisting of ternary or quaternary combinations which are concentrically arranged. The ternary combinations symbolize the dynamic process of development or growth, whereas the quaternary configurations represent a static structural wholeness, or completion.[47]

The ternary and quaternary number symbolism manifested in mandalas can be seen as an expression of the emergence of the renewed personality built on the activation of the ego/Self axis. As a part of the psychic process, the ego/Self axis actualizes in terms of a ternary rhythm: differentiation of that which is nonego is the basis of ego consciousness. In the case of the transformed or renewed personality, structured on the ego/Self axis, the ego recognizes the Self as nonego, or its opposite. The tension thus created by this duality is released in the creation of a third mode of being in which the ego/Self interacts. Jung maintains that this psychological process with the ternary rhythm goes on to be resolved in a "fourth" condition: "The unspeakable conflict posited by duality resolves itself in a fourth princple. The rhythm is built up in three steps, but the resultant symbol is a quaternity."[48] The fourth, or completion, is a beginning of the new process of development on a different level of consciousness.

B. The Major Buddhist Teachings as Formulated in Mandalic Combinations of the Numbers Three and Four

As expressions of the ideational content of the Buddha's experience of the numinous, the essential teachings of Buddhism repeatedly employ in their formulation the mandalic combinations of the numbers three and four. In the doctrine of the Twelve Links of the Chain of Interdependent Origination, the number 12 (3x4) symbolizes the simultaneous occurrence of the process and the goal, or samādhi-paññā.[49]

The dual awareness of the samsāric-nirvānic life which is expressed in the doctrine of Interdependent Origination, and which is pointedly reinforced in the Mahāvagga's account of the Buddha's Enlightenment by the statement that the Buddha thought over each one of the Twelve Links of the Chain of Interdependent Origination both forward and backward,[50] is also clearly stressed in the following formulation of the doctrine:

When this is, that is;
This arising, that arises;
When this is not, that is not;
This ceasing, that ceases.[51]

Symbolically interpreted, "this" and "that" represent all, or any, possible opposites, such as samsāra and nirvāna. In a confrontation with the numinous, or Enlightenment, samsāra and nirvāna are experienced as the unus mundus, or a unitary dynamic reality of interconnected process, and this synthesis is the resolution of the tension created by the duality of the samsāra-nirvāna opposition. Psychologically, to take in "this" and "that" "as-they-are" (yathābhūtañān-adassana) means that the duality arising from these opposites is transcended on a "higher" level, or unitary form of consciousness which represents the "third" in the psychological process. Thus, out of the two-ness of the opposites of samsāra-nirvāna, or arising and ceasing, or this and that, comes the three-ness of their synthesis, or the dhamma of Interdependent Origination.

This simultaneous affirmation, or synthesis of the opposites is, psychologically, the transcendence of the boundary between "I" and the "world." The transcendence of this boundary can be understood to occur as the result of what Jung calls the "transcendent function." The transcendent function is a creative expression of the psyche. It is called "transcendent" because it "facilitates the transition from one psychic condition to another by means of the mutual confrontation of the opposites," of conscious and unconscious.[52] The state of consciousness which is produced by transcendence of the opposites is experienced without losing the awareness of the transcendence that occurs. This state of awareness of transcendence is thus the fourth stage or the completion of the psychic process, or Enlightenment.

The transcended state of consciousness created by the actualization and activity of the ego/Self axis in the Enlightenment experience also finds expression in other major teachings in Buddhism. Combinations of the number 3 and 4, which psychologically represent growth and completion respectively, appear in the doctrine of the Middle Path. The Buddha, in his First Sermon, states that he realized the "Enlightenment of the Middle Path," avoiding the two extremes of "self-indulgence" and "self-mortifcation."[53] Thus, the Middle Path indicates an ongoing process which, out of the tension produced by the two extremes, is resolved in the Middle Path or the third step of development. "Enlightenment of the Middle Path" is the expression of the fourth step of completion, or the awareness of the ongoing experience of paññā.

The realization of the Four Noble Truths is expounded by the Buddha in his First Sermon in terms of the Three Sections and Twelve Divisions (tiparivattam dvādasākāram).[54] The Three Sections constitute the process of realization which consists of (1) coming to an awareness of the truth; (2) deciding to practice the truth; and (3) having accomplished this practice. The realization of each of the Four Noble Truths by the practice of these Three Sections, or that of the Twelve Divisions (3x4), results in the attainment of the "ineffable knowledge of things as they have become" (yathābhūtañānadassana), which is a phrase commonly used to designate the experience of Enlightenment. Thus, we see in this formulation, the reflection of the ternary process of development resolving itself into the quaternary wholeness or completion of Enlightenment.

The teachings of the Three Characteristics of dhamma is a ternary expression of the process involved in the attainment of Enlightenment.[55] Realization of the three aspects of dhamma, namely, impermanence (anicca), dis-ease (dukkha), and no-separate entity (anatta), leads to the fourth step, or panna as the emancipating factor.[56]

Another important Buddhist doctrine is the Seven Factors of Enlightenment (satta bojjhaṅga). The number seven comprises the union and totality of the ternary process and the quaternary completion. Hence, this teaching has been considered as important as that of the Twelve Links of the Chain of Interdependent Origination. They are: mindfulness (sati), discerning the dhamma (dhamma-vicāya), energy (viriya), rapture (pīti), serenity (passadhi), concentration (samādhi), and equanimity (upekkhā).[57]

The quaternary teaching of the Noble Eightfold Way can be replaced or interchanged with the ternary formulation of the doctrine of the Threefold Study. According to Nāgārjuna, (c. 150–250 A.D.), the Threefold Study condenses the Noble Eightfold Way as follows: right speech, right conduct, and right livelihood are self-training or observance of sīla; right mindfulness and right contemplation are self-purification, or the practice of samādhi; right view, right thought, and right effort are self-liberation, or panna.[58] Herein we can see the dynamic developmental aspect of the Threefold Study resolved in the accomplishment of the Noble Eightfold Way, or the quaternary (4+4) formulation of Enlightenment.

Summary

Our study, employing Jung's concept and methodology, has afforded us a psychodynamic understanding of the Buddha's experience of Enlightenment in terms of the individuation process as Selbstverwirklichung, or the innate urge of the Self to realize itself. In selbstverwirklichung, a "Self-centric" condition of the psyche occurs so that the function of the ego can also be described as "Self-centric," instead of "egocentric." This "Self-centric" functioning of the ego is not to be confused with the dissolution of the ego. On the contrary, being Self-centered, the ego functions in the service of the Self, or the source of life. In this way, the ego is replenished by assimilating the contents of the unconscious. The ego thus enriched and strengthened can proceed to a further Awakening. This on-going process of Awakening is also represented by mandala symbolism as found in the major teachings of Buddhism. The essential feature of Buddhism does not consist in life-negation or ego-dissolution, but, rather, in a life-long process of a further Awakening through the integration of unconscious contents into consciousness. Thus understood, Buddhism reveals itself as a pragmatic approach for dealing with dukkha, or dis-ease of life, through the transformation of the ego.

NOTES

1. This article is a further elaboration of the author's paper entitled, "A Jungian Approach to the Ideational Content of the Buddha's Enlightenment" (Presented at the First Conference of the International Association of Buddhist Studies, Columbia University, New York, September 1978).

2. Hui-yüan, Ta-cheng i-chang (The Essentials of Mahāyāna Doctrine), Taishō, vol. 44, no. 1851, p. 864c. This definition of the term "Buddha" by Hui-yüan (523-592 A.D.), a famous master of Ti-lun Tsung, has been widely accepted in both Chinese and Japanese Buddhism. For instance, Shan-tao (613-681 A.D.), a prominent Pure Land master of the early T'ang, employs this definition in his important work entitled, Kuan wu-liang-shou-fo ching su (A Commentary on the Sūtra of the Meditation on Amitāyus), Taishō, vol. 37, no. 1753, p. 246. Since Shan-tao is revered as a patriarch in Japanese Pure Land Buddhism, this definition of the term "Buddha" is well known in Japan.

3. See Mokusen Miyuki, "Living with Duhkha" in East/West Culture: Religious Motivations for Behavior (Santa Barbara: Educational Futures, International, 1977), pp. 57-64.

4. The term paticcasamupāda, or pratītyasamutpāda in Sanskrit, is variously translated into English as follows: "Dependent Origination" in H.C. Warren, Buddhism in Translation, 6th ed. (New York: Atheneum, 1973), p. 82; and also in Nyanatiloka, Buddhist Dictionary, 3rd ed. (Colombo: Frewin & Co., Ltd., 1972), p. 128; "The Law of Dependent-Together Origination" in Th. Stcherbatsky, The Conception of Buddhist Nirvana (Leningrad: Academy of Sciences of the U.S.S.R., 1927), p. 8; "Dependent Production" in J. Takakusu, The Essentials of Buddhist Philosophy (Honolulu: University of Hawaii, 1947), p. 30; "Conditioned Genesis" in W. Rahula, What the Buddha Taught (New York: Grove Press, 1962), p. 52; "The Law of Dependent Origination" in A.K. Coomaraswamy, Buddha and the Gospel of Buddhism (New York: Harper Torchbooks, 1964), p. 96; "Conditioned Co-Production" in Edward Conze, Buddhism: Its Essence and Development (New York: Philosophical Library, 1951), p. 48; and finally, "The Chain of Causation" in Edward J. Thomas, The Life of Buddha (New York: Barnes & Noble, Inc., 1960), p. 76.

Etymologically speaking, the term pratītyasamutpāda is a compound which consists of pratītya and samutpāda. The word pratītya is a gerund derived from the verb prati-i, meaning "to go (the root verb i) toward or against (the prefix prati)," and thus it means "dependent on." The word samutpāda is a noun derived from the verb sam-ut-pad, meaning "to go (the root verb pad) up (the prefix ut) together (the prefix sam)," and thus it means "co-arising." Refer to Sir M. Mornier-Williams, Sanskrit English Dictionary (Oxford: The Clarendon Press, 1899). The term pratītyasamutpāda, therefore, means "origination by dependence of one thing on another," from Franklin Edgerton, Buddhist Hybrid Sanskrit: Grammar and Dictionary, vol. II (New Haven: Yale University Press, 1953), p. 373; and it indicates the "phenomenon" of the dynamic mutual interdependence of each and every dhamma, or event/thing.

5. See, for instance, Ui Hakuju, Bukkyō shisō kenkyū (Studies of Buddhist Thought) (Tokyo: Iwanami-shoten, 1943), pp. 3-8; Yamaguchi

Susumu, et al., Bukkyōgaku josetsu (What is Buddhism? Introducing
Buddhology) (Kyoto: Heirakuji-shoten, 1961), pp. 46-49.
6. For instance, in the Samyutta-Nikāya, XII, 2, 20, the Buddha
addresses his disciples as follows:

> Whether, brethren, there be an arising of Tathagatas
> [an epithet of the Buddha], or whether there be no such arising,
> this nature of things just stands, this causal status, this
> causal orderliness (thitā va sā dhātu dhammatthitatā
> dhammaniyāmatā), the related of this to that (idapaccayatā).
> Concerning that the Tathagata is fully enlightened, that he
> fully understand. Fully enlightened, fully understanding he
> declares it, teaches it, reveals it, sets it forth, manifests,
> explains, makes it plain, saying: "Behold! Conditioned by
> this, that comes to be!" [Mrs. Rhys Davids, trans. The Book of
> the Kindred Sayings (London: Luzac & Company Ltd. Repr. 1952),
> p. 21.]

It should be noted that those words describing the eternal truth
of Interdependent Origination, namely, thitā va sā dhātu dham-
matthitatā dhammaniyāmatā, are also used to designate the eternal
truth of the so-called "Three Characteristics of dhamma," i.e., impermanence (anicca), dis-ease (dukkha), and no-separate entity
(anattā) in the Aṅguttara-Nikāya III, 134. This means that the Three
Characteristics of dhamma can also be regarded as the content of the
Buddha's Enlightenment. H.C. Warren translates these words as follows: "it [each one of the Three characteristics] remains a fact and
the fixed and necessary condition of being" (Buddhism in Translation,
p. x). Lama Anagarika Govinda's German translation of these words
are: "es bleibt eine Tatsache, eine unumstössliche Daseinsbedingung
und eine ewiges Gesetz," or in English translation, "it remains a
fact, an unalterable condition of existence and an eternal law." See
Lama A. Govinda, Die psychologische Haltung der fruhbuddhistischen
Philosophie (Zürich und Stuttgart: Rascher Verlag, 1942), p. 82.
Idem, The Psychological Attitude of Early Buddhist Philosophy (New
York: Samuel Weiser, Inc., 1961), p. 66.
7. The Ariyapariyesana-sutta (the Majjhima-Nikāya I. 167) gives
us an account in which the Buddha, after having attained Enlightenment, hesitated to preach because he thought that mankind would find
it difficult to grasp the dhamma of Interdependent Origination. However, having been asked by Brahmā Sahampati and also out of his own
compassion, the Buddha is said to have decided to preach. For an
English translation of this sutta, see E.J. Thomas, Early Buddhist
Scriptures (London: Kegan Paul, Trench, Trubner & Co., Ltd., 1935),
pp. 23-25. Also see Thomas, The Life of Buddha, pp. 81-82. These
accounts are generally found in the canons which relate to us the
Buddha's biography. See, for instance, the Mahāvagga I, 5, 1-13.
8. Those canons that do relate the content of the Buddha's Enlightenment vary greatly. Certain texts consider the Four Noble
Truths as the content of the Buddha's Enlightenment. See the Vinaya
text of the Mūlasarvāstivādin (Ken-pen shuo i-ch'ieh yu-pu p'i-na-yeh
p'o-seng shih, Taishō, vol. 24, no. 1450, p. 124b), the Vinaya text
of the Dharmagupta (Ssu-fen lu, Taishō, vol. 22, no. 1428, p. 781c)
and so on. In the Buddha's First Sermon, however, as we see later

on, not only the Four Noble Truths but also other important teachings
of the Buddha, namely, the Middle Path and the Noble Eightfold Way,
can also be considered as the content of the Buddha's Enlightenment.
See note 19 below.

9. C.G. Jung, "On the Nature of the Psyche," The Structure and
Dynamics of the Psyche from The Collected Works of C.G. Jung, vol. 8,
eds. Herbert Read, Michael Fordham and Gerhard Adler (New York: Pantheon Books, 1964), par. 420.

10. C.G. Jung, "Psychology and Religion," Psychology and Religion: West and East from ibid., vol. 11, par. 6.

11. Jung also states, "We might say, then, that the term 'religion' designates the attitude peculiar to a consciousness which has
been changed by experience of the numinosum." Quote appears in
ibid., par. 9.

12. Ibid., par. 7.

13. C.G. Jung, Mysterium Coniunctionis from ibid., vol. 14, par.
458.

14. C.G. Jung, "On The Tibetan Book of the Great Liberation"
from ibid., vol. 11, par. 806.

15. C.G. Jung, "Flying Saucers: A Modern Myth," Civilization in
Transition from ibid., vol. 10, par. 646.

16. Ibid., par. 732.

17. C.G. Jung, Psychology and Alchemy from ibid., vol. 12, par.
48.

18. Ibid., par. 403.

19. In the First Sermon, the Buddha states that he has attained
"the Enlightenment of the Middle Path (majjhimā patipadā)" and we
are, thus, given the impression that the Middle Path is the content
of his Enlightenment. He then equates the Middle Path with the Noble
Eightfold Way and goes on to expound the Four Noble Truths in terms
of the Three Sections and Twelve Divisions (tiparivattam
dvādasakāram). In this canon, therefore, any one of the three teachings, i.e., the Middle Path, the Noble Eightfold Way, or the Four
Noble Truths, can duly be regarded as the content of the Buddha's Enlightenment.

20. See, for instance, Marvin Spiegelman, "A Jungian Contribution to the Future of Psychotherapy," International Psychiatry
Clinics 6, no. 3 (1975): 43.

21. C.G. Jung, The Practice of Psychotherapy from Collected
Works, vol. 16, par. 366.

22. See note 8 above.

23. Ibid.

24. C.G. Jung, "On the Nature of the Psyche" from ibid., vol. 8,
par. 416.

25. C.G. Jung, Psychology and Alchemy from ibid., vol. 12, par.
44.

26. C.G. Jung, "Conscious, Unconscious and Individuation," The
Archetypes and the Collective Unconscious from ibid., vol. 9, p. 1,
par. 275.

27. C.G. Jung, Two Essays on Analytical Psychology from ibid.,
vol. 7, par. 266.

28. E.F. Edinger, Ego and Archetype (Baltimore: Penguin Books,
Inc., 1973), p. 104.

29. See notes 6 and 8 above.

30. C.G. Jung, Aion from Collected Works, vol. 9, p. ii, par. 123.

31. The Jātaka, I, 68, 5-76, 17. For an English translation, see Warren, Buddhism in Translation, pp. 71-83.

32. C.G. Jung, "On the Nature of the Psyche" from Collected Works, vol. 8, par. 405.

33. Edinger, Ego and Archetype, p. 5.

34. The Lalita-vistara, a Mahāyāna biography of the Buddha, related to us that Māra came to the Buddha to entice him to enter nirvāna. See A. Foucher, The Life of the Buddha, trans. S.B. Boas (Middletown, CT: Wesleyan University Press, 1963), p. 129. The Mahā-parinibbāna Suttanta (VI, 11-13) also mentions that Mara asked the Buddha to enter nirvāna. For an English translation, see T.W. Rhys Davids, trans., Buddhist Suttas (New York: Dover Publications, Inc., 1969), pp. 114-116.

35. C.G. Jung, "On Tibetan Book of the Great Liberation" from ibid., vol. 11, par. 848.

36. Ibid.

37. Ibid., par. 774.

38. Ibid.

39. C.G. Jung, "Forward to Suzuki's Introduction to Zen Buddhism" from ibid., vol. 11, par. 890.

40. For a discussion on the "Self-centric" functioning of the psyche, see Mokusen Miyuki, "Selbstverwirklichung in the Ten Oxherding Pictures." (A paper presented at the Eighth International Congress of International Association for Analytical Psychology, San Francisco, September 1980).

41. C.G. Jung, "Transformation Symbolism in the Mass" from ibid., vol. 11, par 391.

42. Erich Neumann, "Narcissism, Normal Self-formation, and the Primary Relation to the Mother," Spring (1966): 85.

43. Edinger, Ego and Archetype, p. 6.

44. Edinger, "The Ego-Self Paradox," The Journal of Analytical Psychology 5, no. 1 (January 1960): 8.

45. See note 41 above.

46. Miyuki, "Selbstverwirklichung in the Ten Oxherding Pictures," pp. 12-14.

47. Edinger, Ego and Archetype, p. 188.

48. C.G. Jung, "A Psychological Approach to the Dogma of the Trinity" from ibid., vol. 11, par. 258.

49. The Twelve Links of Interdependent Origination are: ignorance (avijjā), Karma-formation (saṅkhārā), consciousness (viññāna), corporeality and mentality (nāma-rūpa), six bases (āyatana), impression (phassa), feeling (vedanā), craving (tanhā), clinging (upādāna), process of becoming (bhava), rebirth (jāti), old age and death (jarā-marana). See Nyanatiloka, Buddhist Dictionary, pp. 128-136.

50. The phrase "forward and backward" indicates that the Buddha pondered over the conditions from which the samsāric life of dis-ease arises (forward), but also pondered over the way to overcome the conditions of dis-ease (backward) so as to attain nirvāna.

51. Walpola Rahula's translation. See his What the Buddha Taught, p. 53. This is a set verse which is often, though not always, used in connection with the teaching of the Twelve Links of Interdependent Origination and which is to be considered as an older

formulation of the teaching than that of the Twelve Links. See Nakamura Hajime, "Engi-setsu no genkei" ("The Original Formula of the Doctrine of Interdependent Origination"), Indogaku Bukkyōgaku Kenkyū (Journal of Indian and Buddhist Studies) 5, no. 1 (1957): 59-68.

52. C.G. Jung, "On The Tibetan Book of the Great Liberation" from ibid., vol. 11, par. 780.

53. See note 17 above.

54. The Four Noble Truths are the essential message of the Buddha's First Sermon and have been considered as the pillar of Theravadin teachings. They are: The Noble Truth of Dis-ease (dukkha), the Noble Truth of the Uprising-together (samudaya) of Dis-ease, the Noble Truth of the Cessation (nirodho) of Dis-ease, and the Noble Truth of the Path (maggo) leading to the cessation of Dis-ease.

55. See, for example, the Anguttara-Nikāya III. 134. See note 6 above.

56. See Anattalakkhana-sutta (Samyutta Nikāya III. 66), which is translated into English by E.J. Thomas as "Sermon on the Marks of Non-Soul" in his The Life of Buddha, pp. 88-89.

57. See Lama A. Govinda, The Psychological Attitude of Early Buddhist Philosophy, p. 69.

58. Nāgārjuna, Ta chih-ta lun (A Treatise on the Prajñā Pāramitā), Taishō 25, no. 1509, p. 488a.

EMOTIONS AND THERAPY: THREE PARADIGMATIC ZONES[*]

M.W. Padmasiri de Silva

PART I

I

Concepts like "emotions" have traditionally grown within the empirically oriented discipline of psychology and the clinically
oriented field of psychoanalysis. With the development of philosophical psychology, the philosophical investigation of psychological
concepts has been considered a legitimate field of investigation and
study. Though philosophers of very early times (Greek and Indian
thinkers) presented a great amount of material on the nature of the
mind, the charting of the "logical geography of the mind" as a self-
conscious discipline demarcating its boundaries from empirical studies is a recent development.[1]

It has been observed that today the analytic philosopher attempts
to relate the findings of clinical and experimental psychology to
everyday conceptions of psychological terms of the layman.[2] Regarding the relationship between philosophy and the social sciences, philosophers have taken certain distinctive stands: some philosophers
feel that it is the task of analysis to lay bare sources of conceptual confusions, linguistic ambiguities, and excessive claims of
theories built on one track paradigms and to look out for logical
holes between theoretical frames and inferences. In doing this the
philosopher has nothing much to learn from the social and natural
sciences but draw from his own insights from commonsense, linguistic
usage, and logic. Others feel that philosophy should be acquainted
with the variety of empirical investigations and that the scientist
himself should not be blind to the conceptual apparatus linked to his
own work. This two way process of interaction and mutual understanding is a healthy approach to accept and more so in the field of the
study of emotions.

Within the field of philosophical psychology, two interests have
widened from its incessant concern with the body-mind issue: volition and perception to concerns which were earlier hidden in the
periphery like self-deception, rationality, and therapy. This article partly betrays these widening horizons. There is a new feature
which is introduced to these dimensions of inquiry and these are the
Eastern philosophical insights which are entering the spectrum of
Western philosophical discussion.[3]

[*]The following article was the Inaugural Lecture at the Unive
Peradeniya, January 20, 1981.

II

We are interested in two specific questions: <u>What are emotions?</u> and <u>How do we deal with them</u>? In answering the first question, an attempt would be made to examine the concept of emotions and assess the types of framework used for charting out the nature of emotions or affective experience in general. Our main focus is on the kind of frame with a strong therapeutic orientation, as the question "How do we deal with emotions?" is important for us. How would different conceptions of the nature of emotions generate different possibilities for changing, eliminating, or transforming them? Thus in brief the main purpose of this analysis is to explore points of linkage between philosophical theories of emotions and the therapeutic framework of concerns like education and clinical psychology. It would be necessary to extend these strong academically structured lines of inquiry to everyday concerns—how does a person deal with his personal emotional moods and clarify his personal vision in society within the complicated web of attitudes and feelings. This framework of interpersonal relationships colors our moral life, and a primary concern of this paper is to examine the relationship between morality and emotions. Thus in a very general sense we are concerned with the <u>education of the emotions</u>. Such a general concern has important practical implications for a world beset with dualities, dichotomies, and fragmentation—the rift between the technological and the humanistic imagination, artistic and scientific skills, the analytic and the existentialist philosophies, or to use the jargon of Pirsig in <u>Zen and the Art of Motorcycle Maintenance</u>, "the split between the romantic and the classical."[4] Thus the rational investigation of the nature of emotions is not only a legitimate field of inquiry but one which has great relevance and significance for us.

While the physiological and biological foundations of emotion study are important, the present analysis will be more concerned with the psychological and the evaluative structure of emotion concepts. As R.S. Peters points out, the notion of educating the emotions acquires significance only in the light of beliefs, reasons, appraisals, and justifications.[5] By an appeal to understanding and knowledge, people can be made to see situations afresh and see them differently, thus breaking through both emotional and value rigidity. To see things differently is to experience them in a new way, and to experience them in a new way is to enlarge the dimensions of our affective nature.[6]

If the term "emotions" implies merely a state of arousal without any necessary connection with knowledge, understanding or belief, then people can be stimulated or conditioned but not educated.[7] There is a connection between emotions and a class of cognitions rendered as appraisals, which is to recognize certain situations as desirable or undesirable:

> Thus we are not afraid of x unless we take x to be
> dangerous; we are not angry at x unless we take x to be
> acting contrary to something we want; we do not have remorse
> over having done x unless we regard it as unfortunate that we
> did x; we are not grief stricken over x unless we see x as the
> loss of something we wanted very much; we do not have pity for

x unless we take x to be undesirable; and so on.[8]

The role of "thought" in clinical contexts and their significance for therapy has been recently presented in a philosophical study by Jerome Neu.[9] Neu sees two paradigmatic approaches to emotions and therapy in the work of philosophers Hume and Spinoza: Hume and those who follow him treat emotions as essentially "feelings" where "thought" plays only an incidental role; whereas Spinoza and those who follow him consider "thought" (in the broader sense including belief) as central to emotion. In Hume's associationist and mechanistic models of understanding is seen a precursor of the physiologically oriented James-Lange theory of emotions and contemporary behaviorism, while the Spinozistic line of inquiry strengthens the case for analytic therapies like psychoanalysis. If you follow the Spinozistic line of inquiry analytic therapies make philosophical sense. Neu argues that appropriate beliefs offer the basis for discriminating between different emotions (e.g. between anger and fear or anger and jealousy), experiencing them, and also providing interpretative grounds for recognizing emotions as well as transforming them. That knowledge can free man provides a philosophical rationale for the education of the emotions. Knowledge can free man from deleterious emotions, open up parasitic sub-routes, expose stultifying dispositions and generate new perspectives for understanding oneself and others. But "knowledge" of a purely intellectual type is not sufficient.

The analogy we seek for the education of emotions in psychotherapy might give a false impression, that what is involved is merely a negative process of rooting out deleterious emotions and false beliefs. The education of the emotions is committed to a more positive program; it may even derive its finest analogies from art and aesthetics. There is a positive emotional responsiveness which has to be distinguished from mere excitability, sentimentality, apathy, and insincerity.

When one is merely excitable, emotional response has no depth: when one is sentimental, one goes to excess and there is no genuine pathos and so on.[10] True emotional responsiveness is a finer blend of the capacity for objectivity with sensitivity. Discussing the role of emotions on works of fiction it has been observed that: "it is only when we are able to contemplate an object or incident in comparative calm—to have it as an idea rather than as a raw stimulus—that we can be relied upon to respond 'appropriately.'"[11]

The analogies offered by literature are interesting as they provide a corrective to the somewhat over-intellectualized overtones in the Spinozistic mode of inquiry: "...there is certainly an important distinction to be made between knowing certain facts about oneself and other people and the more imaginative type of entering into one's own and other people's more recondite emotions, for which we use the term 'insight.'"[12] There is a kind of "insight" accommodated within Freudian analytic therapy but it has its own limitations.

When we are exploring a concept of "insight" beyond the Spinozistic-Freudian mode, we are perhaps trespassing on an area beyond the paradigmatic zones, a kind of prohibited area. Western analytic philosophers well trained in the nonesoteric art of philosophical discourse generally know their silent zones. There have been a few "cracks in the wall" and the conceptual leakages which are very revealing, and without being unduly esoteric, it may be worthwhile to traverse the outskirts of this silent zone.

III

It may be useful to cite a few examples from our own random discoveries. The analysis of self-deception made by Fingarette opens up an interesting East-West dialogue on the kind of dimension we could use for self-analysis or the understanding of emotions in particular.[13] The paradox of self-deception is to explain how the same person can at the same time "know" and yet "not know," "believe" and yet "not believe" or be "sincere" and "not sincere." Fingarette makes a claim to move from the "cognition-perception" family of concepts to the "volition-action" family of concepts.

Terms like "know," "be aware of," and "be conscious of" are linked by a metaphor; it is the metaphor of seeing: "the essentially passive registration and reflection to the 'mind' of what the world presents to our eyes."[14] Though in recent times philosophers have become suspicious of passive visual imagery in relation to concepts like "know" and "believe," Fingarette claims that no such doubts have been cast regarding the language and imagery of vision in relation to the concept of "consciousness." Terms like "conscious," "aware," "realize," "notice" and "attention" have a passive meaning in every day usage and may be technically described in White's terminology as kinds of "reception concepts."[15] Fingarette instead suggests a model of consciousness as active: "The model I propose is one in which we are doers, active rather than passive. To be specific, the model I suggest is that of skill."[16] Thus to be conscious of something explicitly is to exercise a skill, which he says is a skill of "spelling out."

Though this practice of spelling out is often done in the early stages of life in the adult this is never a significant concern.

> Although the adult can explicitly and systematically continue to cultivate his skill in spelling out, this has not been a traditional concern in the Western world, except among practitioners of religious meditational disciplines. In Asia and Asia Minor, however, the complex doctrines of consciousnes associated with meditational practice embody millenia of experience in the cultivation of this skill. In the Western world, psychoanalytic "free association" may be thought of as a special spelling out technique.[17]

At this point, we are entering the outskirts of an area beyond accepted paradigmatic zones and one which is very much relevant for "emotions and therapy." Recent studies on the philosophy of emotions have emphasized the significance of attention concepts.[18] There are other considerations that have come up for discussion which can be equally significant to understanding emotion concepts from the bases of our own philosophical and religious tradition: the distinction between "depth understanding and breadth understanding," the linkup between character descriptions and emotions, and the relation between morality and psychological traits. There has even been the idea of developing a field called "moral psychology," and finally the distinction between "theoretical knowledge" and "practical knowledge" has been recast in terms of new dichotomies. We find these developments interesting in the light of some research that has been done on the Buddhist perspectives on emotions and therapy. It will be one of the aims of this article to make a preliminary investigation of this subject.

The first window to the East is provided by these crosscutting pathways to self-knowledge. A second point of considerable interest is the approach to ethics and morality in the West dominated by the fact-value dichotomy or what is referred to by Anthony Flew as Hume's fork: all meaningful propositions are either analytical statements like the ones in logic and mathematics or the factual statements based on science and general observation. Statements like, "This rose is beautiful" (as different from "This rose is red") or "stealing is bad" (as different from "stealing is a rare occurrence in this village") are value statements. They do not fall into any one of Hume's dual categories and thus they are arbitrary, subjective, mere expressions of emotion, and lack meaning. As Bernard Williams points out, this deep cleavage between facts and values had a disastrous impact on the variety of legitimate ethical concerns, especially any possible interest in the role of emotions in our moral life. But as was mentioned the "cracks in the wall" in the Western philosophical scene are interesting.

Iris Murdoch's essay on the "Idea of Perfection" in her The Sovereignty of Good[19] once again opens up these refreshing windows to the East. Murdoch's critique is presented more in the form of an impressionistic picture of man with a philosophical brush rather than in the form of a sustained analytic dissection. For this reason it is more suited to explore a paradigmatic zone which will accommodate East-West crosscurrents in philosophy.

Murdoch is disappointed both with the work of Hampshire, Ayer and Hare (the race of philosophers who produce good reasons for ethically significant action) as well as with Jean-Paul Sartre (the tribe of existentialists haunted by pure freedom and basic decisions): "Characteristic of both is the identification of the true person with the empty choosing will, and the corresponding emphasis on movement rather than vision." For these philosophers according to Murdoch, there is no point in talking of "moral seeing" since there is nothing morally to see: "There is no moral vision." According to Murdoch there are two concepts of knowledge we can use in the context of morality: the democratic concept where as rational beings all of us can know the meaning of a word (the impersonal network of language) and the other is a hierarchial one, where an individual's grasp of a moral concept can be placed on any point on a path toward an ideal limit, there is a deepening process in the latter concept: "Knowledge of a value concept is something to be understood, as it were in depth, and not in terms of switching on to some impersonal network."[20]

For the existentialist Jean-Paul Sartre, she has a message: instead of getting sandwiched between total freedom and total derminism as the only alternatives there is something more realistic to know: "...the exercise of our freedom is a small piecemeal business which goes on all the time and not a grandiose leaping about unimpeded at important moments." Thus Murdoch says that, "The moral life, on this view, is something that goes on continually, not something that is switched off in between the occurrence of explicit moral choices."[21] Murdoch throws away a very bright spark by commenting that what happens in between the choices is well described by the term "attention." Instead of considering people as acting with crystal clear intentions, the linkup between morality and attention (or mindfulness to use a term in Buddhist psychology) suggests that the individual undergoes a deeper struggle from obscurity to clarity in the everyday pathways to action. There is an interesting difference between what Fingarette and Murdoch say on the nature of attention; though both emphasize the significance of "attention," Fingarette's emphasis on attention as an activity attempts to leave out the imagery of "vision," but Murdoch prefers the imagery of "vision" to "movement." But there is an interesting congruence: while Fingarette considers the development of consciousness as an activity of "spelling out," Murdoch considers the exercise of freedom, not as "a grandiose process of leaping out," but a small piecemeal process dependent on gradual effort and growth.

The idea that clear vision is a result of moral imagination and moral effort should provide a new lease on life to British moral philosophy so heavily clouded by the fact-value dichotomy. In the field of recent comparative philosophy there has been a very interesting attempt to examine the nature of moral evaluation in Buddhism from the perspectives of Western philosophy; here the author P.D. Premasiri comes to the conclusion that early Buddhism offers a cognitivist position unhindered by the fact-value dichotomy.[22] He does not accept explicitly anything like "moral vision," but rather sees a significant relation between ethics on the one hand and a significant conception of human nature, a theory of reality and a related world view. He would perhaps accept that a disciplined and creative moral life would provide a viable base for the clarity of understanding and the development of knowledge. This work does not discuss in detail the close linkup between psychology and ethics or the role of moral emotions in particular but it shows how an alternative paradigmatic stance on ethics is possible, much different from the dominating ethos of noncognitivism in British moral philosophy.

Thus in summary, the basic questions which concern us are: What are emotions and how do we deal with them? How do different conceptions of emotions generate diverse possibilities for educating them? And what are the basic theoretical approaches in this direction? Apart from the Humean and Spinozistic mode, is there a third mode of confrontation between emotions and therapy?

IV

In our attempt to answer these questions the following strategy will be followed: present some factors which led to a neglect of the philosophy of emotions; make an analysis of the kinds of questions which may be generated in relation to the concept of emotions; and thirdly, clarify how specific theories of emotions offer different implications for therapy or in more general terms, the education of the emotions.

One of the factors which led to a neglect of emotion studies, specially in moral contexts, is the spell cast by the traditional distinction between "reason" and "feeling":

> It is perhaps no more than a commonplace that moral educa-
> tion is in part at least an education of the emotions. Yet
> moral philosophers have often taken this to mean merely that
> we must learn to control them, for if we fail to do so we
> are at the mercy of what is fickle and irrational, and so
> are unable to exercise any control over our lives.[23]

Taylor, who makes these observations, adds that this kind of view leads people to think that emotions do not add to the moral worth of a person. But a careful study of "emotions and morality" will convince us that there is a close connection between emotions and our evaluation of a human being. As students of philosophy our interests should not be limited to the subject of overcoming emotional excesses as such. A more positive attempt to develop one's "emotional sensibility" is necessary. Philosophically, interest may be focused on certain conceptual considerations like what are appropriate and inappropriate emotional responses.

There have been very few philosophical contributions to the study of moral emotions. Two very encouraging attempts in this direction dealing with emotions and our moral life are Strawson's essay on "Freedom and Resentment" and Bernard William's lecture on "Morality and the Emotions." The fact that ethical and religious values color emotion vocabularies and taxonomies was quite evident in an empirical study that we have done in Sri Lanka as a part of the "Emotions and Culture" project of the East-West Center.[24] Such crosscultural studies specially focused on the impact of ethical and religious codes on emotion terms will assure us that our thinking on emotions are not shot through a narrow culture-bound ethos. It might even help us to discover the common humanity behind the web of reactive attitudes and human relations of which Strawson speaks. In fact, in this context Bernard Williams observes:

> It is the points of intersection between the more purely
> evaluational elements in a moral outlook, and an associated
> view of human nature, that provide most fruitfully both the
> sources of understanding and the focus of criticism. Such
> a point of intersection will be found in the moral signifi-
> cance of emotions.[25]

The kind of metaphor which dominates our average usage also prejudices us against the more positive and creative role of emotions: "struck by jealousy," "paralyzed by fear," "driven by anger," "plagued by remorse," "overcome by grief," "drowned by sorrow" and similar darts from Cupid when we are overcome by love.[26] It is said that emotions in these contexts may be compared to the "taming and caging of the wild beast."[27] If emotions are wild, fickle and irrational, they become merely road blocks to be cleared in the weary encounter between reason and feeling.

This is of course not to deny that there are elements of passivity in our experience of emotions, but it is necessary to understand that emotions also involve belief, appraisals, reponsibility, intentionality, and an understanding of social rules and moral norms. The causal structure of emotions cannot be separated from these features. Recent studies have even focused interests in patterns of attention and "shifts of salience." The canalization of passivity is an important issue,[28] but it is necessary to accept the challenge that emotions have a logic and rationale which makes the education of the emotions a meaningful task. Our study of the affective dimension of man from a Buddhist perspective points toward some interesting reminders; apart from the logic of specific emotions and emotion generating contexts, there are interesting existential structures which help us to understand the nature of human emotions, their emergence, their expression, conflicts, and ambivalences too.[29]

Another related reason for the neglect of emotion studies is the general tendency to make emotion synonymous with passion, and specially so in religious and ethical contexts. Apart from the emotions which disorient our perspectives and cloud our visions, there are more positive emotions. Certainly emotional warmth and a concern for others can be combined with such traits as clarity, objectivity, and impartiality. The positive role of emotions in intellectual investigations has been the subject of recent analysis.

Apart from these factors (obstructing the study of emotions), which can be grasped in commonsense situations, there are two other theories which were nourished within academic groves and laboratories. When the use of introspection as a legitimate method of psychology fell into disrepute through a militant behaviorist reaction, there was a strong emphasis on the physiology of emotion study and the study of emotions in relation to animals. This development did not exactly hinder the development of emotion studies but gave it a rather one-track direction, which played some role in the neglect of moral emotions and the role of beliefs in emotion.

Darwin's work The Expression of Emotions in Man and Animals[30] is influenced by his theory of evolution and natural selection. Darwin was interested in the apparent continuity of functions between man and animals, the adaptive function of emotions, the search for universal basic emotions across cultures, and the facial expression of emotions. Darwin's work was a valuable study of its kind, but he was more interested in emotions with clear facial expression and action patterns (e.g. anger, fear, surprise, disgust, happiness, and sadness). Peters says that this restricted the study of emotions where fear and anger came to be considered as paradigms and not pride or jealousy.[31] Peters also mentions that animals do not have a conceptual scheme to experience pride, shame, and regret. It is true that this kind of study led to the neglect of emotions as cognitions and appraisals, a dimension of emotion study very much relevant to our interest in therapy. But Darwin's study did make a contributon to the overall theoretical interest in the concept of emotions, the expression of emotions, and also to what he called the shame-shyness emotions.

Darwin for instance was interested in the question why an occasion which normally causes blushing generated paleness of the face rather than redness of the face:

> For instance, a young lady told me that in a large and crowded
> party she caught her hair so firmly on the button of a passing

servant that it took some time before she could be extricated;
from her sensations she imagined that she had blushed crimson;
but was assured by a friend that she had turned extremely
pale.[32]

Darwin's work on the emotion of shame has received detailed study under a neo-Darwinian revival in the work of Ekman.

Apart from the impact of emotion studies with a strong physiological and biological orientation, behaviorism with its methodological
slogans had an inhibiting effect on emotion studies. Philosophers
have pointed out that the identification of personal experience and
action with its observable expression is fallacious.[33]

A very powerful factor which almost closed the door for emotion
studies in ethical contexts was the impact of the "emotive theory of
ethics." Emotivism in ethics held that moral judgments (e.g. "stealing is bad") had no factual content but merely expressed the emotions
of the speaker with the aim of influencing the emotions of the
hearer.[34] This was not an empirical claim that moral judgments do
really work this way, but a conceptual claim associating moral judgments with the expression of emotions. The preoccupation with the
distinction between facts and values has, according to Bernard
Williams, made philosophers reflect on the most general features of
moral language, specially of evaluative language. He says that concentrated work on such linguistic activities like commendation, evaluation and prescription has pushed the emotions out of the picture.[35]
Thus recent moral philosophy in Britain had not much to say about
emotions.

The role of emotions in ethics is an important subject which suffered setbacks due to the emotive theory of ethics. If one glances
through the Nichomacean Ethics[36] of Aristotle or the ethics of Buddhism as presented in the dialogues of the Buddha there is certainly
a recognition of the moral emotions unhindered by any emotivism. In
our studies of Buddhist psychology, we have discussed in detail the
interlocking of the psychological and the ethical and the use of psychological terms with ethical overtones.[37] The interconnections between the evaluational elements in our moral outlook and an associated
view of human nature referred to by Bernard Williams comes out well
in the third paradigmatic zone which is being explored.

Though the emotive theory has had a baneful effect on the understanding of the relationship between emotions and morality, a close
examination of the diversity of emotions will reveal not merely their
evaluative structure but that there are specific emotions which are
labelled as "moral emotions":

> Most emotions and motives are, as a matter of fact,
> regarded as virtues and vices--for instance, envy, benevo-
> lence, lust, pity. This is presumably because they are
> consonant with, or in conflict with, fundamental moral
> principles such as respect for persons and the consider-
> ation of people's interests. And there are many emotions
> which are conceptually connected with general moral notions--
> for instance, shame, guilt, remorse.[38]

V The Traditional Theory of Emotions

With the development of a viable analysis of the concept of emotions, traditional theories which considered an emotion as a unique inner feeling came in for criticism. George Pitcher makes the following observations:

> The traditional theory which I wish to criticise is that to
> have an emotion is just to have a unique inner feeling or
> group of inner feelings, to undergo a special inner experi-
> ence.... In most versions of this view, for "inner" one can
> read "mental." The feelings that are alleged to be involved
> are just like sensations such as pains, tickles and itches,
> in that they are immediately felt or experienced and have a
> fairly definite duration, but they differ from them in being
> mental rather than physical.[39]

This picture of emotions it was said was not very conducive to
the education of the emotions. An emotion has an object or is directed toward it (agent directed or otherwise). But can sensations
have an object? We can ask for a person's reasons for his emotions
or we can say that it is warranted, unwarranted, justified, appropriate, etc. But we cannot speak of sensations in this manner. This
traditional concept is akin to the Humean version of emotions. It is
also linked to the Cartesian notion of the mind which came in for
sustained criticism at the hands of Gilbert Ryle: "To explain an action as done from a certain motive is not to correlate it with an oc-
cult cause, but to subsume it under a behaviour-trend."[40]
    Ryle's criticism of the traditional theory of emotions had an im-
portant impact on the philosophy of emotions, but his dispositional
theory of emotions does not do justice to the intentional aspect of
emotions and their evaluative structure. Errol Bedford's essay on
"Emotions" is of great interest in this respect: "To assimilate emotion words closely to dispositional words is to give an incomplete
account of their explanatory function; they explain behaviour more
fully than could be done by, saying, in effect, that it was only to
be expected."[41] Bedford goes on to emphasize the evaluative function
of emotion words: "emotion words form part of the vocabulary of appraisal and criticism, and a number of them belong to the more specific language of moral criticism."[42]
    If emotions are not mysterious happenings within some occult psy-
chic passage, but rather come within the range of public criticism
and interpersonal responses, they are said to be directed toward certain objects. To describe the thesis that emotions are about some
state of affairs, the technical term intentional has been used. "I
am angry at John for releasing his cow into my garden" presents an
object of anger, which can be a person, an action, etc. There are
problems about this analysis; and that is, how do we account for "depression," "free-floating" anxiety or "unbound" anxiety of the
Freudian variety, Kierkegardian "dread," euphoria, etc. We can say
that they are "agent directed" as compared with nonagent directed
emotions or following Heidegger that they are emotional moods "about
the whole world."
    The strongest exponent of the "intentionality" of emotions is
Kenny's work, Action, Emotion and Will.[43] There was a long-drawn

debate where the critics attempted to eliminate the possibility of talking in terms of "objects" and present an alternative account in terms of "causes." It seems to us that it is rather unproductive to get immersed in a debate of this sort here, but rather accept that the causal structure of emotion concepts may accommodate a concept of "intentionality."[44]

We have now come across a number of facts of the emotion concept: their object directed nature, the dispositional components, and their evaluative function. While accepting the important physiological and the biological facets of emotions, this article on "Emotions and Therapy" draws more from the psychological and the moral foundations of emotion study.

A fourth aspect of emotions is the "responsibility" of individuals for the emotions they experience and express. If we are to praise and blame people and evaluate their behavior in this light, it is necessary that we search for the link between emotions and the concept of responsibility. We are sometimes indignant with a person for the emotion he feels or guilty about what we feel: "Such emotion concepts as guilt, anger, indignation, irritation, admiration, pride, and others are either universally or often connected with the imputation of responsiblity for actions."[45]

Responsibility is not merely related to outward behavior but the whole range of the psychological and valuational structure which gives form to the nature of emotions: "His evaluations and beliefs, generally his habits of thoughts, many of his choices and decisions—all these and more, affect his capacities and tendencies in emotion."[46] A person's capacity for the rational assessment of his own emotions, the capacity for emotional regulation and the capacity to make more refined descriptions of his emotional states enhances a person's sense of responsibility—all these facets are central to the education of the emotions.

The concept of "responsibility" in relation to emotions has important implications not merely for morality and law but the types of framework used for therapy. At this point the concept of emotions as an object for rational investigation has to face a number of complicated issues: unconscious motivation, sudden breakdowns of competence, clouding of vision, temptation, self-deception, the irrational conservation of pathological emotional traits, etc. Unlike in drug and shock therapies, Shamanistic healing ceremonies, or even behavior therapies, the notion of an agent, a responsible agent capable of "reflexive knowledge," plays an important part in analytic therapies. But how do we place the breakdowns cited above on a continuum of actions, some of which can be praised and blamed, some which can be understood, and others where the "agent" is more like a "patient" and is the object of treatment rather than moral or legal assessment. The notions of praise and blame, excuse, guilt, and responsibility color the use of certain types of emotion words. Strawson, in his essay on "Freedom and Resentment," says that it is very necessary to clarify the kind of relations which may be found between gratitude, resentment, forgiveness, love, and hurt feelings on the one hand and the notions of moral guilt, of blame, and of moral responsibility on the other:

If some one treads on my hand accidentally, while trying to

help me, the pain may be no less accurate than if he treads
on it in contemptuous disregard of my existence. But I shall
generally feel in the second case a kind and degree of resentment that I shall not feel in the first.[47]

Part II
A Third Paradigmatic Zone

The Humean mode of therapy has its focus on feelings, the Spinozistic on thoughts and the Buddhist on attention.

While we do not wish the articulation of the third paradigmatic
zone to look like a new herbarium area laid out by a gardener trying
to amass together some rare varieties of exotic plants, we are exploring the logical features of an idiom and an image different from
the Humean and Spinozist modes, of understanding the nature of emotions and transforming them or eliminating them.

Though "behavior therapy" ingrained in the Humean model makes
limited use of "thoughts" (in spite of its claims to the contrary),[48]
it basically treats the mind like "an associative switchboard" and
gives a central place to the history of learning and conditioning.
Analytic therapy ingrained in the Spinozist model gives a primary
place to thought and beliefs:

> Emphasizing the importance of thought in the classification
> and discrimination of emotional states, the Spinozist view
> illuminates the consequent importance of reflexive knowledge
> in changing those states. If we acknowledge that emotions
> essentially involve beliefs, we begin to see how changing
> beliefs can transform emotions.[49]

Thus psychoanalysis attempts to explain ideogenesis.

The limits of analytic therapy are clearly voiced by Freud himself in "Analysis Terminable and Interminable" and a number of other
papers.[50]   The substitution of conscious control for unconscious
repression is certainly a great step forward, but Freud himself says
that he is merely transforming hysterical misery into common unhappiness.[51] Assuming that this process rests on a lively reenactment of
a traumatic scene, the living through of a repressed setting and the
liberation of energy, it may be said that there is a considerable
process of reeducation. Even if so, it is difficult to extend this
analogy fully to emotions in relation to the world of everyday concerns; in such contexts the rational inquiry into one's emotional
life may turn out to be a highly "intellectual concern" and the warning is graphically presented by Freud himself:

> If knowledge about the unconscious were as important for the
> patient as people inexperienced in psychoanalysis imagine,
> listening to lectures or reading books would be enough to
> cure him. Such measures, however, have as much influence on
> the symptoms of nervous illness as a distribution of menu
> cards in a time of famine has upon hunger.[52]

Our concepts of a third paradigmatic zone will be drawn from our studies of emotions in the psychology of Buddhism: it has a multi-layered structure to understand the relation of emotions to therapy. Certainly the conflict between the Humean and the Spinozist mode of understanding emotions do provide legitimate ways of conceptualizing two therapeutic approaches to understanding emotions. But as it is the case with many dichotomies, it is possible that there are more complex positions which do not fall distinctly into either modes. This is specially the case with the distinction between the Spinozistic rational therapies (which includes psychoanalysis) and the Humean nonrational techniques, which include behavior therapy.[53]

The psychology of Buddhism, which also offers interesting analogies to psychoanalysis as discussed in Buddhist and Freudian Psychology, presents a third paradigmatic approach to emotions and therapy. The philosophical foundation of Buddhism has its own conception of rationality: Buddhism is critical of rationalist metaphysics based on deductive models as found in Spinoza, but it gives a significant place to critical and analytic reason; it is critical of mechanistic theories of therapy as implicit in Hume, but it has a strong empiricist or, in a more broad sense, an experientialist strand;[54] while Freud was confronted with the conflict between descriptive diagnostic categories and normative recommendations, like Spinoza, the Buddha openly accepts the strong link between the ethical and the psychological; while unlike Freud and more like Spinoza, Buddhism offers an ultimate ideal (complete mastery of passions), there is no theological basis (not even its Spinozistic version) for Buddhism. To these crosscutting differences is added the paradigm of nondiscursive discernment in Buddhism, which is firmly rooted in Buddhist meditative culture. Buddhist psychology offers a multilayered approach to the understanding of emotions. Within the limited time available only a brief outline of this approach can be made.

The fact that the image of human nature and the rational understanding of emotions in both Spinoza and Freud offer some significant similarities to the Buddhist psychological insights is the only justification for a comparative study of this sort. The distinctive differences however should make a pointer to a more comprehensive theory of emotions, which will not reject the Spinozist mode, but will both include it and transcend it. This in essence is the primary impulse behind this article, aware of the fact that only the barest outline of such a project may be given within the afforded space.

The Pali term vedanā translated as "feeling" refers to a sensation which can have a physical or mental origin and is described as pleasant, unpleasant, or indifferent. "It is not used, as in the English Language, in the sense of 'emotion' which is a mental factor of much more complex nature."[55] Some psychologists like Magda Arnold adhere to this distinction, "feelings may be considered as affective reactions to sensations," whereas in emotions there is a complex relationship of the subject toward an object.

Feelings in the Buddhist context are hedonic tones which are basically the first reactions to sensations, and this factor plays a significant role in the development of mindfulness:

This, therefore, is a crucial point in the conditioned origin of Suffering; it is at this point that Feeling may give rise

to passionate emotions of various types and it is, therefore,
here that one may be able to break that fatuous concatenation.
If, in receiving a sense impression, one is able to pause and
stop at the phase of Feeling, and make it, in its very first
stage of manifestation, the object of Bare Attention, Feeling
will not be able to originate Craving or other passions.[56]

At this point the person attempts to break the associative links
which convert a sensation into a hedonic tone and thus put a signal
across the lines, which generate complex emotional phenomena. It is
basically an attempt to break through a process of conditioning which
converts sense impressions (phassa) into feelings (vedanā) and feelings into complex emotions.

Though this technique tries to break through associative links it
does not use crudely behaviorist techniques such as, for instance, a
man who attacked handbags conditioned to develop an aversion for it:
"A similar actual treatment involved a man who attacked handbags:
kept awake by amphetamine, he was presented with handbags and then
made nauseous by injection of apamorphine, thus coming to associate
handbags (as the conditioned stimulus) with an unpleasant response."[57] In the development of mindfulness there is no counter-
conditioning by developing aversion instead of attraction, but an
objective process of observation beyond both attraction and repulsion. It is by this process of attraction and repulsion that we
accumulate strong doses of negativities in our emotional makeup, and
it is necessary to develop a stance of equanimity beyond both attraction and repulsion.

At this point one has to anticipate an objection: "Does this
mean that the psychology of therapy here advanced in Buddhism aims to
completely drain off one's emotions?" Though this point will be
taken for detailed treatment as we go along, it must be mentioned
that there are wholesome emotions which should be developed and which
do not emerge on the attraction-repulsion pattern inherent in vedanā.

The objects of mindfulness in Buddhism are of four types: Body,
Feelings, States of Mind, and Mental Contents. What we have referred
to now is the contemplation on feelings. The basic message in the
contemplation on feeling is clearly presented by the Venerable
Nyanaponika: "The curt and simple, but repeated registering of the
nature of feelings just arisen, will have a greater influence on the
emotional life than an emotional or rational counter-pressure by way
of eulogy, deprecation, condemnation or persuasion."[58] In light of
this technique the emphasis on "organized patterns of attention and
focus," instead of beliefs in proportional form in the philosophy of
emotions, is a step in the right direction.[59]

It is at the next stage in the practice of mindfulness, the contemplation of the state of mind (cittānupassanā), that Neu's notion
of the link between thought-dependence and emotions become significant. It is of course presented in the form of a highly generalized
formula: "Herein a monk knows the mind with lust, as with lust; the
mind without lust as without lust; the mind with hate, as with hate;
the mind without hate as without hate; the mind with delusion as with
delusion and the mind without delusion as without delusion...."[60]
The next section on the contemplation of mind-objects continues this
theme on a greater level of complexity focusing specific sense

desires which can dominate our minds, specific states of anger, sloth and torpor, agitation, worry, and doubt.

In this phase of the development of mindfulness there is an emphasis on self-examination and self-knowledge, which makes the education of the emotions a meaningful quest. However, some feel that excessive concern with self-accusations, self-justifications and the "elaborate search for 'hidden motives'" can be often damaging. So that instead of overdoing the Freudian analogies embedded in our concepts of self-knowledge, it may be often useful to let the simple facts of observation speak and make their impression on the mind.

Apart from the levels of hedonic tones and that of complex emotions, there is a third level at which Buddhism offers a therapeutic dimension: The existential structures inherent in the human predicament, man-world polarity, and the dialectic of the inner-outer shadows embedded in man's concern with pride, shame, hurt, depression, wounded narcissism, and emptiness. (The theoretical base for this is found in the concept of the five aggregates of clinging.)

Our study of emotions and therapy will also be presented from the dimension of the existential structures embedded in the emergence and expression of human emotions. Whatever dimension we take, the understanding of emotions is a deeply human concern and is based on a direct experiential route. There is no need to cast a cloud of obscurity on this project by an excessive concern with the vocabulary of para-mysticism. The attempt to separate emotions into those which are disruptive and creative, negative and positive, is facilitated in the Buddhist context by the terms unwholesome (unskillful, akusala) and wholesome (skillful, kusala), which bring an ethico-psychological grounding to the study of emotions. In more common language Buddhism makes a distinction between emotions which are egoistic and nonegoistic taking us all the way to the deep existential structures within which our human relations are cast. Koestler's search for the violet side of the rainbow of emotions,[61] making a distinction between self-transcending and self-assertive emotions, offers some stimulating parallels to Buddhism, though there are some clear differences between the two approaches. What the self-transcending emotions have in common, according to him, is the feeling of integrative participation with others' sympathy or identification. Examples of such emotions are joy, sadness, tenderness, and compassion. Koestler feels that the self-transcending emotions have been neglected by present-day civilization due to self-assertive activities like domination and competition. While Buddhist meditative culture would be quick to discern shades of attachment in sadness and differentiate self-pity from positive compassion, the search for the violet side of the rainbow or the self-transcending emotions is certainly the basic ethos of the psychology of emotions in Buddhism.

It was mentioned that the Humean mode emphasizes feelings, the Spinozistic mode thought (belief) and the Buddhist mode that of attention, as methods of the therapeutic confrontation of emotions. This does not mean that the psychology of Buddhism neglects the role of feelings and beliefs. Rather it considers the emergence of feelings an important point at which attention should be focused, the point at which a reaction to sensation is converted into a hedonic tone. Unlike feelings, thought can be used as an instrument of therapeutic transformation. But as thought itself can be colored by memory, imagery or unwholesome dispositions, the development of "bare attention" has a more unique function. Attention (mindfulness) has an unparalleled therapeutic function in breaking through the "attraction-repulsion" structure of hedonic tones and also beliefs which are wrong and colored by memory and egoistic projections. More than everything, unwholesome beliefs are colored by man's attachment to his sense of the ego.

The development of attention is basically formulated as a therapeutic technique in the "Discourse on the Foundations of Mindfulness" (Satipatthāna Sutta). The word sati in its Buddhist usage has the notion of referring to the present by way of attention or awareness. In the Buddhist usage (as different from its Western counterpart) the kind of attention recommended is grounded in the Buddhist meditational culture, and it is referred to as good, skillful, or right (kusala). Mindfulness has to be specially directed to associative thinking, the capacity to generalize from experience and the development of abstract thinking which influence the cognitive and affective structures of our daily experience. Sometimes "bare" attention is directed to details of experience and at other times to the deeper structural aspects of experience. The many faces of egoism would form the deep structural bases for understanding the nature of emotions.

The context in which the word "attention" is used, the conceptual surroundings and the ethico-psychological scaffolding in Buddhist terminology, gives a special focus to the use of attention concepts in Buddhism, but will also color the question, "What are appropriate and inappropriate emotional responses, and the whole question regarding the justification of emotions?" Thus it would be necessary to give a brief sketch of the Buddhist analysis of emotions in its psychological and ethical dimension. Therapeutically, the Buddhist mode accepts the claim that conditioning is a significant mechanism, but it would try to break through these associative links by a process of directing awareness to it, rather than any counter-conditioning. The role of beliefs in the Spinozistic mode is important, as we have strong ideological bases (ditthi) which color our emotions, but rational understanding, logical elucidation and intellectual understanding have limits. Specially in the task of breaking through unwholesome habits and attitudes, attention is a more powerful instrument than thought.

An acknowledgement of the limits to the power of thought and the spell of imagination may be found in Neu's study of Spinoza: "Awareness of inadequacy does not drive out or destroy the idea, but the false belief gives way to an acknowledged imagination once we know the causes of the thought."[62] Spinoza uses the example that though the sun is far away, we think it close by, and even when we intellectually realize this fact, the spell of the illusion at the level of the imagination is strong; the Buddha would use the example that, though at the intellectual level we can be aware that the ego is a construction made of the five aggregates (body, feelings, perceptions, dispositions, and consciousness), at the imaginative level the idea persists like the scent of a flower seen in the past.[63]

Emotions in Buddhist Perspective

Emotions in Buddhism have to be examined in the light of three
lifestyles: the layman who has made a compromise with life but seeks
a righteous way of life, the monk who has severed himself from secular pursuits, where the call to liberate from the predicament of human suffering is urgent, and the perfected arahat. Whatever the
lifestyle we deal with, there has been a mistaken view among Buddhists that emotions always interfere with the spiritual life, that
they are unwholesome states which are ethically undesirable, and that
they are states of agitation and imbalance to be mastered. Though a
large number of contexts discussed in Buddhist texts fall into this
category, there are emotions which can be wholesome and creative. As
we have mentioned elsewhere, in a study of emotions in Buddhist perspective, "It may be that there is an emotional aspect of man that
distorts his reasoning, feeds his prejudices and darkens his vision;
but should we not look for an emotional facet in man that expands
one's horizons of thinking, breaks through our egotism, sharpens a
healthy sense of the tragic and evokes the ennobling emotions of sympathy and compassion for fellow men?"[64] Even regarding the unwholesome ones, there is something more than their blank rejection and
elimination, and that is a mastery attained through a subtler process
of rational investigation, diagnostic study, and by a development of
the way of mindfulness. In this sense, we can speak of the "education of the emotions," a healthier and a more lasting way to wellbeing and happiness.

In relation to the life of the layman, we have discussed elsewhere the Buddhist parallels to the Kierkegaardian distinction between "erotic love" and "conjugal love": for Kierkegaard, marriage
is the truest transformation of romantic love, while pure erotic love
is based on the enigmatic, the secretive, and the surprising; conjugal love stands for candor, open-heartedness, revelation, and understanding.[65] The Buddha also discusses how components like respect,
concern, guidance, and sympathy color the emotional warmth of domes-
tic felicity and the human relations of a family.[66]

The recluse, though intent on a more sustained path to liberation,
expresses concern for fellow beings, deep sympathy, and compassion.
The recluse is also capable of developing a zest for liberation (the
desire for spiritual growth which is eliminated after perfection).
There are also instances in Buddhist texts where people who attained
great heights of spiritual development appreciated scenic beauty.

Finally, the claim that the perfected saint is "beyond good and
evil" is a misguided notion. As P.D. Premasiri points out in his
study of Buddhist ethics, the Buddha was not indifferent to such distinctions:

On the contrary, it was after his enlightenment that he claimed
to know with full confidence what is kusala and akusala, and
spent the rest of his life in instructing others about these
distinctions. Does it then mean that the conduct of the Buddha
does not conform to such distinctions? This too is not plausi-
ble, for it is said: "The Tathāgata is one who has discarded
all states that are akusala and possessed of states that are
kusala."[67]

128

The role of emotions in relation to the arahant has been discussed by
Nathan Katz in a recent article:

> Rather than saying, as some might, that all emotions are
> worldly...we would prefer to employ the Buddha's more ana-
> lytical and less categorical approach, and say something like:
> depending on the attitude one holds toward them, some emotions
> could be said to be worldly; and some such as mettā, samvega
> and karunā, would be nibbānic, which is to say those emotions
> appropriate to an arahant; and the other emotions could be
> either worldly or nibbānic, depending upon their context and
> one's relation to them.[68]

If one is aware of the ethico-psychological frame in which the Buddhist theory of emotions is cast, then according to contexts we can
discern their appropriateness. The rest of the discussion will be
spent on outlining the ethico-psychological frame of the Buddhist
theory of emotions, and examining the logic of "appropriateness" (of
justification) in the light of the Buddhist world view.

Pleasant feelings (sukha vedanā) and painful feelings (dukkha
vedanā) are affective reactions to sensations. When we make a judgment in terms of the hedonic tone of these affective reactions, excited in us are certain dispositions to possess the object (greed),
run away from it (fear), destroy it (hatred), and similar tendencies.
The situation perceived and evaluated generates a meaning for the individual according to which he responds, and basically this would be
how emotion works. According to the emergence of hedonic tones a
person is either attracted by an object or repelled by it; he feels
attraction (sarājjati) for agreeable material shapes and he feels repugnance (byāpajjati) for disagreeable material shapes. An individual thus possessed of like (anurodha) and dislike (virodha) approaches pleasure-giving objects and avoids painful objects. Our
attitudes which have been formed in the past influence our present
reactions to oncoming stimuli, and these attitudes are often rooted
in dynamic personality traits. Thus while emotions have significant
causal histories, the Buddha attempts to formalize the patterns in
the causal history of emotions by speaking of different types of dispositional activity, some of which work at an unconscious level
(anusaya), an unconscious level not just rooted in traumatic events
but extending beyond to innumerable lives. The latter idea is hard
to communicate to the West, and the only analogy (though inadequate)
is Freud's concept of the "archaic heritage of mankind."[69]

If the word "unconscious" is too specifically Freudian, we can
refer to them as deep-rooted proclivities. Pleasant feelings excite
the proclivity towards sensuous greed (rāgānusaya), painful feelings
arouse the proclivity to express anger and hatred (patighānusaya).
There are a number of other such proclivities like the ones exciting
conceit, craving for existence, skepticism, ignorance, etc. As a
consequence of their pertinacity they provide the structural bases
for the complicated web of human emotions which are unwholesome.

The distinction between emotions which are wholesome and unwholesome rests on the dual bases of motivation or what are referred to as
motivational roots (mūla). The motivational aspect of emotions is
divided into two groups, wholesome (kusala) and unwholesome

(akusala). The unwholesome roots are greed (lobha), hatred (dosa), and delusion (moha), while the wholesome roots are nongreed, nonhatred, and nondelusion. Greed generates the approach desires in the form of the drive for self-preservation (bhava-tanhā) and the drive for sensuous pursuits (kāma-tanhā), while hatred generates the avoidance desires in the form of the drive for annihilation and aggressive tendencies (vibhava-tanhā).

The Buddhist analysis of craving according to which the drive for self-preservation and self-destruction emerge from the same root of the ego illusion is an extremely rich psychological hypothesis, which can account for a great deal of ambiguity and ambivalence in our emotional lives. For instance, take the enigmatic question of Sigmund Freud in examining the death instinct—how can one who is infected with such a great amount of self-love consent to his own destruction? Freud came to the verge of solving this puzzle when he saw a link between wounded narcissism (injured self-love) and the state of depression described in Mourning and Melancholia, but this insight was not integrated into his complete system, as it possibly could have been done. Buddha's psychological insight lay in pointing out that such apparently contradictory attitudes like narcissistic self-love and self-hatred, and contradictory or ambivalent attitudes like the desire to live and the desire to annihilate oneself—all stem from a basic ego illusion. Koestler's search for the "violet side of the rainbow" is pursued by the Buddha with a great deal of perspicacity. A detailed study of the theoretical frame for distinguishing between self-centered and self-regarding motives, self-surrender and self-confidence, as well the nature of self-display, self-effacement (pathological) and the nature of nonselfish activity has been made elsewhere in a comparative study of the Buddhist concept of Bhavatanhā and the Freudian concept of the ego instinct.[70]

Broadly, craving provides the affective root of motivation and delusion provides the cognitive root of motivation:

> Non-greed and non-hate may, according to the particular
> case, have either a mainly negative meaning signifying absence
> of greed and hate: or they may possess a distinctly positive
> character, for example: non-greed as renunciation, liberality;
> non-hate as amity, kindness, forbearance. Non-delusion has
> always a positive meaning: for it represents the knowledge
> which motivates the respective state of consciousness. In
> their positive aspect non-greed and non-hate are likewise
> strong motives of good actions. They supply the nonrational,
> volitional or emotional motives, while non-delusion represents
> the rational motive of a good thought or action.[71]

Thus it will be seen that nongreed and nonhatred are the affective sources of healthy and positive emotions, while nondelusion provides the rationale for them. While differing types of social structures stimulate the varying types of psychological drives, the six roots of motivation provide a general base for distinguishing emotions which should be cultivated and those that should be eliminated or transformed.

Emotions and the Logic of Justification

Resentment is a natural emotion when our feelings are hurt; so is gratitude when we appreciate a deeply felt act of kindness; perhaps forgiveness is as natural as resentment, when we understand the context of action and develop an attitude of "live and let live"; now this is the complicated "web of feelings and attitudes," of gratitude, resentment, forgiveness, love and hurt referred to by Strawson. It is this range of interpersonal relationships which brings into focus the significant relationship between emotions and morality, and specially so when we move from mere resentment to moral indignation: "Just as there are personal and vicarious reactive attitudes associated with demands on others for oneself and demands on others for others, so there are self-reactive attitudes associated with demands on oneself for others."[72] It is in this manner that obligation, guilt, remorse, and shame emerge in interpersonal relations.

Though we can thus understand the naturalness of the complicated web of human feelings and attitudes, there do emerge questions regarding the appropriateness of these emotions in relation to varying contexts. This brings in the controversial issue regarding the justification of emotions. Is it correct to express one's anger on certain occasions? As Russell remarked, is jealousy an inappropriate reaction in all contexts? Can we make a case for a justifiable feeling of pride rather than conceit on some occasions? Are there occasions when it is better to develop a sense of equanimity rather than express grief, dejection, or depression? The approach to these questions need not be dominated by a wildly ascetic view of emotions or a narrowly puritanical one, but rather a clinical dimension where questions of wellbeing, health and happiness become important.[73]

Can emotions be described as "good" and "bad" or be described in more cautious terminology as "appropriate" and "inappropriate"? These words have to be used carefully; if one is mistaken about the facts, then it is unfounded (e.g. "I thought that A had stolen my book when I had merely misplaced it; my anger is unfounded"). Emotions can be irrational, as when someone shows a strange fear of rats. Emotions can be excessive or disproportionate ("I felt depressed when I lost my pencil").[74] The logic of justification is an issue directly related to the therapeutic confrontation of emotions.

As it is not possible to examine the whole range of emotions involved in this article, it would be better to discuss a selected range of emotions which are directly related to our study. Resentment and anger emerge in natural contexts:

If someone treads on my hand accidentally, while trying to help me, the pain may be no less acute than if he treads on it in contemptuous disregard of my existence. But I shall generally feel in the second case a kind and degree of resentment that I shall not feel in the first.[75]

In one sense of the word "appropriate" we can say that when one is resentful on such an occasion, anger is an appropriate emotion. We can compare this with another situation: A person vies with another for an award in sports, and it was a fair competition, but the loser

feels angry at the winner. The first instance offers a case for
"righteous indignation" in the words of Aristotle. This would be a
mean between malice and envy. Aristotle also says that incontinence /iṅ'kan
in anger is less disgraceful than incontinence in desire, as anger is ₜₐₙₐₙₛ/
amenable to reason up to a point.
Consider Spinoza's position on this question: n。不àの制

> All emotions of hatred and evil....therefore, the man who lives
> according to the guidance of reason will strive as much as
> possible to keep himself from being agitated by the emotions
> of hatred....and, consequently....will strive to keep others
> from being subject to the same emotions. But hatred is in-
> creased by reciprocal hatred, and, on the other hand, can be
> extinguished by love....[76]

In may be objected to Spinoza's position that if there is a case
for justifiable resentment and one is not stirred by this the person
is stupid or a coward. There are a number of issues involved here.
If there are grounds for justifiable resentment, one should not go to
sleep. One should inform the person concerned that a wrong was done
but need not become furious, one can be firm but need not get agitated, and finally feel for the wrongdoer as a fellow human being and
seek his transformation. The way of openness, vigilance, and firm-
ness can finally lead to understanding and transformation. This
would be the attitude reflected in the Buddhist mode to this question. Basically, accumulated hatred is unwholesome and a passing
state of anger should be mindfully handled. There is an interesting
aside to Aristotle in the Buddhist reflections on the relative lia-
bilities of hatred and greed: if one is within the five precepts,
"greed" may not generate consequences as disastrous as "hatred," however, hatred may be a passing phase, as it is more reactive, but
greed is more deep-rooted and harder to master.[77]
Unlike in the case of anger, the emotions of fear, shame, and
sorrow have both unwholesome and wholesome facets. As a detailed
analysis of these emotions has been presented in my Introduction to
Buddhist Psychology,[78] there is no need to reproduce this analysis
again. Briefly to sum up the contents of this study, emotions may be
considered inappropriate in two contexts, those which obstruct the
ideal of good life sought by the layman and those that interfere with
the path of perfection sought by the recluse, while those that further the life perspectives of the layman as well as the life ideals
of the recluse are appropriate. Fear, for instance, can emerge from
excessive desire and craving; they are to be eliminated; fear of
leading a bad life when considered as a healthy sense of "moral dread
and shame" may be profitably cultivated. Sorrow which leads to
lamentation and grief over losses to attachment may not be profit-
able, but the impact of genuine tragic situations can bring about a
spiritual alertness. The emotion of samvega can be an invigorating
kind of existential stirring. A similar approach may be used to distinguish compassion which is of an unbound nature from the narrow expressions of erotic love and lust.
The logic of justification of emotions in the Buddhist context
has to follow the lines of demarcation between the wholesome and unwholesome emotions. Detailed determination of the nature of the

appropriateness of emotions should pay heed to context, intentionality, personal responsibility, and nature of the "world view,"[79] a complete study of which cannot be attempted here.

Emotions and Their Basic Existential Structure

Frank Tillman has worked out an interesting concept, a way of plotting out the abstract narrative structure of emotion enactments, and the initial frame can be used with modifications to understand the nature of different types of emotion. Emergence of emotions in the Buddhist perspective can be understood in the light of more generalized frames.[80] But at a more basic level, what we call the "existential structures" of emotions, provide the ground-level climate for the emergence and expression of emotions, and these levels have to be reached by a kind of discernment well rooted in Buddhist meditative culture.

A ground level emotion like "emptiness" provides an interesting illustration, as it involves the total person—there is a crucial link between the notion of emptiness and the doctrine of egolessness (anattā). Emptiness in the Buddhist context has a dual edge—one pointing to the staleness, vacuity, boredom and identity illusions generated by the ego (the five constituents which go to make the individual); the other points toward the lack of attachment, stillness, tranquility, and silence. It was looking at the second facet that Erich Fromm remarked, "He is filled because he is empty."

The experience of vacuity, boredom, and loneliness has been graphically presented in contemporary literature.[81] Prototypes of this experience have been common in clinical situations. Emptiness in the negative sense has two manifestations, there is emptiness with a simple "e" and Emptiness with a capital "E." The first refers to the little pools of nonbeing—experiences of dashed expectations, distance, absence, change, otherness, repulsion or regret; the latter refers to the basic hollowness within oneself. To use an example of Kierkegaard, there are two types of boredom. In one form a person can be bored with a talk, a book, or a play. This is a superficial kind of boredom. One can also be bored not with any specific object, but with oneself. This is referred to as a nameless emptiness. More specifically, it is the sort of feeling a person has when he loses any sense of meaning in life.

In the context of Buddhism, there are two approaches, one is the negative encounter with the vacuity and boredom in one's life; the other is the positive realization of this experience, and a transformation of this emotion into a positive insight regarding the nature of reality. The positive insight would be the lack of an inner essence or a permanent self. It is due to a kind of spiritual poverty that modern man is incapable of converting this negative encounter into a more positive insight into the nature of reality. Edward Conze, analyzing the term śūnya (emptiness) says that the Sanskrit root helps us to understand how the word becomes a synonym for notself. This connection between the self and emptiness belongs to the existential structures which color our emotional lives. To quote from one of my earlier writings:

The Sanskrit word śūnya is derived from the root svi (to swell). Śūnya means, literally, relating to the swollen. In the remote past, our ancestors had a sense of the double meaning of words. They often deliberately used verbal roots with opposite meanings. Conze says that svi conveyed the idea that something which looks "swollen" from outside is "hollow" from inside.... Unless the so-called self receives positive identifications, it manifests as a void or hollow;[82]

thus reminding us of T. S. Eliot's hollow men and stuffed men of our age.

Conclusion

Our interest in emotions is wedded to their therapeutic orientation. In this light the paradigmatic Humean approach centered on "feelings," the Spinozistic approach based on "thought" (beliefs) and the characteristically Buddhist approach based on "attention" have been outlined. In raising the question about the "appropriateness" of emotions to their specific contexts, an outline of the pyschological framework in the Buddhist theory of emotions was made, a task which is related to distinguishing between emotions which are therapeutically wholesome and those which are not. In this process we brought out the evaluative texture of emotion concepts as well as their basic existential structure. The existential structure of emotions is of crucial significance for what may be called Buddhistic therapeutic procedure, and in attempting to elucidate this point, a sample study of a ground level emotion, that of "emptiness" was made. The analysis of "emptiness" as an emotion betrays quite clearly its dual-edged nature: one pointing toward boredom and vacuity, the other pointing toward stillness and tranquility.

Finally, it must be said that emotions do not fall into one neatly classified, natural class.[83] In the context of Buddhism, the dominating therapeutic orientation gives a certain degree of order to the role of emotions. But Buddhism also offers a multilayered therapeutic structure accepting a variety of emotion types: emotion types range, for example, from the specific context of bound ones, the motivationally generated ones, those linked to dispositions and character traits, to those deep, existential, total orientations of a global nature, like "Care," "Angst" and "Emptiness."[84]

NOTES

1. See Gilbert Ryle, The Concept of the Mind (New York: Penguin, 1964).
2. See Donald Gustafson, ed., Essays in Philosophical Pyschology (New York: Doubleday, 1964), pp. xi-xix.
3. The "Philosophy East-West Comparative Study Program" at the University of Hawaii has been promoting projects of this sort over the years.
4. Robert M. Pirsig, Zen and the Art of Motorcycle Maintenance (New York: Bantam, 1976).

5. R.S. Peters, "The Education of the Emotions" in Feelings and Emotions: The Loyola Symposium, ed. M.B. Arnold (New York: Academic Press, 1970).

6. Ibid.

7. Ibid.

8. W.P. Alston, "Emotion and Feeling" in The Encyclopedia of Philosophy, vol. 2, ed. Paul Edwards (New York: Macmillan, 1967), p. 481.

9. Jerome Neu, Emotion, Thought, and Therapy (Los Angeles: U. of California Press, 1977).

Out of print
B & N available

10. See Albert Welleck, "Emotional Polarity in Personality Structure" in Feelings and Emotions. Also see R.W. Hepburn, "The Arts and the Education of Feeling" in Education and the Development of Reason, eds. Dearden, Hirst and Peters (London: Routledge and Kegan Paul, 1972).

11. B.J. Rosebury, "Fiction, Emotion and Belief," British Journal of Aesthetics (Spring 1979).

12. Peters, "The Education of the Emotions."

13. Herbert Fingarette, Self Deception (New York: Humanities Press, 1969), p. 44.

14. Ibid., p. 35.

15. Ibid., p. 36.

16. Ibid., p. 38.

17. Ibid., pp. 44-45.

18. See Amelie O. Rorty, "Explaining Emotions," The Journal of Philosophy (March 1978): 150; Ronald de Sousa, "The Rationality of Emotions," Dialogue 18 (1979): 53.

19. Iris Murdoch, The Sovereignty of Good (London: Routledge and Kegan Paul, 1970). Emphasis in quotations from this book are mine.

20. Ibid., p. 29.

21. Ibid.

22. P.D. Premasiri, "Moral Evaluation in Early Buddhism: From the Perspectives of Western Philosophical Analysis" (Ph.D. dissertation, University of Hawaii, 1980).

23. Gabriele Taylor, "Justifying the Emotions," Mind 84 (1975).

24. This material is being prepared for publication by the Cultural Learning Institute of East-West Center, Hawaii, and is being edited for this purpose by Jerry D. Boucher.

25. Bernard Williams, "Morality and the Emotions" (Inaugural Lecture, Bedford College) in Williams, Problems of the Self (London: Cambridge U. Press, 1973).

26. See Robert C. Solomon, "Emotions and Choice," Review of Metaphysics (September 1973).

27. Ibid.

28. Peters, "The Education of the Emotions."

29. The role of "existential structures" and the nature of "ground emotions" will be discussed in the concluding sections of this article.

30. Charles Darwin, The Expression of Emotions in Man and Animals (Chicago: U. of Chicago Press, 1965).

31. Peters, "The Education of the Emotions."

32. Darwin, Expression of Emotions.

33. See Alastair MacIntyre, "Behaviour, Belief and Emotions" in Interpretations of Life and Mind, ed. Marjorie Grene (London:

Routledge and Kegan Paul, 1971).

34. See the writings of C.L. Stevenson and D.M. Hare.

35. Williams, "Morality and the Emotions."

36. See J.A.K. Thomson, trans., The Ethics of Aristotle (London: George Allen & Unwin, 1959).

37. Padmasiri de Silva, An Introduction to Buddhist Pyschology (New York: Macmillan, 1979).

38. Peters, "The Education of Emotions."

39. G. Pitcher, "Emotion," Mind 79 (1965).

40. Ryle, The Concept of Mind.

41. Errol Bedford, "Emotions," in Essays in Philosophical Psychology.

42. Ibid.

43. Anthony Kenny, Action, Emotion and Will (London: Routledge and Kegan Paul, 1963).

44. See Padmasiri de Silva, "Two Paradigmatic Strands in the Buddhist Theory of Consciousness" in Metaphors of Consciousness, eds. R.S. Valle and Rolf Von Eckersberg (New York: Plenum Pub., 1980).

45. Edward Sankowski, "Responsibility of Persons for their Emotions," Canadian Journal of Philosophy (December 1977).

46. Ibid.

47. P.F. Strawson, "Freedom and Resentment" in Studies in the Philosophy of Thought and Action, ed. Strawson (London: Oxford U. Press, 1968).

48. Neu, Emotion, Thought and Therapy.

49. Ibid., p. 118.

50. Sigmund Freud, Collected Papers, vol. V, ed. James Strachey (London: Hogarth Press, 1950), p. 316.

51. Sigmund Freud, Complete Works, vol. II, ed. James Strachey (London: Hogarth Prss, 1950), p. 305.

52. Freud, "'Wild Psychoanalysis,'" Complete Works, vol. XI.

53. Jerome Neu also contrasts the "mythical" and "symbolic" structure of shamanistic healing with psychotherapy, especially how the shamanistic healing provides a conceptual scheme to the patient to reintegrate an otherwise alien experience. It is not possible to discuss here this discussion of the therapeutic encounter; for an analysis of the Buddhist attitude to healing rites, see Padmasiri de Silva, "Doctrinal Buddhism and Healing Rituals" in de Silva, Buddhist and Freudian Psychology, 2nd ed. (Colombo: Lake House Investments, 1978).

54. For an interesting discussion of the empiricist strands in the early Buddhist tradition, see Ivan Strensky, "Gradual Enlightenment, Sudden Enlightenment and Empiricism," Philosophy East and West (January 1980).

55. Nyanaponika Thera, The Heart of Buddhist Meditation (London: Rider & Co., 1965), p. 65.

56. Ibid., p. 69.

57. Neu, Emotion, Thought, and Therapy. Neu discusses this point with reference to the work of Eysenck.

58. Thera, The Heart of Buddhist Meditation, p. 70.

59. See Rorty, "Explaining Emotions."

60. Thera, The Heart of Buddhist Meditation, p. 112.

61. See Arthur Koestler, The Art of Creation (London: Pan Books, Ltd., 1966); Koestler, Janus (London: Hutchinson, 1978).

62. Neu, Emotion, Thought, and Therapy, p. 96.

63. Woodward, trans., "The Sermon to Khemaka," Kindred Sayings, vol. III (London: Pali Text Society, 1954), p. 130.

64. See de Silva, Emotions in Buddhist Perspective, Sir D.B. Jayatilleke Memorial Lecture, Colombo, 1976 (Kandy: Buddhist Publication Society, 1976).

65. Padmasiri de Silva, Tangles and Webs (Colombo: Lake House Investments, 1976), chapter 2.

66. See T.W. Rhys-Davids and C.A.F. Rhys-Davids, trans., "The Sigalovada Sutta" in Dialogues of the Buddha, vol. III (London: Pali Text Society, 1957).

67. Premasiri, "Moral Evaluation in Early Buddhism."

68. Nathan Katz, "Does the 'Cessation of the World' Entail the Cessation of Emotions? The Psychology of the Arahant," Pali Buddhist Review 4, no. 3 (1979).

69. See de Silva, ed., Buddhist and Freudian Psychology, pp. 39, 64-67.

70. Ibid., chapter 4.

71. Nyanaponika Thera, Ahbidhamma Studies (Kandy: Buddhist Publication Society, 1965), p. 79.

72. Strawson, "Freedom and Resentment," p. 86.

73. See Stuart Hampshire, Spinoza (Harmondsworth: Penguin Books, 1951), chapter 4.

74. Taylor, "Justifying the Emotions."

75. Strawson, "Freedom and Resentment."

76. Spinoza, Ethics, ed. James Gutmann (New York: Grosset, 1963), p. 223.

77. Nyanaponika Thera, The Roots of Good and Evil (Kandy: Buddhist Publication Society, 1978), p. 27.

78. See de Silva, An Introduction to Buddhist Psychology.

79. A "world view" has significant consequences for emotion concepts. See the discussion of "Never in Anger" in R.C. Solomon, "Emotions and Anthropology: The Logic of World Views," in Inquiry.

80. Frank Tillman, "Understanding Emotion" (Paper written at the University of Hawaii, 1979). The author was kind enough to show me a copy of this paper.

81. This is discussed in Padmasiri de Silva, Positive and Negative Encounters with Emptiness (S.L.B.C. Lecture, Colombo, The Expanding Mind Series, 1980).

82. See de Silva, Introduction to Buddhist Psychology, p. 121.

83. Rorty, "Explaining Emotions."

84. The therapeutic framework of the Buddhist concept of emotions outlined here will form part of a forthcoming work entitled, Emotions and their Shadows.

PART TWO

Psychological Implications of Japanese Buddhism

Illusion and Human Suffering:
A Brief Comparison of Horney's Ideas
with Buddhistic Understanding of Mind

Akihisa Kondo

The salvation of man from his suffering has been one of the deepest yearnings of man from the beginning of his life on the planet.
Serious efforts have been made since then to find out the cause of
suffering so that certain therapeutic methods can be found. It took,
however, many centuries until the causes of physical suffering, the
organic diseases, were determined and it was really then that modern
medicine began to develop.

In the case of mental suffering, the situation was worse. It was
only at the beginning of this century that revolutionary pioneering
work made by Sigmund Freud proceeded to open the way to understanding
the causes of mental suffering. His ideas of the unconscious, of the
structure of mind consisting of libido, superego, and ego, governed
by conflict and regulated by defense mechanisms, of transference, and
of the psychosexual development of the child, have created a deeper
understanding of the human mind and helped to establish a more effective therapeutic approach to mental suffering.

However, as time went on and the degree and range of therapeutic
experiences increased, it was found that his ideas were too biologically inclined, mechanistic, and deterministic to explain the total
phenomena and potentialities of the human mind, resulting in relatively limited therapeutic efficacy. Among those who took a critical
attitude toward Freud, Karen Horney was one of the most determined
critics. Though she highly valued Freud's contributions, especially
as to the unconscious, transference, resistance, and free association, she developed her own ideas about the human mind based on personal clinical experience.

Horney believes in the existence of the real self, common to all
human beings and intrinsically unique in each individual, which is
the source of growth, or the inner central force that enables each
person to realize his given potential as a human being. Hence, she
believes each individual, if given favorable conditions, can grow
toward self-realization, expressing his genuine feelings, thoughts,
wishes, and interests, developing his intrinsic capacities, and relating himself to others spontaneously. But the actual conditions in
life are so manifold that a favorable condition for growth is not always present. Under adverse circumstances, especially surrounded by
people who are domineering, intimidating, hypocritical, peevish, er-
ratic, overindulgent, indifferent (and there is no end to our list),

the child experiences a feeling of insecurity, and the sense of being left alone helplessly in a world permeated with hostility. Horney calls this primary feeling of insecurity that the child feels, "basic anxiety." In order to allay his basic anxiety, the child can move toward people for affection, or away from them, or against them in the act of fighting and rebellion. As the child is driven by his need for security and safety, these moves become rigid and compulsive, hence neurotic. And, as the child is not only compulsively driven by one of these trends but also by the other contradicting trends, he suffers from conflicts which Horney called "basic conflicts." After vacillation, eventually he will choose one of the trends as his predominant attitude toward others in order to solve his conflicts. Once a predominant attitude is established, it will not only serve as a defense for the child against conflicts and basic anxiety but as the center of his early integration, or a crutch for his identity, which he strongly needs in the absence of real self-confidence.

It is at this point that imagination plays a greater role, though it is a fact that it is always functioning more or less in any kind of activity of the human psyche. The predominant trend with its specific needs, inhibitions, sensitivities, and values is idealized by dint of the imagination to create an idealized self-image. Other contradictory trends are isolated or glorified so that they will not be felt as the causes of conflicts. Thus in the idealized image, aggressiveness becomes manliness, bravery, heroism, omnipotence; compliance or dependent attitudes are transformed to devotional life, pacifism, goodness, saintliness; and aloofness or resigned attitudes are idealized as independence, serenity, loftiness, wisdom.

Since his idealized image is a device to relieve himself from anxiety and conflict, the neurotic individual adheres to and depends upon it in dealing with actual situations in life, even if it is nothing but a product of his imagination. However, as he struggles desperately for actualizing his idealized image, he has to experience the gap between actual accomplishments and idealized self-image, thus throwing him back in the arms of anxiety again. Being exposed to such a gap, he has to invent something by which he can get a feeling of absolute security. Here again, imagination plays a most decisive role. Like a magic wand, imagination helps the individual to identify himself with his idealized self-image, so much so that he will no more become conscious of the gap by which he felt insecure. In other words, the idealized image now becomes his idealized self—a pseudo, false, neurotic self in contrast to his real self. This idealized self is naturally an illusion, but, for the neurotic individual who is desperately in need of his identity, whatever it may be, it is real or at least has an equivalent value of the real self as long as he can depend on it as the center of his life. As he feels his identity in the idealized self, efforts will be made to express or actualize it in life situations. In the process of actualization of the idealized self, the following neurotic characteristics in its structure will come to be expressed more openly.

In the individual's relation with others, he imagines, expects or assumes that others will take and treat him in terms of the same image as he has for himself—his glorified self. Because of his grandiose image of himself, he feels others should fulfill his demands and expectations, and that he is entitled to act in such a way. Horney calls these self-righteous, ego-centered demands "neurotic claims." Claims are made in total disregard to realistic feasibility, the need of others, or the necessity of effort and endurance. This unrealistic attitude is closely related to his basic imagination-oriented attitude. Claims vary with the nature of the predominant trend that prevails in the individual's idealized self or his neurotic personality. In the case of the expansive, aggressive type of individual his claim on others will be for absolute obedience, unconditional surrender, immunity from any sort of criticism, admiration of his supremacy, or special privileges of various kinds. With the self-effacing, dependent type the claim will be for total acceptance, limitless affection and care, monopolizing other's devotional love, or perfect understanding and help. With the self-limiting, resigned, withdrawing type the claim may be for freedom from any sort of intervention, or freedom from restrictions, rules, and limitations. Whatever the claim may be, when he is frustrated the neurotic individual reacts with hostility and indignation, feelings of being abused or unfairly treated, and when these feelings are repressed he will suffer from depression, irritability, dismay, self-pity, chronic feelings of discontent or some other type of psychosomatic symptoms.

When he is frustrated, he reacts not only to others but also to himself. The individual has to find how weak and incompetent his actual self is in fulfilling the demands of his idealized self. The demands of the idealized self, since they are deeply connected with the need for security, are always stringent and coercive. They are made relentlessly as an order comprised of "shoulds," in complete disregard of actual conditions and feasibility. These "shoulds" vary with the prevailing trend in the idealized self. With the expansive type, he feels he should always be strong, wise, invincible, infallible—in short, omnipotent. With the self-effacing type, he should be always generous, humble, loving, understanding, hypersensitive to others' feelings, self-sacrificing. And with the resigned type, he should be always serene, undisturbed, untouched by external affairs, lofty, transcendental. Though these "shoulds" are tyrannically imperative demanding their absolute and perfected fulfillment, confirming in Horney's words a "tyranny of shoulds," they are doomed to be frustrated in the realities of life as they are the products of fantastic illusion. Reactions to frustration are intense self-hate, self-criticism, guilt feeling, depression, despair. Besides these direct reactions to frustration, the individual who is constantly under the tyranny of "shoulds" suffers from a feeling of strain, chronic exhaustion, hypersensitivity to criticism that disturbs his relation to others, and the deadening effect of the "shoulds" on the spontaneity of feelings, thoughts, and beliefs.

When the individual finds his identity in a fantastic, idealized self, he can feel pride in his imagined self as a substitute for real self-confidence. The kinds of pride vary with the prevalent trend of the neurotic self, such as pride in an absolute self-sufficiency, omniscient intellectual capacity, immunity, invulnerability, lovableness, compassion, humbleness, goodness, fairness, serenity, purity, sublime loftiness, independence, freedom. Those attributes sound glorious and make the individual become totally unaware of his anxiety, powerlessness, and inferiority, at least for the time that he is absorbed. But, as they are the products of his illusion, they are intrinsically fragile. When his pride is hurt, whatever kind it may be, the neurotic individual suffers from shame or humilitiation. He feels ashamed when what he actually does, thinks, or feels does not live up to his neurotic pride's standards. He feels humiliated when his pride is injured by others. Often, because of his pride in invulnerability, the aggressive expansive type of individual does not allow himself to feel shame at all, while the self-effacing type of person tends to be overwhelmed with the feeling of shame that overshadows his reaction of humiliation. When those reactions of shame and humiliation to hurt pride are not experienced directly as such, rage and fear are experienced as secondary reactions. Rage directed to others will be expressed in retaliation, and rage at him-self will result in self-hatred. Fear is not only experienced in a humiliating situation, but also in anticipation of such a situation—anticipatory fear or anxiety. In order to restore hurt pride, measures are taken such as retaliation, losing interest in people and things that may evoke humiliation, forgetfulness, and denial. Also, in order to protect pride from dangers in the future, avoidance is taken as a defensive measure. For the neurotic person pride serves as a value system or a measuring rod to determine what to like or ab-hor, reject or accept, love or hate, do or not do, attack or escape, glorify or feel shame—in short, his way of life.

When his neurotic, grandiose, idealized self is established, with its pride as a measuring rod and its system of "shoulds" as an en-forcing agent, the neurotic's attention is bound to be drawn to the state of his actual self. It is an embarassing sight viewed from such a vantage point. His actual being is so powerless in measuring up to the demands of the "shoulds" and living up to a lofty pride that he has to despise and hate his actual self. Pride and self-hate form in fact an inseparable entity, which Horney called "the pride system." Though self-hate is generally an unconscious process, it operates or is expressed in the form of relentless demands on self, self-accusation, self-contempt, self-frustration, self-torment, and self-destruction.

In the process of actualization of the idealized self, the neu-rotic individual exerts his whole energy, which could have been used for the development of his real self, for fulfilling the orders of "snoulds" to satisfy his neurotic pride, thereby furthering separa-tion from the real self, which Horney called self-alienation. It is the most detrimental effect of neurosis. Self-alienation deprives a person of his genuine, spontaneous feelings, wishes, outflow of ener-gies, sense of values, lively sensations of the body, and a secure feeling of identity, which are the expressions of the real self. The above mentioned neurotic characteristics contribute to this effect. The relentless order of "shoulds" drives a person to become compul-sive, tense, and rigid, like automation, removed from his autonomous spontaneity. Pride takes the place of his genuine feeling. Also, as pride works as a governing value system, the individual loses his genuine values and alertness to respond to his real self. Self-hate makes him deny or reject his actual self through which the real self is expressed and developed. It must be noted, however, that though very little of the real self is operating under the pressure of the neurotic, pseudo-self, there is a realistic possibility for the real self to develop itself and become the central source for growth if a favorable condition, such as psychoanalytic treatment, is applied.

The neurotic individual suffers from symptoms, compulsively driven by conflicts and anxiety. These neurotic sufferings, whatever they may be, are basically the inevitable consequences of his neurotic growth, which, in his illusion, were made by assuming the idealized self as his identity while sacrificing the development of his real self. Therefore the therapeutic process is one in which the therapist helps the patient's effort to liberate himself from illusions about himself, thus enabling him to realize and develop his real self. In this sense, it is a "disillusioning process," as Horney correctly put it. But though it is evident to the therapist as his goal, it is not so with the patient. In the sessions, what he wants is relief from his symptoms, unpleasant situations, disturbing problems, or other items of his immediate concern, without changing his neurotic structure. Rather, the patient wants to protect and preserve or sometimes strengthen his neurotic structure by the aid of therapy. He feels, even unconsciously, that to examine and renounce the idealized self which he has taken as the center of his existence, is deadly detrimental to his feeling of security and identity, however illusory that "self" may be. Blockage or resistance, which hinder the progress of therapy, will emerge in many forms and vary with the specific type of neurotic trends, such as reactions of belligerence, hostility, appeasement, flattery, apathy, indifference, flirtation, panic, physical symptoms, and so on. Those reactions or defense mechanisms are to be elucidated in connection with the claims, "shoulds," pride, and needs of the idealized self specific to the patient for his self-understanding. Horney streses the importance of emotional experience instead of intellectual understanding. As the therapy progresses and the patient's insight deepens regarding the illusory nature of his neurotic self and its ramifications, the time will come when he experiences a flow of his constructive force, the expression of his real self. Then, with more hope and enthusiasm, he will advance toward mobilizing his real self. But, as his neurotic self is so chronically ingrained, it has a tremendous inertia that maintains the status quo and resists against the newly generated constructive force of the real self—so much so that he has to experience quite a turbulent period of ups and downs. It is in this period that a final battle is going on between the destructive force and the constructive force, or the neurotic illusory self and the healthy real self, respectively. The therapist must be attentive to being a strong ally of the patient's real self by pointing out what it is fighting against, and for what aims it is fighting. After passing through this critical period the patient will become much more clear about the right path that he really wants to take, with more conviction about his ability to live without depending on illusions. The path he chooses is the path for his growth, for his self-realization.

It is quite evident that, in Horney's theory of neurosis, illusions taking the forms of a grandiose idealized self, the arrogant claims, the relentless "shoulds," the fantastic pride, play the leading role in the formation of neurotic phenomena including neurotic suffering. Horney gives us a vivid picture of the neurotic personality whose mind is haunted and driven by illusions, and shows how illusions mislead the human mind to the extent of despair and self-destructiveness. It is true that Freud observed various forms of illusionary expression in the neurotic defense mechanisms such as projection, introjection, identification, reaction formation, undoing, transference, and so on which produce the "as if" effect in any given situation. He even used the word "illusion" in the title of a book—The Future of an Illusion[1]—in which he critically discussed the nature of religion, concluding that it is an illusion, a product of a collective compulsive neurosis. But Horney was more positive in asserting that the essential core of neurosis is the establishment of an idealized self which is nothing but an illusion; therefore, the therapeutic help necessary for liberating a neurotic person from his sufferings could be made by a disillusioning process, which, in her case, is the psychoanalytic process.

The notion of illusion as a tool for understanding psychic phenomena or the function of the human mind may be of rather recent achievement in Western culture. However in the East, especially in Buddhist tradition, it is not only a familiar concept but also one of the basic notions evidenced from the very beginning of Buddhist history. Actually the whole practice and training in Buddhism is dedicated to the attainment of enlightenment, an awakening of the real self by a process of breaking through the beclouding illusions of the human mind.

The structure of the human mind, according to Buddhist understanding, consists of the following kinds of consciousness: 1) the consciousness of sight; 2) the consciousness of hearing; 3) the consciousness of smell; 4) the consciousness of taste; 5) the tactile consciousness, corresponding to respective sense organs; 6) the mental consciousness; 7) the seventh consciousness of manas; and 8) the eighth consciousness of ālaya or the store-consciousness. Among them, the group of consciousness from the first to the fifth covers the sensory perceptions and impressions; the sixth consciousness, the mental or intellectual one, perceives, interprets, and coordinates those sensory impressions by means of words or concepts, producing the images of sense objects or materials as well as the image of the "I," the ego or the self, the subject that stands against the object image, the external world. Though so far the above psychic processes can be experienced by the mind in the conscious level, the seventh manas consciousness and the eighth ālaya consciousness belong to the unconscious realm.

Actually manas is the unconscious source of self-consciousness, for ego formation, that urges and enforces the sixth intellectual consciousness to establish the image of ego and cling to it. It is always working in one's mind, even while one is unconscious or asleep. It operates and serves as the integrating, stabilizing, and balancing center of one's mind, one's individuality, or one's so-called identity. That is because it erroneously takes the eighth ālaya consciousness as the substance for the notions of ego.

The eighth ālaya consciousness is a sort of reservoir into which all kinds of experiences from the beginningless past flow in as seeds or potentialities to be activated by circumstances in the present, and also in which all the effects of present experiences are stored as seeds or potential to be actualized in the endless future.

It is a torrent of consciousness in which incessant transformation, the birth and death of the seeds takes place. It stores defiled seeds which are tainted by illusions, the cause for suffering, as well as immaculate seeds which, being called Buddha nature, will produce the fruit of enlightenment, liberation from suffering. It also expresses itself by actualizing the seeds and potential of the forementioned seven kinds of consciousness, to the effect that it becomes the source of all kinds of phenomena in this world. In other words, the whole world, both internal and external, is the multifarious and differentiated forms of self-expression of the ālaya consciousness. However, it is in this very process of differentiation that illusion plays a significant role as cause for human suffering.

The seventh manas consciousness, as it takes the ālaya consciousness as a constant, permanent, and concrete entity to depend on, sets up the notion of ego or selfhood, an illusion that does not correspond with the ever dynamically changing reality of the ālaya consciousness. As soon as the illusory notion of ego is established, it is objectified and produces the following basic inclinations that govern the human mind. First is the inclination for believing in the permanent existence of the ego, which is actually the product of projection of the notion of ego, another product of illusion. Second is the pride for the ego. It is arrogance based on the deceptive belief of the permanent existence of one's ego, or one's being. Therefore, pride is also an illusion. It deprives the human mind of the capacity for compassion for others. Third is the inclination for self-love or tenacious attachment to oneself or one's ego. The proud ego built on projection becomes the object of affection, endearment, and attachment. It is the deep source of fear of death because death is supposed to annihilate the existence of the most beloved one, one's ego.

These tendencies, even though they are operating in the unconscious, exert an overall influence over the functions of the sixth intellectual consciousness. The intellectual consciousness establishes the image of ego or self, assuming it as reality and a subject against which the external objects stand. The world it develops is the world of dichotomy, discrimination, and discrepancy resulting in conflicts. It also perceives, interprets, understands, judges, coordinates the information about its objects conveyed by the five kinds of sense consciousness, makes decisions, resorts to actions. But, at every moment of its functioning, the intellectual consciousness is under the powerful emotional influence of the manas consciousness. Its perception, interpretation, understanding, and judgment are so tainted and distorted by the projection of the ego-centered tendencies of the manas consciousness, that the images of the so-called objects become far away from reality. Yet these imagined objects, the illusory phenomena, are erroneously believed to be of real, certain, unchangeable, concrete, dependable, and permanent nature, exactly in the same way as the ego or self is believed, namely by way of projection. It is of course an illusion to believe that way. But the structure and the tendencies of the human mind are such that it is driven by burning desires and cravings of the ego and for their fulfillment, by chasing and possessing these objects. Even when they are fulfilled, pleasure does not last so long, and after a while more desires and increased cravings haunt the mind. The mind also suffers from anger and hatred when frustrated. Thus, human life, whether one likes it or not, is doomed to repeat this vicious circle of suffering until death comes, as long as one lives in the illusions of his mind.

Of all the illusions the human mind produces, the most fundamental one is the illusion of ego which the manas consciousness creates in relation to the ālaya consciousness. As has been observed, from the very moment the notion of ego is assumed to be reality, the dichotomous world of subject and object begins to develop, accompanied by attachment, cravings, desires, anger, hatred, sorrows, and other emotions. Besides, as long as the defiled seeds are prevailing in the ālaya consciousness to delude the mind, there will be no end for human suffering. However, there are also undefiled, immaculate, genuine seeds contained in it to be ripened for the attainment of enlightenment. With all of these factors in mind, the Buddhist approach for helping people from their suffering aims at disillusioning the basic illusion about ego, transforming the ālaya consciousness by cleansing the defiled seeds and developing the clean, genuine seeds. These aims, of course, can not be achieved by mere intellectual understanding which is always under the influence of the manas consciousness. By the intensive practice of meditation one may experience the process of disillusionment by total participation of body and mind, and finally accomplish the transformation of the ālaya consciousness to the Wisdom of the Great Mirror, the manas consciousness to the Wisdom of the Essential Equality of All Beings, the intellectual consciousness to the Distinguishing Wisdom, and the sense consciousness to the All Accomplishing Wisdom.

In explaining potentialities for growth, Horney used a simile of an acorn, in her book Neurosis and Human Growth.[2] An acorn is a seed that grows into an oak tree. Similarly a human being is bestowed with potential, the seeds for self-realization. In the same spirit the word "seed" is used by the Buddhist to denote the potential for enlightenment, or for realization of Buddha nature. Horney takes the real self as the central inner force and the deep source for growth. Likewise, the ālaya consciousness, with its dynamic force of self-actualization, is believed by Buddhists to be the deepest source of transformation from ignorance to enlightenment.[3] Also according to Horney, under unfavorable situations, one's real self tends to be prevented from healthy growth and obliged to create neurotic images, one's illusions about oneself, by the pressure of anxiety. In the case of the ālaya consciousness, though it is true that the external conditions, if unfavorable, will hamper the development of the genuine, untainted seeds it contains, and promote proliferation of the defiled, tainted seeds, it has an inner obstacle in the form of the manas consciousness. As the manas consciousness has an illusion of ego, all the seeds tend to be colored by the notion of ego unconsciously. This internal block can be compared with the inner resistance which the neurotic self makes against the real self, what Horney called "central conflict." The arrogant pride attached to the image of ego by the manas consciousness is also identical with the haughty system of pride which a neurotic individual attaches to his idealized self. And a neurotic's adoration, adherence, and devotion to his glorified neurotic self is the exact equivalent of ego's blind self-love and glutinous attachment. Neurotic claims and ego's fer-

vent desires and tenacious cravings are not so different so far as
their ego-centered tendency is concerned. As regards the cause of
suffering, Horney's understanding that they are the outcome of the
neurotic personality living in the illusion of the idealized self is
almost the same as Buddhist understanding, that they are the inevitable sequence of karmic human life which is based on a false illusion called ego. Their understanding of suffering is such that it is
quite natural that they both make the same approach of a disillusioning process in helping people get rid of their suffering. So far we
have observed similarities.

But a question arises: "Though both are talking about the significance of illusion, isn't it true that their understanding on the
causation of illusion is different?" It is true that Horney understands that the illusory image of idealized self is built out of
anxiety and, for Buddhists, the illusory notion of ego comes out of
the illusion of the manas consciousness. But if we examine the
nature of anxiety about which Horney talks, especially in connection
with basic anxiety, we can find that anxiety is caused by want of
security. Since security means preservation of one's ego or self,
anxiety is inseparably related to ego. Even a child feels anxiety
when his ego is in danger. Though his intellectual consciousness is
not mature enough to be aware of it, the manas consciousness is
working, if we use Buddhist terms.

Also we may further raise a question: "Isn't what Horney talked
about concerning the neurotic, abnormal mind, while Buddhist understanding is related to the normal human mind, and thus they are not
talking about the same thing?" Apparently it seems that they are
talking about different subjects. But if we look back and compare
the characteristics of the neurotic mind with those of ego, we can
not necessarily conclude that they are talking about different things
as it seems. Since the neurotic mind is always at work to preserve
the illusion of ego by measures which are also of illusory nature,
while the ordinary human mind is absorbed in chasing for the fulfillment of the desires of ego by measures which, they believe, are not
illusory. The difference is the distinction between a person who is
dreaming and another who is dreaming in his dream. They have in common the fact that they are living the illusion of ego. Actually the
neurotic mind is enormously ego-centered as Horney often pointed out.
But, regrettably enough, the ordinary human mind is also ego-
centered, if not more. Perhaps it is a matter of difference of quan-
tity but not of quality. In other words, what Horney and the
Buddhist school are stressing is the fact that the illusion of ego
deceives the human mind and misleads it to suffer from the vicious
cycle of suffering, regardless of whether they are neurotic or of existential nature. Therefore, disillusionment is the process of
therapy. Methods vary depending on the difference of culture, tradition, and the therapist's individuality--from the gradual one that
helps the individual get disillusioned with his neurotic image and
then become aware of his real self to be liberated from the illusion
of ego, to the radical one that attacks ego itself directly and uproots the illusion of ego by penetrating intuitive experience of enlightenment.

Making a brief comparison of Horney's idea with Buddhist understanding of mind it is quite impressive to see that, although

Horney's contribution was made specifically for understanding the
neurotic mind, her approach is almost identical with the Buddhist approach for understanding the human mind which was developed in the
period of the third or fourth century, spanning differences of culture and time. Besides her elucidation of the meaning and role of
illusion in the neurotic phenomena, her idea of real self which she
emphasized in her last book[4] is a great contribution because it is a
notion, I believe, that could be developed, deepened, and enriched by
further research and exploration to become one of the basic concepts
in understanding the human mind.

NOTES

1. Sigmund Freud, The Future of an Illusion, ed. James Strachey
(New York: W.W. Norton & Co., 1975).
2. Karen Horney, Neurosis and Human Growth: The Struggle Toward
Self-Realization, 1st ed. (New York: W.W. Norton & Co., 1950).
3. G. Hosaka, Yuishiki Konpon Kyori (The Fundamental Principles
of Vijñapti-mātra), 1st ed. (Tokyo: Komeisha, 1960). K. Yokoyama,
Yuishiki no Tetsugaku (Philosophy of Vijñapti-mātra), 1st ed. (Kyoto:
Heirakuji Shoten, 1979).
4. Horney, Neurosis and Human Growth.

The Meaning of Death in
Psychoanalysis, Existential Phenomenology, and Dōgen Zen

by
Steven Heine

I

The central concern of Buddhism, according to Dōgen,[a] is "the great matter of life and death (daiji shōji)[b]...for the changes of impermanence pass swiftly and time waits for no man."[1] Clarification of the meaning of death in its interrelationship with life provides essential access to an understanding of the nature and structure of impermanence (mujō)[c] and to genuine realization of nonself (muga).[d] Death is significant existentially as the extreme yet all-pervasive and unavoidable possibility of one's own impossibility which, if resolutely encountered, liberates man from egocentric fixations and attachments by directly pointing, ontologically, to the perpetual process of arising-desistence, generation-destruction that characterizes nonsubstantive reality unbound by static substratum or duration.

The twofold interaction between life and death paradoxically encompasses two seemingly contradictory dimensions: (1) the interpenetration of life and death, being (u)[e] and nothingness (mu)[f] as inseparable and interdependent phenomena comprising the totality of each and every moment of being-time (uji)[g]; (2) the independence or absolute difference between life and death as discrete and complete phenomena in and of themselves without reference to passage from one state to the other. On the one hand, Dōgen stresses that the here-and-now manifestation of life and death together constitutes nirvāna. Yet he also maintains that birth alone and death alone are the full disclosure of being-time. Furthermore, Dōgen adds that from a third and perhaps deeper perspective, life itself is no-life and death itself is no-death; life and death each are thoroughly self-negating and nonsubstantial.

Despite the profundity and uniqueness of Dōgen's reflections on death, his thoughts are generally expressed cryptically and ambiguously, and frequently in a theoretically fragmentary form, although they seem to convey the culmination of Zen spiritual emancipation. Therefore, it is helpful to clarify and amplify, highlight and illustrate Dōgen's views by reference to three conceptions of death in psychoanalysis and existential phenomenology: Freud's notion of the ongoing battle of "life against death," of the instinctual tendency toward unity, preservation, and proliferation in opposition to the instinct for destruction and dissolution; Heidegger's phenomenological disclosure of "Being-towards-death" as Dasein's ownmost and uttermost potential grounded in the primordial and inalterable finitude of its Being; and Sartre's view of the distinction between life and death as two inseparable and fundamentally unrelated phenomena.

The aim of using these three modern Western standpoints to examine and evaluate Dōgen's thought is not strictly comparison; rather,
this study is prior to and sets the stage for comparative analysis.
The central focus here is the uncovering of the subtlety of Dōgen's
understanding. Any contemporary explication of Dōgen, however, presupposes an interpretive perspective and framework that relies on
Western scholarship and theory. Acknowledging that, I will critically expose three hermeneutic stances to clarify the multiple and paradoxical dimensions of Dōgen's thought, thereby laying the groundwork
for possibly returning, in an admittedly circular fashion, to a more
direct and straightforward comparison between Dōgen and any of these
modern thinkers. Therefore, I will first reconstruct how Freud,
Heidegger, and Sartre have interpreted death as well as the ideological connections between them, then examine Dōgen's understanding in
light of their respective views as expressed in passages of his
"Genjōkōan"[h] fascicle, and finally point out the hermeneutic significance of this study for comparative philosophical psychology.

II

Freud's discovery of the significance of death for the formulation of his psychoanalytic theory—in addition to the more conspicuous and accessible phenomena of ego, libido, and sexuality—marks the
transition from his scientific-clinical approach to his speculative-
mythological quest for the unifying and universal conception underlying biological and cultural as well as psychological behavior.
Confronting the various meanings of death revealed during psychoanalysis, he is forced to revise, expand, and deepen his previous theoretical outlook by seeking its metaphysical foundations, a problem he
resolves in terms of the duality of fundamental instincts at the
basis of all personal concerns and attitudes and intersubjective relations: the "battle of the giants" of life and death, which can
never be fully appeased or subdued, waged in every id, and projected
violently by the development of civilization onto a world-wide scale.

Freud is led to his postulation of the death instinct—along with
and equal to the life instinct—through the observation of two distinct and seemingly contrary human tendencies, which he maintains
have a unified source: repetition-compulsion and sadism-masochism.
First, in Beyond the Pleasure Principle, Freud is perplexed by the
compulsion of his patients to unconsciously resist psychoanalytic
treatment in that they "repeat the repressed material as contemporary
experience instead of, as the physician would prefer, remembering it
as something belonging to the past."[2] The infantile yet "demonic"
need to recreate even the most unpleasurable experiences and responses with the directness of the immediate present is an obstacle
to treatment because the patient, rather than recognizing what is repeated as a forgotten remnant of the past, clings to it as if it were
current reality, thereby never overcoming or becoming detached from
it. This compulsion is reflected psychologically by the child's insistence on the identical reenactment of a game or retelling of a
story, refusing the introduction or addition of different elements
which would upset the uniformity of the ritual, and biologically by

the migration of certain fish and birds to former localities of the species and the embryo's recapitulation of earlier stages of life.

On the basis of such examples of the repetition-compulsion, Freud concludes that there is a wishful and inevitable urge in life to recede to and restore "an earlier state of things"[3]--by which phrase Freud seems to suggest an inert and inanimate realm ontologically (rather than logically or chronologically) prior to the existence of living substances. He finds that there is a necessity internal to life itself to seek death. Thus, "the aim of all life is death,"[4] and the developing complexities and proliferating varieties of living organisms represent life's ever more complicated detours in pursuing and reaching its ultimate goal of returning to the inorganic state; life struggling paradoxically and most energetically against threats to itself which would aid the rapid attainment of its innermost aim.

In The Ego and the Id, Freud relates the psychological-biological tendency to remove tension and reestablish the primordial state of constancy and nondisturbance to human hostility, hatred and aggression directed (frequently simultaneously) both outwardly at the external world and inwardly at oneself. The drive to actively destroy and dissolve life, reflected in sadism and masochism which aim at the destruction of the sexual partner or one's own ego, he claims, has the same instinctual basis as the tendency to passively recede from life. The result of this speculative synthesis is the full-fledged doctrine of two instincts, which are present together in every particle of living substance, though in unequal proportions, so that any given substance might be the principal representative of one over the other: Eros, consisting not only of uninhibited and sublimated sexual instincts, but all energies for self-preservation and unification; and Thanatos, which strives not only for the termination of life, but for the inanimate state before the emergence of life.

> The emergence of life would thus be the cause of the continuance of life and also at the same time of the striving towards death....The problem of the origin of life would remain a cosmological one and the problem of the goal and purpose of life would be answered dualistically.[5]

Although, as Freud acknowledges, most impulses would seem traceable back to the "clamor" of Eros in its diverse and overlapping manifestations, the "mute" yet omnipresent energies of death suggest that there is an undercurrent and ongoing struggle against life, in which life itself is ironically and tragically the tool as well as the victim.

Human existence is thus a perpetual conflict and compromise between the two cosmic trends that control it, which are fused, blended, and alloyed with each other in every possible instance, and are metapsychologically related to guilt and anxiety manifest in the complex interaction of the tripartite structure of id, ego, and superego. The battle between life and death waged in the id leaves the ego vulnerable to and afraid of the threat to its existence whose aim it is to protect. Internal anxiety about the possibility of its ultimate negation and nonexistence, which it paradoxically seeks as the partial representative of the death instinct, and which is compounded by dangers from the outside world, is both encouraged and repressed by the ego. The ego at once serves the death instinct and attempts to stifle it (repetition-compulsion), eventually becoming its victim. Inner aggressiveness is first displaced and partially defused by being projected against others (sadism), and then harnessed by the superego and cruelly turned back inwardly (masochism). "The fact remains," Freud reports, "as we have stated it: the more a man controls his aggressiveness, the more intense becomes his ideal's inclination to aggressiveness against his ego. It is like a displacement, a turning round upon his own ego."[6]

Aggression is objectified to remove the ego's anxious tension concerning the life-death struggle, and then internalized to pacify his own guilt. The ego's participation in the battle for and against life exposes it to self-imposed punishment. To avoid this tragedy, aggressiveness is again in circular fashion turned outwards—destroying some other thing instead of itself, a vicious process which constitutes the history and evolution of civilization. The intolerable yet ever-regenerating sense of guilt reflected in the tension between the superego and ego is the discontent of culture, carried out in and between societies through continuing conflict and violent interaction. Just as death attempts to destroy life by using life, life attempts to subdue death by causing its own death rather than another one's, and thereby achieves its true aim, which in fact is death. Life must attempt to repress death, yet this very act of repression does not stifle, but rather aggravates the destructive drive.

Despite the profound interrelatedness between life and death on every level and stage of existence, which suggests that neither instinct can be separated from nor analyzed without its dependence on the other, Freud insists on a dualistic interpretation of the instincts. The question arises, however, that if the aim of life is the recreation of the equilibrium before the actual dichtomy of life and death, then are not death and life ultimately united in terms of a dynamic dialectical interplay which allows for apparent and provisional differences between them? Also, can there be a way of life that does not repress death but accepts and affirms its inevitability without invariably wreaking chaos and random destructiveness? Norman O. Brown has maintained that Freud really intended such a conclusion beyond dualism, although he was never able to fully develop or articulate it because of a stubborn pessimism that inhibited his methodology:

> Freud is thus moving toward a structural analysis of organic life as being constituted by a dialectic between unification or interdependence and separation or independence. The principle of unification or interdependence sustains the immortal life of the species and the mortal life of the individual; the principle of separation or independence gives the individual his individuality and ensures his death.[7]

The formulation of a view not simply of life against death but of the full interdependence between them as the basis of their apparent discord, a notion which collapses the provisional duality into fundamental ontological belonging-together is the task of Heidegger's analysis of Dasein's Being-towards-the-end.

III

Heidegger's implicit phenomenologico-ontological critique of the Freudian psychoanalytic approach to the meaning of death functions in two interrelated aspects:[8] methodological, in terms of Heidegger's hermeneutic distinction between the existenziell (everyday factual decisions) and existenzial (underlying factical structure) levels of inquiry; and metaphysical, by his disclosure of the unified yet multidimensional totality of Dasein whose encounters with the boundary-situations (Grenzsituationen) of death, anxiety, and guilt reflect its finite and nonsubstantial basis as an integral and dynamic temporal presence, rather than an objective entity present-at-hand (vorhanden).

Freud seems to admit his methodological shortcomings when he writes in Beyond the Pleasure Principle , "what follows is speculation, often far-fetched speculation, which the reader will consider or dismiss according to his individual predilections."[9] Heidegger challenges the Freudian and other scientific (biology, medicine), social-scientific (psychology, biography) and quasiscientific (theology, theodicy) stances which either gather information and data about death as the objectifiable demise of a living substance or take off on speculative flights about the cosmological origins and importance of death. These approaches never recognize or question the central methodological presupposition that they are dealing with constantly abiding entities which happen at one time to reach an endpoint.

Heidegger's means of overcoming such a pitfall in Being and Time is through (1) a phenomenological separation of the particular existenziell ways Dasein does or has reacted to death as an actual event in its life, and the impartial and invariable existenzial basis and constitutive meaning of its finite being; and by (2) simultaneously acknowledging the hermeneutic circularity or interpenetration between these investigative levels in that Dasein always factically possesses a view and grasp of its Being beyond its factual circumstances, and can proceed back and forth between the concrete decisions it makes and the genuinely founded self-understanding it seeks and is already involved in disclosing. Heidegger's approach, in contrast to the Freudian, is neither a strictly rigorous scientific procedure nor an unjustifiable speculative flight out of touch with its concrete sources because it is based on the transcendent possibilities of Dasein's hermeneutic circle, and it avoids the dichotomies of dualism/monism, realism/idealism which reflect a fixation with substance ontology.

The metaphysical consequence of Heidegger's exposing the methodological limitations of social science is to ontologically reveal Dasein not as a substance which undergoes death as its termination, but as the perpetual process of dying-as-nothingness (Dasein's thoroughly nonsubstantial ground without substratum or self-constancy). Heidegger interprets death not merely in opposition to life but fully integrated with all dimensions of the finite totality of Dasein. Perhaps, as Brown suggests, this was the direction in which Freud was headed when he says that the aim of life is death. For Freud, however, the repression of death is problematic and inevitable, tending to destroy life as much as the unrestricted death instinct. According to Heidegger, it is the Freudian viewpoint which is problematic rather than death itself because it reflects an effort to resist death due to an attachment to existence seen as constant actuality. Heidegger maintains that anxiety and guilt are not based on a death instinct; rather all three contingencies arise from primordial nothingness or nullity--the nonsubstantive, unified, and dynamic structural basis of Dasein.

Death, along with the interrelated phenomena of guilt and anxiety reveals the undercurrent powerlessness and precariousness of Dasein which occupies an open yet bounded realm defined and delineated by inherent limitations and intrinsic constraints. Dasein has not been granted asbolute presence but exists on an always tenuous borderline; the ultimate conditions under which it can act are not at its disposal and are continuously being taken away from it. Its potential for self-illumination and self-understanding is perpetually clouded by the lurking and perplexing unknowable and unforeseeable, that which is concealed and not brought forth by any amount of decisive volition.

Hurled into the world of definite circumstances and environment, Dasein projects itself upon possibilities largely determined by the conditions of its facticity, including its imminent and inevitable end as the final and unmistakable factor. The totality of Dasein is always permeated by the possibility of its ultimate and unavoidable impossibility. Even inauthentic Dasein concedes a sense of certainty about the fact that it is forever passing away, although it considers death an actual state when man will no-longer-be-there, something which will invariably happen in the future but has not yet taken place, to be fearfully awaited rather than resolutely anticipated. Certainty of the end is objectified on empirical grounds alone: death has been observed, and there is ample and undeniable evidence of its occurrence.

The transformation to an authentic conception takes place when death is no longer misrepresented as a one-time event which happens to Dasein as a culmination or even conclusion. Rather, dying is the way to be which Dasein authentically takes over as soon and so long as it dwells anticipatively toward (not expectantly at) its end.

> In death, Dasein has not been fulfilled nor has it simply disappeared: it has not become finished nor is it wholly at one's disposal as something ready-to-hand. On the contrary, just as Dasein is already its "not-yet," and is its "not-yet" constantly as long as it is, it is already its end too. The "ending" which we have in view when we speak of death does not signify Dasein's Being-at-an-end, but a Being-towards-the-end of this entity.[10]

Thus, death is the ownmost and nonrelational possibility which is in each case individually interiorized as mine (je meines) never to be taken over and experienced by anyone else. Death is also the uttermost possibility of existence because it is the inescapable, ultimate, and unsurpassable impossibility of Dasein, and therefore the possibility which is purest and furthest removed from actuality.

Anxiety continually pursues and threatens everyday Dasein, for the most part submissive to the interpretation of self and world as two interacting yet basically separable substantive entities of subject and object. The uncanny feeling of not-being-at-home forces Dasein to confront the "nothing and nowhere" at its very basis—to realize that it is not present-at-hand—which is so disturbing to the obstinate self-assurance and seemingly obvious conception of con-constancy. Anxiety, so close and potentially oppressive that it stifles the breath and creates an overwhelming claustrophobia, does not come from a definite direction; nor does it result from an absence, denial, or elimination of entities. Rather, it suddenly reveals the pervasive finite dependence of nonsubstantive Dasein on a nonobjectifiable world no longer represented as a random gathering of vorhanden entities. Authentic guilt, more fundamental than any notion of indebtedness, moral or legal failure and omission or unfulfilled responsibility, discloses nothingness in that the choice of any specific possibility means that countless others must be overlooked, discounted or left unknown, unacknowledged, and unexplored.

The true meaning of nullity, Heidegger concludes from his analysis of Dasein's contingency, is neither mere privation in the sense of a lack, flaw, or imperfection or a state which Dasein had at one time but since lost or surrendered or has not yet had but could still achieve. It is neither a condition that happens once or occasionally and from which there is reprieve nor an obscure quality that attaches itself to Dasein and might eventually be eliminated. Heidegger calls into question the entire Western metaphysical (or onto-theological) tradition and its derivative standpoints (including the Freudian) which have misconceived the genuine significance of negation revealed by death because of a fixation with constant actuality which confuses the multiple and profound dimensions of nothingness with privation. "Has anyone," he asks rhetorically, "ever made a problem of the ontological source of notness, or, prior to that, ever sought the mere conditions on the basis of which the problem of the 'not' and its notness and the possibility of that notness can be raised?"[11] Heidegger maintains that the clearest resolution of this disturbing philosophical oversight is to interpret nothingness factically as the perpetually encountered borders, the eerie and indefinite yet forbidding and overbearing horizons of Dasein's intrinsic confinements that strip bare any attachment to substance and/or eternalism. From the Heideggerian standpoint, the primordial significance of nothingness is the unthought and unspoken meaning embedded in Freud's phrase, "an earlier state of things."

In examining Heidegger's view of Being-towards-death-as-nothingness, however, a question arises concerning his initial point that death individualizes Dasein if it is authentically anticipated: under what circumstances can the arrival of death ever be foreknown since it is in every case sudden and unexpected; and why is death above all "mine" when it is nothing other than my ultimate loss? Such a challenge to Heidegger's conception is taken up in Sartre's uncompromising distinction between life and death.

IV

Sartre concurs with Heidegger's focus on disclosing the pervasiveness of nothingness and the possibilities for freedom inherent to

existence. He also agrees that phenomenology must seek to uncover
man as an ontological totality rather than a mere collection of random parts. Yet, in contrast to Heidegger's emphasis on unveiling the
Being of man rather than prescribing a way for him to act, Sartre asserts that phenomenological ontology must serve an existentially
therapeutic function. Sartre also distinguishes the existential psychoanalysis he attempts to formulate at the conclusion of Being and
Nothingness, which reveals the original human choice prior to and
manifested in every particular action, from Freudian psychoanalysis
which he maintains gathers empirical evidence about man's psychic
complexes.

Furthermore, Sartre attempts to refute Heidegger's notion that
death provides the best clue as to the fundamental meaning and structural basis of existence. He argues that death is neither the individual's ownmost possibility to be anticipated nor the boundary or
"final chord" which permeates and underlies the entire melody of
life. Rather, death is an absurdity which is the absolute cessation
and dispossession of life that ultimately undermines and negates--
without contributing anything to--its meaning.

> Thus we must conclude in opposition to Heidegger that death,
> far from being my peculiar possibility, is a contingent fact
> which as such on principle escapes me and originally belongs
> to my facticity. I can neither discover my death nor wait
> for it nor adopt an attitude toward it, for it is that which
> is revealed as undiscoverable, that which disarms all
> waiting....[12]

Sartre argues that death cannot be anticipated at every moment
precisely because it can occur at any unknown moment without fore-
warning. Awaiting death does not lessen the suddenness or surprise
of its advency, or alleviate the finality of its effect. To engage
in a wait for death is self-destructive because it negates justifiable and worthwhile waiting and takes on, in retrospect, an absurd
character in its hopelessness and futility. One can only expect a
specific death and not the entire dying process. Nor can death, when
it does arrive, be interiorized by the individual as a particular
possibility and unique responsibility for freedom. To say that my
death is irreplaceable and unique is a truism; so are all experiences, responses, attitudes, decisions, and emotions I have without
exception, from the mundane to the tragic. "Thus death is not my
possibility of no longer realizing a presence in the world but rather
an always possible nihilation of my possibles which is outside my
possibilities."[13] Death does not authenticate man; only if one is
already free does he approach death authentically.

Therefore, death does not bestow meaning on life for its only
function is to remove all meaning from existence, to which nothing
more can happen inwardly or outwardly. Sartre does not maintain that
there is no meaning whatsoever associated with death, but that this
is always ascribed after the fact by the Other, who makes your death
supposedly meaningful by whatever ideas he attributes to it in hindsight based solely on the needs of his life. Life alone decides its
own meaning, though it may be founded on an interpretation of
another's death.

In his challenge, however, Sartre seems to misunderstand Heidegger's subtle hermeneutic distinctions between anticipation and expectation, facticity and factuality. Heidegger would indeed agree with Sartre that idle awaiting of death is inauthentic and fruitless, and that is by no means the position he espouses. It is the openness to futural factical possibilities grounded in finitude, of which death is the most fundamental and peculiar factual example, which Heidegger stresses. Furthermore, Sartre's own standpoint seems problematic in that he asserts that death does not reveal finitude, which is already apparent "because [the for-itself or human reality] makes itself finite by choosing itself as human,"[14] yet also asserts that freedom is total and infinite. But if freedom is complete, why is there a sense of lack and a desire (recalling Heidegger's notion of primordial Being-guilty-of-finitidue) to choose and achieve it? Does not Sartre need to clarify the relation between death, nothingness, and finitude?

Sartre's innovation is that he rediscovers the Freudian dichotomy of life and death and restates it without the apparent inconsistency whereby Freud points to the dialectical interplay between both phenomena—the position more fully developed by Heidegger free of Freudian ambivalence. Are these approaches to death themselves completely separable, or is there an underlying ideological unity which resolves their discrepancies? All three standpoints will be useful in interpreting Dōgen's multidimensional and paradoxical conception of death.

V

Dōgen stresses that the permeation of death throughout the aspects and phases of life must not be overlooked, denied, or inauthentically transcended. He challenges previous Buddhist philosophical or metapsychological conceptions that reflect either substantialism in analyzing the structure of phenomena (the Abhidharma notion of actual entities dichotomized in terms of conditioned and unconditioned realms) or eternalism in depicting enlightenment (Mahāyāna, particularly Japanese Tendai, doctrine of absolute Buddha-nature beyond yet manifested in time). Such notions, Dōgen maintains, betray an attachment to self-constancy in failing to penetrate, clarify, and find freedom in terms of rather than by fleeing perpetual encounter with death each and every moment, which discloses the impermanent and nonsubstantive basis of human and natural existence. Death is the urgent, immediate, and unavoidable signpost of nonself which disavows any attempt to divorce impermanence from existence and betrays claims of eternity that bypass this fundamental interrelatedness.

Dōgen's dissatisfaction with traditional views that discount the full ontological significance of existentially realized transiency is poetically expressed in the opening paragraph of "Genjōkōan" (which in most editions, apparently according to Dōgen's own editing, is the introductory fascicle of his philosophical opus Shōbōgezō[1]). Dōgen notes that although the Buddhist Way is originally unbound by such bifurcations as life/death (ontological), delusion/enlightenment (existential), sentient beings/Buddhas (soteriological), abundance/shortage (axiological), the continual unfolding of birth and demise, generation and extinction is pervasive and irreversible. "Even though this [ultimate nondifferentiation] has been spoken," he writes, "blossoms scatter in sadness, and weeds spring up in dismay."[15] The subjectively experienced reality of impermanence generates a twofold sense of dejection and despair or of longing and aspiration in the pursuit of liberation, attitudes which themselves must be either uprooted or cultivated even while they cannot alter the course or resist the incessancy of change. Any attempt to stifle contingency is ontologically untenable, existentially deficient, and soteriologically unsatisfactory. Dōgen does not propose a final "solution" to death, but demands genuine realization which penetrates to the true meaning of death-as-impermanence prior to a fixation with substantiality. It is the tendency to deny impermanence in the thought that there are no blooming flowers or falling leaves in the world of the "true nature of dharma" (hōsshō)[j] that must be abated, and not the temporal vicissitudes themselves.

In emphasizing the open and unrestricted encounter with death as a pointer to primordial nothingness, Dōgen appears to be in accord with Heidegger's analysis of Being-towards-the-end. For both thinkers, nullity revealed by dying, vicissitude, sorrow, and loss leads away from the habitually ingrained and traditionally accepted preoccupation with constant actuality and toward the unity, dynamism, and nonsubstantiality of existence. The contingency of death is neither a mere human condition in contrast to an Eternal power, nor a partial and temporary drawback of man or an unfortunate yet correctible flaw, nor a psychological or factual emotional problem, but the universal and ultimate nature and structure of reality.

Dōgen would probably agree with the Heideggerian critique of Freud which argues that while resistance to death is problematic, the recognition and acceptance of dying is not. It is not a death instinct which is destructive, but the refusal to confront one's death; death itself is not a cause for nihilism, despair, or fatalism, but a unique affirmation beyond relative attitudes of optimism and pessimism, satisfaction and discontent. Yet, Dōgen does not fail to express the Freudian point that life is generally a struggle to eliminate certain (unenlightened and self-destructive) tendencies and manifestations which would devour the unifying and harmonizing qualities of life if left unchallenged. The complexity and ambiguity of human reactions to death-as-destruction, captured by Freud's theory of instincts, is suggested by Dōgen's reference to the continaul arising of weeds—symbolizing destructiveness which itself must be dissolved—despite the apparent attainment of enlightenment. Like Heidegger, however, Dōgen seeks to uncover the primordial basis of this one dimension of death, without resorting to the view that it is an impulse embedded in living substances.

Dōgen diverges from Heidegger in his naturalistic orientation, represented by the falling flowers, which stresses that subjective response is awakened equally by the transiency of all phenomena, free of distinction between personal and natural, human and nonhuman, or between the temporal and spatial dimensions of existence. He also highlights a more existentially positive or affirmative view of the possibilities for renewal and regeneration which death, itself transient and shifting, represents when he quotes Zen master Ju-ching's words, "Reuin attained enlightenment when he saw the peach blossoms in bloom, but I attained it when I saw them falling."[16] Dōgen notes,

for example, that a withered plum tree (baige)[k] withstands and en-
dures harsh and variable conditions, and invariably returns anew, reflecting the total detachment and selfless imperturbability of the
vigorous and nonsubstantial activity manifest in both living and dying. Dōgen also seems to agree with Sartre and Freud, in contrast to
Heidegger, that an analysis of death must have practical (therapeutic
or soteriological) intentions and implications. Although Heidegger's
distinction between the existenziell and existenzial levels may be
ontologically fruitful and significant, Dōgen's emphasis is on radical transformation of the concrete everyday (existenziell) world
through full (existenzial) awareness of the meaning and structure of
death—a task Heidegger considers outside his disciplinary framework.
"To study the Buddha Way," Dōgen says, "is to study the self. To
study the self is to forget the self."[17] Learning the Way of nonsubstantiality necessarily involves self-forgetfulness (renouncing a
notion of self as a constant entity), which is nothing other than
cultivating the transient, unenduring self.

A deeper divergence, however, is that Dōgen maintains, almost in
direct opposition to Heidegger and affinity with Sartre, that a
clearcut distinction between life and death must be recognized and
portrayed in addition to their dialectical unity. Dōgen points out
that to say life becomes or turns into death, just as firewood is reduced to ash and winter turns to spring, implies a subtle clinging to
the notion of a substratum underlying change. "It is a mistake to
think you pass from life to death."[18] Certainly a transformation
from life to death takes place, but it is the impermanent process itself—and not any enduring or substantive entity which supposedly
undergoes change—which Dōgen seeks to expose. Furthermore, he cau-
tions that if the identity between life and death is simply or one-
sidedly asserted, however flexibly or dialectically, then it would be
necessary to claim that death again becomes life, that man is reborn
after his demise, or that ash returns to firewood and spring to
winter in reverse sequence, a position which is factually inaccurate
and factically misleading and inappropriate. Yet, in exploring the
difference of life and death, Dōgen does not merely accept the
Sartrean view that death is completely irrelevant for understanding
and interpreting life.

VI

In Dōgen's doctrine of the "abiding dharma-position" (jū-hōi),[1]
paradoxically encompassing "before and after...[and] cut off from before and after," the difference and nondifference of life and death
are at once integrated and set off against one another in terms of a
step-by-step deepening of perspectives:

Firewood is reduced to ash, and cannot become firewood
again. So, one should not hold the view that ash is succeeding
and firewood is preceding. One must know that firewood abides in
the dharma-position (hōi) of firewood [in which] there is succeeding and preceding. Although there is before and after, it
is cut off from before and after. Ash is in the dharma-

position of ash [in which] there is succeeding and preceding.
Like the firewood which does not become firewood again after
it has been reduced to ash, so man is not born anew after his
death. Because it is established by Buddhist Dharma not to
say that life becomes death, [the Dharma] speaks of nonarising.
Because the Buddhist tradition has established the doctrine
that death does not become life, [the Dharma] speaks of non-
cessation. Life is a position of time and death is a position
of time. For example in regard to winter and spring, it is
not said that winter becomes spring or that spring becomes
summer.[19]

In this and related passages, Dōgen maintains first of all that
life and death are not separable but occur simultaneously and instantaneously within each moment. At the transformative occasion between
firewood and ash or between winter and spring, life and death, before
and after, past and future, actuality and potentiality emerge as the
holistic present moment, constituting in unison the total dynamic activity (zenki)[m] of the dharma-position. There is no existence without its inevitable and immediate extinction. Consequently, life
should not be clung to and affirmed nor death feared and negated.
Also, life and death together should not be rejected and escaped from
nor should nirvāna, conceived as the resolution to the problem of
life and death, be sought outside of impermanence itself. In the
"Shōji" fascicle Dōgen asserts, "This present life and death itself
is the life of Buddha."[20] If life and death (shōji) is either des-
pised or abided in with attachment, the Buddha Way is lost and one is
left only with the appearance of Buddha. At this stage, Dōgen concurs with Heidegger's insistence that death-as-nothingness rooted
within the conditions of life is not a mere hindrance or gap to be
surpassed to obtain a supratemporal, suprahistorical truth. "Realizing that both life and death are a combination of various conditions
being manifested before your eyes, you utilize a way of complete and
unrestricted freedom."[21]
The first dimension of jū-hōi refers to the aspect encompassing
the totality of simultaneous and interpenetrating manifestations of
life and death. The second dimension--its apparent opposite--is the
directness and spontaneity "cut off from before and after," without
duration or substratum. Dōgen emphasizes that there is no substantive "it" which is first firewood and then ash. There is neither a
reversal of sequence from ash back again to firewood nor a forward
sequential movement of an underlying objective entity. Because no
orderly motion from t1 to t2 or vice versa of an entity can be asserted, the immediate manifestation of death must be different from
the immediate manifestation of life--they are not consecutive changes
of an essentially constant being.
Does this standpoint contradict the first dimensions of the
dharma-position? Dōgen seems to express a Sartrean view of the independence of life and death in order to avoid a possible pitfall that
the Heideggerian view of interdependence posits an actuality which
includes its potentiality, which would be a reversal of the substan-
tialist view but not the refutation and surpassing of it. A conception of life-death as sequentially-related occurrences of a time span
stretching from beginning toward the end implies that the entity

which contains them consists of a stable or enduring substratum, and it is not necessarily liberated from the average view of contingency which, Dōgen notes, holds that life is like a tree that begins with a seed, grows, and finally perishes, and that death is the tree itself no longer alive, as if life were the first activity and death the second. Such a notion tends to fabricate a bifurcation between life and death as well as between the object and the life-death process it undergoes.

To eliminate that misleading duality, Dōgen turns to a Sartrean distinction between life and death as a corrective to the Heideggerian stance, not simply to contradict it but to deepen and enhance that dimension. Life and death, he argues, each possess before and after and are harmoniously interdependent in that they are determined by the influences they simultaneously receive and project. Yet they are also unbound by past and future because they manifest absolute and nonsubstantive presence without reference to any other tense or relative phase of time, or even to each other. "Life is neither coming [along] or going away, neither already here nor becoming. Rather, life is the manifestation of total dynamic activity, and death is the manifestation of total dynamic activity."[22] Examining impermanence from the perspective of impermanence itself--and not as a spectator overlooking change--directly discloses the vigorous dynamism of nonself, of which death is a unique and complete manifestation in itself, just as is life.

Dōgen's concurrence with Sartre, however, would be limited in that Dōgen does not only reject, but attempts to include and surpass the Heideggerian view; he does not negate death as meaningless for life, but emphasizes that from the standpoint of each element, life and death are unimpeding, nonsequential stages which manifest the totality and nonsubstantiality of temporal events. "Life is not obstructed by death, and death is not obstructed by life."[23] In contrast to Sartre, and because he has already shown that death is integral with life, Dōgen discloses death as separable from life, but by no means wholly outside the living process. In contrast to Freud, death is not the return to a constant state in opposition to life, but complete dynamism in itself here-and-now.

Furthermore, Dōgen seems to avoid a contradiction between the views of interdependence (Heideggerian) and independence (Sartrean) by pointing to a third and more fundamental dimension of the dharma-position--that the activity of jū-hōi is neither life nor death. This dimension does not indicate that neither phenomenon occurs nor that reality is essentially static. Rather, the time of no-life and of no-death is the spontaneously durationless and perpetually renewed impermanent/nonsubstantial renewal of existence unbound by categorization in terms of eternity and transiency, now and then, presence and absence, being and nothingness, life and death. Freedom from life-death ("no-life, no-death") is to flexibly maneuver through the shifting perspectives of "life is death (which is nirvāna)" and "life itself, death itself" without attachment to any one standpoint as referring to constancy or fixated actuality. The third dimension points beyond any particular standpoint, thus allowing for multiple and interacting perspectives so long as they are seen as partial and springing from a nonsubstantive basis.

To summarize Dōgen's view of death, when man is struggling

against the "weeds" of unenlightenment and to preserve the scattering blossoms of illumination—even after the so-called attainment of enlightenment or through continuing development beyond Buddha—he is using death to destroy death. However, the Freudian awareness and attempted overcoming of death-as-destructiveness is surpassed by the Heideggerian realization that both enlightenment and unenlightenment are evanescent and and without substratum, and therefore essentially null. Yet, this stage of realization is itself one-sided and to be surpassed by the Sartrean insight into the durationless moment where life (encompassing death) does not pass to death nor death (encompassing life) to life; at that impermanent occasion, life is total and complete and death is total and complete. The relativity of life and death on this level ultimately reveals the truly groundless and meaningless experience from which all conceptions of death in their partiality are derived.

VII

Heidegger's attempted overcoming of Freudian speculation on the death instinct, and Sartre's challenge to Heidegger's notion of Being-towards-death seem to highlight the multiple layers and central paradox of Dōgen's conception of the meaning of death. If some modern methodology or terminology is to be used in analyzing Dōgen, then it is imperative to clarify precomparatively which ones are appropriate and for what reasons as well as the shortcoming each has. The fact that no single Western standpoint is adequate in examining Dōgen suggests the need for exploring a variety of interpretive models to uncover his view without obfuscating its complexity, reducing it to or identifying it with any particular framework, or unacknowledgingly superimposing that stance on his. Dōgen's understanding of death is above all not a collection of viewpoints, but these models can be used to show the essential and integral meaning underlying and giving coherence to shifting and paradoxical perspectives.

That the combination of these three Western standpoints also falls short of conveying the full depth of Dōgen's thought—although together they do seem to reflect most of his central ideas—indicates some of the directions and difficulties for comparative philosophical psychology. Using Freud, Heidegger, and Sartre as hermeneutic to discuss Dōgen does not necessarily impair or limit dealing with these thinkers in another context as the object of straightforward comparison, if the distinction between the two methods and aims is recognized and maintained; the two contextual planes may be complementary or even necessary corollaries, but they are distinct and separable approaches.

After uncovering the foundations of Dōgen's thought in terms of three Western thinkers, it is then possible to engage in direct comparison in a way that is mutually challenging and dialogical, and not defensive or apologetic. That is, to proceed from neutral through critical reconstruction and examination to constructive evaluation. One question in that context is, how does Dōgen highlight and deepen our understanding of three modern reflections on death and the conflicts between the respective disciplines of psychoanalysis, phenomenological ontology, and existential psychoanalysis? Further, does the multidimensionality of Dōgen's view suggest a fundamentally more comprehensive and universalizable outlook than any of the Western thinkers, or an inconsistency and ambiguity to be rethought and revised? Does Dōgen have a flexibility and variety of perspectives arising from a deeper foundation which exposes a partiality or limitation in either Freud, Heidegger, or Sartre?

Comparative dialogue should not be static, but must force a continuing clarification of positions, not necessarily on different grounds, for the original ones may be valid, but through expanding and refining theoretical means of argument, illustration, and justification to resolve the ideological issues that emerge in the process itself.

NOTES

1. A paraphrase of Dōgen's frequently repeated expression of his primary motivation and inspiration in the quest for Buddhist Dharma, particularly in his autobiographical-exhortative works, such as Zuimonki,[n] "Hōkyō-ki,"[o] "Shushō-gi."[p] In his monumental philosophical opus Shōbōgenzō, particularly "Genjōkōan," "Uji," and "Busshō"[q] fascicles, Dōgen expounds on the metaphysical basis of death in terms of the unity of impermanence and nonsubstantiality. See my doctoral dissertation, "Existential and Ontological Dimensions of Time in Heidegger and Dōgen" (Temple University, 1980) for an examination of Dōgen's conception of death and dying in relation to being-time and Buddha-nature and in comparative light with Heidegger's Daseinanalytik of ecstatic temporality and historicality.

2. Sigmund Freud, Beyond the Pleasure Principle, trans. and ed. by James Strachey (New York: W.W. Norton and Company, Inc., 1961), p. 12.

3. Ibid., p. 30.

4. Ibid., p. 32.

5. Freud, The Ego and the Id, trans by Joan Riviere, revised by James Strachey (New York: W.W. Norton and Company, Inc., 1960), pp. 30-31.

6. Ibid., p. 44.

7. Norman O. Brown, Life Against Death, The Psychoanalytical Meaning of History (Middletown, Conn.: Wesleyan University Press, 1969), p. 105.

8. Martin Heidegger, Being and Time, trans. by John Macquarrie and Edward Robinson (New York: Harper and Row, Publishers, 1962). Heidegger does not explicitly refer to and attempt a refutation of Freud. It is not clear whether Heidegger, at the time of the publication of Being and Time in 1927, was aware of Freud's speculative writings on death (referred to above) from the early 1920s. However, his discussion in paragraph 49 (Part II, chapter I), "How the Existential (Existenzial) Analysis of Death is Distinguished from Other Possible Interpretations of This Phenomenon" seems applicable to the Freudian as well as other modern standpoints.

9. Freud, Beyond the Pleasure Principle, p. 18.

10. Heidegger, Being and Time, p. 289.

11. Ibid., p. 332.

164

12. Jean-Paul Sartre, Being and Nothingness, An Essay in Phenomenological Ontology, trans. by Hazel E. Barnes (New York: Philosophical Library, 1956), p. 545. It should be noted that Sartre uses the
terms "fact" and "facticity" in different senses then Heidegger.
13. Ibid., p. 537.
14. Ibid., p. 546.
15. Dōgen Zenji, Shōbōgenzō (Treasury of True Dharma-Eye) in
Nihon Shisō Taikei,ʳ eds. Terada To'oru and Mizuno Yaoko, vols. 11
and 12 (Tokyo: Iwanami shoten, 1970 and 1972), 1st vol., p. 35
("Genjōkōan"). My translation.
16. Ibid., p. 36 ("Genjōkōan").
17. Ibid., p. 218 ("Udonge").ˢ
18. Dōgen, Shōbōgenzō in Dōgen zenji zenshūᵗ (Complete Works of
Dōgen Zenji), ed. Ōkubo Dōshū (Tokyo: Chikuma shobō, 1970), p. 778
("Shōji"). The "Shōji" fascicle is not included in Terada/Mizuno
88-chapter edition, although it is found in the 92- and 95-chapter
editions of Shōbōgenzō.
19. Dōgen (Terada/Mizuno edition), p. 36 ("Genjōkōan").
20. Dōgen (Ōkubo edition), p. 778 ("Shōji").
21. Dōgen (Terada/Mizuno edition), pp. 78-79 ("Shinjingakudō").ᵘ
22. Ibid., p. 275 ("Zenki").
23. Ibid., p. 276 ("Zenki").

Kanji

a. 道元

b. 大事生死

c. 無常

d. 無我

e. 有

f. 無

g. 有時

h. 現成公按

i. 正法眼蔵

j. 法性

k. 梅華

l. 住法位

m. 全機

n. 隨聞記

o. 寶慶記

p. 修証記

q. 仏性

r. 日本思想大系

s. 優曇華

t. 道元禪師全集

u. 身心学道

THE HUMAN SITUATION AND ZEN BUDDHISM[1]

Richard J. DeMartino

I. The Human Situation

A. The Predicament or "Question" Inherent in the Human Situation.

Human existence in its critical, non-bio-physiologically distinctive feature, is, initially, self-conscious—or, in the appellation
here to be preferred, ego-conscious—existence. Adam and Eve in
Paradise before eating of the fruit of the tree of knowledge (i.e.,
of dualistic, reflective self—or ego—consciousness) are neither, in
this non-bio-physiologically distinctive sense, "human" beings nor in
"human" existence. For man, in this meaning, is not directly born
into human existence. From this perspective, the infant is not yet
human; the idiot is never quite human; the wolf-child is only on the
edge of being human; and the unreachable psychotic (while unreachable—or unreached) is perhaps no longer human.
    Not that the infant, the idiot, the wolf-child, or the psychotic
is ever sheer animal. The not-yet (or pre-) ego-consciousness of the
infant, the never-to-be (or therefore, aborted) ego-consciousness of
the idiot, the incomplete (but capable of being completed) ego-
consciousness of the wolf-child, and the deranged (or deteriorated)
ego-consciousnes of the psychotic all receive their particular determination from what would be the norm of their developed and unim-
paired being. This norm is that ego-consciousness which seems, under
usual circumstances, to appear before the age of five in a child
born of a bio-physiologically-human lineage and reared in a reflec-
tively-human culture or society. Foregoing at this time any account
of its onset and development, let us proceed immediately to an analysis of its nature and to an examination of its implications for the
human situation.
    Ego-consciousness means an ego reflectively conscious (or reflec-
tively aware) of itself. Put another way, ego-consciousness designates—or denominates—that being with the once actualized and
thereafter re-actualizable capacity to be aware of its being aware,
or, consequently, with the once actualized and thereafter re-
actualizable capacity to be reflectively aware of its be-ing. This
reflective awareness (or reflective consciousness) of itself and of
its be-ing is expressed as the affirmation of itself, "I" (that is,
"ego"), or, "I am" ("ego sum"). For the reflective consciousness of
being conscious—and, hence, of be-ing—coincidentally attests to (or
harbors) the be-ing of reflective consciousness. Aware that I am
aware, I am aware that I am—and that my awareness "is."
    The ego's reflective (or "self-") affirmation of itself, its be-

ing, and its consciousness, moreover, constituently entails the ego's individuation of itself--i.e., the ego reflectively discriminated from not-itself, whether some visible or tangible "other," or simply its own invisible, intangible negation, not-I, or, non-ego. "I" or "I am" means not alone that "I am alive" but that "I am I," or obversely, that "I am not not-I"; which, again, may mean that "I am not you--or any 'other,'" or, that "I am not dead." This discriminate, reflective affirmation-individuation of itself also involves, however, a bifurcation of itself.

In the ego's reflective affirmation of itself, it is both an active subject-affirmer and a passive object-affirmed. As active subject or affirmer it performs the act of affirming itself. As passive object or affirmed it is an existential fact presented to itself. The reflective awareness and affirmation of itself in which it indeed emerges or appears is at once an act undertaken by the ego and a fact given to the ego. For the ego as active subject-affirmer is not chronologically prior to itself as passive object-affirmed. This means, further, that its individuation does not precede its bifurcation. Immediately when there is ego-consciousness, there is the ego; and immediately when there is the ego, it is already object as well as subject, as much imparted to itself as it is the activator of itself. A living, active subject with freedom and responsibility, the ego is simultaneously a passive, given object, destined, determined, and without responsibility. This is the initial nature and structure of the ego in its dualistic, reflective ego-consciousness. This is the beginning-situation of man in his non-bio-physiologically distinctive human existence, a situation that may be characterized as that of contingent--or conditioned--subjectivity.

Conditioned subjectivity--despite its being conditioned--is, nonetheless, subjectivity. The emergence or advent of ego-consciousness marks the emergence or advent of subjectivity. Existence comes to be peculiarly "human" existence precisely through subjectivity. It is just as subject that the ego is aware of--and thereby "has"--a self: its-self. So, too, it is as a subject encountering--and acknowledging--the subjectivity of others similarly aware of and "having" themselves, that the ego can learn to control, to discipline, and to train itself, and, as a consequence, to develop and to mature itself, thereby to become an increasingly responsible person. The infant, however, is not yet a person, the idiot never quite a person, the wolf-child merely a could-be person, and the unreachable (or unreached) psychotic perhaps no longer a person.

Again, it is as a subject that the ego is aware of, and thereby has, a world--its world; i.e., the spatial-temporal realm in which it seemingly has its place or topos along with other existents. Furthermore, in its reflective awareness as a subject, the ego can, in the freedom of its subjectivity, ever rise above and transcend--at least in some measure--any conditioned or given object aspect of itself or its world. In expression of its inalienable integrity as a subject-person, the ego usually has--with regard to either its world or itself--the residual option of resisting and saying, "No!"

Also as subject, the ego can "go out of" itself emphatically to participate in--or, actually, to "take on"--the subjectivity of another subject in friendship, compassion or love. As subject, moreover, the ego can come to have a grammatically pliable language, nonverbal (or nonlinguistic) symbols, and entertain abstract meaning; can formulate and answer questions; can critically reason, doubt, and understand; can reflectively hope, aspire, envision, and judge—e.g., can be dissatisfied and continually strive for improvement; can pre-plan, fashion, and make multiple use of tools; can have ideals, values, and a conscience; can defer, in order to consider and weigh, decisions; can work voluntarily; and can be creative, expressing itself in (or through) not alone concrete but also theoretical or ideational objects, modes, or activities that may go far beyond the elemental demands of pure utility. Indeed, it is uniquely as subject that it can "have" an object.

In its subjectivity, the ego thus simultaneously "has"—and can rise above—itself and its world; can be "humane" and can love "in spite of"; can critically reason, understand, and appreciate; can ponder and decide with accountability; can have and pursue ideals; can create innovatively (or "for the first time"); and can be productive apart from the pragmatic motivation of brute necessity. This is the greatness of the ego in ego-consciousness. This is the dignity of man in human existence.

Yet, precisely as subject, and this is another component of its greatness, the ego realizes that its subjectivity is a conditioned or contingent subjectivity. Free, as subject, to transcend almost any given object aspect of itself or its world, it has not the freedom—as ego—to transcend its subject-object structure (or matrix) as such. For even as a subject transcender, it remains inextricably linked to the object that is transcended. In its dualistically reflective consciousness, the ego as a subject is unalterably bound to itself and to its world as the objects of which it is conscious. As the reflecting subject, the ego activates itself and "has" its world. As the reflected-upon object, however, it is given to itself in all of its particularity and finitude as part of the world in which it finds itself. Capable of having an object only because it is a subject, it cannot be a subject except that it also is—or has—an object. It is in this sense that reflective self or ego-consciousness is not simply "existential" in that, in its subjectivity, it is the reflective consciousness of be-ing (and especially of its be-ing—and of its being a subject), but is also "ontological" in that it of necessity incorporates as well the objective—or "objectified"—being of that of which it is reflectively conscious (and especially the objectified-being of itself as concurrently both "object-being" and "subject-consciousness"). To reiterate: reflectively aware that it is aware, it is aware that it is—and that its awareness "is." For this reason, dualistically reflective human—or ego—consciousness shall herein be characterized as "onto-existential."

Object-related, object-dependent, and object-conditioned, the ego is, additionally, object-obstructed. For in its subjectivity, the ego as a dualistically reflective subject does not have access to itself as subject; its access to itself is always unavoidably as an object. Expressed slightly differently, by virtue of the very reflective subjectivity in which it is aware of and "has" itself, the ego is separated and cut off from itself. That is, in the reflective awareness of its be-ing and of its being aware, the ego as subject "that is aware" is never the object version of itself "of which it is aware." This means that in its reflective, subject-object consciousness, the ego cannot contact, know, be, or "have" itself in full and genuine in-dividuality. The specific reason for this is that any effort by the reflecting ego-subject in this direction removes it as a perennially regressing subject from its own grasp, leaving in its stead simply some reflected objectification of itself. Forever encountering in front of itself, so to speak, an object-shadow of itself and cognizant that it is the subject-caster-and-seer of—or "behind"—that shadow, each time that the reflecting ego-subject tries to step back in order to see itself as the caster-seer, it still sees, of course, no more than the object-shadow that is being cast before it. Ever elusive or evasive to itself in its subjectivity, the ego thus "has" itself solely as object. Although it knows itself "to be" a subject and will normally resent—and resist—any transgression upon its subjectivity, the dualistic ego can never know itself "as" a subject. Divided and dissociated in its centeredness, it is, consequently, beyond it own "prehension," fractured, obstructed, and alienated from itself. Just in having itself, it does not really have itself; just in knowing itself, it does not really know itself. Hence the compelling appropriateness of the age-old injunction addressed to the ego to "Know Thyself!"

As with the ego's awareness and having of itself, so with its awareness and having of its world—which is, actually, one concomitant of its awareness of itself: the having is a limited or incomplete having; the knowing is a limited or incomplete knowing. In the ego's reflective awareness and having of its world, the world, once more, is object. In its reflection as a subject, the ego may conceive of the world as a supposed "totality" in which it is itself located or contained. But just as the reflected aspect of itself included in that world is an object aspect, so, too, is the world so conceived an object to the ego as subject-conceiver. Accordingly, whether in the functioning reflective ego's perceptual awareness or in its conceptualization, the world is object, from which the ego as subject is left distant, discrete, and estranged.

It is exactly this—the diremptive dichotomy of its subject-object structure and functioning—that constitutes the inherent onto-existential ambiguity, conflict, and, in fact, contradiction of the ego in ego-consciousness. Bifurcated and disjoined in its unity, the ego, while confined by, cannot be sustained or fulfilled in itself. Insulated and excluded in its relatedness, it is at once restricted to and shut off from a world in which and to which it belongs. Thus, in its very knowing and having (which is unable fully either to know or to have) and in its being bound and conditioned by (even as it is segmented and isolated from) itself and its world, the ego is rent by a double cleavage, split with-in as well as with-out. Never pure subject in its subjectivity, never absolutely free in its freedom, the ego is neither the reconciled nor incontrovertible ground of itself or its world, both of which it has—yet does not truly have; both of which it knows—yet does not truly know. This is the peculiarly human predicament of the ego in its dualistically reflective ego-consciousness. This is the burden and the misery of man in his non-bio-physiologically distinctive human existence.

B. <u>Some of the Modes Pursued by the Ego in its Attempt to Deal with its Predicament</u>

Among the ego's primary onto-existential manifestations of its predicament are its parallel anxieties about having to live and having to die. These intertwined anxieties concerning its having to live and its having to die are, however, but two expressions of the ego's single, more fundamental root-anxiety: namely, the anxiety with regard to its overcoming the gnawing inner and outer hiatus that prevents it from authentically being its-self. As in knowing and having itself, the ego does not genuinely know or have its-self, so in being itself, it "is" not genuinely its-self. The anxiety relating to life stems from the necessity to contend with and to resolve this contradiction. The anxiety relating to death arises from the possibility that life may end before a resolution has been obtained. It is uniquely the ego in ego-consciousness that confronts, in order "to be" truly, the need to find and to fulfill itself. This is an indwelling imperative that is not yet present to the infant, that will never become present to the idiot, that may become present to the wolf-child, and that perhaps is no longer entirely present to the unreachable (or unreached) psychotic. With respect to the natural completeness of an animal, however, it is wholly nonexistent.

It would be meaningless—assuming that it were possible and that articulate language were not itself an outgrowth (or at least another concomitant) of reflective ego-consciousness—to ask a young animal, for example, a kitten, what it intends or would like to be when it grows up. The human child, on the other hand, confronts not only externally but internally as well precisely this question. For simple bio-physiological growth or maturation does not as such constitute the growth, maturation, or fulfillment of the human subject or person as human subject or person. Undoubtedly, motherhood, in its various dimensions, comprises more of a measure of trial and tested completion for the human female than does fatherhood, in its various dimensions, for the human male. Accordingly, the reply of the little girl, "I am going to be a mother," would be acceptable. Whereas if the little boy were to answer, "I am going to be a father," this would probably not be considered responsive, and might actually provoke some consternation.

But even when recognizing that its connotation far exceeds the purely bio-physical, human motherhood still does not encompass the fullest realization of the human female as a human person. In fact, no possible role, function, or vocation can ever definitively satisfy the human—male or female—as a human person. The ego, however, constrained by its constituent contradiction to seek its fulfillment, is beguiled by that contradiction into this very deception.

Available to itself—even as it contemplates its own subjectivity—strictly in terms of some object semblance of itself, the ego naturally comes to confuse being fulfilled with "being something." In its endeavor as subject to cope with its task of finding itself, the ego is led to envisage some object-image of itself. Through this image it hopes at once to be able to prove (or to validate) itself to itself and to gain recognition and approval from other egos—or, if not the the allegiance of, then to secure control over or at least independence of other egos. For in its inner and outer alienation, the ego tends to respond to the limitation imposed upon it by the subjectivity of other egos as a challenge, if not an outright threat.

Relying on its particular object-image to establish itself and to deflect or to overpower this challenge (or threat), the ego may eventually come to take that limited, finite impression alone to be the whole of itself—its ground, its source, and its ultimate meaning, by which it is to be sustained, and through which it is to be fulfilled. Much (or indeed all) of its subjectivity is now devoted (or actually subordinated) to the content or contents necessary to actualize the vision—e.g., wealth, power, prestige, status, masculinity, femininity, religiosity, knowledge, moral perfection, artistic creativity, physical beauty, popularity, individuality, or "success." Virtually identifying with these contents, the ego comes to focus more and more upon them and upon the conception of itself that they elicit and nourish. In this growing fixation and attachment it easily falls prey to the arch delusion of ego-centricity. Ever in search of—yet ever elusive to—itself, the ego, object-dependent and object-obstructed, comes to be object-dominated and object-deluded.

Whether the object-image envisioned becomes an actuality, is overtly but pretentiously feigned and affected, or remains a wishful or fanciful ideal, the basic deception involved is the same. The ego in its unqualified fulfillment is never merely any object-feature of itself or its manifest subjectivity—neither its body, mind, talents, position, personality, "charisma," goodness, social or biological function, profession or vocation, class, culture, nation, race, nor species. However truly great the husband, wife, parent, ruler, scientist, humanitarian, thinker, worker, patriot, artist, professional or business man—or woman, however much richer such an ego is, however much more it is "in possession of" itself, it does not have itself consummately as an ego-subject, nor has it, therefore, realized itself wholly as a human person.

Despite its expressing commendable subjectivity in going out of and giving itself in love, creativity, devotion to a moral ideal, or dedication to a laudable task, the ego continues to be bound to and dependent upon the object element entailed in the expression—the specific loved one, artistic activity, ethical ideal, cause, commitment, or work. Inexorably ensnared in its predicament of contingent subjectivity, the ego, not capable of being a subject without an object, is ineluctably circumscribed or curtailed by the object. Hence the ego's ambivalence in _eros_ or _philia_ of the hidden or open hostility toward that which is loved. This hostility together with the pride and special interest of the ego as subject in the love, creativity, or morality, corrupt and defile that love, creativity, or morality, engendering within the ego deeply burrowed qualms concerning its impurity, guilt, or, if religiously oriented, sin.

The ego, functionally and structurally in need of an object to be a subject, can never reach complete fulfillment in or through an object. Any such object-related fulfillment, while bearing its own rewards, will be limited, temporary, or tarnished. In these latter instances, in spite of the enviable richness of its subjectivity, the heralded abundance of the contents of its life, the lasting and applauded merit of its accomplishments and successes, in its heart of hearts the ego is left unfulfilled. Unable to sustain itself within

itself in its greatness or success, and continually vulnerable to
agonizing feelings of its own unworthiness, guilt, or sin as regards
its very achievements, it may come to know melancholy and despondent
moments of loneliness, frustration, or despair, conceivably most
trenchant and poignant precisely in the hour of its crowning
triumph—or shortly thereafter, after the roar of the crowd has faded
and dimmed. Inwardly plagued by restlessness, insecurity, or a con-
tempt and even hatred of itself, it may outwardly exhibit symptoms of
any number of psychological or psychosomatic disturbances.

Yet, it is not uncommon for the ego to manage to contain these
pangs of disquietude and to finish out its life in this general condition. As it does so, however, it faces the ever present danger
that the smoldering deep-seated uneasiness may erupt and surge forth
in an anguish or dread that is uncontainable. This could occur
should the ego no longer be able to rationalize away its sense of un-
deservedness or its sense of guilt, should it become morbidly uncertain of the divine forgiveness of its sin, or should the components
needed to maintain its object-image otherwise come to be lost, destroyed, or unavailable, or should they, while persisting, prove disillusioning, grow empty and sour, or simply cease to be engaging.
Finally, some ordinary occurrence in daily life can precipitate the
stark and sobering realization that not only is every imaginable content transitory and ephemeral, but so, too, is the ego itself. Continuously susceptible in youth as well as in age to illness and
infirmity of body and mind, it must die.

Intellectually, the inevitability of its death is, of course,
known to the ego all along. Its actually experiencing, however, the
prospect of its own non-being as a shattering (onto-)existential
shock thoroughly punctures its illusion as to the feasibility of its
attaining its consummation in terms of any object-image. The traumatic anxiety about having to die is irrefutable testimony to the inability of any object aspect or object content to satisfy the human
ultimately as human. Caught inextricably in the double anxiety of
having to live and having to die, the ego at some time in its life
and at some level of its being undergoes the excruciating torment of
the most piercing indecision of all: to be or not to be.

This singularly probing misgiving—the uncertainty of the ego
whether to endure any longer its struggle for fulfillment—is, perhaps, the profoundest indication of its plight: nothing it can do
can resolve its contradiction. For as long as the ego remains simply
an ego, the contradiction inherent in it also remains.

In full and honest recognition of its situation, the ego may
have the courage and the strength to take its negativities upon itself and to continue to strive "to be" in spite of its limitations as
a contingent subject. Although often an endeavor of heroic character, this in no wise constitutes conclusive consummation. While
accepting, bearing, and suffering can be their own affirmative manifestations of meaningful subjectivity, the fulfillment they adumbrate
is, at best, preliminary and anticipatory. At worst, it is again illusory, involving, in this instance, a subject-illusion.

In enduring and withstanding, the ego sometimes thinks that it
is itself assuming and upholding total responsibility for itself and
its existence. Forgetting that as object it is a passive, given fact
beyond appropriation by its own acts or decisions as subject, it

succumbs to the delusion of hubris. Blinded by this delusion, it dares, even in the throes of the overwhelming catastrophes of its life, to declare, nonetheless, that it is "the master of its fate," that it is "the captain of its soul."

This self-deceptive posture, moreover, is usually maintained through the suppression of almost all emotion, warmth, compassion, or love. For the same ego-will that disciplines and steels itself against its negativities tends to become rigid, brittle and unyielding, fearful of ever relaxing its tautness lest it collapse and crumble in toto. Yet, exactly this unremitting strain keeps it constantly precarious, under the lingering peril of snapping and breaking down. Overwrought, over-responsible and over-repressed, it may precipitously abandon itself to just the opposite extreme.

In contrast to taking upon itself and forbearng the negativity of its intractable predicament, the ego instead undertakes to disavow or to shun that negativity. It seeks "to be" no longer in spite of, but in a would-be disregard of its entrapment as a conditioned subject. Held in the bondage of an object-dependence and object-constriction, the ego contrives to elude rather than bear that bondage either by refusing to admit the importance of, by conjuring to forget, or by venturing to deny altogether the object aspect as such.

Ignoring the nature or components of its acts and decisions, the ego would now immerse itself in a flood of doing, acting, and deciding—if not in search of an avenue of distraction or escape, then expressly for the sake of doing, acting, and deciding. In the latter case, aspiring to a noncontingent subjectivity free from all object constraints, the ego, misled by an implied fallacy of reductionism, falls under a twofold misapprehension. On the one hand presupposing that as active subject its sheer subjectivity will reduce the object aspect, on the other hand it fears that unless it is unintermittently active as subject, it will itself be reduced to object.

Whatever the motivation, however, subjectivity bereft of the significance of its object content ceases to be subjectivity of any import or value. It soon tends to degenerate into aimless activity (or adhering to a strict routine) simply to "keep busy," vacuous "having fun," impulsive "spontaneity," indulgent assertiveness, irresponsible nonconformity, arbitrary willfulness, wanton caprice, or unbridled libertinism and licentiousness. Almost without exception, this sort of spurious—or "pseudo"—subjectivity is unable to provide other than merely diversionary interests and satisfactions or momentary and fleeting "thrills"—and even these gratifications steadily weaken and begin to turn acrid and arid in the next moment. In frenzied desperation, the ego is driven to heighten the intensity of this "supposed" subjectivity—more and more "action," more and more pleasure-seeking, more and more unconventionality, more and more "getting away from it all," more and more alcohol, narcotics, and sex in their sundry abuses and perversions.

The process is pathetically vicious. Incapable of being eradicated, the object aspect ingrained in the subject-object structure and functioning of the ego is rendered further and further poverty stricken, destitute, and useless, while the subjectivity of the ego, denied in turn any significant object element, becomes increasingly meaningless, empty, and dissolute. Unmindful of the fact that it can never be a subject unless it also is or has an object, the ego in its desire to reduce the object aspect through a misconceived abandonment to subjectivity, succeeds only in reducing itself as a whole. Left ensnared in the exact impasse it had sought to avert, it still has looming before it the abyss—and the despair—of the yawning inner and outer hiatus that frustrates and thwarts it from fully being itself.

Failing in its alternate endeavors "to be" and unable to tolerate the anxiety or the burden of a continued contending with this seemingly impossible task, the ego may have the temptation—even the compulsion—to give up all additional effort. Virtually choosing "not to be," in the power of its subjectivity it tries to evade its strait by yielding, forgoing, or jettisoning that subjectivity. Albeit through secular or religious idolatry, cynical negative indifference, slavish submission to collective conformity, psychological regression to the unawakened dependency of its infancy, or outright psychotic disintegration, the ego would circumvent its predicament by surrendering its freedom and responsibility—and with them itself as a human subject.

For the human person as person—that is, for the ego in ego-consciousness—this, too, entails a double deception. For not only is the forsaking of subjectivity itself a contorted expression of subjectivity, but the ego in its ceasing to be a bona fide subject ceases to be a bona fide ego. Any relinquishment by the ego of its subjectivity results of necessity in a purely negative diminution, impairment, or forfeiture of itself as ego. In the blind superstition or obsequiousnes of idolatry, in the nihilistic denial of the meaning and value of whatever act or decision, in the abject adjustment to the mass-crowd, in the attempted return to the womb, or in the retreat and withdrawal into a psychosis, the human person as human person is to that extent demeaned or even destroyed. Abandonment of subjectivity is as misguided and as futile as abandonment to subjectivity.

Finally, no longer able to cope with, endure, or escape its fragmentation and unsettlement, the ego, out of an agonizing sense of helplessness in its felt aporia, may choose "not to be" not through the discarding of its subjectivity, but through the deliberate discarding of itself. In the intolerable anguish and despondency of the unviability and apparent unresolvability of its basic contradiction—in whichever of its manifestations, the ego resorts to its summary annihilation in suicide.

Thus, whether efforts that would aim at (or grope toward) resolution, acceptance, surrender, avoidance, or abandonment, the ways in which the ego assays to deal with its primal contradiction are, in their outcome, at best (under the perpetual hazard of collapse), transitory, partial, or fragmentary, and, at worst (under a misconception or illusion), nihilistic and destructive. Not that the ego ordinarily pursues any single mode exclusively. In its actual life it usually combines several—in varying degrees, and with varying predominances. Irrespective, however, of their being positive or negative, responsible or irresponsible, profound or superficial, all stem from the one fundamental longing of the ego, caught in the inner and outer alienation of its intrinsic contradiction, to find and to fulfill, to really know, to come home to, and to fully be and have its-self—in and with its world. This longing and its quest for fulfillment constitute the central and ultimate concern of the ego in ego-consciousness. This quest and this fulfillment constitute the existential beginning and the consummate end of Zen Buddhism.

II. Zen Buddhism

A. Chinese "Origins": The Relation of Zen Buddhism to the Predicament or "Question" Inherent in the Human Situation

According to its tradition, Zen (or Ch'an)[2,a] Buddhism in effect first began to function in China when a perplexed sixth-century Chinese, Shen-kuang, discontent with his learned and erudite Confucian and Taoist study, heard of the presence at a nearby Buddhist temple of a Zen teacher from India and undertook to visit him. The Indian master, Bodhidharma, sitting cross-legged facing a wall, continued sitting, and did not take heed of the caller. Shen-kuang, resolute out of a deep disquietude, kept returning, but still was not acknowledged. One night, in spite of a blinding snowstorm, he again went there and decided literally to "stand fast." At daybreak, the snow reached his knees. Moved, Bodhidharma then inquired the purpose of this action. In tears, the Chinese begged the Indian teacher, would he not grant the benefit of his wisdom to help troubled beings. Bodhidharma replied that the way was unbearably difficult, involving the greatest trials, and not to be attained by those lacking in perseverance or determination. Hearing this, Shen-kuang took out a sword he was carrying, cut off his left arm, and placed it in front of the Indian monk. Not until that moment did Bodhidharma accept Shen-kuang as a student, giving him the new name Hui-k'o.[3,b]

To interpret this account--most probably legendary--in what may be considered its representative or "symbolic" meaning for an understanding of Zen Buddhism, straight way to be observed is that an unsettled and distraught ego moves toward the teacher. The Zen master waits, as it were, for a questing ego to come to him. Further, he is apt not to accord an instantaneous overt recognition. On the surface, his early responses sometimes appear to be slighting, if not rudely discouraging. This seeming inattentiveness--or even rejection--is, however, but a manner of ascertaining the earnestness or seriousness of the involvement. When the master has been assured of the ultimacy of that seriousness, open acknowledgement and reception are immediately forthcoming.

It is, accordingly, just the all-compelling and unrelenting perplexity that led him to approach and to keep returning to Bodhidharma, to defy and withstand a snowstorm, and then without hesitation to amputate his arm that establishes Hui-k'o symbolically as the first Zen "student." Perturbed and distressed in his innermost contradiction that is unrelieved by classical learning, Hui-k'o goes to Bodhidharma in search of alleviation and resolution, and is ready, in that pursuit, to stake his entire being.

Whatever the historicity of this incident, it is precisely this primordial quest born of the underlying human predicament that constitutes, when brought before--or evoked by--a Zen teacher, the existential beginning of Zen Buddhism. Lacking this, although one sit in cross-legged meditation for decades at innumerable Zen temples and give oneself over to countless interviews with a myriad of Zen masters, one remains, notwithstanding, a student of Zen in name alone. For Zen Buddhism neither is in itself—nor can be converted into—any objective or disengageable content to be studied as such psychologically, religiously, philosophically, sociologically, historically, or culturally. On the contrary, the only valid component of Zen Buddhism is one's concrete life and existence, its central contradiction and incompleteness, and, in distinction to the mere longing, the actual search for—and attainment of—its genuine reconciliation and fulfillment. If what goes under the designation of Zen Buddhism does not direct itself to and undertake to resolve this cardinal problem of the ego in ego-consciousness, regardless of any claim it may make to hoary orthodoxy, it no longer deserves to be called Zen Buddhism.

Accepted as a properly motivated Zen student, Hui-k'o, expectantly, inquired after the truth. Bodhidharma declared that it was not to be attained other than through one's Self.[4] Hui-k'o, nevertheless, presented his plaint: his heart-mind was not at peace; would not the master please pacify it.

Here is further confirmation that Hui-k'o's impelling vexation stemmed from his inner—as well as outer—contradiction. The Chinese term, hsin, herein rendered as heart-mind, can mean heart or mind, but is more than either alone. The Greek, psyché, or the German, Geist, probably approach it more closely. In the preferred terminology of this presentation, it may be taken to be the ego as subject. The ego as subject in its situation of conditioned subjectivity, plagued by disquietude and unrest, pleads for pacification.

Bodhidharma, in anticipation, had already begun his guidance and instruction in declaring that a resolution was not available apart from one's Self. Not yet comprehending, and in keeping with his felt sense of helplessness—or even desperation, Hui-k'o persisted and described his distress, requesting Bodhidharma to alleviate it.

B. Zen's Methodology: The Zen Manner of Dealing with the Human Predicament

What was Bodhidharma's response? Did he delve into Hui-k'o's past—his personal history, parents, early childhood, the time when he first became aware of the disturbance, the cause, symptoms, and accompanying circumstances? Did he explore Hui-k'o's present—his occupation, marital status, dreams, likes, and interests? Did he, in spite of the fact that he was reputedly himself in that posture, say anything about sitting in the full-lotus position? or about engaging in any sort of so-called dhyāna or zazen[5] practice? No! Bodhidharma's response was: "Bring forth your heart-mind and I shall pacify it for you!"[6]

Eschewing all the fortuitous particularities of Hui-k'o's life— past or present—Bodhidharma plunges immediately and incisively into the living core of the human quandry itself. The ego, caught in the clutches of its basal contradiction and split—which it can neither resolve nor endure—is called upon to produce not anything it may feel to be its problem, but itself as apparent sufferer of the problem. Bring forth the ego-subject that is troubled! Bodhidharma, and Zen Buddhism after him, is aware that finally and fundamentally it is not that the ego has a problem, but that the ego is the problem. Show me who (or what) is disturbed, and you shall be pacified. For although the Zen challenge or demand is ostensibly directed to the dualistic or problematic ego-subject, it is really a call for (and an attempt to trigger the awakening of) the nondualistic or nonproblematic True Self.

Commencing thus with Bodhidharma and continuing ever thereafter, the basic, unveering approach of authentic Zen Buddhism—whatever the form or mode of its methodology in word, deed, or gesture in any instance—has been just such a straightforward, unswerving assault upon the contradictory dualistic subject-object structure and functioning of the ego in ego-consciousness. The exclusive aim has remained throughout to overcome the divisive inner and outer cleavage separating and removing the ego from its-self and its world in order that it may fully be and truly know who and what it is.

To give some further examples: Hui-neng (seventh century), considered to be the Sixth Chinese Zen Patriarch in the lineage of Bodhidharma, when visited by a troubled peripatetic monk, asked simply but pointedly: "What [or who] is it that thus comes?"[7],[c] It is reputed that it took the monk, Nan-yo (or Nan-yüeh), eight years before he could answer.[8] On another occasion, to another quester, this same Hui-neng inquired: "What is the original face that you have prior to the birth of your father and mother?"[9],[d] That is, what are you "beyond" the temporal-spatial—or subject-object—matrix of your ego in ego-consciousness?

Lin-chi[e] (ninth century), the founder of a major school of Zen Buddhism still flourishing in Japan[10] (where he is known as Rinzai), is reported to have declared:

> "There is one true man without a title on the mass of red-colored flesh; he comes out and goes in through your sense gates. If you have not yet borne witness to him, look, look!"
>
> A monk came forward and asked, "Who is this true man without a title?"
>
> Rinzai came down from his chair, and taking hold of [the monk's] chest, demanded, "Speak, Speak!"
>
> The monk hesitated, whereupon, letting him go, Rinzai exclaimed, "What kind of dirt-scraper is this true man without a title!" So saying, Rinzai went back to his room, leaving the monk to chew the cud.[11]

In trying to help the ego actualize this "true man without a title"—which is to say, to truly know and be its-self (or now, better, its-Self[12])—there arose among a number of Zen teachers—notably those of the Lin-chi or Rinzai School—the use of what is known, in Japanese, as the kōan.[13],[f] This is a development especially of the eleventh and twelfth centuries, when Zen (or Ch'an) Buddhism, having acquired great esteem and wide renown throughout China, attracted many who no longer came out of any salient or pressing need. Masters of the preceding epoch would probably have reacted with the same out-

ward indifference and disregard as did Bodhidharma. These later
teachers, however, in their sincere and compassionate desire to help
all inquirers, began themselves to initiate their instructional relation to the caller by means of a formally presented kōan.

The Chinese Sung master who was a pioneer in the effort to utilize the kōan somewhat systematically, Ta-hui (twelfth century), addressed a certain convocation as follows:

> Whence are we born? Whither do we go? He who knows this
> whence and whither is the one to be truly called a Buddhist.
> But who is this one who goes through this birth-and-death?
> Again, who is the one who knows not anything of the whence and
> whither of life? Who is the one who suddenly becomes aware of
> the whence and whither of life? Who is the one, again, who,
> facing this koan, cannot keep his eyes fixed, and as he is not
> able to comprehend it, feels his internals altogether put out
> of order as if a fiery ball swallowed down could not readily
> be ejected. If you wish to know who this one is, apprehend him
> where he cannot be brought within the fold of reason. When you
> thus apprehend him, you will know that he is after all above
> the interference of birth-and-death.[14]

The express purpose is invariant: to know and apprehend who one
is "outside" the fold of reason—that is, "outside" the subject-
object realm of the dualistic ego. In furtherance of this goal, the
kōan, a kind of question, problem, challenge, or demand proffered by
and upon the initiative of the master, is intended to serve two interrelated functions. The first is to penetrate to the root and to
quicken at its source the deeply buried or deceptively concealed underlying concern of the ego in ego-consciousness. The second is,
while stirring this fundamental longing and its quest, to keep them
properly grounded and directed. For it is not sufficient that they
simply be aroused. They must, in order to avoid the many pitfalls in
which they may become attenuated or go astray, also be carefully
guided and even nourished.

In the earlier or pre-kōan phase of Zen Buddhism, the caller generally came, out of the provocation of his own life experience, already bestirred by some acute or "crying" urgency. Normally,
however, the exigency, question, or concern had not yet been plumbed
to its uttermost depth. Though kindled naturally, known neither in
its root-source nor in its primal nature—and so without an adequate
form, it could easily become veiled or deflected. Despite a genuine
intensity and seriousness, the longing and quest were hence likely to
be blind, amorphous, or confused, in need of a correct grounding and
focus.

When, in this period, the student, during an encounter with the
master, would receive a piercing challenge or command—for instance,
"Bring forth your heart-mind!" "Who is it that thus comes?" "What
is the original face that you have prior to the birth of your father
and mother?" "When you are dead, cremated, and the ashes scattered,
where are you?"[15] or, simply, "Speak! Speak!"—the effect, often,
was to supply precisely the appropriate orientation and guidance.
Even so, such charges, questions, or demands were not referred to as
kōans. These spontaneous, unstructured exchanges between master and

student were termed mondō, or, in Chinese, wen-ta, literally, question and answer. But since these mondō-exchanges were intended, on the part of the master, to incite, to ground, to fuel, and to direct the primary concern of the ego, many of them were used, subsequently, either as kōans or as the basis of kōans.

In its two-tiered function, the formal kōan may, consequently, be regarded as a deliberate and calculated expedient employed to secure a result formerly obtained naturally or without contrivance. Expressed otherwise, it could perhaps be maintained, irrespective of the technical terminology and distinctions of Zen Buddhism, that the earlier student had his own natural kōan, natural as to the burning substance, although wanting a proper form of focus; whereas, in the later period, when the inquirer approached neither with a suitable form of the question nor yet viscerally fired to its all-consuming content, the master himself sought to foster both elements by incipiently implanting—or "in-fusing"—such a "question," as it were, from without. In this instance, the kōan, rather than being partially natural, was totally "given."

But, once more, it must immediately be emphasized that so long as the "question" or kōan continues to be simply "given," the exertion expended upon it will be an exercise in futility, and there will be no Zen Buddhism. In its character and composition, however, as well as in the proper mode of its application and usage, the kōan is meant to safeguard against exactly this danger. For by its very nature the kōan does not permit itself to be fitted into any dualistic subject-object scheme of the ego in ego-consciousness. It cannot even be meaningful, must less "solved" or satisfied, if struggled with as an object external to the ego as subject. This is strikingly illustrated by what, in the kōan system, is one of the most widely employed beginning kōans—"Mu," or, in Chinese, "Wu."

The background of this kōan, like that of so many others, is a previously recorded mondō-exchange. The ninth-century Chinese master, Chao-chou (Japanese, Jōshū), on being asked whether or not a dog possessed the Buddha-nature, replied, "Mu!" (Taken in its literal sense, "It does not!") As a formal kōan, however, this monosyllabic response is removed from the conceptual confines of the prompting inquiry, and is presented as the undiminished (or Eternal-Infinite[16]). Self-expression[17] of Chao-chou's (or the presenting master's—or, indeed, the student's very own) Buddha-nature for the student to "see" or to "become." The kōan is, "See Mu!" or, "Become Mu!" Clearly, this kōan-injunction can have no application or relevance, and can in no way be handled or dealt with, within the matrix of any subject-object dualism.

Similarly, when the kōan is the question culled from one of the aforementioned mondō-exchanges, "What is the original face that you have before the birth of your parents?" or when it is the kōan subsequently preferred to "Mu" as an initiating kōan by the eighteenth-century Japanese master, Hakuin, because it contained more of a "noetic" element, "Hear the sound of one hand!" these queries or problems cannot be answered or met (and, indeed, have no meaning) within the subject-object framework of dualistic ego-consciousness, its intellection, or logic. For whatever the noetic element that a kōan may, in effect, have, to come to its understanding or resolution is impossible if it is approached as an object-question or object-problem by the ego as subject, epistemological or otherwise.

Whether "Mu," the "sound of one hand" (which is "No-hand"), "Where are you after you have been cremated?" or one's "original face" (which "is prior to" time-and-space), the kōan, natural or given, provides nothing tangible, nothing to grasp, nothing to take hold of as object. Should the student try to objectify it, under the careful and alert master his maneuver is sharply repudiated and any worked out (or thought-to-be) solution unceremoniously rejected.

Sometimes, however, for example in the kōan system as it has evolved in Japan, when a kōan is differentiated and taken as one particular kōan among other such differentiated (or particularized) kōans, the result inevitably is some objectification of the kōan. As a consequence, some objectified aspect of the form or content of the kōan may yet remain in--and so vitiate--the approved offering with respect to that kōan. To filter this out and to broaden and deepen what may be termed the partial or restricted "glimpse" or "insight" of the student, another kōan is given, and then another, and another. Improperly applied, this kōan system (especially when it is not finally undercut by its own ultimate negation-fulfillment) can become its own impediment and may eventually succumb to a variant of the very danger that the kōan was specifically intended to guard against.

The only unrestrictedly valid content of the kōan is the contending ego itself, its being and its nonbeing, in and with its entire world. The authentic quest to solve the kōan is the quest of the ego split or divided from itself and its world to come to its own ultimate reconciliation or resolution. Actually, if considered from the side of its origination, the kōan is an articulation or expression of that resolution. Whether the student is initially aware of it or not, his genuine grappling with the kōan is the attempt to fulfill himself, not by partially or temporarily transcending his dualistic subject-object structure and functioning with regard to some specific object--not even some differentiated, particularized kōan, but by breaking-through the dualistic and subject-object format per se, which means with regard to any or every object. Accordingly, in either case--natural or given--the kōan struggle or effort[18,g] must finally remain misguided and in vain if undertaken by the ego as subject setting about to deal with or handle its problem as object, or if the result is a provisional and restricted overcoming of the subject-object duality with respect to some particular object within the subject-object matrix rather than an (Infinite-)Eternal overcoming of that duality with respect to the subject-object matrix as such. For, as has already been seen, it is no other than the underlying--or all-pervading--onto-existential dichotomy between subject-and-object, which means the subject-object scheme itself, that is the problem of the ego.

Historically--or traditionally--Zen Buddhism has not expended too much effort to try to explain this intellectually, conceptually, or analytically, as has been a major intention of this brief, summary exposition. Rather, Zen has usually preferred to hit the ego solidly and directly--in the natural mondō-exchange or in the formal, given kōan--with demands or challenges that the ego in its subject-object disjunction can never meet. These baffling onslaughts as expressions in word, deed, gesture, or even "silence" of a compassionately honed fulfillment, constitute Zen's peculiar manner of declaring—and endeavoring to get the ego to grasp—that in no way can the ego ever complete itself within itself, that it cannot possibly—in terms of its subject-object structured-functioning—resolve the contradiction that is this subject-object structured-functioning itself.

The preliminary objective of the kōan, consequently, is to impel and incite not merely noetically, but affectively and physically as well, what in the parlance of Zen Buddhism is referred to as the "great doubt"[19,h]—and to do this so that the ego in and with its world becomes totally or onto-existentially the "great doubt block"[20,i] itself. Unless the ego (with its world) does come to be the "great doubt block" itself, it cannot be said to have arrived at—or to have actualized—the "great doubt."

Toward this provisional (as well as toward its final) end, the kōan was combined with the already existing practice—in Zen methodology—of sitting cross-legged in a form of sustained "integrated-concentration," called, in Japanese, zazen.[21,j] This discipline of seating oneself with legs crossed, each foot up on the opposite thigh, spinal column straight, hands palms-up or otherwise overlapped in front, with breathing—even, slow, and deep—centered in the lower abdomen, in a kind of "contemplation" or "meditation" was prevalent in India long before Buddhism. It was supposedly in this posture that Gautama came to his own ("negation-")[22] fulfillment under the Bodhi-tree—when he happened to look up and to "see" ("without-seeing")[23] the morning star. It was also in this position that Bodhidharma was reported to have been seated when visited by Hui-k'o. About a century later, however, Hui-neng rebelled against what he recognized to be the purely formalistic and quietistic corruption of this practice. As a result, not much mention is made of it immediately following him. Nevertheless, it is uniformly agreed that a majority of Zen monks and students of that era must have taken to it at some time or another.

With the natural kōan, the inner dynamic of this "concentration" derives from one's already churning internal disturbance or uneasiness. The thrust, orientation, or focus is most likely to be that suggested—or "indicated"—by the master during a recent exchange. The student, after such an interchange, is understandably prone to carry its effect into the "meditation hall"[24,k] and to "sit" with it in zazen.

In the case of a formal or given kōan, on the other hand, the ego, not yet roused to the same exacting intensity with regard to its plight, usually lacks the necessary "concentrating (or 'concentrated') power" to "attack"—or "to get into"—the kōan. Accordingly, there arose in conjunction with the kōan and zazen, in the Lin-chi or Rinzai school, especially in Japan, what are known, in Japanese, as the sesshin[25,l] and sanzen.[26,m]

Depending on the monastery, one week of the month six or eight times a year is devoted wholly by the monk or student to zazen—and his kōan. Customarily arising at 3 A.M., he continues in this zazen—except for light work chores, sūtra-chanting, meals, a lecture, interviews with the master, and short rest periods, which may be omitted—until 10 P.M., or later, for seven consecutive days. This period is called a sesshin, and the daily compulsory and voluntary visits—from two to five—to the master, sanzen. [27]

Under the stimulation of such a regimen with its taut and serious atmosphere, the given kōan may begin to take effect. The student, prodded and aided by the staff of the head monk when dozing appears, exertion wanes, or soreness and stiffness set in, and spurred, inspired, goaded, or even driven by the master, finds himself to be more and more caught by his kōan. As his successive responses to it tendered to the teacher are consistently undercut and dismissed, he becomes increasingly dislodged, shaken, and unsteady in whatever assurance or complacency he may have possessed at the outset. Gradually, having less and less to offer, yet incessantly hounded with the same unrelenting demand for an answer, the student grappling with the kōan, unable as a some-one to deal with his problem as a something, experiences a frustration and despair very close to (if not the same as) that known by the ego in its untutored aspiration to find and to fulfill itself.

The inability of the ego as a subject to come to terms with the kōan as an object is, in fact, precisely the inability of the ego as ego in its subject-object bifurcation to resolve the onto-existential contradiction which is the bifurcation. For the student, the given kōan, also, is now, like the natural kōan, a mode or expression of the actual question or quandary of the ego itself, and the struggle of its resolution an equally torturing life-and-death struggle. The kōan thus comes to be, as regards the student, a living crisis, taking over as the central and exclusive concern of his entire being. His confronting it is, indeed, his confronting his own predicament in all of its immediate and burning urgency. Not able to cope with it, he truly "feels his internals altogether put out of order as if a fiery ball swallowed down could not readily be ejected."

This explains why the monk or student, when he has not yet arrived at a solution, may resist seeing the teacher, and why, for the compulsory sanzen visits, he may occasionally have to be pulled, dragged, or, as once witnessed, forcibly carried by four other monks out of the meditation hall and into the interview.

The master's relentless insistence upon a response to the kōan does not in any sense issue from an external, strange, or heteronomous authority. Quite the reverse; an authentic teacher is an embodiment of the actualized optimum ("negation"-)fulfillment of the agonizing ego itself. His demand for a resolution of the kōan, natural or given, is, in reality, the critical mandate of the longing-questing ego for its own resolution. The refusal to see the master arises from the incapacity of the ego to face itself in its acute lack and insufficiency, tellingly mirrored, as it were, by its consummate completion in the person of the teacher. Staying away affords a temporary respite from having to encounter in full and uncompromising honesty the imperative of its own inner conflict for mitigation and relief. Having had, during preceding audiences, its various offerings (whether misdirected, fragmentary, or delusive) sloughed off and discarded, the ego fights to keep itself sheltered and to avoid not only the embarrassment of disclosure in its already partial nakedness but also the torment of a further or complete exposure in total nakedness. For the threat to the ego of such a total naked exposure in its bared root-contradiction could appear to it to be a threat to its very existence, carrying with it the terror of possible insanity or death.

Expressed in more Zen-like metaphor, the ego, denuded or deprived of the function of every other aspect and part of itself, is left clinging by its teeth to a branch overhanging a precipice. Holding on to this last remnant of itself, it feels that it may be able, if only for a little while, to salvage or to preserve itself, albeit in an almost intolerable condition. In such a critical circumstance, to be forced to engage itself unsparingly in the person of the teacher and receive the obligatory commands: "Speak!" and "Speak quick!" can be for it, indeed, a trying ordeal. And this all the more so when it realizes that should it decide, before the master, to stay put and not respond, it may even be denied the use of those teeth. This lattermost denial, it somehow senses, is an absolute necessity that it must inevitably undergo—but one which it is seemingly unable to undergo.

The master's persistent divesting or proscribing is never, of course, an unredeeming or nihilistic negation. What is methodically and rigorously pared away is that which the ego as subject is able to hold on to or to deal with as object. This also encompasses those contents that could (or do) contribute to a limited or qualified ful-fillment. So long as the ego as subject continues to be or to cling to an object—any object, its besetting contradiction and predicament as ego will likewise continue. The aim, therefore, is to eliminate every available objectified (or objectifiable) constitutent— including the very mind and body—toward the end of baring and expos-ing in its unadorned diremption the inwrought dualistic subject-object structure and functioning of the ego as such. For without an objectified component, the ego, unable to be a subject, becomes itself untenable. Yet, it is just to this radical and fundamental moment that Zen wishes to drive, and there to challenge, in the words of a recent teacher:[28] "Without using your mouth, without using your mind, without using your body, express your Self!

Pressed to this extremity, the nature of the student's quest and struggle begins to be altered. His zazen, hitherto undoubtedly a struggling with and a concentrating upon the natural or given kōan as an object, is now shorn of the objectified kōan as well as of all other objectified content, itself rendered objectless. This is but the continuation of the process started when the kōan began to have its effect and to enter into the student's "internals," eventually to permeate his whole being. Becoming less and less external, it became less and less accessible for ordinary contemplation or meditation. At last, it has been overtly stripped of every conceivable object as-pect. Nonetheless, it obdurately persists, unsettled and unresolved; and persisting along with it, there is the unremitting exhortation from the master (as from the ego itself) for settlement and resolu-tion.

As with its kōan, so with itself: the ego, in a chafing-living-bind that it can neither compose, endure, abandon, or escape, is un-able to advance, unable to retreat, unable to stand fixed. Still, it remains under the impelling admonition to move and to resolve. Sys-tematically and mercilessly disallowed the use of all its contents, powers, resources, abilities—or, in sum, its very mind and body—it faces notwithstanding the commanding imperative of the teacher to present and express itself.[29] In this apparent cul de sac, the ego undergoes a felt anguish of supreme futility and helplessness that ordinarily could lead to suicide. In the Zen situation, however, this anxiety and despair never become submerged under any such stark, negative hopelessness.

Unlike the destitute ego in a presuicidal state, the student with a true master has before him the undeniable assurance of a possible resolution to his problem. The teacher, manifesting the genuine love and compassion of an all-embracing (or nondualistic) reconciliation, encourages and reassures not alone through any especially expressed or intended love, but simply by his being. The student somehow realizes that the master is the student even more than the student is himself. In this, he also feels the teacher to be participating as much as himself in the harrowing trial with its suffering and distress. The master is thus for the student the authority, reconciliation, and love of the supernal consummation of the student's own existence.

The student, on the other hand, is for the teacher at once the teacher himself, although another, whom the teacher must, out of his love and compassion, hurl into the tormenting pit of the utterly raw and exposed inner contradiction. On his part, the master is obliged to tear away all remaining layers and to probe directly into the central core of the wound; for not until it has been rigorously unshrouded and onto-existentially actualized in and of itself can it proceed to heal.

Prior to that actualization, the pain and anxiety of the ego in its ostensible prostration do not derive from the wound or contradiction as such, but issue from the ego as subject-bearer of the wound. Purged, from without, of all object content, the ego, from within, still not subjectless (and so still not really objectless) continues to function as an ever-regressing subject, tenaciously retaining its grip. When, however, the ego can cease to be an ever-regressing subject and become transfixed—or transmuted—as the unwrought subject-object root-contradiction in itself, then the contradiction supports and bears itself, and the exterior or simply felt negativity of the ego—precisely as a regressively functioning subject—is left behind.

So the necessity, according to Zen, for the ego, physically as well as mentally, to come to be this radical contradiction or "great doubt block." The "great doubt" (or "great doubt block") is nothing other than the intrinsic predicament of the ego in ego-consciousness thoroughly and climatically exacerbated. The penultimate purpose of the kōan—as well as of the accompanying methodology of zazen, the sesshin, and sanzen—is, consequently, to get the ego to arouse, to accentuate, to bring entirely to the fore, and then (rather than as a regressing subject to bear the burden of) to crystallize locked-in-itself-nonregressively the dualistic contradiction that, as ego, it veritably is.

Hence, in order for the ego to plumb itself exhaustively as ego, it has to expend itself and actualize its ultimate limit not in terms of any recurrent or insurmountable extrinsic failures or impossibilities, but in terms of its own constituent structural and functional antinomy. As an ever-object-oriented-subject, for the ego to approach this actualization, it is necessary that every possible content for its object-orientation in some way be spent, depleted, or otherwise obliterated. Unable as subject to make any further effort away from itself toward some external objectification, it may then undergo the critically needed transformation—not remaining as a regressive-subject and simply reversing its orientation inwardly upon itself as object in introspection, but becoming radically and conclusively its nonregressing root-contradiction in and of itself. Solely when it has become that contradiction-in-itself does it finally come to be subjectless and objectless. For as that actualized core-disjunction-in-itself, reflective ego-consciousness is arrested and checked. Ceasing to entail a fluid, regressive, conditioned subjectivity and objectivity, the ego is now, without subjectivity or objectivity, a solid, undifferentiated, all-inclusive, existential (or onto-existential) block.

This is not—and is not to be confused with—the pre-ego-consciousness of the infant, the nonemergent ego-consciousness of the idiot, the uncompleted ego-consciousness of the wolf-child, the deteriorated ego-consciousness of the psychotic, the numbed ego-consciousness of the anesthetized, the lethargic ego-consciousness of the stupor, the quiescent ego-consciousness of dreamless sleep, the suspended ego-consciousness of the trance, the inert ego-consciousness of the coma, the bewitched ego-consciousness of the fantasy, the enchanted ego-consciousness of the daydream, the immersed ego-consciousness of empathetic creativity, the suggestively induced ego-consciousness of the hypnotized, the captivated ego-consciousness of the possessed (or "pre-possessed"), the excessively saturated (or drugged) ego-consciousness of intoxication, the dogmatically suffused ego-consciousness of the indoctrinated (or "brain-washed"), or the overly stimulated ego-consciousness of a high-pitched (or "whipped-up") frenzy. This is, rather ego-consciousness "in itself"—i.e., "in" and "as its own radical diaeresis—stayed and impacted. It is neither vacant nor blank; nor does it cancel itself and dissolve. While blocked and constricted, lacking active discrimination between subject and object, itself and not itself, it is not at all dull or lifeless. It is, indeed, most sensitive. Moreover, being as yet unresolved, its struggle continues, although no more by or of the ego merely as ego. Ego has at last become kōan, and both have become the struggle and "concentration" itself, the "great doubt block" itself, the root-contradiction itself, subjectless and objectless.

This is the ego unequivocally exhausted as ego. No longer subject or object, it is no longer able to strive or attempt. In contradistinction to the no more than seeming helplessness of the presuicidal state, this is consummate existential helplessness itself, in which even suicide is impossible. As long as the ego as subject can carry out any reflectively intentional act, albeit its own destruction, it is not truly helpless.

Similarly, it is this situation in which the ego is acutely or unregressively its in-fixed antinomy that constitutes the definitive dilemma, the definitive impasse, the definitive cul de sac, the definitive nihilism of the indistinguishableness of the positive and the negative (e.g., of meaning and meaninglessness, or of value and valuelessness), the definitive aporia of "no exit." This is the ego's constituent plight utterly and unabashedly excoriated, dispossessed of every veil and integument. This is ultimate negativity itself (although as yet in its penultimate form), beyond any merely dualistic or negative negativity.

This maximum negativity, it is ever to be remembered, while a necessary antecedent and not alone negative, is still a precondition. It is not yet resolution or fulfillment. Becoming the "great doubt block," that is, the root-diremption in its root, is not the final end.

Having ceased to be a chronically receding subject "caught up" in its subject-object disjunction, the ego is now, in and as that disjunction itself, functionally and structurally disabled and immobilized. Its being objectless and subjectless is a negativity of an exhaustive bondage and obstruction, in which subject and object in their contradictory, dualistic polarity totally impede and impound each other in an all-comprehensive, helpless clog. Being thus negatively objectless and subjectless, having neither body nor mind, is not sufficient. Without body, without mouth, and without mind, there must be expression. The root-contradiction—great-doubt-block remains to be in-divisibly broken up and resolved.

It is, however, solely when this great-doubt-block has been actualized that it can then be "uprooted."[30] It is precisely in this condition of the most intense, most delicate tension, that some chance event of daily life, or perhaps some action, exclamation—or even "silence"—of the master, can suddenly spark the basic and revolutionary upheaval in which this root-antimony—great-doubt-block instantaneously breaks up in what is at the same time a break-through.

C. The Zen Resolution: The Nature of the Zen "Answer" to the "Question" of Human Existence

Just as the ego in ego-consciousness is, in its genesis, both an act and a fact, so its consummate extirpation and resolution also have the quality of act as well as of fact, but now neither relatively so nor sheerly of the ego as ego. For in and as the root-disjuncture—great-doubt-block, ordinary ego-consciousness is, in effect, already transcended. Notwithstanding that the great-doubt comprises a negative absence of distinction with regard to subject and object, positive and negative, itself and not-itself, it nevertheless incorporates the entire realm of being—including the very dualism of being and nonbeing. As the root-abscission in its root, it is the abyss of being, or, more correctly, the abyss of the antimony between being and non-being, between existence and nonexistence. But although negatively the dissociation and abyss, it is this same root-core that is—positively—the ground and the source.

Approached from the ego, this core is the irrefragable extremity or unsurpassable limit—the innermost center of the disseverance that is ego-consciousness. Crystallized as this center, the ego is expended but not yet "actively" consumed. Further, so long as the root-core remains in terms of the ego-contradiction, even though exhausted, it continues to be that root negatively—as the root-barrier, root-circumscription, or root-impediment. Actualized as such, the ego is only "as if dead." When, however, this negative root-core—bursting—"uproots" and "turns" on itself, then the ego really dies the "great death,"[31,n] which is at once the "great birth" or "great awakening."[32,o]

The "great death" is the ego dying-to-itself in its crystallized ultimate negativity. In no sense a relative, nihilistic destruction

or expiration into a vacuous (or hollow) void, emptiness, or nothingness, this abrupt "uprooting" and "reversal" is, on the contrary, the
break-up and dispelling of the contradiction, of the abyss, of the
aporia. The annulment or negation of an exhaustive but unawakened
negativity, it is—precisely as such—positive. The negative dissolution is a positive resolution. The negation of the ego in the
axial antithesis of its dualistic ego-consciousness is a negation of
a negation that is, positively and affirmatively, a resolution and
fulfillment. The ego in dying to itself as ego in its core antinomy
or great-doubt-block, is born or "awakens" to its "uprooted" (and
"uprooting") Self as an ego-less—or Self-less—Self.

Again to be underscored is that the root-contradiction in its
root is not here any metaphysical or ontological postulate. It is an
urgent and burning actuality. So, its "bursting" and "turning upon"
itself is also a concrete reality. The breaking-up and dissolving of
the consolidated ingrained disjunction is a direct and im-mediate reconciliation. What was the constricted and obstructed ultimate limit
is now the freely functioning primeval source and ultimate ground.
The center, no longer the locked-in (or in-fixed) blockage of a non-
regressive dualistic ego, is, in sharp contrast, the unbounded
center-less center of the ego-less or Self-less Self. Root-limit,
"reversing" or "turning on" itself, becomes the limit-less-limit of
the ground-less-ground and the source-less-source. This radical,
cataclysmic "uprooting," "reversing," or "turning" by, of, and at the
root-core, is called in Zen, in Japanese, satori.[33,p]

The satori break-up and dissipation of the expended and arrested
ego in its root-contradiction at the root is the awakening of the
ego—or, better, of the root—to its "ground-abyss" in its Self-less-
Self. This awakening to its (Selfless-)Self is at once the awakening
of its (Selfless-)Self. From the perspective of ego-consciousness in
its core-antimony-great-doubt-block, the total break-up, disintegration, or "death" is an awakening and breakthrough to its Self. From
the opposite perspective, however, the awakening and breakthrough to
its Self is the awakening and opening up of its Self. This is, ver-
ily, Self-awakening: that which awakens is that which is awakened,
that by which it is awakened, and that to which it is awakened. Act
as well as fact, this Self-awakening is in its Self the ground, the
abyss, and the prius of act and fact.

As "abysmal source" (or "ground-abyss")—never unilaterally dynamic or static—this Self is in no wise a dead identity or an ideal,
abstract universality or oneness. Nor is it an "exclusive nondual-
ity," a "false sameness,"[34,q] or a "one-sided emptiness."[35,r] Its-
Self the ground-source, abyss, and prius of the static and the
dynamic, while it continues to remain its-Self, it is forever giving
rise to new expression of its-Self. Indeed, awakened to its Self, it
realizes that the very subjectivity of the ego as subject—even in
its contradictory duality—really derives or springs from its Self.
Likewise, the unfathomable font of the longing and quest of the ego
to overcome its estrangement and to complete and fulfill itself is
also its (Selfless-)Self. Broken off from (in its "relation" with)
its-Self, the ego longs and quests to "return" to its-Self. In its
diremptive contradiction of having yet not having itself and its
world, the ego is actually in the unsettled (and "unsettling") condition of neither being nor having its True—or Self-less—Self.

In its dualistic, reflective consciousness, the ego in addition to being disjoined from itself, the other, and its world, is, moreover, cut off and obstructed from what may be termed its primordial "ground-source-abyss." That is, the ego's dualistically differential individuality, fragmented from within and isolated from without, is ungrounded, and so unsustainable. Such an individuality, rent within, insulated without, and strange to its own source, can never genuinely know or affirm itself because it never is or has itself genuinely. Solely in dying to itself as ego and awakening to its-Self as a nondualistic or Self-less Self is its truly autonomous in-dividuality attained for the first time. For as a nondualistic Self-less-Self, it is at once Itself and Not-Itself—and so at once Everything and Nothing. It is, in this sense, both un-divided and in-divisible. Expressed still otherwise, ceasing to be a mere ego, it is hereafter what may be designated an "ego-less," "form-less,"[36,s] or "Empty"[37,t] ego—or, hence, a Self-ego, or ego-Self.

The underlying predicament of the onto-existentially contradictory subject-object structure and functioning of the dualistic ego is resolved only when that living root-contradiction breaks up and dies to itself at its root, awakening in resolution and fulfillment in and as its Self as a Self-ego. As Self, the ground-less-ground of itself as ego, it is at last free from the cleavage of any inner or outer divisive duality. No longer laboring "to be" out of the negative abyss of an unreconciled, bifurcated core, it now both is and issues forth from its Self-less-Self as the abysmal source of itself as subject and object.

In difference to the conditioned subjectivity of initial ego-consciousness, no more does object bind, obstruct, circumscribe, or curtail subject. Nor do subject and object, as in the great-doubt-block, immobilize each other in the depth of their antagonistic duality. Uprooted and overturned in their centrally impacted dualistic opposition, they are henceforward rooted and centered in their non-dualistic ground-of-no-ground. Re-rooted and re-centered, they cease to impede in mutual contradiction and become, instead, the free flowing expression or manifestation of that ground-less-ground.

From the standpoint of the ground-source-abyss in and of its Self, exactly this free and continuous flow out of its Self as subject and object is its "return," unhindered and unhampered, to its Self, through time-and-space, but in Eternity-Infinity. That is to say, albeit through time-and-space, it is never simply time-and-space, but is always time-less-time and space-less-space—or, consequently, Eternity-Infinity. Again to be stressed is that this is Self-less or Form-less Self-manifestation: that which manifests is that which is manifested, that through which it is manifested, and that of which it is a manifestation.

As an awakened-subject manifest (or actualized) as the opening-up—or "dis-closing"—of its source-less-source or source-abyss, it is a pure or conditioned Self-subject, as its object is a pure or un-conditioned Self-object. Just as subject is an expression and function of its Self, so, too, is object equally an expression and function of its Self. As pure, unconditioned (subjectless-)subject and (objectless-)object, subject is, indeed, object (even as it continues to remain subject), as object is, indeed, subject (even as it continues to remain object). Their duality, no longer contradictory or

merely dualistic, is henceforth a reconciled, noncontradictory, nondualistic duality. Moving unobstructed and unimpeded in the absolute
freedom of unconditioned subjectivity, subject mirrors object and is
mirrored by object, as object mirrors subject and is mirrored by subject. That which mirrors is that which is mirrored, that from which
it is mirrored, and that in which it is mirrored. Ego, ego-
consciousness, and its subject-object duality, becoming trans-rooted,
trans-centered, and trans-formed, are now the noncontradictory, nondualistic duality of a subject-less, object-less, ego-less ego--or,
in short, a Self-ego.

Its Self as Self the ground-abyss of itself as ego, Self-ego is
simultaneously with form and without form. It is form-less-form. As
inexhaustible ground-source-abyss, it is (in its-Self) without (any
"de-finite" or fixed) form--which Formlessness is also not a fixed
form. Neither theoretical nor abstract, this Formlessness is its
Self the fountain-spring of form--as, also, of form-less-ness. Because Formless, it is able in actual existence to give rise to, to
express its-Self in, and to be all forms--or, all form-less-forms.

In its awakened Self-awareness and fulfillment as Self-ego, it is
and has the form of itself as Self-ego. As ground-source-abyss, on
the other hand, it is never simply the form of itself as Self-ego.
Itself and not-itself as a form-less-form, Self-ego is coincidentally
its own being and its own nonbeing in time-less-time and space-less-
space. It is, in another word, actualized <u>ekstasis</u>: "beyond" itself
(and not-itself); "beyond" its being (and its nonbeing).

That is, whereas the ordinary ego affirms itself by dualistically
negating or excluding its negation, "I am I because I am not not-I,"
the Form-less or Self-less Self-ego affirms its Self by nondualist-
ically affirming or including its negation, "I am I because I am not-
I." Put slightly differently, while the ego's dualistic negation or
not-I stands outside of and against the ego's I, thereby limiting and
indeed threatening it, the (Self-less-)Self-ego's nondualistic nega-
tion(-affirmation) or Not-I stands as a constitutive element (or dimension) within the ego-less or Self-less I, thereby un-limiting,
completing, or "full-filling" it in what is actually (however paradoxically) an "emptying-filling." So it is-without-being, as it
does-without doing.[38,u] It may, consequently, freely assert in unconditional affirmation: "I am" and "I am not"; "I am I" and "I am
not I"; "I am not I therefore I am I"; "A rose is not a rose is a
rose"; "I am not that I am!" Unconditional Self-affirmation is, accordingly, an unconditional Self-affirmation-negation--or Self-
negation-affirmation.

This nondualistic Self-affirmation-negation (or Self-negation-
affirmation) may be considered, as well, to be the nature--or <u>logos</u>--
of Love. For reconciled to and completed in its Self as a Form-less
or Self-less Self, Self-ego is the other, as the other is its Self.
The duality between itself and other being but one aspect of the
duality of subject and object, just as Self-ego realizes itself to be
an unfolding of its-Self, so it realizes the other similarly to be an
unfolding of its-Self: "I am I," "Thou art thou"; "I am Thou," "Thou
art I."[39]

Nor is this nondualistic-duality confined to a reflectively human
other--or, for that matter, to any specific object. Rather, it obtains unrestrictedly (or, again, nonexclusively) with respect to the

Self-ego and the entire formless universe. This accounts for what in Buddhism is referred to as the "reciprocal permeation (or inter-penetration) between thing-and-thing,"[40,v] or, the "mutually inter-dependent [and, hence, totally In-dependent] co-origination of all things"[41]—since each thing in its-Self is also No-thing and at the same time Every-thing. In the words of the renowned Chinese Taoist, Chuang-tzu: "Heaven, earth, and I arise together; all things and I are one."[42] This could also be expressed as: "When I see the flower, I see my Self; the flower sees my Self; the flower sees the flower; the flower sees its Self; the flower sees me; its Self sees my Self; my Self sees its Self." Or, more succinctly: "When I see the flower, I see Nothing-that-is-Everything; the flower sees Nothing-that-is-Everything; Nothing-that-is-Everything sees Nothing-that-is-Everything."

    A rose
    By any other name
    As sweet
    As
    No-Rose
    No-Name
    All Names.

Here is living, creative Love in consummate activation and ful-fillment—ever expressing its (Self-less-)Self, ever that which is expressed. That which expresses is that which is expressed, that out of which it is expressed, and that for the sake of which it is ex-pressed. And this even as—or just because—it is a Form-less (or expression-less) Self-expression that both is and is not. Here, at last, is total and unconditional Negation-Affirmation of subject and object, of itself, of the other, of the world, of being (or of the very matrix of being-and-nonbeing); for here, at last, is total and unconditional Negation-Affirmation of its Self, in its Self, by its Self as a Self-less Self, which, in the resolved paradox of its non-duality—or nondualistic-duality, is-yet-is-not, has-yet-has-not, does-yet-does-not, and knows-yet-knows-not. This is not to be con-fused, however, with "I live, yet not I, but Christ [or Buddha—or any intended 'other'] liveth within me." This is, rather, I-yet-not-I live-yet-do-not-live—which, incidentally, is what is meant "to be" a Buddha.
    Thus being-while-not-being and having-while-not-having, it "is" the "original face" that it "has" prior to the birth of its parents. Moreover, doing-without-doing, it "sees Mu," "hears the sound of one hand," and can "present its-Self" without using its body, mouth, or mind. Again, in knowing-without-knowing and in being-without-being, it "apprehends who and where it 'is' after its cremated ashes have been scattered."
    This, then, is human existence reconciled and fulfilled beyond the dualistic onto-existential contradiction of its ordinary ego-consciousness. This, now, is Man thoroughly actualized as Man—(Un-)Self-consciously at once fully being (in-and-through not-being), knowing (in-and-through not-knowing), and having (in-and-through not-having) him-Self and his world, able (in-and-through a doing that is coincidentally a not-doing) to "transform mountains, rivers, and the

great earth, and reduce them into [him-]Self," and to "transform
[him-]Self and turn it into mountains, rivers, and the great
earth."[43]

This, in my understanding, is the relation between Zen Buddhism
and the human situation.

> Love is
> When Nothing touches Its-Self
> And all springs forth
> In Formless Form.

> Love is
> When you and I
> And I and you
> And I and I
> And you and you
> In Nothingness
> No longer--two--
> Emerge
> In naked presentation
> Self to Self
> And Self in Self.

> This .... is
> When love .... is.

NOTES

1. Written originally in the summer of 1957 for a conference on
"Zen Buddhism and Psychoanalysis," and later published in a book with
that title; see Erich Fromm, D.T. Suzuki, and Richard DeMartino, Zen
Buddhism and Psychoanalysis (New York: Harper and Row, 1960), pp.
142-171. This article had been appreciably revised for this present
publication.

2. Ch'an is the first syllable of the Chinese ch'an-na[al] (pronounced in Japanese zenna), a phonetic transcription of the Sanskrit,
dhyāna, a specific mode of "contemplation" or "concentration."

3. This rendition is taken from the Ching-tê Ch'uan-têng Lu (The
Record of the Transmission of the Lamp), vol. 3.

4. See my discussion of Zen's methodology (II,B) and of Zen's
resolution (II,C).

5. See my discussion of kōan practice and fn. 21.

6. Ching-tê Chu'an-têng Lu, vol. 3.

7. Wu-teng Hui-yüan (A Composite of the Five Lamps), vol. 3.

8. Ibid.

9. Shūmon Kattō Shū (A Collection of "Zen Entanglements").

10. The other is the Ts'ao-tung[el] (in Japanese, Sōtō) school.

11. Quoted from Daisetz T. Suzuki, Living by Zen (Tokyo:
Sanseido, 1949), p. 23.

12. Again, see the section on Zen's resolution (II,C).

13. In Chinese, kung-an, literally, public document or testament.

14. Quoted from Suzuki, Living by Zen , pp. 171-2.

15. Quoted from ibid., p. 189; see also fn. 5.

16. See my discussion of "Eternity-Infinity" in section II,C.
17. See my discussion of Self-expression as unconditional Negation-Affirmation in section II,C.
18. Technically, kung-fu (in Japanese, kufū).
19. Tai-i; in Japanese daigi or taigi.
20. Ta-i-t'uan; in Japanese, daigidan or taigidan.
21. In Chinese, tso-ch'an, literally, "sitting-dhyāna," but perhaps better rendered as "Zen sitting."
22. See my discussion of negation and emptiness (section II,C) and of Negation-Affirmation (also section II,C).
23. See my discussion of unconditional Self-affirmation-negation in the last few pages of this essay.
24. Ch'an-t'ang; in Japanese, zendō, literally, "Zen-hall."
25. In Chinese, she (sometimes, chieh)-hsin, "concentralization of the heart-mind," or, "heart-mind concentralization."
26. In Chinese, ts'an-ch'an, "to pursue the Zen quest."
27. This account is broadly generic and presents none of the finer, more technical distinctions.
28. The recent Japanese Zen teacher, Shin'ichi Hisamatsu.
29. Another form of this kōan-command employed by Shin'ichi Hisamatsu is: "When whatever you do [or do not do] will not do, what do you do!?"
30. In the words of Hakuin, "[It is] at the base (or root) of the Great Doubt [that] there is the Great Awakening." For another translation, see Isshū Miura and Ruth Fuller Sasaki, Zen Dust (New York: Harcourt, Brace & World, 1966), p. 47.
31. Ta-ssu; in Japanese, daishi or taishi.
32. Ta-wu; in Japanese, daigo or taigo; also Ta-ssu i-fan.[nl]
33. In Chinese, wu, literally, awakening or apprehending; in Japanese satori.[pl]
34. O-p'ing-teng; in Japanese akubyōdō.
35. P'ing-k'ung; in Japanese, henkū.
36. Wu-hsiang; in Japanese, musō.
37. K'ung; in Japanese, kū: a translation of the Sanskrit, śūnya.
38. In Chinese Taoism this is expressed as wei-wu-wei.
39. It is interesting, in this connection, to read from the young John Dewey: "Love is the complete identification of subject and object, of agent and function, and, therefore, is complete in every phase." (John Dewey, The Study of Ethics [Ann Arbor: George Wahr, 1897], p. 143.)
40. This is a formulation of Chinese Hua-yen Buddhism: shih-shih wu-ai (in Japanese, jiji-muge).
41. This is a formulation of early Indian Buddhism: in Sanskrit, pratītya-samutpāda; in Pāli, paticca-samuppāda.
42. The Book of Chuang-tzu, chap. 2.
43. See Suzuki, Living by Zen, pp. 26-27.

a. 禪

a'. 禪那

b. 景德傳燈錄

c. 五燈會元

d. 宗門葛藤集

e. 臨濟宗

e'. 曹洞宗

f. 公案

g. 工（功）夫

h. 大疑

i. 大疑團

j. 坐禪

k. 禪堂

l. 攝（接）心

m. 參禪

n. 大死

n'. 大死一番

o. 大悟

p. 悟

p'. 悟り

q. 惡平等

r. 偏空

s. 無相

t. 空

u. 爲無爲

v. 事事無礙

PART THREE

Psychological Implications of Sanskrit Buddhism

Prasaṅga and Double Bind

Gustavo Benavides

I

First formulated in 1956[1], the "Double-Bind" theory of schizophrenia has become much more than a therapeutic instrument for the
treatment of psychic disorders. Dealing as it does with central
problems in the areas of theory of communication, psychotherapy, and
logic, the double-bind theory can now be considered as an interdis-
ciplinary (or rather "predisciplinary") paradigm capable of explaining the logical foundations of human behavior.[2]
Briefly stated, the components of a double-bind situation are,
according to the Palo Alto research team, the following:

(1) Two or more persons; (2) Repeated experience; (3) A
primary negative injunction; (4) A secondary injunction
conflicting with the first at a more abstract level, and
like the first enforced by punishment or signals which
threaten survival; (5) Perception of the world in double-
bind terms.[3]

This first formulation has been simplified and reduced to three basic
points: (1) the individual is involved in an intense relationship;
(2) he is caught in a situation in which contradictory messages are
being received; and (3) metacommunication is impossible. A situation
such as this, then, is considered to cause the type of behavior which
is usually labelled as "schizophrenic." There has been, however, a
tendency to replace the purely psychiatric aspects of the double bind
theory by a more general utilization of this concept in seemingly unrelated fields such as play and humor theories,[4] literature,[5] and
creativity in general. In fact, once the psychiatric limits of the
concept were overstepped, the world began to be seen as a system of
inescapable double-binds. From this point of view we can reformulate
the principles mentioned above, replacing the family or interpersonal
situation by a more "existential" one. Double-binds, then, would occur whenever a person (1) experiences himself as part of the system
which is the world; (2) is caught in a series of situations in which
paradoxical messages from and about the world are being received; and
(3) is incapable of escaping from it.
These three basic points can be expanded: we can say that the
first characteristic of a double-bind situation (that which states
the interpersonal and intense character of the situation) is obviously present in our awareness of being part of the world. In the same

way, the contradictory character of the message which constitutes the world, as well as the image we have of ourselves, and of the relation between the world and ourselves, is present outside of a "pathological" situation. The third point, the impossibility of metacommunicating, is also present, since we know that any utterance is part of the universe of discourse which we call "world."

Although not in these terms, an "existential" view of the double-bind situation has already been formulated by Arthur Burton, who equates the problem of schizophrenia with the problem of reality, saying that "the Absurd is the double-bind par excellence and the model for all others."[6] In a more restricted way, Winfried Kudszus[7] has referred to the culturally and socially determined contexts with which the double-bind theory is concerned.

Our aim in this article shall be more modest: we will attempt to show the similarities between the content-free therapy developed by the Palo Alto group with the equally thesis free (prasaṅga as opposed to svatantra) therapeutic argumentation of the Madhyamaka school of Buddhism.

II

Interesting parallels can be found between psychotherapeutic and "religious" ways of dealing with pathological or nonpathological ways of approaching reality. In principle, one basic distinction can be made based on the content, or lack of it, of the religious, philosophical, or psychological schools under examination. Any hypothetical theory starts with a set of premises about "reality," and also about the ideologically determined, and ideologically determining, goal to be achieved. Similarly, a religious doctrine starts with a basic conception of the world, of Man ("Man" generally, and not "Woman"), and of a desirable "spiritual" realization. On the other hand, it is possible to think of at least one example of a "doctrine" that claims not to have any thesis of its own (nāsti ca mama pratijñā),[8] with a method consisting in the systematic reductio ad absurdum ("necessary consequence" prasaṅga)[9] of the opponent's arguments, and, paradoxically, no aim.[10] The psychotherapeutic counterpart—the double-bind approach—has as content the theory of Logical Types, as method the so-called "symptom prescription" (a reductio ad absurdum in fact), and as aim the disappearance of the paradoxically originated and paradoxically prescribed symptoms.

If we were to continue looking for religious-therapeutical parallels, we could find, still within Buddhism, a system, the Svātantrika-Madhyamaka,[11] that is less extreme than the Prāsaṅgika-Madhyamaka, since it uses independent arguments (svatantra). (It is interesting to notice how the extremism of the Mādhyamikas—despite their name—has to give way to a more conventional view, even if this conventionality refers only to the procedure to be followed in dealing with the adversary-patient.) Other Buddhist schools, especially those dealing with the Tathāgatagarbha[12] theory, would be closer to psychological theories postulating some kind of "Absolute/Self," even if this concept, as Lamotte remarks, is "plus brāhmanique que bouddhiste."[13]

In any case, to subject psychological (or psychotherapeutic) theories and religious doctrines to the same questions can be illuminating, provided that the questions are addressed to the logical and methodological presuppositions of the doctrines and theories in question. In this sense, we can agree with Ricoeur's observation about the rules underlying any discourse: "the most poetic symbolism, the most sacred, operates with the same semic variables as does the most banal word in the dictionary."[14] In our case, however, the "semic variables" are understood not only within the restricted limits of linguistics or poetics, but in the wider context of semiotics.[15]

III

The perception of the world in double-bind terms is due fundamentally to its temporal nature. The immediate message we receive from the world is the one stating its existence, an existence which at first seems to be immune to time. On the other hand, the most superficial examination of anything reveals its basic temporality. "Things," then, affirm themselves, while at the same time pointing to their intrinsic impermanence (anitya). This self-destroying semiosis (signs, as dharmas, are born only to die) can be considered, using the framework of the double-bind, as the reason for seeing the world as a systematic double-bind. In this sense, the first component of a double-bind situation, that of "relationship," is unnecessary (or redundant), since any situation in which there is an object-subject split, whether interpersonal or intrapersonal, presupposes already a "relational" situation. The impossibility of metacommunicating is also an inextricable aspect of the problem, since metacommunication in an absolute way would imply some kind of "transcendence," which in this case would mean a type of discourse utterly unintelligible to the very participants in the process. "Meta-" solutions of any type are at best only provisional compromises, which after a brief and illusory existence have to return to the universe of discourse they have never left. In the case of Buddhism, the only instance of a "meta-" instance would be that of nirvāna, a "concept" which because of its paradoxical character has been the object of endless discussions.[16]

Nāgārjuna's statement in the Mūlamadhyamakakārikā XXV,20:

nirvānasya ca yā kotih samsāranasya ca/
na tayor antaram kimcit susūksmam api vidyate//

The limits of nirvāna are the limits of samsāra
between the two there is not the slightest difference,[17]

indicates the impossibility of assuming a transcendental realm. Nirvāna as opposed to samsāra would be the ontological equivalent of the opposition between the therapist's own arguments and goals and the opponent-patient's arguments-symptoms. In the Mūlamadhyamakakārikā we can see how Nāgārjuna treats a world that is subject to the "self-perpetuating oscillation" caused by paradoxical injunctions. To remedy this Nāgārjuna does not postulate a solution, trying to

show, for example, how the phenomenic world has an "absolute" or
"blissful" substratum. Nor does he uncover a realm where being and
nonbeing, or their various combinations, are finally reconciled in a
coincidentia oppositorum.[18] He, on the contrary, subjects the entire
(Buddhist) universe of meaning to an examination (parīksā) through
which the inconsistencies of our logically constructed world are un-
masked. In the twenty-seven chapters of the Madhyamakakārikā we see
how a world that is generally perceived as a loosely connected collection of contradictions and paradoxes is shown to be a tightly organized system in which everything is proved to be impossible. In
order to do this, Nāgārjuna pushes to their logical conclusions the
paradoxes whose existence we only guess, and demonstrates that they
are indeed present, and that they are inescapable.

As an example of this technique we can refer to the tenth chapter
(Agnīndhana parīksā), where Nāgārjuna examines the perplexing relationship between wood and fire. He starts by saying that:

> If fuel and fire were the same, then the agent
> and the act would also be the same. If fire is
> other than fuel, then fire should exist without
> fuel.

> yad indhanam sa ced agnir ekatvam kartrkarmanoh/
> anyaś ced indhanād agnir indhanād apy rte bhaver//1.[19]

Nāgārjuna concludes:

> Fire does not depend on fuel; fire is not indepedent
> of fuel. Fuel is not dependent on fire; fuel is not
> independent of fire.

> apeksyendhanam agnir na nānapeksyāgnir indhanam/
> apeksyendhanam agnim na nānapeksyāgnim indhanam//12.[20]

In this case, using the problems of "relation" and "causality," he
transforms an everyday puzzle into an unsolvable problem, which he
uses at the end of the chapter to illustrate the relationship between
"self" and "entities." In the twelfth chapter (Duhkha parīksā), an
"existentially" relevant problem is examined in a similar fashion.
Here, duhkha (translated as "sorrow," "suffering," "unhappiness") is
said not to be "self-caused; other-caused; both; noncausal" (svayam
krtam parakrtam dvābhyām krtam ahetukam),[21] a characteristic which
duhkha shares with all other "beings."

As we can see, what is relevant for Nāgārjuna is not so much the
concepts or objects under examination as the argumentation[22] itself.
Wood, fire, the Tathāgata, the sense organs, nirvāna, are all examined and disposed of in the same way. This is due to the fact that
all these concepts belong to the same universe of meaning, or to the
same universe of symptoms which Nāgārjuna wants to turn against itself. Nirvāna, the Tathāgata, the Four Noble Truths are not ex-
empted, because they are, even more than the other concepts, subject
to the "oscillation"[23] caused by paradoxical injunctions, and also
because to leave them "unexamined" would have as consequence their
reification, and their becoming "views" (drsti).

The technique of not using any own arguments (or propositions) is
clearly stated in the Vigrahavyāvartanī,[24] a prose work in which
Nāgārjuna defends himself against the criticisms of a Naiyāyika by
merely showing the contradictions of his opponent without presenting
any of his own. The reductio ad absurdum method works as a mirror in
which the opponent-patient can see his own logically entangled
reasoning. Acting as psychotherapist, Nāgārjuna had, in the
Mūlamadhyamakakārikā, "prescribed the symptom," showing that the
world is indeed constituted by paradoxes; now, in the Vigrahavyāvartanī, he makes clear that he is, in fact, only showing, and not
presenting any view:

> This statement is not endowed with an intrinsic
> nature. There is therefore no abandonment of
> position on my part.

> na svābhāvikametadvākyam tasmānna vādahānirme/.[25]

> If I had any proposition, then this defect
> would be mine. I have, however, no proposition;
> therefore, there is no defect that is mine.

> yadi kācana pratijñā syānme tata esa me bhaveddosah/
> nāsti ca mama pratijñā tasmānnaivāsti me dosah//29.[26]

IV

Hans Sachs, a disciple of Freud, is quoted as saying that "an
analysis terminates when the patient realizes that it could go on
forever," a statement that has been called:

> strangely reminiscent of the Zen Buddhist tenet that
> enlightenment comes when the disciple realizes that
> there is no secret, no ultimate answer, and therefore
> no point in continuing to ask questions.[27]

An extreme application of this view can be found in the technique of
certain psychotherapists who not only "prescribe" or "schedule" the
symptoms,[28] but who also try to convince the patient of the absolute
impossibility of getting rid of them.[29] Through this "negative therapy," the patient is confronted with his own mental constructions
and, in the case of symptom "prescription" or "schedule," told that
in fact his problems are his own creations. In the second and more
extreme case, the patient is told that he is the problem, because he
sees himself and the world as problematic. His world is not seen "as
it is," as the tautological[30] discourse that can not be otherwise,
but as a paradox-ridden discourse that oscillates between "is," "is
not," "can be," "cannot be."
Āryadeva, in the tenth chapter of his Śataśāstra, says:

> On account of the absolute purity. On account of the

refutation of the ātman, there is no individual. On
account of the refutation of Nirvāna, there is no liberation; how is it possible to say that man obtains liberation? (We say that) there is liberation only according
to the worldly truth.[31]

To postulate nirvāna is to fall into the four alternatives of "existence," "nonexistence," "both existence and nonexistence," and
"neither existence nor nonexistence";[32] whereas, as Āryadeva says in
the Catuhśataka (chapter XVI), "He who has no thesis stating existence, nonexistence and (both) existence and nonexistence cannot ever
be criticized."[33] He who "cannot ever be criticized" would be the
one who, in the framework of the double-bind theory, does not see the
world in terms of "symptom" and "cure," having therefore gained a
kind of insight with no content.

    As mentioned before, Hans Sachs' remark about an analysis that
could go on forever, has been compared with the cryptical remarks
made by Chinese and Japanese Zen masters. After having examined,
however briefly, some of the teachings of the Mādhyamikas, it would
seem unnecessary to refer to these late developments, since in India
we can already find systematic examples of the no-thesis approach to
reality. On the other hand, a comparison with Ch'an and Zen can be
illuminating, because in their scriptures we can find in a condensed
way, as it were, the basic tenets of the Middle Way School. Another
important aspect which is emphasized by these schools is the practical one (although one should not forget that similar stress of the
"mystical praxis" and paradoxicality can be found in the Kālacakra
system, as shown in the studies of Helmut Hoffmann).[34]

    In the logia of Lin-tsi we can see the logical conclusion of the
no-thesis, no-proposition "position": "...if I were to hold to the
tradition of the lineage of our patriarchs and disciples, I simply
would not open my mouth, and you would not be able to put your foot
in it"(1a).[35] Silence, the "silence of the saints" (āryatūsnīmbhāva), is not understood in this text as "ineffability," or "incom-
municability" (anabhilāpya), but in a much more radical sense: one
keeps silent because there is nothing to talk about.[36] To talk is to
"put your foot in your mouth"; it is to forget that, as Lin-tsi says,
"every search is sorrow" (17b),[37] and that the ideal of the wise is
"to keep oneself in the everyday...."(13a).[38] To do otherwise is to
be caught in the double-bind situation from which the therapeutic
double-bind, prasaṅga-like, "liberates" us.

V

    A final point, however, should be made. The theorists of the
double-bind have concluded that as a result of the absurdity of a
situation, a person may react in three basic ways, which correspond
to schizophrenic subgroups. One can become "obsessed with the need
of finding clues, of giving meaning to what is going on in and around
oneself" (paranoia). Or, instead, one may choose "to comply with any
and all injunctions with complete literalness and abstain overtly
from any independent thinking" (hebephrenia). Or, finally, one can

"withdraw from human involvement" by becoming either unapproachable, autistic (stupurous catatonia), or by engaging in hyperactive behavior (agitated catatonia).[39] These basic reactions correspond, however, not only to the pretherapeutic situation, but also, partially, to the posttherapeutic and "mystical." A situation of "perfect adjustment" is, in a certain sense, a case, mild or not, of "hebephrenia," whereas the "silence of the saints" (āryatūsnīmbhāva) can be understood as a case of "catatonia." In any case, one should not romanticize psychiatric or "mystic" solutions. The creative aspect of pre- and posttherapeutic double-bind situations should always be kept in mind.[40] In fact, one argument against considering "mystical silence" as a form of catatonia is the existence of mystical poetry, in which, through the use of paradoxes and—what is usually less emphasized—tautologies,[41] tension and creativity are being preserved.

NOTES

1. See also G. Bateson, D.D. Jackson, J. Haley, J.H. Weakland, "Toward a Theory of Schizophrenia," Behavioral Science 1 (1956): 251-264, reprinted in Gregory Bateson, Steps to an Ecology of Mind (New York: Ballantine, 1972); G. Bateson, "Minimal Requirements for a Theory of Schizophrenia," Archives of General Psychiatry 2 (1960): 477-491; in Bateson, Steps, pp. 244-270; G. Bateson, D.D. Jackson, J. Haley, J.H. Weakland, "A Note on the Double-Bind 1962," Family Process 2 (1963): 154-161; Bateson, "Double Bind—1969," Steps, pp. 271-278. Two anthologies on the Double-Bind have been published: Paul Watzlawick and John H. Weakland, eds., The Interactional View: Studies at the Mental Research Institute Palo Alto, 1965-1974 (New York: Norton, 1977); and Carlos E. Sluzki and Donald C. Ransom, eds., Double Bind: The Foundation of the Communicational Approach to the Family (New York: Grune Stratton, 1978). For reviews see, P. Watzlawick, "Review of the Double Bind Theory," Family Process 2 (1963): 132-153; J.H. Weakland, "'The Double Bind Theory' by Self-Reflexive Hindsight," Family Process 13 (1974): 269-277, rep. in Sluzki and Ransom, eds., Double Bind, pp. 302-314, and in Watzlawick and Weakland, eds., The Interactional View, pp. 241-248; J. Haley, "Development of a Theory: A History of a Research Project," in Sluzki and Ransom, eds., Double Bind, pp. 59-104; D.H. Olson, "Empirically Unbinding the Double Bind: Review of Research and Conceptual Reformulations," Family Process 11 (1972): 69-94; R. Rabkin, "Critique of the Clinical Use of the Double Bind Hypothesis," in Sluzki and Ransom, eds., Double Bind, pp. 287-306; G. Abeles, "Researching the Unresearchable: Experimentation on the Double Bind," in ibid., pp. 113-149. For rather critical reviews see, Silvano Arietti, Interpretation of Schizophrenia (New York: Basic Books, 1974, 2nd ed.), pp. 97-101: "Double-Bind situations are a characteristic of life, not of schizophrenia...we must emphasize...that double-bind situations represent not necessarily pathology, but the complexity of human experience" (p. 99); cf. J.P. Spiegel and N.W. Bell, in S. Arietti, ed., American Handbook of Psychiatry (New York: Basic Books, 1959) I, p. 134.
2. Cf. Paul Watzlawick, J.H. Beavin, D.D. Jackson, Pragmatics of

Human Communication: A Study of Interactional Patterns, Pathologies, and Paradoxes (New York: Norton, 1967).

3. G. Bateson, et al., "Toward a Theory of Schizophrenia," Bateson, Steps, p. 207.

4. William F. Fry, Sweet Madness: A Study of Humor (Palo Alto: Pacific Books, 1963).

5. Widfried Kudszus, Literatur und Schizophrenie: Theorie und Interpretation eines Grenzgebiets (Tubingen: Niemayer, 1977); idem, Einleitung: Literatur und Schizophrenie: Forschungsperspektiven, pp. 1-12; idem, Literatur, Soziopathologie, Double-Bind: Uberlegungen zu einem Grenzgebiet, pp. 135-165.

6. Arthur Burton, "Schizophrenia and Existence," Psychiatry 23 (1960): 385-394; see also S. Arietii, Interpretation of Schizophrenia, pp. 99-101.

7. In Kudszus, Literatur und Schizophrenie:

Die immer noch verbreitete Ansicht, es handle sich bei dieser Theorie um eine pragmatische Deskription persönlicher Interpretationsprobleme, trifft bestenfalls deren Anfangsstadium und vereinzelte Epigonalformen. Im übrigen betrifft die Double-bind-Theorie komplexe multipersonale Situationen bis hin zu kulturell und gesellschaftlich determinierten Zusammenhängen.

Another interesting interpretation is the one given by Anthony Wilden and Tim Wilson, "The Double Bind: Logic, Magic, and Economics," in Sluzki and Ransom, eds., Double Bind, pp. 263-286.

8. Nāgārjuna, Vigrahavyāvartanī XXIX; cf. K. Bhattacharya, The Dialectical Method of Nāgārjuna (Delhi: Motilal Banarsidass, 1979), p. 23: "If I had any proposition (pratijñā), then this defect (dosa) would be mine. I have, however, no proposition (nāsti ca mama pratijñā). Therefore, there is no defect that is mine (tasmān naivasti me dosah)"; the Sanskrit text, edited by E.H. Johnston and A. Kunst (originally published in the Mélanges chinois et bouddhiques 9 (1951): 99-152) is reproduced in Bhattacharya's Dialectical Method of Nāgārjuna, part II, p. 29.

9. On prasaṅga(h), cf. Erich Frauwallner, Die Philosophie des Buddhismus (Berlin: Akademie Verlag, 1956, rep. 1958), pp. 221-222 (on Buddhapālita); cf. A.K. Warder, Indian Buddhism (Delhi: Motilal Banarsidass, 1980), p. 378.

10. Some recent publications on the Madhyamaka are J. May, "On Mādhyamika Philosophy," Journal of Indian Philosophy 6 (1978): 233-241; D.D. Daye, "Major Schools of Mahāyāna: Mādhyamika," in C.S. Prebish, ed., Buddhism: A Modern Perspective (University Park: Pennsylvania State U. Press, 1975); Samdhong Rinpoche, ed., Mādhyamika Dialectic and the Philosophy of Nāgārjuna (Sarnath: The Dalai Lama Tibetan Indology Series, 1977).

11. On this school, see Frauwallner, Philosophie des Buddhismus, pp. 224-241; A.K. Warder, Indian Buddhism, pp. 428 ff.; L. de La Vallée Poussin, "L'Auteur du Joyau dans le Main," Mélanges Chinois et Bouddhiques 2 (1932): 60-67; Y. Kajiyama, "Bhāvaviveka and the Prāsaṅgika School," in S. Mookerjee, ed., The Nava Nalanda Mahavihara Research Publication, vol. I (Nalanda: Nava Nalanda Mahavihara Research Institute, 1957), pp. 289-331; Nathan Katz, "An Appraisal of

the Svātantrika-Prāsaṅgika Debates," Philosophy East and West 26 (1976): 253-267.

12. On this concept see David Seyfort Ruegg, La théorie du Tathāgatagarbha et du Gotra: Études sur la Sotériologie et la Gnoséologie du Bouddhisme (Paris: École Française d'Extrême-Orient, 1969).

13. Cf. Etienne Lamotte, L'enseignement de Vimalakīrti (Vimalakīrtinirdeśa) (Louvain: Bibliothèque du Muséon, 1962), pp. 54-56 (56); Ruegg, La théorie du Tathāgatagarbha, p. 2. On the Ātman-Brahman, cf. K. Bhattacharya, L'Ātman-Brahman dans le bouddhisme ancien (Paris: École Français d'Extrême-Orient, 1973), p. 1; Paul Horsch, "Buddhismus und Upaniṣaden," Pratidānam: Indian, Iranian, and Indo-European Studies presented to F.B.J. Kuiper (The Hague-Paris: Mouton, 1968), pp. 462-477.

14. Paul Ricoeur, Le conflit des interprétations (Paris: Seuil, 1969), p 78.

15. For applications of semiotics to Buddhist and Indian studies see, Linnart Mäll, "Une approche possible du śūnyavāda," Tel Quel 32 (1968): 55-62; D.S. Ruegg, "Mathematical and Linguistic Models in Indian Thought: The Case of Zero and Śūnyatā," Wiener Zeitschrift für die Kunde Südasiens (1978): 171-181; idem, "The Study of Tibetan Philosophy and its Indian Sources," Proceedings of the Csoma de Körös Memorial Symposium, ed. L. Ligeti (Budapest: Adadémiai Kiadó, 1978), pp. 377-391, esp. pp. 388-389; A.M. Piatigorsky and D.B. Zilberman, "The Emergence of Semiotics in India: Some Approaches to Understanding Lakṣaṇā in Hindu and Buddhist Philosophical Usage," Semiotica 17 (1976): 255-265. For a semiotic approach to psychiatry see J. Ruesch, Semiotic Approaches to Human Relations (The Hague-Paris: Mouton, 1972).

16. On nirvāna, cf. L. de La Vallée Poussin, Nirvana (Paris: Beauchesne, 1925); Th. Stcherbatsky, The Conception of Buddhist Nirvana (Leningrad: Academy of Sciences of the U.S.S.R, 1927, and reprints); some information can be found in G.R. Welbon, The Buddhist Nirvana and its Western Interpreters (Chicago: University Press, 1969). Shozen Kumoi, "Der Nirvana-Begriff in den kanonischen Texten des Frühbuddhismus," Festschrift für Erich Frauwallner, Wiener Zeitschrift für die Kunde Südasiens, XII-XIII (1968-1969), pp. 206-213; B.S. Yadav, "Nirvana, Negation, and Nonsense," Journal of the American Academy of Religion 45 (1977): 451-471. On the paradoxicality ("double-bind" character) of Buddhism, see A.K. Chatterjee, "Insight and Paradox in Buddhist Thought," T.R.V. Murti Festschrift, (Emeryville: Dharma, 1977), pp. 141-151; A.L. Herman, "A Solution to the Paradox of Desire in Buddhism," Philosophy East and West 29 (1979): 91-94.

17. Nāgārjuna, Mūlamadhyamakakārikā, ed. J.W. de Jong (Madras: Adyar, 1977), p. 39.

18. Cf., for instance, St. Schayer, "Das Mahayanistische Absolutum nach der Lehre der Mādhyamikas," Orientalische Literaturzeitung (1935), cols. 401-415. A coincidentia oppositorum interpretation of the Madhyamaka goes against the fourfold negation of the catuskoti (see note 32, infra); indeed, an "absolutistic" interpretation goes against the letter and the spirit of this school.

19. Mūlamadyamakakārikā X,1,14.

20. Mūlamadyamakakārikā X,12,15.

21. Mūlamadyamakakārikā XII,1,16.

22. Cf. R.H. Jones, "The Nature and Function of Nāgārjuna's Arguments," Philosophy East and West 28 (1978): 485-502.

23. On the "oscillation" caused by paradoxical injunctions, see P. Watzlawick et al., Pragmatics of Human Communication, p. 217, and A. Wilden and T. Wilson, "The Double-Bind: Logic, Magic, and Economics," in Sluzki and Ransom, eds., Double-Bind, p. 276. The vaibhāsika and sautrāntika interpretations of nirvāṇa [referred to in our article "Tautology as Philosophy in Nicolaus Cusanus and Nāgārjuna," in Buddhist and Western Philosophy, ed. Nathan Katz (New Delhi: Sterling, 1981)] could be understood as the "oscillating interpretations caused by the paradoxical injunction that is nirvāṇa."

24. Nāgārjuna, Vigrahavyāvartanī, trans. K. Bhattacharya, see note 8, supra.

25. Vigrahavyāvartanī XXIV; Bhattacharya, Dialectical Method of Nāgārjuna, pp. 19, 26.

26. Vigrhavyāvartanī XXIX; Bhattacharya, Dialectical Method of Nāgārjuna, pp. 23, 29.

27. Watzlawick, Pragmatics, p. 244; the similarities between the double-bind approach and "mysticism" are mentioned by Ben-Ami Scharfstein, "Salvation by Paradox: On Zen and Zen-like Thought," Journal of Chinese Philosophy 3 (1976): 209-234, esp. 229. On the problem of "sense" and "nonsense" in Zen see T. Izutsu, "Sense and Nonsense in Zen Buddhism," Eranos 39 (1970): 183-215; Chung-ying Cheng, "On Zen (Ch'an) Language and Zen Paradoxes," Journal of Chinese Philosophy 1 (1973): 77-102; M.E. Levin, "Comments on the Paradoxicality of Zen Koans," Journal of Chinese Philosophy 3 (1976): 281-290, and the response by Cheng, "Rejoinder to Michael Levin's 'Comments,'" ibid., pp. 291-297.

28. Cf. Luciano L'Abate and Gerald Weeks, "A Bibliography of Paradoxical Methods in the Psychotherapy of Family Systems," Family Process 17 (1978): 95-98; M. Andolfi, "Paradox in Psychotherapy," American Journal of Psychoanalysis 34 (1974): 221-228; J.R. Newton, "Therapeutic Paradoxes, Paradoxical Intentions, and Negative Practice," American Journal of Psychotherapy 22 (1968): 68-81; D.E. Raskin and Z.E. Klein, "Losing a Symptom through Keeping It," Archives of General Psychiatry 33 (1976): 548-555; D.D. Jackson, "A Suggestion for the Technical Handling of Paranoid Patients," Psychiatry 26 (1963): 306-307; Watzlawick et al., Pragmatics, pp. 236-240.

29. Watzlawick et al., Pragmatics, pp. 247ff.

30. Cf. Gustavo Benavides, "Tautology as Philosophy in Nicolaus Cusanus and Nāgārjuna," in Buddhist and Western Philosophy, ed. N. Katz (New Delhi: Sterling, 1981).

31. Āryadeva, Śataśāstra, chap. X, "Refutation of the Void"; cf. Giuseppe Tucci, Pre-Diṅnāga Buddhist Texts on Logic from Chinese Sources (Baroda: Oriental Institute, 1929), p. 89; L. de La Vallée Poussin, "Le Nirvana d'après Āryadeva," Mélanges Chinois et Bouddhiques 1 (1931-1932): 127-135: "Lieu terrible, comment est-il objet d'affection? ... Si dans le nirvana manque toute inclination et toute chose aimable, le nirvana sera un lieu plus terrible que les choses impermanentes... On n'obtient pas le nirvana" (p. 129).

32. On the catuskoti see, A. Wayman, "Who Understands the Four Alternatives of the Buddhist Texts?" Philosophy East and West 27

(1977): 13-21; D.S. Ruegg, "The Uses of the Four Positions of the Catuṣkoṭi and the Problem of the Description of Reality in Mahayana Buddhism," Journal of Indian Philosophy 5 (1977): 171. (In this important study Ruegg refers to the semiotic approach of L. Mäll, as well as to the writings of Julia Kristeva. S.S. Chakravarti, "The Mādhyamika Catuṣkoṭi or Tetralemma," Journal of Indian Philosophy 8 (1980): 303-306; R.D. Gunaratne, "The Logical Form of Catuṣkoṭi: A New Solution," Philosophy East and West 30 (1980): 211-239.

33. Āryadeva, Catuḥśataka, chap. XIV: sad asat sadasac ceti sadasan neti ca kramah/ eṣa prayojyo vidvabhir ekatvadisu nityaśaḥ//21; cf. P.L. Vaidya, Études sur Āryadeva et son Catuhśataka (Paris: Geuthner, 1923), p. 114; trans. p. 159; also G. Tucci, "La versione cinese del Catuḥçataka di Āryadeva..." Rivista di Studi Orientali X (1923-1925), pp. 521-563 (557). Chapter XVI, 25: sad asat sadasac ceti yasya pakso na vidyāte/ upālambhaś cireṇāpi tasya vaktum na śakyate//25; Vaidya, Études, p. 128, trans. p. 167; Tucci, "La versione cinese," p. 567; also Ruegg, "The uses of the four positions," p. 9, note 39.

34. Helmut Hoffmann, "Das Kālacakra, die Letzte Phase des Buddhismus in Indien," Saeculum 15 (1964): 125-131; "Die Polaritätslehre des späten Buddhismus," Eranos 36 (1967): 361-378.

35. Paul Demiéville, Entretiens de Lin-tsi, Traduits du Chinois et Commentés (Paris: Fayard, 1972), p. 21.

36. Guy Bugault, La Notion de "Prajñā" ou de Sapience Selon les Perspectives du "Mahāyāna", (Paris: Institut de Civilisation Indienne, 1968), pp. 194-195; we find ourselves in complete agreement with Bugault's radical interpretation.

37. Demiéville, Entretiens de Lin-tsi, p. 104.

38. Ibid., p. 71.

39. Watzlawick et al., Pragmatics, pp. 218-219.

40. Cf. J.S. Kafka, "Ambiguity for Individuation: A Critique and Reformulation of the Double-Bind Theory," Archives of General Psychiatry 25 (1971): 232-239; L.C. Wynne, "On the Anguish, and Creative Passions, of Not Escaping Double Binds: a Reformulation," in Double Bind, eds. Sluzki and Ransom, pp. 243-250; also Ludwig von Bertalanffy, "General Systems Theory and Psychiatry" in American Handbook of Psychiatry, ed. S. Arietti (New York: Basic Books, 1966), III, chap. 43, rep. in L. von Bertalanffy, General Systems Theory: Foundations, Development, Applications (New York: Brazillier, 1969), pp. 205-221.

41. Joachim Seyppel, "Mystik als Grenzphänomen und Existenzial: Ein Beitrag zur Uberwindung ihrer Definitionen," DVJ 35 (1961): 153-183. Seyppel's is the only study of mysticism that emphasizes the importance of both paradox and tautology in mystical language.

N.B. Dr. Peter Sohn, Berlin, has brought to our attention the similarities between Homeopathic Medicine and the approaches that have been discussed above; see Samuel Hahnemann, Organon der Heilkunst (1st ed., Dresden, 1810; 6th ed., Leipzig, 1921; rep. Ulm, 1958), esp. p. 63. We have not been able to consult Georg Bayr, Kybernetik und Homöopatische Medizin (Heildelberg, 1966).

PARATANTRA AND PARIKALPITA AS EPISTEMOLOGICAL CONCEPTS IN YOGĀCĀRA BUDDHISM AND HOLOGRAPHIC PSYCHOLOGY[*]

Stephen Kaplan

The Problem as Context

This article begins by raising two questions: how do we see a world and where do we see a world. The questions of how we see a world and where we see a world are not separate inquiries. As we will disclose, they are interrelated questions whose resolutions are drawn from an understanding of the nature of perception. Perception is one of the fundamental problems within psychology upon which schools are compared to each other. Realist schools are differentiated from idealist schools and behaviorists are distinguished from rationalists over the question of perception. Perception, which is so fundamental to our existence as to be virtually definable of our existence, is an unresolved issue. It is the issue which will establish the context and the parameters for the ensuing discussion of holographic psychology and Yogācāra Buddhism.

Holographic psychology is a theory which is rooted in neurophysiology and neurophysiology is an empirical science. Yogācāra Buddhism is a form of Buddhism which is often classified as idealism. Immediately, our endeavor must confront the fact that holographic psychology and Yogācāra Buddhism are viewed as diametrically opposed in their fundamental presuppositions. Holographic psychology begins its work by focusing on neurological components and their functions, thereby affirming the existence and significance of objects and matter. On the other hand, Yogācāra Buddhism, understood as idealism or as idealistically inclined, discounts the existence and/or significance of objects and matter in favor of the existence and significance of mind and consciousness. The difference as stated between these two positions is metaphysical: it is a question of how reality is defined.[1] This alleged metaphysical difference is not however an obstacle to our comparative study. Our task is to unravel what each position says about the nature of perception, particularly, the nature of our perceptual images—how and where they arise. Holographic psychology may want to deny an ultimate status to consciousness, although this is certainly not evident from its leading spokesman, and Yogācāra Buddhism may want to deny the real existence of brains; but

---

[*]This article was first presented at the panel on Buddhist and Western Psychology, chaired by Nathan Katz, at the 1980 Annual Meeting of the American Academy of Religion, Dallas, Texas, November 6-9, 1980.

nonetheless, both focus upon the nature of our perceptual experience.
Thus we will unfold the confluence of Yogācāra Buddhism and holographic psychology by examining their understanding of perceptual experience, while accepting, for argument's sake, that this confluence
is rooted in diverse metaphysical positions. Our task is not to
tackle the metaphysical issue, although we may lay the foundation for
such an endeavor. Rather, our task is to show that both Yogācāra
Buddhism and holographic psychology maintain that our perceptual
experiences—the perceptual images which we experience—are mental
constructions which appear but do not exist anywhere. The confluence
between these two positions arises not as the result of the identity
of their metaphysical presuppositions; but rather it arises in spite
of the putative divergence of their metaphysics.

The relationship between our initial questions of how and where
we see a world and the significance of these questions can be il-
licited by citing the causal theory of perception and the contemporary Identity Thesis. The causal theory of perception informs us
that perception is dependent upon an uninterrupted causal sequence
commencing with the external object and terminating within the individual's brain. For example, what we see of the world is consequent
upon the reflection of light off an object and the transmission of
the reflected light to the eye(s) of the individual. The reflected
light forms an image on the retina. This image is subsequently
transformed into neurological patterns which can be relayed throughout the brain. The last element within this causal series is the
transmission of the neurological information to the appropriate
neurological centers for vision. This causal theory of visual perception terminates the sequence in the occipital lobe of the brain,
which is roughly speaking in the back of our heads. If at any point
in this series the sequence is interrupted, then the perception of
the visual object will not occur.

Understanding the nature of visual perception as a causal sequence originating at an external object and terminating in a
posterior section of our brain leaves us with the impression that the
last element of explanation in the question of how we see an object
is also the answer to where we see our image of the object. From
this perspective our seeing the image of the object occurs in the
occipital lobe—it occurs in the brain. Bertrand Russell has said:

> Whoever accepts the causal theory of perception is
> compelled to conclude that percepts are in our heads,
> for they come at the end of a causal chain of physical
> events leading, spatially, from the object to the brain
> of the percepient. We cannot suppose that, at the end
> of this process, the last effect suddenly jumps back to
> the starting point, like a stretched rope when it snaps.[2]

The Identity Thesis endorses the notion that "percepts"—perceptual images—are in our heads. The Identity Thesis states that consciousness is a brain process.[3] In other words, all that we normally
associate with our mental life is, in fact, claimed to be identical
with and hence reducible to particular brain states. Thus, following
upon the causal theory of perception, the Identity Thesis proclaims
that our seeing of objects is spatially and temporally identical with

particular brain processes. Our visual perception of an object takes place at the same time and in the same place as the appropriate neurological processes involved within the "last" element of the causal sequence. For the Identity Theorist, the seeing of the world is a brain process and this takes place within our skulls.

The contemporary Identity Thesis is telling us that we do not see the world as we believe we see the world. We do not see the world "out-there" in front of us. According to the Identity Thesis our perceptual life is a "Grand Illusion." The "Grand Illusion" is that we believe that we see things and hear things "out-there" or that we feel things at the point of contact between our body and the object, but we are told that this is not the case. We are told that the images that we see are not "out-there" in the world; but rather they are located within us. According to the Identity Theorist, only the naive and unsophisticated, who not understanding the role that the sense organs, the nervous system, and brain processes play in perception, believe that they are cognizant of the panorama that appears in the world before them—in front of them. It is the naive and unsophisticated who succumb to the "Grand Illusion" which makes us believe that what we see or hear we really see or hear "out-there" and not "in-here."

We can succumb to this call for scientific and philosophical sophistications expounded by the Identity Thesis, but that leaves us in the peculiar position of having to deny that which seems indubitable—that when I open my eyes, I look out and see a world in front of me. It is our unquestioned feeling that the visual-perceptual images which we have of the things in the world appear to be located within the world—to be located "out-there." Our visual perceptions, as well as our other sensory perceptions, appear to us to be projected. The term "projection of images" is intended to indicate that the mental images of which we become aware appear at the locus of that which we believe initiates the perception. For example, the feeling of a pain in my foot appears to be in my foot and not in my brain. The mental images of the people in this room appear out-there in front of me and not in my head. Our perceptual images seem to be projected. This notion of the projection of our perceptual, mental images leaves us with the idea that the "mind," at least as it refers to our perceptual images, is projected. The consequence of our acceptance of the apodictic feeling that perceptual-mental images are projected is the reversal of the proverb, "He is out of his mind." In the light of the notion of projection, it is more appropriate to say "he is out of his brain, but not out of his mind." His mind is constantly projected "out-there" when he perceives things "out-there."

We have questioned the Identity Thesis position that our seeing the world exists within our brains only to arrive at the position that our minds are out of our brains. We should realize that to accept the Identity Thesis is to accept the notion that when we drive down the highway at 50 miles per hour the sight of the car which we are tailgating takes place within our brain. How comfortable would we feel driving at 50 miles per hour when we realize that we are not looking out through our eyes, past the windshield to the car in front of us: but rather, the image of that car exists within our brains—within our occipital lobe? On the other hand, do we really want to say that our perceptual images are projected? Do we want to say that our minds are "out-there" while our bodies are "over-here?" The notion of the projection of the mind leaves us with the schizophrenic feeling that our individuality is bifurcated. The questions of how we see the world and where we see the world have answers, but these answers seem less than totally satisfactory.

The Buddha's Response

The questions with which we have been wrestling are certainly not new ones. In the Śūraṅgama Sūtra, the Buddha, in a dialogue with Ānanda, raises questions about the nature of perception and the perceiving, discriminating mind (citta). This issue is not a matter of idle sophistry. Rather, the Buddha says: "...if you do not know where lies the perception of sight and where the activities of the mind originate, you will never be able to subjugate your worldly attachments and contaminations."[4] According to the Buddha, how we understand our perceptual experience reflects our attitude toward and attachments to the world.

The crux of the dialogue between the Buddha and Ananda in the Śūraṅgama Sūtra centers upon the question of the locations of the discriminating, perceiving mind. The Buddha asks Ānanda, "Referring to your eyes and mind, do you know their secret hiding place?"[5] Ānanda has no trouble fixing the location of the eyes and the other senses: they are on the surface of the body. However, Ānanda's response that the perceiving mind is hidden within the body illicits a series of inquiries from the Buddha as to how the mind could be lodged within the body. Ānanda, recognizing the import of these questions, acknowledges that the mind is not within the body. Stirred by this conclusion, Ānanda postulates that the mind may be outside the body: like a lamp, the mind might illuminate objects outside the body. The Buddha points out that the mind and the body have a mutual correspondence. We are told, for example, that that which the mind perceives is often felt by the body and that which the body feels is perceived by the mind. Therefore, in light of this mutual correspondence, the Buddha finds the notion that the mind is outside the body unacceptable.

Ānanda, undaunted by these two rejections and still certain that the mind must have some location, posits that the mind is concealed in the sense organs like a crystal bowl covering the eyes. This suggestion fares no better at the wit of the Buddha than the first two ideas. Why, if the mind is concealed within the eye is it unable to see the eye? Ānanda then proposes that when the mind meets an object there is a manifestation of the mind. The Buddha responds:

Ānanda, your interpretation that the perceiving mind
has a substantiality of its own at the point where
the object and thought meet, would put fetters to your
mind. ...if we grant that your perceiving mind has some
kind of substantiality, is it one body or many bodies?
.... If it is one body, then if you bind one limb the
others will feel bound.... if the perceiving mind is

considered to be many bodies or involved in many bodies, it would mean that there must be as many personalities, and the question would arise, which of these localized perceiving minds rightly belongs to you.... Therefore, Ānanda, you must see that your suggestion that where-ever the mind happens to meet outer objects, there is localized a manifestation of mind is unreasonable.[6]

Another idea which is presented suggests that the mind exists between the sense organ and the object of sense. This notion has nothing to offer except the combined problems of the previous ideas. Thus, Ānanda is left to conclude that the perceiving mind has no location. The Buddha agrees to this saying:

Ānanda, as to what you have just said that the essence of the discerning, perceptive, conscious mind has no definite location anywhere the meaning is clear; it is neither in this world, in the vast open spaces, neither in water, nor on land, neither flying with wings, nor walking, nor is it anywhere.[7]

The Buddha has informed us that the mind does not exist within the body, it does not exist at the sense organs, and it does not exist outside the body. The mind does not exist in any of those locations: it cannot be said to exist in any locale. Yet the manifestations of the mind present the world of phenomena. We can perceive the world only when the perceiving mind manifests.[8] Thus, we experience the manifestation of the mind, but it does not exist as a substantial entity and it does not exist in any location. We now can ponder how the mind can manifest without existence and without location. It is with this question in mind that we turn to holographic psychology and Yogācāra Buddhism.

The Holographic Model

Holographic images appear yet they do not exist. We can see them; we can describe them; but we cannot locate them anywhere. They have no locus. Holographic images are the products of an optical-imaging technique known as holography: they are three-dimensional optical artifacts. Holography refers to the technique by which a coherent light source reflected off an object can be stored on photographic film and subsequently can reproduce an image of the object three-dimensionally. A hologram refers to the film upon which the information necessary to reproduce the complete image of an object is recorded. It is derived from the Greek words holos meaning complete or whole, and gramma meaning a writing. A hologram thus writes the whole, or we may say that it contains the whole picture. It contains the whole picture in the sense that the image of the object which is reconstructed has all the visual properties of the original scene.

Holographic images appear three-dimensional. They appear solid and tangible. Like our three-dimensional perceptual world, holographic images exhibit parallax effect. In other words, if a hologram reproduces two images, an anterior image which partially conceals a posterior image, one can change one's vantage point in order to see around the anterior image and thereby view the entirety of the posterior image. Parallax effect cannot be reproduced by photography. Photography, in contrast to holography, presents two-dimensional images which only offer one vantage point. Photography presents optical artifacts backed upon two-dimensional paper or projected upon a two-dimensional surface. Holographic images are not presented on any sort of two-dimensional surface. They appear as three-dimensional images.

The position of this paper is that holographic psychology offers valuable insights into the nature of our perceptual processes. Holographic psychology, with specific reference to perception, postulates that the manner in which the nervous system operates resembles the processes that describe holography.[9] In other words, this theory maintains that the neurological processes which play a role in perception can be described, as regards certain essential points, by the same principles as those which describe holography. The claim is that the mathematical formulations that describe holography are structurally identical to the mathematical formulations that describe the neurophysiological components which play a role in our perceptual lives. Holography produces holographic images: our brain and nervous system produce holographic-like perceptual images.

A brief description of how holograms are produced will help elucidate the nature of holographic images and will provide us with a background from which to understand holographic psychology.[10] In order to create a hologram, a laser beam is aimed at a half-silvered mirror which splits the beam. Lasers, and not ordinary sources of light, are used to produce holograms. Lasers are coherent light sources and do not contain the multiplicity of frequencies that compose ordinary light. Once the laser beam is split, half of the laser is used as a reference beam. The reference beam does not reflect off the object, but rather is directed toward the film. At the film, the reference beam will converge with the other half of the laser beam which is reflected off the object—the object or scene beam. The convergence of these two beams of light on the film create interference patterns. These interference patterns are like the ripples created by throwing stones into a pool of water. The waves will interact with each other setting up patterns of neighborhood interactions, known as superposition. The superposition—the intereference patterns of the two halves of the laser beam—is recorded on the film. This is the hologram. The interference patterns which the hologram records appear meaningless. No discernible object can be discovered by looking at the hologram. (In this regard, a hologram is also unlike a photograph in which, on the negative, an image of the object can be seen.)

In order to reconstruct an image of the original object, a light source of a similar nature as that which was used to construct the hologram is directed at the holographic film.[11] This illumination of the hologram will produce an image of the original object by reconstructing the original wave patterns that were reflected off the object. That which was originally coded onto the hologram in the form of interference patterns is decoded from the hologram by passing the reference beam through the hologram. Theoretically speaking, we can say that the superposition of wave forms onto a film can be mathematically analyzed by convolutional integers. These equations, such as Fourier equations, which describe the original interference patterns, are reversible equations. Therefore, the interference patterns coded onto the hologram can be decoded from the hologram so that the original pattern of light reflected off the object is reproduced. This process will allow us to see the holographic image.

The hologram, although it contains all the information necessary to reproduce the image, stores this information in interference patterns. Interference patterns and not images exist on the hologram. These patterns are spread across the entire hologram. Thus each part of the hologram contains all the information necessary to reproduce the whole image while the entire hologram only reproduces one holographic image. Any single part of the film can be used to reconstruct the entire holographic image.[12] One can rip a hologram in tenths and each piece still would be able to reproduce the entire image. In this context, we should note that the image which is reconstructed is never seen on the hologram since the image does not exist on the hologram. The image is always reconstructed from the interference patterns which are recorded on the hologram and this reconstruction process results in an image that always appears at a distance from the hologram. In other words, the holographic image always appears projected.

The type of holographic image with which we are concerned in holographic psychology is called a virtual image.[13] An understanding of the nature of the virtual image is essential if one is to understand the ensuing comparison. The virtual image is a type of holographic image such that, at the spot at which the viewer sees the image, there does not exist any light source already reconstructed from the hologram. In other words, if the holographic image appears to the viewer to be located in a space which is prior to the interference of the reconstructing reference beam with the holographic film, then the viewer sees the virtual image.[14] It must be realized that where the virtual image appears the reconstructing reference beam has not yet passed through the film from which the holographic image is produced. The process by which the virtual holographic image is reproduced—the passing of the reconstructing reference beam through the film—has not yet occurred and does not occur at the place where the viewer claims to see the image. Therefore, in the location in which the viewer claims to see the virtual-holographic image nothing has been decoded from the hologram: no image of any sort exists in the area at which the viewer claims to see the image. Nothing exists, yet something appears—the holographic image.

Holographic psychology posits that our perceptual and mnemonic images are constructed projections from neurological processes. These processes are structurally akin to the processes by which holographic images are created.[15] Therefore our perceptual images are like holographic images. Only an outline of holographic psychology can be offered here. A discussion detailing the complexities of the neurological components and the evidence in support of the holographic position as opposed to alternative theories is beyond the scope of this article.

Our outline of the holographic theory starts with the position that the sense organs, and their corresponding neural transmissions, record and convey their data in frequency domains. Little photographs and phonographs are not found floating around the nervous system. Rather the nervous system transforms information into frequency codes which maintains the relative harmonics of the information without the literal point-to-point correspondence which characterizes photographs and phonographs. These neural frequency codes are being compared to the laser--to a frequency of light. Second, the holographic position also proposes that an essential part of the nervous system's analysis of its neuronal messages transpires at the intercellular level--the junctional microstructure. The junctional microstructure refers to the interlacing network of axons and dendrites that connect neurons together at their synaptic intervals. Neuronal messages traversing this interlacing junctional network create multiwave front activities. The convergence of waveforms at the junctional microstructure produces the superimposition of neural patterns. These superimposed neural patterns are like the interference patterns created on a hologram by the convergence of the scene beam and the reference beam. Third, the interference patterns which traverse the junctional microstructure can be recorded into the junctional microstructure either permanently as memory traces or temporarily as the result of the hyperexcitability of the traversed region.[16]   This encoding process allows previous neural interference patterns to be accessible for interaction with subsequent neural transmissions. Thus, the configurational alterations of the junctional microstructure record the relevant data like the holographic film records the revelant interference patterns needed to produce holographic images. Finally, the interaction of the organism's encoded neural interference patterns with a current neural transmission from the sense organs produces perceptual images like those created from a hologram when a reconstructing reference beam is passed through it.

This holographic theory maintains that the production of perceptual images is consequent upon information from both the sense organs and existent, neural holographic patterns. Therefore, perceptual images are constructions. They are constructions reflecting not only the information received by the sense organs, but also the state (nature) of the organism that processes this information.[17] The constructed perceptual images are not to be found in the neural interference patterns which in no way resemble the images produced. Like holographic images the constructed perceptual images are projections. Thus, we perceive what we have constructed and our constructions appearing projected are believed to be independent, objective realities. The things appearing "over-there" are individual fabrications whose projected nature allows us to believe that they exist when in fact they only appear.

Yogācāra Buddhism: Paratantra and Parikalpita

The mind which manifests and the form (ākāra) in which it manifests is paratantra svabhāva. Paratantra is the presenting of our constructed-projected images (vikalpa). It is, according to Yogācāra Buddhism, one of the three aspects (svabhāvas) which describe the nature of experience. Paratantra literally means that which is dependent upon or subject to another. This svabhāva is the relative aspect: it is dependent upon causes and conditions (pratyaya).[18] Paratantra svabhāva is distinguished, on the one hand, from the parikalpita nature and on the other hand from the parinispanna nature. The former is the purely imagined nature. It is the mental fabrication which results from the imposition of names or signs and from the imposition of objectness or existence upon that which only appears (asatkalpa, abhūtaparikalpita).[19] The manner of cognizing paratantra which insists that that which appears is other than an appearance and is, in fact, imagined to be a real, external object (vastu) is parikalpita svabhāva.[20] Parinispanna is that manner of cognizing paratantra in which the falsely imputed objectness is realized to be never existing[21] and therefore the nonexistence of the duality of subject and object (grāhaka-grāhya) is uncovered.[22] It is that aspect which is without discriminations (nirvikalpa) and as such without impurities (samklesa). Parinispanna is the perfected nature and is identified with paramārtha.

Our explanation of the three svabhāvas is intended to illuminate our initial questions which focused upon developing an understanding of the nature of our perceptual images and the location of the perceiving mind. We are not concerned with the question of whether there are truly existent, solid material objects which stimulate our perceptions, whether there is a store-house consciousness (ālaya) which gives rise to our perceptions, or even whether there is a universal holographic domain from which all spatial-temporal objects and perceiving minds are explicated thereby providing the appearance of the world. Our intention is to employ the notion of the three svabhāvas, in particular paratantra and parikalpita, in order to understand our perceptual experience. It is with this in mind that we shall turn to Vasubandhu's Trisvabhāvanirdeśa.

Vasubandhu in the Trisvabhāvanirdeśa, a text devoted to the explication of the three svabhāvas, explains these three natures by comparing them to the construction of an illusory elephant which is conjured by means of a mantra.[23] "The elephant is the kalpita svabhāva, its form is the paratantra (nature) and the elephant which is not existent there is regarded as the parinispanna."[24] In the analogy, the paratantra svabhāva refers to the form (ākāra) by which and as which the elephant appears. "Something" is seen and what is seen is a mental construction (vikalpa) which is the form of the elephant. There is only an appearance; there is no elephant.[25] The form of the elephant is the asatkalpa (the unreal construction) of the mind. The mind (citta) constructs and projects this appearance (prātibhāsika) enabling it to be presented—to be present. Therefore, this presentation which is described as asat or abhūta (unreal) establishes the mind as that which manifests. Paratantra is the manifestation of the mind. It is the presentation of the asatkalpa.[26] These presented images are not other than the mind, yet the paratantra svabhāva appears with the nature of duality: it appears as the mind and the constructed image. But Vasubandhu tells us that ". . . this duality is completely nonexistent; there is only the appearance (of it)."[27] The duality cannot be real because all that has manifest is a mind. The appearance does not become other than mind. Thus paratantra svabhāva is that aspect of experience in

which the mind dependent upon causes and conditions constructs images. Herbert V. Guenther makes this point as follows:

> It is precisely this state which is indicated by the
> "relative," not the relation that holds between two
> terms or connects two events. It is a stage in which
> subject and object are given together because subject
> qua subject means to function, and to function means to
> relate oneself to an object which is given together with
> the subject as a possibility of positive and negative
> judgments. . . . It is important here to note that the
> "relative" (paratantra) is one unitary event, and it is
> not the relation between two things.[28]

Parikalpita svabhāva refers to the way or the manner in which
that which appears is taken or understood (yathākhyānam).[29] This
mentally fabricated aspect is the demand that the "unitary event" in
which the mind manifests as subject and object is the duality of a
subject encountering an object (grāhaka and grāhya as vastu).[30] The
imposition of the duality of subject and object separates that which
appears, for example, the ākāra of the elephant, from the mind which
is, in fact, the constructed, appearing ākāra of the elephant. In
other words, that which the mind manifests in paratantra svabhāva is
imagined in the parikalpita aspect of experience to be the objects
which are available for our perception (vastu); and hence, as objects
for our perception, they are imagined to be other than the perceiver.
Thus the "one unitary event" in which subject and object are presented is here imagined to be the duality of a subject facing an independent, existing object.

This imposition of duality can be understood to be problematic in
two ways. In one sense, the bifurcation of this "unitary event" into
the duality of subject and object allows one to assume that the object within this experience is a real, external object. In the case
of our analogy, the nature of parikalpita is to demand that there is
a real elephant. In the case of our normal perceptual experience,
the insistence that that which appears to us is an independently
existing, real object is parikalpita. Janice Willis frames this
issue rather clearly:

> It is here that we find the Yogācāra's important epistemo-
> logical point that in every ordinary cognition, what is
> cognized is not an accurate portrayal of an object exist-
> ing outside the mind but merely an object-like mental image
> (vijñaptimātra) of that; only a "conceptualized" object,
> one that is solely the product of constructive imagination.[31]

The second aspect of this parikalpita dilemma lies in the bifurcation of experience such that the subject who experiences is imagined to be distinct from that which is experienced. From this
perspective the issue is not whether there is a real elephant "over-
there" or an independent object "over-there" which is being directly
experienced. Here we can accept that there is no elephant "over-
there." We also can accept that what is normally experienced is not
an independent object "over-there" but rather a mentally constructed

image. However, the impositions of the parikalpita svabhāva are not
totally eliminated by removing the belief in the existence of the
elephant or in removing the belief in the experience of an independent object "over-there." For example, while accepting that there is
no real elephant "over-there," the parikalpita svabhāva still would
be operative by insisting that there is an "illusory appearance over-
there" apart from and independent from the subject. In other words,
even if one realizes that there is no real elephant "over-there,"
parikalpita svabhāva is still operative if we insist that there is an
illusory elephant "over-there"--at a distance from me, the subject
who sees it. There is no illusory elephant "over-there." Likewise,
there are no mentally constructed images of objects "out-there" which
we can then perceive from our vantage point "over-here." The mind
constructs appearances, be they the illusory elephant or images of
objects. These images are never independent of the mind. They are
never "over-there" to be perceived by the mind which is "right-here."
The belief that the images constructed by the mind appear to be located "over-there" as distinguished from the knower who is "right-
here" is the mental fabrication which describes the parikalpita
svabhāva.

Conclusion: The Confluence of Yogācāra Buddhism and Holographic
Psychology

We now can illustrate these two aspects of the parikalpita
dilemma in terms of our holographic model. In the holographic situation a three-dimensional image appears projected "out-there." The
first parikalpita mistake is the assumption that what is seen is a
real object. Those more sophisticated realize that there is no real
object existing "over-there." However, one who readily admits that
no real object exists "over-there" will still maintain that the image
of the object exists "over-there." The holographic image is believed
to be "over-there," apart from and independent of the seer; and
therefore, the image is imagined to exist there. It must be remembered that at the locus at which the image is seen--where the image
is said to exist--the light which reconstructs the image has not yet
passed through the film. The holographic image is seen as being in a
location which is prior to the interference of the reconstructing
reference beam with the holographic film. No "image-thing" exists
there.

Analogously, we have said that our perceptual-mental images are
constructed by holographic-like processes. These images do not exist
within the brain. Interference patterns that in no way resemble our
perceptual images exist within the brain. Nor do our perceptual
images exist "out-there." No "thing," no matter how ethereal, is
projected out of our brains and into the world "out-there" so that
they can then be perceived. There is no reason to assume some mysterious power by which mental images coalesce in front of us. No
such process exists within optical holography. Rather, we should
realize that our perceptual images, like images in a hologram, are
not such that we can affix a spatial location to them. Assigning
perceptual images a location is a mental fabrication.

At this point we again can say that that which manifests is para-tantra. It is dependent upon causes which lead to its arising and its arising is our mental constructions (vikalpa). Parikalpita re-fers to the way it appears or, we can say, the manner in which it ap-pears to us. Our mental constructions always appear to be located. Whether we believe we see real objects or mental images we nonethe-less see them as having a locus. However, our mental images have no more of a locus than do holographic images. Just as we cannot see the holographic image unless we see it somewhere, so also our mental constructions cannot be seen without seeing them as appearing some-where.[32] The imposition to the holographic image or to the mental-perceptual image is not part of that which has been constructed: the image has no location. The imposition of location is a mental fabri-cation: it is parikalpita svabhāva.

Thus we now can see that to ask where the perceiving, discrim-inating mind is located is to ask a question which is only applicable within the domain of parikalpita svabhāva. Or we can say that it is a question which only arises within the domain of the holographic-perceptual image which appears but does not exist. The image does not exist on holographic film, it does not exist within the brain and it does not exist "out-there" where it seems to appear. The imposi-tion of existence to that which appears and the imposition of loca-tion to that which appears are two sides of the same coin and both are fabrications of our imagination. Therefore, to ask about the lo-cation of the mind and its perceptual images is to fall prey to these fabrications--to the imagination which is parikalpita. We cannot establish the location of the mind because this notion that our per-ceptual images have location is merely a product of the imagination: it is parikalpita svabhāva and parikalpita has no existence. In conclusion, our problem is not to find an answer to the question which we have raised; rather, our problem is asking the question and demanding that it be a real question. The question is the pari-kalpita dilemma.

NOTES

1. Our enterprise is willing to acknowledge this metaphysical difference. However, I am not ready to defend it. First, I think that the label of idealism which has been applied to Yogācāra, in particular the Yogācāra of the Vasubandhu contingent, must be care-fully reexamined. Second, it is unclear whether the label of mater-ialism is applicable to holographic psychology when holographic psychology is viewed in the context of holographic physics as it pre-sently is being proposed by David Bohm and Karl Pribram. Bohm, a physicist, and Pribram, a neurophysiologist, are proposing a holo-graphic model which encompasses both physics and neuropsychology and which claims to overcome the distinction between materialism and idealism. See Karl H. Pribram, "The Problems Concerning the Struc-ture of Consciousness" in Consciousness and the Brain, ed. Gordon G. Globus, et. al. (New York: Plenum Press, 1976); and David Bohm, "Quantum Physics as an Indication of a New Order in Physics: Part B," Foundations of Physics 3 (1973).
2. Bertrand Russell, Analysis of Matter (New York: Power Publi-

cations, 1954), p. 320.

3. For a discussion of the Identity Thesis as it is being represented here see, for example, U.T. Place, "Is Consciousness a Brain Process?" in Introduction to Philosophy of Mind, ed. Harold Morrick (Illinois: Scott, Freeman and Company, 1970). Other works by U.T. Place, J.J.C. Smart, or James Cornman also would be helpful.

4. The Śūraṅgama Sūtra, trans. Wai-Tao and Dwight Goddard, A Buddhist Bible, ed. Dwight Goddard (Boston: Beacon Press, 1966), p. 113.

5. Ibid., p. 113.

6. Ibid., pp. 118–119.

7. Ibid., p. 121.

8. Ibid., p. 135.

9. The leading exponent of the holographic theory of the brain is Dr. Karl H. Pribram, Stanford University. This position is based upon the research both of Dr. Pribram and of numerous others. We should note that a theory of this magnitude which explains the nature of brain functions is not proven with one piece of evidence. This position is based upon the accumulated findings of many researchers and upon theoretical considerations which resolve previous problems within neurophysiology. Given the evidence and the theoretical considerations, the holographic theory of the brain appears to this author as a reasonable scientific position. For a full treatment of holographic psychology by this author see "Māyā, Mind and Holography" (Ph.D. dissertation, Temple University, 1980).

10. It should be noted that there are several types of holograms. The exact methods and means of production and of reconstruction vary according to the type. However, the purpose of the following account is to give an overview of holography, and therefore, we will avoid references to specific types of holograms except where essential.

11. Actually, it should be noted that a holographic image can be made to appear using any "reasonably coherent" light source as a reference beam. For example, the light from an ordinary light bulb which is not in phase can be used to present a holographic image.

12. When smaller and smaller sections of the original film are used to reconstruct the image, one decreases one's possible vantage points from which to view the image and one will lose some detail while the depth of focus increases.

13. Using a transmission hologram as an example, the presentation of the virtual image is produced when the holographic film is illuminated with a reference beam which makes the same angle with the hologram as the original reference beam made with the film. (We should note that if the reconstructing reference beam passes through the hologram at the same angle as the original scene beam, then a real image will be reproduced.) In the case of the virtual image, the reference beam when it illuminates the hologram will generate spherical waves which diverge. The divergence of the waves creates the appearance that the waves are generated from a focal point on the side of the hologram away from the viewer.

14. In addition to virtual images there are also real image holograms. The difference between them depends upon the manner in which the hologram is illuminated when reconstructing an image. Since our concern is with virtual images we will not digress into a

224

discussion of real images. For a discussion of this subject see
Irwin Stambler, Revolution in Light: Lasers and Holography (Garden
City: Doubleday & Co., 1972).

15. Pribram is not maintaining that all neurological processes
are holographic. It would be absurd to reduce the enormous complexity of all nervous system functions to one type of mathematical ab-
straction. This does not destroy the holographic theory; but rather,
it places it in a wider context. See Karl H. Pribram, "How Is It
That Sensing So Much We Can Do So Little?" in The Neurosciences:
Third Study Program, eds. Frances O. Schmitt and Frederic G. Worden
(Cambridge, Mass.: The MIT Press, 1974), p. 253.

16. For a full discussion of this process see: Karl H. Pribram,
Marc Nuwer and Robert J. Baron, "The Holographic Hypothesis of Memory
Structure in Brain Function and Perception" in Contemporary Develop-
ments in Mathematical Psychology, eds. R.C. Atkinson, D.H. Krantz,
R.C. Luce and P. Super (San Francisco: W.H. Freeman and Co., 1974).

17. For a concise description of the constructed nature of perception and opposing theories see: Karl H. Pribram, "Holography and
Structure in the Organization of Perception" in Images, Perceptions
and Knowledge (Dordrecht-Holland: D. Reidel Publishing Co., 1977),
pp. 171-178.

18. See Vasubandhu, Triṃśikā, verse 21, Sylvain Lévi, ed., Deux
Traités De Vasubandhu: Viṃśatikā et Triṃśikā (Paris: Librairie
Ancienne Honore Champion, 1925).

19. The term asatkalpa, appears frequently in Vasubandu's
Trisvabhāvanirdeśa; while abhūtaparikalpita is used in Madhyānta-
Vibhaṅga and commentaries. I take the terms to be synonymous and to
mean "nonexistent or unreal construction. There is a mental construction, but it is not real."

20. See Vasubandhu, Triṃśikā, verse 20, Sylvian Lévi, ed.

21. Vasubandhu, Trisvabhāvanirdeśa, ed. Sujitkumar
Mukhopandhyaya (Visvabharati: Visvabharati Bookshop, 1939), verse 3:
tasya khyāturyathākhyānaṃ ya sadā vidyamānatā/ jneyaḥ sa pariniṣpan-
nasvabhāvo 'nanyathāthātvataḥ// (Hereafter, this text listed as TSN.)

22. TSN, verse 33: dvayasyānupalambhena dvayākāro vigacchati/
vigamattasya niṣpanno dvayabhavo 'dhigamyate//

23. See TSN, verses 27-30.

24. TSN, verse 28: svabhāvaḥ kalpito hasti
paratantrastadākṛtiḥ/ yastatra hastyabhāvo 'sau pariniṣpanno isyate/

25. TSN, verse 27.

26. TSN, verse 4.

27. TSN, verse 27: māyākṛtaṃ mantravaśātkhyāti hastyātmanā
yathā/ ākāramātraṃ tatrāsti hasti nāsti tu sarvathā//

28. Herbert V. Guenther, "Saṃvṛti and Paramārtha in Yogācāra according to Tibetan Sources" in Two Truths in Buddhism and Vedānta,
ed. M. Sprung (Dordrecht-Holland: D. Reidel Publishing Co., 1973),
pp. 94-95.

29. TSN, verse 2: yatkhyāti paratantro 'sau yathā khyāti sa
kalpitaḥ/ pratyayādhīnavṛttitvātkalpanāmātra bhāvataḥ// Our interest
here is with the second half of the first line of the śloka.
Mukhopandhyaya translates it "the form in which it (the Appearance)
manifests itself is called the Imaginary;" I believe that the translation "the form in which it (Appearance) manifests" is somewhat misleading especially since in later verses the term ākāra is also

translated "form" yet it applies to paratantra and not kalpitah svabhāva. In light of this, I have taken the phrase yathā khyāti to mean how, or the way, it appears. This phrasing is intended to emphasize the subjective impositions of the kalpita-svabhāva.

30. Vasubandhu, Trimśikā, verse 20, Sylvain Lévi, ed.: yena yena vikalpena yadyad vastu vikalpyate/ parikalpita evāsau svabhāvo na sa vidyate/

31. Janice Dean Willis, On Knowing Reality (New York: Columbia University Press, 1979), p. 26.

32. This is why Vasubandhu says that paratantra exists as an error. (See TSN, verses 12, 15, 26). It appears as an error because it is only recognized when it appears as a subject viewing an object. It is also why Vasubandhu says that once you remove the imposition of parikalpita, then the form of duality which is paratantra vanishes. That is not to say that paratantra no longer exists but "it certainly does not appear as an error." (See TSN, verses 32, 33, 34).

PART FOUR

Psychological Implications of Tibetan Buddhism

Buddhist <u>rDzogs-chen</u> Thought and Western "Daseinsanalyse"[*]

Herbert V. Guenther

Western psychology has been plagued throughout its history by reductionism whose aim is to reduce all and everything to one level of explanation, be it rational or mechanistic. The root of this reductionism is to be found in the Cartesian dichotomy of <u>res extensa</u> and <u>res cogitans</u>, troublesome substances of an allegedly material and mental kind, which by some mysterious activity jump over a metaphysical gulf to project out of themselves what is then observed. So too it is absolutized into the dualism of body and mind, which strictly operate in what can be described as quantitative terms. Collateral to and supporting this reductionism is Newtonian mechanism, which reduces the world to trajectories of single material points whose impulse has to be provided from outside. Hence, within this framework of reductionism measurement and quantification are of paramount importance, and this has led to the illusion of objectivity.

The very utterance of the word "objectivity" has an almost magical effect on those who hear it and, unnoticeably, succumb to its lure with the attending myth of power and control. It is true, classical mechanism as a mere thought model has been and still is useful for specific and limited areas such as closed systems. It is also correct that reductionism is rational in the sense that it presents a certain organized knowledge which, however, leaves out and, as a matter of fact, ignores more than it can or is willing to accommodate within its limited perspective. The world in which man as participant lives, does not merely consist of the pure motion of a particle or a wave packet; it includes encounters, exchanges, challenges, and stimulations of many kinds. But what reductionism overlooks is that there are no closed systems, except perhaps in a laboratory, and that the world as we understand it—without understanding, awareness, cognition no world and, inversely, no understanding, awareness, cognition without world—is itself a hierarchy of levels. This is to say that it includes, or rather is suffused with, value. We live in what Sir Geoffrey Vickers has called the "appreciated world," and it is through value appreciation that man is actively and creatively

[*]This article was first presented at the panel on Buddhist and Western Psychology, chaired by Nathan Katz, at the 1980 Annual Meeting of the American Academy of Religion, Dallas, Texas, November 6-9, 1980.

participating in the shaping of his world.[1] Unfortunately, even
"value" is being reduced to the quantitative and quantifiable. For
instance, George Edwin Pugh's The Biological Origin of Human Values--
the title of which betrays the reductionist trend--talks about "primary values," which he understands to be food and sexuality, and are
claimed to be genetically fixed; and "secondary values," such as
ethics and other forms of behavior which arise when solving the
problems created by primary values. This recent reductionism is but
a restatement of the old reductionism propounded by Sigmund Freud and
Karl Marx who conceived of work (to get food) and sexuality (to be
relieved from the boredom of work) as making up all of man's life.

We may deplore and reject such "downward" reductionism into materialism, but nothing is gained by praising and accepting an "up-
ward" reductionism into what may be termed the world of the spirit.
As is well known this reductionism has found its most profound expression in German classical idealism, which also contributed to its
distortion so easily discernible in modern epistemological theories.
The latter have made spirit synonymous with "mental activity" or
"mind" and, in so doing, fallen heir to the prejudices on which ob-
jectivism has thrived. It is significant that this kind of reductionism has been enthusiastically pursued by those philosophers in
the West and East who thought that they would do their tradition a
service by repeating reductionist notions that had evolved in the
Western world. Because of the difficulties connected with mind,
psychology, which is true to its tradition and commitment to method
rather than attempting to solve the problem, has correctly rejected
mind in the sense of a Cartesian substance. Instead psychology has
dismissed mind in the sense of an interiority as an illusion and
adopted the attitude of chosen ignorance--talking about what it does
not know. Though not subscribing to this extreme kind of reductionism, C.G. Jung, one of the great figures in psychology and psychotherapy, is reductionist in maintaining a causal-mechanistic
perspective. This is seen in his notion of archetypes, hidden away
in the recesses of the mind and acting as causes and regulators or
forces of and in actual phenomena. Jung has borrowed the term
"archetypes" from Plato and developed their plurality as a world-
forming principle. In this respect he went beyond Plato, but not far
enough.[2] Therefore this reductionism--most conspicuous in the archetype which he calls the Self (the definite article betrays the hypos-
tatization)--also conceals the actual individual in his or her world
and, even more so, the dynamic emergence of the appreciated world
with the experiencer installed in it. It is this reductionism, so
common in all branches of science-and psychology wants to be counted
as a science--that, until most recently, has been responsible for a
certain dogmatism (Jung's theory of archetypes is no exception) and
for a widespread admiration for that which one does not understand in
order to make up for the emptiness created by dogmatic narrowness.
This is easily recognizable in Jung's expatiations on Far Eastern
thought of which he learned by hearsay from his friend Richard
Wilhelm, and which he promptly generalized--another way of reducing
all and everything to one level of explanation. It may be mentioned
in passing that Jung did not know any Oriental language and hence was
unable to check the validity (or even correctness) of what he was
told or read in dubious translations.[3]

Whether it be of the objectivist kind which attempts to reduce
man to one object among other objects or to the subjectivist kind
which reduces man to a subject separate from the world; in terms of
psychology, a mechanistic instinct-oriented reduction or a no less
mechanistic psychic-apparatus-oriented reduction—no reduction can
ever provide an adequate and hence more satisfactory understanding of
man's living reality. Moreover, there is always something inhuman
about reductionist interpretations which occur in many guises. I refer here only to the "here and now" spirit, which epitomizes the
autonomy of a static and stationary self. It was the dissatisfaction
with these mechanistic reductions that led Medard Boss to turn to
Ludwig Binswanger's "existential analysis" based on the thought of
Martin Heidegger with whom Boss eventually developed a close friendship. In order to avoid any misunderstanding concerning the term
"existential" it may be pointed out that Heidegger's so-called "existentialism" in no way resembles Jean-Paul Sartre's "existentialism,"
which is a mood psychology and basically a restatement of the obso-
lete Cartesian dualism. Boss' "Dasainsanalytic" perspective—the
term "Dasein" being one of the key notions of Heidegger's philosophy—enabled him to see man always installed in a world such that he
and the world are inseparable. Thus, not only is man shaping his
world and being shaped by it, man and world require each other for
their very being.[4] "Indivisibility" (dbyer-med) is one of the key
terms in rDzogs-chen thinking which, with its discussion of gnas-
lugs, a "being-there mode," in certain respects resembles the
Daseinsanalyse by Boss. Sensitive to Indian (Hindu-Buddhist) thinking and because of his knowledge of Hindi, Boss could acquire first-
hand information which made him see similarities and discrepancies.[5]

The importance of the "being-there mode" (gnas-lugs) forces us to
reconsider the validity of the traditional "what is" question. We
must admit that such a question fails to focus the problem of man's
living reality, which cannot be divorced from its ontological implication or simply be reduced to something ontic. The reductionist
question of the "what is" has to be replaced by a dynamic (evolu-
tionary) question which asks, "By which process is all that is, coming about?"; or using the more philosophical diction, "How does Being
occur without necessitating a reference to a thing occurring?" This
new question is of a higher order in the sense that the "how" makes
the "what" possible, though not necessarily in a temporal sequence.
From this viewpoint of the "how," Being avoids becoming narrowed down
or even reduced to a being and continues letting beings be; that is,
in more precise terms, letting beings come and be-there as what they
seem to be. Thus Being turns out to be pure process, more fundamental than its ephemeral end state or structure, which, by implication,
is resolved into dynamic structuring.

The new question about the "how" also brings into foreground the
significance and importance which experience-as-such has in a person's life. It, too, is not so much a "what" into which the act of
experiencing congeals, but a configurative ongoing process. Its dynamics exhibit, roughly speaking, dual characters. One aspect or
pole of attention is its prereflective, prepredicative, nonthematic
operation in the sense that its configurative complexity of interlacing constituents is as yet undisturbed by reflective, predicative,
thematic considerations which, as a rule, tend to change the texture

of the complexity of experience-as-such. It is this reflective, predicative, thematic aspect that constitutes the other pole of attention. It should be borne in mind, however, that this distinction
between two aspects of or directions in experience does not involve
the classical distinction between something at rest (a static phenomenon or thing) and something in motion (a dynamical phenomenon or
motion). Rather, the prereflective, prepredicative, prethematic is
itself already a "primary motility" existing for us as living beings
(who should, despite our being embodied, not be dealt with as static
entities) as a solicitation to be responded to. One is immediately
reminded of Nernst's discovery of "zero point energy," which states
that microphysical particles are still vibrating when, according to
the kinetic theory of matter, they should be completely at rest.
This also brings to mind de Broglie's waves whose oscillations can
hardly be interpreted as vibratory displacements of corpuscular entities. This analogy from modern physics may help to clarify and understand the unity of what is termed the "initially (atemporally)
pure" (ka-dag) and the "spontaneously present" (lhun-grub); the first
comparable to "zero point energy," the latter to "vibration" and
"radiation" which as pure energy, is spontaneously present. The
analogy becomes even more poignant when we take into account that
what is termed "initially (atemporally) pure" is also stated to have
nothing about it that would enable us to pinpoint it as either this
or that. The best we can say about it is that it is open-dimensional
(stong-pa), having a field character (dbyings) and being an opening-
up (go-'byed).[6] That which has been termed "spontaneously present"
is also stated to be "luminating" or "radiant" (gsal-ba) pervasive of
the whole "field" of Being. Furthermore, when it is stated that the
"initially (atemporally) pure" and the "spontaneously present" are
indivisible (dbyer-med), this can only indicate the fusion of two
contrary concepts into a single dynamic notion, which in its very dynamics is an ongoing process. This opening up (stong-pa) and luminating (gsal-ba) in their indivisibility (dbyer-med) tallies with
what in Daseinsanalyse is termed "Lichtung." Indeed none of its
English renderings by openness or clearness can convey the dynamics
of the German noun.

Included in this indivisibility of the opening up and the
luminating-illumining is what is termed "excitatory intelligence"
(rig-pa)[7] which is as much opening up as it is luminating-
illumining. In this sense it can be said to comprise both resonance
and a tuning in to the dynamics of Being, and being its dynamic ener-
gizing principle. It is this "excitatory intelligence" that relates
the universe to the individual as the experiencer of the universe,
and also relates the experiencing individual to the universe. In
resonating with the universe man also becomes responsible for the
universe. Thus each individual is a complete universe and the multiplicity of individual universes is the direct outcome of the iso-
tropic multifrequenced lumination eliciting the appropriate resonance
and, by implication, also dissonance.

The atemporal, dynamic ground or reason for man's being-in-a-
world-by-being-his/her-world is a vector equilibrium referred to by
the terms "facticity" (ngo-bo), "actuality" (rang-bzhin) and "resonating concern" (thugs-rje).[8] Each of these vectors—meaning-bearing
connectives, not eternal essences—has its specific modality such

that facticity is an opening up, actuality is lumination, and resonating concern is excitatory cognitiveness. Klong-chen rab-
'byams-pa says of these world-experience-occasioning vectors:[9]

> Since in the facticity (of Being) which is initially
> (atemporally) pure, (the actuality [of Being] which is)
> spontaneously present, is there as lumination from deep
> within (Being), the excitatory intelligence of (Being's)
> facticity which is initially (atemporally) pure--this
> facticity constituting one aspect of the indivisibility
> (of the atemporally pure and the spontaneously present)
> is such that it is neither substance nor quality. In
> (this facticity-cum-actuality) the subtle sheer lucency
> of (Being's) actuality which is spontaneously present, is
> there as an inner lumination. (That is to say), the fac-
> ticity of (Being's) coming-into-presence remains open
> (opening-up) and the actuality of the opening-up is lum-
> ination, the energy of this lumination is the excitatory
> intelligence. (Thus) the gestalt (sku) (through which
> Being expresses itself in its being cognized) and the
> pristine cognition (ye-shes) (which is cognizing Being's
> gestalt) have been such that since their atemporal begin-
> ning they could not be added to or subtracted from each
> other. This is what is meant by the indivisibility of
> Being's facticity, atemporally pure, and Being's actuality,
> spontaneously present.

In support of this presentation Klong-chen rab-'byams-pa quotes
the Rig-pa rang-shar chen-po'i rgyud (p. 632):[10]

> The ground is said to be twofold:
> The ground as ultimate (in being) initially (atemporally)
>   pure, and
> The ground as variety (in being) spontaneously there;

the Kun-tu bzang-po klong-drug-pa'i rgyud (p. 176):

> As to (Being's) facticity, (this is) initially (atemporally)
>   pure (and hence)
> As to (Being's) actuality, (this is) spontaneously
>   present;

and the Mu-tig phreng-ba zhes-bya-ba'i rgyud (p. 513):

> (Being's) facticity, initially (atemporally) pure
>   defies any predication;
> (Being's) actuality, spontaneously present, is complete
>   as to any (auto-)presencing.

This vectorial triad constitutes a unity--unity always implies
more than one--and its dynamics can be seen as an identity transformation of Being such that Being's auto-presencing is Being itself. A
difficulty may seem to arise with the manner in which actuality and
resonant concern are related. Does Being's actuality give rise to a

resonating concern? Or does the resonating concern come first,
causing the multifrequenced lumination of Being's actuality? Indeed
we cannot sort out what is "cause" and "effect," nor do we have to.
All we can do is to compute the probability of what forms the fluctuations will assume. Because of the importance this triad has in
the dynamics of what we have termed experience-as-such, it may be
graphically stated as follows:[11]

(Being's) facticity (ngo-bo)

actuality (rang-bzhin) ⟵⟶ resonating concern (thugs-rje).

But while the use of nouns easily lends itself to a concretiza-
tion into "things"--after all, nouns stand for things--the intercon-
nectedness can be more appropriately indicated by descriptive
adjectives, which can be used without there being any "thing" having
the properties so described. There are two sets. The one may be
said to have ontological implications and is as follows.

initially (atemporally) pure (ka-dag)

spontaneously present (lhun-grub) ⟵⟶ all encompassing (khyab-pa).

It will be remembered that any resonating concern is, in terms of
a response to a challenge, a total response; it is excitatory (which
is characteristic for every living organism) and such excitatoriness
is cognitive (rig-pa). Hence the term "all encompassing," that is,
including everything without being terminated by anything, and "ex-
citatorily cognitive" such that the universe can "think itself into
existence as a standing out in profile," are interchangeable. This,
then, points to the operational or functional character of Being:

opening up (stong-pa)

luminating-illumining (gsal-ba) ⟵⟶ excitatory (rig-pa).

Reflection on these diagrams shows that concrete man may be seen
as a feedback circuitry wherein the locally operative forces are
structurally regenerative and restabilizing so as to cope with continuous complex processes.

Of specific importance is what has been variously termed "resonating concern," "all encompassing" or "excitatory," each in its own
way highlighting intelligence as, if we may say so, the basic stuff
of the universe. This "excitatory intelligence" indicates the fact
that excitation lies at the root of every aspect of actual cognition;
it also points out the inherent capacity of any living organism or
system to be either in a more excited or less excited state. Excitation is intimately connected with and related to radiation, which is
described in terms of light values or "pure colors," representing a
force field reflecting the level or intensity of excitation. Con-
comitantly, excitation is related to feelings of pleasure and happi-

ness--an increase in excitation leads to pleasure and, quite literally, also radiates into its environment. Thus in a more excited state such as, for instance, love, a person is less aware of the object of his love as a means to a personal end; rather, he is more aware of its intrinsic value and uniqueness, defying any attempt to subsume it under distinct thematic categories. Therefore, the more excited state is a total response in harmonious vibration. Its cognitive operation is termed ye-shes, "pristine cognition."

In marked contrast is the less excited state whose cognitive operation is termed sems--as this term renders the Indian term citta, it has usually been translated as "mind," although the indigenous works dealing with citta make it abundantly clear that it is a term for what we nowadays call a feedback mechanism. In relation to ye-shes it presents the organism's excitatory capacity as having dropped to an all-time low and approaching a state of random behavior as exemplified by a human being swayed by wayward emotions. Any response on this level is a very narrow one. It prescinds from man's Being-ness and ultimately reduces him to a mechanical device, hailed in some circles as the last word about man's existence. On this level, whatever is perceived is perceived in the subject-object relation-ship in which everything serves as a means to a subjective end. Pre-cisely because this state prescinds from man's humanity it has been experienced and described as a going astray ('khrul-pa), a becoming lost in a world where, not merely figuratively, the light has gone out. A representative of such a state is termed sems-can "having a mind," that is, he or she being a sentient being. However, it should be noted that the term "sentient being" (sattva) is the Indian equiv-alent for the Tibetan sems-can; while the Indian term emphasizes a static notion of "being" (sat), the Tibetan term emphasizes the dy-namics of a feedback operation (sems). In any case, anyone, whether we conceive of him as an ontic being (sattva) or as someone having a mind (sems-can), is inexorably drawn into a divided state in which one pole or construct becomes the subject or ego and the other pole becomes the object. Such a divided state which proliferates into further divisions and subdivisions, is the outcome of a decline in excitation which involves a decrease in pleasure. Therefore "having a mind," which is tantamount to lacking pleasure, constitutes what is so aptly termed samsāra--a running around in circles, a groping in the dark, an unceasing source of frustrations. It is a total situ-ation and as such totally different from a world or universe in which excitation is operative. This does not mean that samsāra is totally without excitation--if this were the case samsāra would be a closed equilibrium system with monotonously increasing entropy coming to a dead end as both physical and spiritual death. That samsāra has not yet done so is ample evidence that it is not a closed system. Actually, samsāra is merely a decline in excitation, not its absence; hence it can be recharged or revitalized. This recharging, in over-simplistic terms, is a tuning-in into the very dynamics of Being and may be initiated by the system itself when it has reached a critical point.

The apparent contrast between excitation and loss of excitation reflects complements, not opposites, which remain separate from each other. The world of excitation in which pristine cognition (ye-shes) operates and the world in which mind (sems) operates--a low level stirring of excitation, if not a near equilibrium state of dullness (gti-mug), citta, avidyā, moha being synonymous--are fluctuations of the openness of Being such that each world emerges out of and presents the interaction between Being's presence and resonating concern with it.

The emergence of a state of which it is possible to say that it "has a mind" and which is felt as a deficiency state, is thus seen as a "vacuum fluctuation." It comes out of Being's openness and itself dynamically presents a continual and pulsational flux of sensations, perceptions, feelings, all of them setting up certain resonances. Selectively they accommodate certain aspects of the environing field in which they operate; gradually they establish the relatively permanent demarcation of a perceiving, apprehending subject and a perceived, apprehended, or apprehendable domain in which the perceiving subject's body is one among many other objects. In this process which goes on playfully, creatively, even aesthetically (at first), a map is drawn up which henceforth will enter and shape all future perceptions in a thematic (and representational) framework. Part of this play is the creation of the appearance of separate, sequential instances or frames of reference. Pursuing its own game this creative play is forgetting or becomes progressively unaware of the fact that it is playing a trick on itself. It is in "moments" of being-in-a-less-excited-state that objects as relative to a subject are construed and avidly sought, while in "moments" of being-in-a-more-excited-state this dichotomy is suspended in what can only be indicated by the paradox of there being something which is not even something. This is because it is not relative to anything at all and hence cannot even be referred to as a "moment," since it was already before there was any time. Thus a more excited state and a less excited one are meanings which the play takes on in ever shifting perspectives. From one perspective the play may be seen as a fluctuation or pulsation within a certain framework; from another perspective as a play engaged in by Being on itself--ceaselessly going on like waves in the ocean with their crests and troughs, all of them "contained" in the ocean whose pulsations they are. And so, what in a wave are its crest and trough, are in a human being's existence nirvāna, the light that shines, and samsāra, the light that has gone out.

Since excitation is cognitive, any decline in excitation is a loss in cognition and corresponding lowering in the existential mode. Thus:[12]

> By not recognizing the emergence of Being's auto-presencing from out of Being's (openness), the construct of an apprehending subject (or ego/Self) is generated and thereby one roams about in samsāra.
> By not recognizing the five distinctive (frequencies in) the glow of Being's (actuality) as a self-(present) glow in five pure colors, one becomes involved in (the duality of) an objective situation and owner of the objective situation, an apprehendable (object) and apprehending (subject) and thereby Being's auto-presencing is set up as the deceptive presence of samsāra (such that):
>   (a) by not recognizing Being's facticity as open, (its

pervasive) excitatory intelligence does not break from (and rises above) this ground;[13]

    (b) by not recognizing Being's actuality as luminating, one goes astray into the body (as lived by a person) and (the world of) physical objects;

    (c) by not recognizing Being's resonating concern as ceaselessly operative, (all) understandings (that go with such concern) turn into the feedback mechanism "mind";

    (d) by not recognizing Being's dynamic potential as constant, its dynamics is turned into the defeat (of being static); and

    (e) by not recognizing Being's charismatic activity as unlimited, one lingers on and roams about in the heights and depths of samsāra and is engrossed, like in a dream, in the many deceptive presences of individual bodily existences, the four types of birth-forms, the (individual's) status (in such a world), and the pleasures and sorrows (that go with misconstruing Being's activity as personal acts).

This lengthy passage again emphasizes the existential problem of how it is that man finds himself in a world—a total situation. It also implies that man is a being who is both an object in the world among other objects and also a subject for whom the world is the world. Here, the "indivisibility of openness and excitatory intelligence" (rig-stong dbyer-med) provides a cue. The inherent dynamics of the intelligence which permits it—quantum-like—to jump to a higher state of excitation or to drop to a lower state, is truly an excitation of the field, the openness of Being. Hence this "intelligence" is in no way independent of it. This means that man's being is a being-to-the-world, an opening up, as well as a presence-to-himself. For if man were (as subject) unaware of this being-to-the-world and opening-up-to-Being, the world (as object) would not be for him. It also follows from the above that any decline in excitatoriness, a stepped-down "intelligence" involves a narrowing of the field, a loss in openness. Hence what we call mind (sems), which is but stepped down excitatoriness (ma-rig-pa), operates in narrowly circumscribed domains (yul). In a certain sense, it also operates through a medium which, for us as embodied beings, is our body (lus)—not as it is known by the anatomist or physiologist, but as it is lived as the base of operations. Inasmuch as the domain which we call world is closed-in openness and so too what we call mind is stepped-down excitation, we may see in this feature a similar relationship as the one which exists between nonthermal radiation (which is spread over a wide range of wavelengths) and thermal radiation (which is strongly peaked to a narrow range of wavelengths), as well as radiant energy and ponderant energy (mass).

Conversely, stepped-up excitation termed "pristine cognition" (ye-shes) is pervasive of its "field" in the latter's sheer lucency. This pristine cognition, too, is intentional in character but unlike mind it does not intend objects, but formal gestalts (sku) through which the meaningfulness of Being becomes comprehensible. It must be remembered that wherever there is cognition—in rdzogs-chen thought it is the excitation of the field "Being" and hence everpresent—there is meaning involved; on the stepped-up level of excitation it is commensurate with Being itself. This is indicated by the recurrent phrase that sku (formal gestalt) and ye-shes (pristine cognitiveness) can neither be added to nor subtracted from each other as separate entities. When it is further stated that, in phenomenological diction, sku is the founding stratum (rten) and ye-shes the founded (brten-pa), the two statements together point to the fact that, in terms of a living individual, man's body (whether as a "thing" or a gestalt) is itself coexperienced simultaneously with the sensuous perception of the content such as, for instance, his "environment" (the domain of objects) or the very meaningfulness of Being-qua-Existenz. On the other hand, Existenz (as formal gestalt, sku) or man's body (lus) is that with which a cognition takes place and by means of which what is perceived is recognized in a meaningful manner (ye-shes) or in a manner which becomes ever more meaningless (sems). Graphically this is as follows:[14]

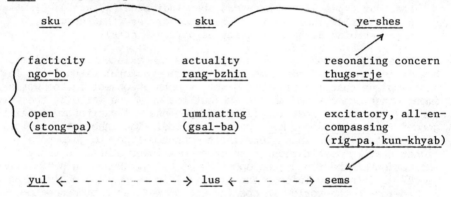

	sku		sku		ye-shes
facticity		actuality		resonating concern	
ngo-bo		rang-bzhin		thugs-rje	
open		luminating		excitatory, all-encompassing	
(stong-pa)		(gsal-ba)		(rig-pa, kun-khyab)	

yul ← - - - - - - - - → lus ← - - - - - → sems

This diagram shows that there is a close relationship between rdzogs-chen ideas (open/opening up, luminating-illumining, being-there mode) and Boss' key terms: world-openness, clearing, world-disclosing, Dasein. It also shows that on the level of what is rendered as "mind" (sems) there is, from the viewpoint of Being as a dynamic system, a marked self-constriction and self-narrowing of the openness to the world, that is, Being as a whole. It should be noted that a system can be anything of interest: a geometric figure, a fundamental particle, a crystal, a plant, a human being, the earth, the whole universe; it can be abstract or concrete, finite or infinite, static or dynamic. According to Boss, self-constriction is most conspicuous in mental patients—according to rdzogs-chen thought we all might be listed as mental patients with various and varying degrees of narrowness. Furthermore, the diagram also bears out the fact that man is not an isolated entity (a windowless monad of a Leibnizian or Cartesian type), but rather is always in-and-with-(a)-world or, as Boss sees it, man is fundamentally open (stong-pa) to the world and also in the relations to world (including man's fellow beings). Therefore, man's relatively bounded state can be overcome precisely because this possibility is ever-present as the cognitive-spiritual thrust (shes-rab) whose development ensures the transition from a stepped-down excitation (ma-rig-pa—avidyā is not the negation of vidyā but merely is "not-quite-what-it-could-be") to a "stepped-up" excitation, which approximates the "stuff of which the universe is made"—pristine cognitiveness (ye-shes; the Indian equivalent jñāna, does not convey the atemporal primordiality as indicated by the Tibetan ye in ye-shes). However, rdzogs-chen thought goes beyond Daseinsanalyse in suggesting that not only man but the entire universe can be regarded as a vacuum fluctuation. This image represents a spontaneous plus/minus polarization of the vacuum in such a way that the sum of all values over the whole fluctuation always remains zero.[15]

NOTES

1. Geoffrey Vickers, Values Systems and Social Process (London: Tavistock Publications, 1968). Quoted in Erich Jantsch, Design for Evolution (New York: George Braziller, 1975), pp. 106ff., 189ff.

2. For an assessment see Carl Friedrich von Weizsacker, The Unity of Nature (New York: Farrar-Straus-Giroux, 1980), pp. 248ff.

3. A trenchant critique of Jung's incomprehension of Eastern thought is offered by Hans Jacobs, Western Psychotherapy and Hindu-Sadhana (London: George Allen & Unwin, Ltd., 1961), passim.

4. For a general account of Medard Boss' work, see Donald S. Valle and Mark King, Existential-Phenomenological Alternatives for Psychology (New York: Oxford University Press, 1978), pp. 308ff.

5. Medard Boss, A Psychiatrist Discovers India (Calcutta: Rupa Co., 1966).

6. Zab-mo yang-tig II,102; mKha'-'gro yang-tig II,70; Theg-mchog rin-po-cha'i mdzod I, 387f.

7. mKha'-'gro yang-tig I,462.

8. Zab-mo yang-tig I,213, 225, 286, 289ff, 365. Theg-mchog rin-po-che'i mdzod I,391; II,19. Tshig-don rin-po-che'i mdzod, p. 28. mKha'-'gro yang-tig II,71, and elsewhere in rdzogs-chen literature.

9. Theg-mchog rin-po-che'i mdzod I,278.

10. This and the following work are to be found in rNing ma'i rgyud bcu bdun. Collected Nyingmapa tantras of the Man nag sde class of the Atiyoga (rdzogs chen) (New Delhi: Sanje Dorje, 1973), vols. 1 and 2, respectively.

11. Here and in the following diagrams, ‖ means an identity transformation, and ⟵⟶ means complementarity as well as symmetry transformation. On these technical aspects see Joe Rosen, Symmetry Discussed, Concepts and Applications in Nature and Science (Cambridge: Cambridge University Press, 1975).

12. Zag-mo yang-tig II,71.

13. sems or ma-rig-pa.

14. Here ↗ means "stepped-up excitation"; ↙ means "stepped-down excitation"; ‹- - - - - -› means representational, thematic fragmentization; and ⌢ means symmetry transformation.

15. For a scientific view of this idea see Edward P. Tryon, "Is the Universe a Vacuum Fluctuation?" Nature 26 (1973): 386-387.

On the Phenomena of the "Feminine" according to
Tantric Hagiographical Texts and Jungian Psychology

Nathan Katz

I. The Question: Its Scope and Our Methodology

It was no accident that when Oxford Orientalist W.Y. Evans-Wentz
brought to Western awareness some obscure ritualistic and yogic
translations from Tibet in 1927 he asked the great Swiss Psychiatrist, Carl Gustav Jung to provide introductions and psychological
commentaries for two of the four volumes he published. There are, on
the apparent level at least, striking similarities between Jung's
psychological theories and Tibetan Buddhist thought. It shall be the
purpose of this article to see if these similarities, intuitively apprehended by Evans-Wentz (and to a lesser degree by Mircea Eliade and
others), are merely superficial resemblances or if they go deeper.
Although most scholars of Tibetan Buddhism today would find
Jung's a dubious hermeneutic indeed, it is our intention to take up
these questions again. In order to do so, we shall not concern ourselves overmuch with Jung's own attempts at interpreting Tibetan Buddhism for Western audiences; we are not so concerned with Jung as a
hermeneutic for Tiben texts as we are with comparing two more or less
systematic human images, as taken from Jung's and Tibetan writings.
Our sources, therefore, shall be Tibetan hagiographical texts and
Jung's specifically psychological writings, leaving his ventures into
Eastern thought more or less to the side. Our purpose in so doing is
to avoid fitting Tibetan thought into Jungian categories, which tends
to become an extremely monological methodology. Rather, by treating
each as systems on their own (and not merely applying the categories
of one onto the other), we would hope to develop a dialogue between
them, thereby avoiding superficial or prejudiced comparisons, and to
arrive at some fundamental issues with which both Jung and the
Tibetan writers are concerned.
The focus of this article shall be on the phenomena of anima
(Jung's "female within male") and mkha' 'gro ma (Skt. ḍākinī), the
demoness-like beings who magically inspire and initiate Vajrayāna
adepts to whom Herbert V. Guenther has applied Karl Jasper's term,
"ciphers of transcendence."[1] After delineating the basic concepts
involved in understanding both the anima and the mkha' 'gro ma, we
shall consider three areas in which they appear to overlap: (1) the
function of inspiration; (2) their position in the subject/object (or
conscious/unconscious) dichotomy; and (3) the symbolic concreteness
(in this case, of contrasexuality) of which both Jungians and
Tibetans are fond.

II. The Rationale for a Discussion of Jung and Buddhism

For Jung and all schools of Buddhism, over-identification with the ego is the fundamental human problem. Ego as a reference point for relation with the external world is flatly denied by Buddhism; Jung would have us recenter our personality at a point which "....no longer coincides with ego, but...midway between the conscious and unconscious."[2] When there is an unwarranted identification of self with the persona (personality as presented to the world), which by its nature excludes the unconscious, the unconscious intrudes upon consciousness and neurotic symptoms develop. Jung's solution would be to break down the narrowly defined persona, with its insistence upon ego as its center, thereby expanding and restructuring the notion of self to include unconscious archetypal materials and relocating its center as separate from the conscious ego. Thus our problem, according to Jung, is not ego per se but the erroneous identification of self with ego, the former uncontainable in the latter.

Buddhism would accept Jung's analysis of the problem in so far as it goes. Buddhism agrees that man falsely identifies with ego; yet upon closer analysis finds ego to be totally lacking. Unlike for Jung, the problem is not, as has often been said, that humans have an ego; the problem is ego itself. Buddhism does not speak of the destruction or relocation of the ego; rather, it asks us to see that one may be in the world without continual reference to some point of relation between self and other. Whereas the individuated person, according to Jung, becomes conscious of archetypal images in relation to the conscious ego, the Buddhist ideals (arahant, bodhisattva, mahāsiddha) deny the possibility of such a relation entirely and speak rather of a spontaneity of cognition-action without reference to self or other. In the Vajracchedikā prajñāpāramitā sūtra,[3] for example, the bodhisattva (the ideal of Mahāyāna Buddhism) is admonished to produce the cognition-action of nonabidingness; that is, in leading all sentient beings to nirvāna (the goal of the bodhisattva), no thought of beings, nirvāna, or self may arise. This seemingly paradoxical statement means that once the category of relation is existentially negated, one may be in the world without any reference points to relate self and other. This mode of cognition-action is at the same time the culmination of the perfection of wisdom (prajñā-pāramitā) and the generation of the great compassionate heart (mahakaruṇācitta), indicating that the possibility of spontaneous cognition-action arises when the fiction of self has been left behind. In Buddhist terms, this is called the generation of bodhicitta, or thought of enlightenment, and is the starting point for the practice of Vajrayāna Buddhism, the main form to be considered in this article. Thus, whereas for Jung cognition is always intentional and referential (i.e., for there to be cognition of the unconscious the ego must become aware of an archetype), Buddhism, by claiming ego to be purely fictitious in the first place, offers the possibility of a spontaneous cognition-action without reference points.

Despite these very important differences in assumptions, we feel that there remains a rationale for a comparison of Jung and Buddhism, particularly in the realm of inspiration and symbolism. Jung does not seek merely to restructure the ego to a more balanced accommodation with the external world; he indicates that there is a fundamental problem in identifying oneself with ego, a notion which Buddhism would second. (This, however, does not mean to indicate that the term "ego" means the same for Jung and Buddhism. In fact, it does not.) We hope to elucidate just where the similarities and differences occur by phenomenologically investigating the anima and the mkha' 'gro ma.

III. Anima

In Jungian psychological theory, the anima is the most accessible of the archetypal contents of the unconscious. It is a multivalent and multifunctional image. At times it is a counterbalance to the persona to the extent that the individual identifies himself with the persona:

> The anima is an unconscious subject-imago analagous to the persona. Just as the persona is the image of himself which the subject presents to the world, so the anima is the image of the subject in his relation to the collective unconscious, or an expression of unconscious collective contents unconsciously constellated by him. One could also say: the anima is the face of the subject as seen by the collective unconscious.[4]

And at other times the anima is the "...personification of the unconscious"[5] in its entirety. It functions as a source of neurotic symptoms when there is over-identification with the persona.

> To the degree that the ego identifies with the persona, the anima, like everything unconscious, is projected onto the real objects of our environment. She is regularly to be found, therefore, in the woman we are in love with....The more normal a person is, the less will the daemonic qualities of the anima appear in the objects of his immediate environment...the more sensitive a person is, the closer these daemonic projections will come, until in the end they break through the family taboo and produce the typical neurotic complications of a family romance.[6]

And also as a psychic helpmate, a wisdom imago:

> My psychological experience has shown time and again that certain contents issue from a psyche more complete than consciousness. They often contain a superior analysis or insight or knowledge which consciousness has not been able to produce.[7]

As with any archetype, the anima cannot be known in itself, but only as it presents itself to consciousness. It appears always as a contra-sexual image, although psychiatrist James Hillman[8] has taken Jung to task on this point, claiming that it is just as likely for anima to appear to a woman (rather than animus) as to a man in certain cases.[9]

The anima is relatively accessible because it is everything the conscious self is not. In Jungian therapeutic practice, the anima is the first of the archetypal (i.e., collective) images to come to consciousness, following the shadow, which is personal. As such it plays the role of mediator between consciousness and the unconscious, as well as being the most likely culprit in the genesis of psychopathology. The anima is an autonomous complex and as such, a dissociation of the conscious self is required for it to become known. This dissociation may be pathological, as Jung describes:

> The forces that burst out of the collective psyche have a confusing and binding effect. One result of the dissolution of the persona is a release of involuntary fantasy, which is apparently nothing else than the specific activity of the collective psyche. This activity throws up contents whose existence one had never suspected before. But as the influence of the collective unconscious increases, so the conscious mind loses its power of leadership. Imperceptible it becomes the led, while an unconscious and impersonal process gradually takes control. Thus, without noticing it, the conscious personality is pushed about like a figure on a chess-board by an invisible player. It is this player who decides the game of fate, not the conscious mind and its plans.[10]

Or it may be a deliberate, constructive aspect of Jungian therapy, wherein the therapist and patient work toward a form of dissociation:

> The psyche not being a unity but a contradictory multiplicity of complexes, the dissociation required for our dialectics with the anima is not so terribly difficult. The art of it consists only in allowing our invisible partner to make herself heard, in putting the mechanism of expression momentarily at her disposal, without being overcome by the distaste one naturally feels at playing such an apparently ludicrous game with oneself, or by doubts as to the genuineness of the voice of one's interlocutor.[11]

When one becomes aware of the anima, either by neurotic disturbances or by deliberate therapeutic dissociation, its autonomy becomes apparent because it is truly archetypal or, put differently, because it cannot be identified with the personal, conscious self. James Hillman makes this point:

> "My" anima expresses the personalistic fallacy. Even though anima experiences bring with them a numinosity of person, the feeling of a unique inwardness and sense of importance (exaggerations and mythologization of mood, insight, or fantasy), to take these experiences literally, as literally personal, puts anima inside "me." The heightened subjectivity of anima events is "anything but personal" because it is

archetypal (CW, 14, 469)...to take the archetypal literally as personal is a personalistic fallacy. So, when under the domination of anima our soulfullness makes us feel most uniquely "me," special, different, called—this is precisely the moment when, as Jung goes on to say in the same passage, "we are in fact most estranged from ourselves and most like the average type of <u>homo sapiens</u>."[12]

The most common response to the discovery of the anima is fear because the existence of autonomous complexes within one's psyche is inherently frightening, because one can no longer imagine consciousness to be the master of the self, and "it is normal for man to resist his anima because she represents...the unconscious with all those tendencies and contents hitherto excluded from conscious life."[13] These contents have been excluded because the conscious self finds them generally unpleasant and they become "partial personalities (that) have the character of an inferior woman or an inferior man, hence their irritating influence."[14]

The anima exists in relation to the persona or self as consciously presented to the world. The relationship between the anima and the persona is compensatory,[15] and when the disparity between conscious and unconscious becomes inflated, pathological projection of the unconscious ensues. These projections can lead to psychotic conditions, as Jung writes:

The effect of projection is to isolate the subject from his environment, since instead of a real relation to it there is now only an illusory one. Projections change the world into the replica of one's own unknown face. In the last analysis, therefore, they lead to an auto-erotic or autistic condition in which one dreams a world whose reality remains forever unattainable....The more projections interpose themselves between the subject and environment, the harder it becomes for the ego to see through its illusions.[16]

However, these projections are also potential teachers, mirrors which reflect to us our true psychological condition, useful friends on Jung's path to individuation. As Emma Jung tells us:

One function of the anima is to be a looking glass for a man, to reflect his thoughts, desires, and emotions.... That is precisely why she is so important to him, whether as an inner figure or projected to an actual, other woman; in this way he becomes aware of things about which he is still unconscious.[17]

Thus the anima could "...function (as guides to the depths of the unconscious) if only man and woman can learn to relate to them within themselves in an open and constructive way," as Jungian psychiatrist June Singer[18] writes. As such the anima is a wisdom imago, as well as a psychologically disturbing character. In itself it is neutral; all that remains in question is our relation to it, our refusal to identify the totality of our psychic being with the persona, which according to Jung is the negation of egocentricity.[19]

The anima is also an image of power. It is precisely because it has such capabilities for disturbing us that it has the potentiality for healing us. Jung very perceptively writes:

> The thing that cures a neurosis must be as convincing as the neurosis; and since the latter is only too real, the helpful experience must be of equal reality. It must be a very real illusion, if you want to put it pessimistically. But what is the difference between a real illusion and a healing religious experience? It is merely a difference in words.[20]

The healing process then becomes a reappropriation of the power of the anima into the image of the self. This is done, as has been noted, by the therapeutic dissociation of the persona and the recognition of the anima as an autonomous, powerful complex. Thus the anima is recognized:

> "She" (a literary anima figure) is a mana-personality, a being full of some occult and bewitching quality (mana), endowed with magical knowledge and power. All these attributes naturally have their source in the naive projection of an unconscious self-knowledge.[21]

After the anima is so recognized, her power can be appropriated:

> Through this process the anima forfeits the daemonic power of an autonomous complex; she can no longer exercise the power of possession, since she is depotentiated. She is no longer the guardian of treasures unknown;...but a psychological function of an intuitive nature.[22]

Jung then points to a very interesting phenomenon after the power of the anima has been appropriated:

> Well then: who is it that has integrated the anima? Obviously the consciousness, and therefore the ego has taken over the mana. Thus the ego becomes a mana-personality. But the mana-personality is a dominant of the collective unconscious. The well-known archetype of the mighty man in the form of a hero, chief, magician, medicineman, the ruler of man and spirits, the friend of God. This masculine collective figure who now rises out of the dark background and takes possession of the conscious personality entails a psychic danger of a subtle nature, for by inflating the conscious mind it can destroy everything that was gained by coming to terms with the anima.[23]

The anima always appears as a concrete image. It is not a thing which, at depth, can be known; rather, it is known as it presents itself to consciousness, formal and concrete. This could be said of any of the archetypes, since to be conscious means, for Jung, for an image to appear before the conscious self: consciousness is always intentional and referential. The reference of the consciousness of anima must therefore be a concrete image of the anima and never the anima itself. Ira Progoff makes this point when he writes that "....on the question of what they (the archetypes) are in themselves, Jung states that we must remain silent."[24] The concreteness of the anima is extended to include actual women when they function as an anima.[25]

One's encounter with the anima brings about a recentering of the personality, a readaptation to life. This process may by either psychotic degeneration, when one's private reality is projected upon the public reality indiscriminately, or it may involve a nonegoistic mode of being. This transformation is decribed thus:

> If we picture the conscious mind, with the ego at its center, as being opposed to the unconscious, and if we now add to our mental picture the process of assimilating the unconscious, we can think of this assimilation as a kind of approximation of conscious and unconscious, where the center of the total personality no longer coincides with the ego, but with a point midway between the conscious and unconscious. This would be the point of new equilibrium, a new centering of the total personality, a vital center which, on account of its focal position between conscious and unconscious, ensures for the personality a new and more solid foundation.[26]

This idea of a nonegocentric recentering of the total personality, in which Jung goes beyond his psychoanalytic colleagues who would rather attempt to affirm the readjusted ego's centeredness, indicates that a fundamental problematic involved in all neurotic pathology is the identification with ego (or persona, of which the ego is the center) itself. As Jung writes, "Reality sees to it that the peaceful cycle of egocentric ideas is constantly interrupted by ideas with a strong feeling-tone, that is, by affects,"[27] which have their origin in the unconscious. This journey towards nonegocentrism is called by Jung the process of individuation, wherein persona is not so rigidly defined as in a neurotic condition and unconsciousness is allowed into dialogue with consciousness. This individuated person is able to integrate the contents of the archetypes, to gain their power and learn from their perspective. It is somewhat paradoxical that the individuated person feels himself to be the least "individual," because he is able to appreciate that the psyche is truly collective at bottom and in no sense personal. It is the substratae of consciousness and not merely repressed personalistic contents, as other psychoanalytic schools believe. As Jung writes:

> [The archetypes] personify those of its contents which, when withdrawn from projection, can be integrated into consciousness. To this extent both figures represent functions which filter the contents of the collective unconscious through to the conscious mind....The reason for their behaving in this way is that though the contents of anima and animus can be integrated, they themselves cannot, since they are archetypes. As such they are the

foundation stones of the psychic structure, which in its
totality exceeds the limits of consciousness and therefore can never become the object of direct cognition.
The effects of anima and animus can indeed be made conscious, but they themselves are factors transcending
consciousness and beyond the reach of perception and
volition.[28]

The point to be noted is that Jung does not intend his archetypes to
be "merely psychological." He writes that "....the archetypes...have
a nature that cannot with certainty be designated as psychic."[29]

Jung here has opened up two very crucial questions, with which we
shall conclude our discussion of the anima: (1) the question of private and public realities generally, and how it relates to the psychotic or the yogin; and (2) the dilemma of the means of knowledge of
psychic substructure: obviously one cannot know the ground of consciousness in the same way that one knows an external object.

Jung only hints at a solution to the first question in his later
and more speculative writings. In his introduction to the Chinese
alchemical text, The Secret of the Golden Flower,[30] he indicates that
it is perhaps the fundamental bifurcation of reality into private and
public sectors that is, at bottom, the root cause of all psychological disorders. However, the remarkable notion is nowhere systematically incorporated into his psychological theory.

Jung is aware of the problems involved in treating the psyche as
an ordinary object of investigation. He writes:

Man thinks of himself as holding the psyche in the hollow
of his hand. He dreams of making a science of her. But
in reality she is the mother and the maker, the psychical
subject and even the possibility of consciousness itself.
The psyche reaches so far beyond the boundary line of consciousness that the latter could be easily compared to an
island in the ocean. While the island is small and narrow,
the ocean is immensely wide and deep, so that if it is a
question of space, it does not matter whether the gods are
inside or outside.[31]

Thus Jung is aptly raising the question of the very possibility
of the scientific (i.e., "objective") investigation of the psyche,
which has been the task of the psychologist in the West. Some of the
implications of this question shall be drawn out in our comparison
with Tibetan notions of the psyche and the means of knowing it. It
seems, however, that Jung is aware of the shortcomings of his own
methodology for resolving questions as to the nature of the psyche
itself. His conclusion, therefore, has been to avoid making claims
about its fundamental nature, a position in which we find a refreshing honesty.

IV. mKha' 'gro ma

We shall be dealing with the phenomenon of the mkha' 'gro ma

largely as it appears in the hagiographies (rnam thar) of the grub
chen (Skt. mahāsiddha), the "saints" of Vajrayāna Buddhism, traditionally eighty-four in number. We shall be working both with canonical texts[32] and their modern adaptations,[33] as well as some of the
few hagiographies which have been translated into Western
languages.[34] These rnam thar texts are from a relatively early
phase of Vajrayāna literature, wherein the mkha' 'gro ma are depicted
fiercely. In later purely Tibetan writings, they often take on a
more pacific character. Also, whereas in the early writings the
mkha' 'gro ma usually appear spontaneously, in later sādhana texts
one finds instructions for their visualization and worship. We have
thus limited our scope because we find stronger parallels for comparison with the anima in these early writings, most of which are of
Indian origin.

The rnam thar are "introductory" tantric texts, as they can be
read by all without specific empowerments, and are vastly popular as
homiletic as well as meditative texts in Tibet. They are
hagiographies in the special sense of accounts of the spiritual
development of the adept. They are written in a language called in
Sanskrit sandyābhāṣā, "twilight language," richly symbolic and multivalent in meaning. As Lama Govinda writes:

> In the symbolic language of the Siddhas, experiences of medi-
> tation are transformed into external events, inner attainments
> into visible miracles and similes into factual, quasi-
> historical events. If, for instance, it is said of certain
> Siddhas that they stopped the sun and the moon in their
> course...this has nothing to do with the heavenly bodies...but
> with the "solar" and "lunar" currents of psychic energy, and
> their unification and sublimation in the body of the yogin.[35]

The grub chen or mahāsiddha are the ideal humans of Vajrayāna
Buddhism, and as such hold a similar position as the arahant in
Theravāda Buddhism and the bodhisattva in Mahāyāna Buddhism.[36] They
indicate a convergence of the Appolinarian and Dionysian trends in
Indian religions, of the ecstatic and the ascetic, of the upāsaka
(layperson) and the bhiksu (monk), of intellectual and popular religions. Rebelling against the formalism of bodhisattva practices at
the great monastic universities of India of the fourth to eleventh
centuries C.E., the Vajrayāna sees in the grub chen the highest ideal
of Buddhism, a going beyond the monasteries into the world, yet remaining aloof from it.

The word siddha (grub pa) comes from the root sidh, "to be successful," as in Siddhārtha. Thus mahāsiddha, of which grub chen is
the Tibetan translation, means "great successful one," commonly
translated in early scholarship as "great sorcerer" or "great magician." Their practices, or sādhana (from the same root), lead to
certain "accomplishments" or siddhi (dngos grub), many of which seem
magical in nature while others, such as mahāmudrāsiddhi (phyags rgya
chen po) are clearly spiritual. A "typical" rnam thar of a grub
chen, if such a thing could be said to exist, might include the following motifs: (1) birth in varied castes: brahmin (Saraha), kingly
(Indrabhūti), thief, (Nāgabodhi), dancing-girl (Sahajasiddhi); (2)
unusual accomplishments in early career: abbot at Nālandā University

(Nāropa), translator of Buddhist Sanskrit texts (Marpa), powerful sorcerer (Mi la ras pa); (3) turning point involving renunciation of previous vocation (Nāropa, Mi la ras pa, Tilopa, Indrabhūti, etc.); (4) initiation into Vajrayāna practices, usually by a mkha' 'gro ma; (5) meeting the guru; and (6) attainment of the highest siddhi and the working of miracles.[37] We shall outline the role of the mkha' 'gro ma through some of these and other rnam thar motifs, especially at the turning point and initiation stages, where the influence of the mkha' 'gro ma is virtually universal.

Probably the most famous encounter with a mkha' 'gro ma is interpreted by Herbert V. Guenther in his account of the life of the pandit Nāropa, who occupied the prestigious and learned position as gatekeeper (analagous to dean) of Nālandā, the greatest of the Buddhist monastic univerities.

> The vision which induced Nāropa to resign from his post and to abandon worldly honours was that of an old and ugly woman who mercilessly revealed to him his psychological state. Throughout the years he had been engaged in intellectual activities which were essentially analytic and thereby had become oblivious to the fact that the human organ of knowledge is bifocal. "Objective" knowledge may be entirely accurate without, however, being entirely important, and only too often it misses the heart of the matter. All that he had neglected and failed to develop was symbolically revealed to him as the vision of an old and ugy woman. She is old because all that the female symbol stands for, the emotionally and passionately moving, is older than the cold rationality of the intellect which itself could not be if it were not supported by feelings and moods which it usually misconceives and misjudges. And she is ugly, because that which she stands for has not been allowed to become alive or only in the undeveloped and distorted manner. Lastly she is a deity because all that is not incorporated in the conscious mental make-up of the individual and appears other-than and more-than himself is the old ugly and divine woman, who in the religious symbolism of the Tantras is the diety rDo-rje phag-mo Vajravārāhī) and who in a psychological setting acts as "messenger" (pho-nya).[38]

A similar account of the mkha' 'gro ma presenting the adept with that which is psychologically most abhorrent to him is found in the rnam thar of Abhyāharagupta:

> Once, as he was sitting in the temple cloister, there appeared a young maiden who dropped a piece of beef near to him which was dripping in blood, shoved it to the ācārya and said: "I am a Candāla (out-caste) maiden, but eat what is slaughtered for you." But he answered: "I am a Bhikshu of purer order, how shall I eat meat which is extraordinarily offered to me?" But she sank back and disappeared in the court below. That was...Vajrayoginī (a popular mkha' 'gro ma) who gave him the beef.[39]

Not only do the mkha' 'gro ma reveal to the adept his state of mind,
which is neurotic becaue of the defilements of attraction and/or
aversion (as to the bloody beef), rooted in ignorance (ma rig pa,
Skt. avidyā), but they also positively direct the adept in his journeys. We read of the brahmin Rāhulabhadra (later called Saraha or
mDa'bsnun) who is directed by four brahman girls offering cups of
beer to leave his caste position and live with an arrowsmith
woman.[40] Three beautiful visionary women tell Marpa that he must
make a third arduous trip across the Himālayas to India to complete
his training with Nāropa.[41] Marpa is so told that although he has
mastered the phyag rgya chen mo (mahāmudrā) teachings, he has
neglected the drong 'jug practices and had better attend to them.[42]
Mi la ras pa is advised by the mkha' 'gro ma as to his disciples.[43]
This advice comes in the form of direct visions, as with Nāropa and
Abhyāharagupta, or in dreams.[44]

The term mkha' 'gro ma is composed of the syllables mkha', or
"space" (Skt. ākāśa), 'gro meaning "to go," and the feminine particle
ma. Guenther[45] explains the etymology thus:

> The Tibetan explanation for the word is that "sky," "celestial
> space" is a term for "no-thing-ness" (stong pa nyid, Skt.
> śūnyatā) and "to go" means "to understand." The Dākinī is
> therefore an understanding of no-thing-ness. It is a fine
> example of "embodying" language.

Govinda[46] explains the term by telling us that since mkha' means
space or ether, or that which makes movement possible, 'gro means "to
go" and ma is a feminine particle, therefore mkha' 'gro ma means a
"heavenly being of female appearance who partakes of the luminous nature of ākāśa."

The role of the "feminine" in the lives of the grub chen is enormous. The Grub thob brgyad cu rtsa bzhi'i gsol 'debs is a poem by
rDo rje gdan pa which contains entreaties (gsol 'debs) to the eighty-
four grub chen,[47] and in it fully fifty-six of them are praised for
keeping company with women. Two grub chen, Saraha[48] and Lavapa,[49]
are said to be born of mkha' 'gro ma. We find Kukuripa[50] living with
a mkha' 'gro ma who appeared to the world as his pet dog. The
attainment of mahāmudrā by Vaidyāpāda is dependent upon his taking up
residence with a candāla, or outcaste woman.[51] rDo rje dril bu pa is
instructed by his guru, Dārikapa, to study the Cakrasamvara cycle of
teachings with a hideous female swine-keeper, and later becomes guru
of a beer-seller-girl.[52] We hear Saraha singing in his dohā (a
Bengali mystical song):[53]

> Oh, I am a brahmin.
> Together with a magician-girl I enjoy.
> I don't see caste or no-caste.
> As one who lives as a bhiksu with shaved head,
> I wander together with a consort.
> There is no division between attachment and
>   non-attachment;
> Impurity is simply a mental fabrication,
> And this is not known by others.

Dārikapa, a king, becomes the servant of a harlot.[54] Putaloki in the same verse "...won the harlot and perfection."[55]

The most important roles of the mkha' 'gro ma in the grub chen stories are that of inspiration, as discussed, in the biblical sense of God "inspiring Abraham to err," and teaching and initiating the grub chen. In some cases this is done indirectly, as in the story of Biwapa of the Sa skya pa lineage, to whom a mkha' 'gro ma in the form of a common woman appears and admonishes him for considering giving up his Vajrayāna practices;[56] or in the case of Kānha who is directed by mkha' 'gro ma to a place where spontaneous initiation occurs.[57]

An account of a more direct initiation by a mkha' 'gro ma is a motif in the rnam thar of Tilopa as found in the Chos 'byung of Pa dma dkar po and as recounted by Hoffmann.[58] Seeing an ugly crone on the road, Tilopa recognizes her as a mkha' 'gro ma. She tells him to give up the pāramitāyāna (the bodhisattva practices) and study the tantric teachings. After he accepts her as his guru, she gives four major empowerments to Tilopa: (1) the Cakrasamvara-mandala empowerment, after which time Cakrasamvara became the yi dam (tutelary deity) of the bKa' brgyud pa lineage founded, in part, by Tilopa; (2) the bskyed pa'i rim pa, or utpattikrama, method for transmuting the five poisons into the five wisdoms; (3) the rdzogs pa'i rim pa, or sampannakrama, the attainment of bde chen, or mahāsukha ("great bliss"); and (4) the initiation of how to act like a "mad drunkard" (smyon pa), the highest Vajrayāna empowerment.[59] The mkha' 'gro ma then tells him to seek further teaching from the "queen of the mkha' 'gro ma."

> After long trials and tribulations he finally made his way
> to the court of the Dākinī queen, whose palace walls of
> metal gave forth tremendous heat and brilliance. But
> neither this nor other terrors dismayed him, and he forced
> his way into the enchanted palace, passed through an end-
> less succession of splendid apartments until finally he
> reached the queen of the Dākinīs, who sat on her throne
> of superb beauty, loaded with jewels, and smiling gently
> at the gallant adept. But he kept repeating his magic
> formula (given to him by his guru dākinī) ripped off the
> jewelery and clothing of the queen and raped her...in the
> end he was seen in a lonely place in an aura of light
> surrounded by twelve lamps and twelve women. With this
> the master was recognized, and he now disseminated secret
> teachings in certain mystic verses (Vajra-Dohā), and from
> that time on he is said to have been able to walk on the
> heavens. With this he had become equal to the Dākas and
> the Dākinīs.[60]

Such potent symbolism lends itself to the danger of misinterpre-
tation, as the great modern teacher, bLa ma Mi pham said that those
who take tantric texts too literally end up only with too many children![61] The Hevajra-tantra clearly tells us that mind produces and
maintains the mkha' 'gro ma,[62] and that the "homes" of the various
mkha' 'gro ma are the various cakras, or psychophysical energy centers.[63] Thus we may speculate that when Tilopa is said to rape the
queen of the mkha' 'gro ma, the reference is to the arousal of

spiritual energies. Govinda explicates a similar passage:

> In one of the most controversial passages of Anangavajra, it
> is said that all women should be enjoyed by the sādhaka (prac-
> titioner) in order to experience the mahāmudrā. It is clear
> that this cannot be understood in the physical sense, but
> that it can only be applied to the highest form of love which
> is not restricted to a single object and which is able to see
> all "female" qualities, whether in ourselves or in others as
> those of the Divine Mother (shes rab kyi pha rol tu phyin pa).[64]

We find other grub chen receiving teachings directly from the
mkha' 'gro ma. In the rnam thar of Padmasambhava, we find tales of
his receiving the abhiṣeka (empowerment) of Avalokiteśvara in the
stomach of a mkha' 'gro ma.[65] Tilopa received teachings directly
from the dharmakāya of Ye shes gyi mkha' 'gro ma.[66] Nāgārjuna receives alchemical teachings from a mkha' 'gro ma.[67] Kasoripa:

> ...conjured up Vajrayoginī [yoginī, rnal 'byor ma =
> mkha' 'gro ma[68]] and saw her face. On her inquiry what
> he wanted, he said that he wished to reach her stage,
> whereupon she lowered herself into his soul and he at
> once obtained the Siddhi.[69]

The mkha' 'gro ma are multivalent symbols. They appear in many
different forms; we find Beyer citing the Tse dbang kun khyab lo
rgyus:

> I the Lotus Ḍākinī instantaneously change my state and
> become the Lion-Faced Ḍākinī, very fierce, holding aloft
> a chopper and skull bowl, my body embraced by the Father,
> the Black Slayer of Death (gShin rje gshed), who holds a
> copper-iron wheel.[70]

As well as offering empowerments, teachings, and magical powers (as
we shall see), Beyer notes that, "In ritual invocations, it is recognized that dākinīs can be evil as 'pollutors and demons of madness'
or as 'misleading demons.'"[71]

mKha' 'gro ma may also take different forms to teach the adept
equanimity and nondiscrimination. We read:

> (Buddhaśānti and Buddhaguhya) went to Potala mountain
> (equated with the spinal cord in yogic treatises), at the
> foot of which the goddess Tārā was reciting the dharma
> before the Nāgas (sea-serpents). She appeared to them as
> an old woman looking after a herd of cattle. In the middle
> of the mountain, Bhrutī was preaching the dharma to a num-
> ber of Asuras (anti-gods) and Yakshas (nature spirits).
> She appeared to them as a girl looking after a flock of
> goats. On the top of the mountain both of them saw a
> stone image of Avalokiteśvara. Buddhaśānti was of opinion
> that they had not yet developed ability to visualize
> Avalokiteśvara in his godly form.[72]

mKha' 'gro ma may also be actual women. In the rnam thar of King
Indrabhūti,[73] he is inspired by the religious accomplishments of his
sister, Lakṣmīṅkārā, who is also a grub chen. We read of Buddhaśrīj-
ñāna who studies with a candālā girl named Jātijālā.[74] Two of the
female grub chen, Sahajasiddhī and Mandāravā become mkha' 'gro ma.[75]
Mi la ras pa is able to see in a young farm girl all the qualifica-
tions of a mkha' 'gro ma, and he takes her as his disciple.[76] In one
case, that of the grub chen Kukuripa, the mkha' 'gro ma is a dog.[77]

The mkha' 'gro ma also play such roles as: (1) sources of magical and spiritual powers; (2) testers of the grub chen; (3) guardians
of the gter ma, or hidden texts; and (4) biographers of the grub
chen.

As sources of power, the mkha' 'gro ma enable Nāgārjuna to provide for the entire monastery at Nālandā by magical means.[78] They
also assist Padmasambhava in his sorcery duel with non-Buddhists at
Buddha Gaya by giving him "...a leather box with iron nails containing instructions for feats of sorcery to defeat his opponents."[79]
When the grub chen Vyāli was unsuccessfully practicing alchemy, a
mkha' 'gro ma knocks some chemicals into his potion, which then becomes successful, telling him: "The essence of life and nature, the
secret of immortality, cannot be found in dry intellectual work and
selfish desire, but only by the touch of undiluted life in the spontaneity of intuition."[80]

As testers, a mkha' 'gro ma, incarnated as a girl, Ras chung ma,
tests the power and motives of Mi la ras pa.[81]

The mkha' 'gro ma are also guardians of the gter ma, texts hidden
by Padmasambhava and other tantric authors until humanity is ready
for these esoteric teachings. Padmasambhava entrusts some of these
hidden teachings to the mkha' 'gro ma for safekeeping.[82] The mkha'
'gro ma Ye shes mTsho rgyal holds the texts of the legend of the
great stūpa, also composed by Padmasambhava.[83] The same mkha' 'gro
ma also records the rnam thar of Padmasambhava,[84] much as the mkha'
'gro ma Ras chung ma is the author of the rnam thar of Mi la ras
pa.[85] The role of the mkha' 'gro ma in the quests of the gter ton
("discoverer of gter ma") is discussed by Hoffmann.[86]

An interesting phenomenon is that when a grub chen has attained
great spiritual heights, his relationship with the mkha' 'gro ma
undergoes a reversal. Rather than being compelled, inspired, and em-
powered by them, he now becomes their teacher. Padmasambhava spends
several time periods teaching the mkha' 'gro ma,[87] and they chose him
as their tutelary rather than vice versa.[88] Mi la ras pa is sustained by the mkha' 'gro ma during periods of fasting and meditation.[89] The great Tibetan historian, Pa dma dkar po, described Mi la
ras pa as "king of the mkha' 'gro ma,"[90] indicating this new relationship between the adept and the mkha' 'gro ma, much as Hevajra is
described as "rejoicer of the dākinīs."[91]

Certain yogic practices are the special province of some of the
mkha' 'gro ma. The rite of gcod, which involves psychic dismember-
ment and self-sacrifice and has been likened to a deliberate, self-
induced schizophrenic episode, was founded by Machig Labdron, who
"....is pictured as a naked white dākinī, beating a drum and blowing
a thighbone trumpet, one leg raised and turned in the posture of a
yogic dance."[92] One of the six yogas of Nāropa, gtum mo, or the generation of psychic heat, is called "the warming breath of the mkha'

'gro ma."[93]

Summarizing, the major functions of the mkha' 'gro ma in the hagiographical accounts of the grub chen are (1) inspiring and directing the grub chen; (2) directly or indirectly bestowing empowerments to the grub chen; (3) the patron of the grub chen, and in cases of very great spiritual achievement on their part, this relationship is reversed; (4) the source of power of the grub chen; (5) guardians of gter ma; and (6) biographers of the grub chen. The mkha' 'gro ma may appear in visions, dreams, meditations, and as actual women. They are revered as perceptors of particular yogic practices (i.e., gcod and gtum mo), and may be demonical as well as beneficent.

Their role in the lives of the grub chen is enormous, as the Bengali teacher Saraha sings in his Dohā-kośa:

> There how should another arise,
> Where the wife without hesitation consumes the householder?
> This yoginī's action is peerless.
> She consumes the householder and the Innate shines forth,
> There is neither passion nor absence of passion.
> Seated beside her own, her mind destroyed,
> Thus have I seen the yoginī.
> One eats and drinks and thinks what occurs to be thought.
> It is beyond the mind and inconceivable,
> The wonder of the yoginī.
> Here Sun and Moon lose their distinction,
> In her the triple world is formed.
> O know this yoginī,
> Perfecter of thought and unity of the Innate.[94]

V. Comparisons and Conclusions

Our comparisons of the phenomena of the anima and of the mkha' 'gro ma reveal striking similarities, both in the appearance of the "feminine" and in their psychological function in the lives of those on Jung's path to individuation or of practitioners of Vajrayāna Buddhism. As tempting as it might be to delve into how Jungians and tāntrikas understand these phenomena, that would be well beyond the scope of this article.[95]

From the descriptions we have seen, the first striking parallel between anima and mkha' 'gro ma is their contrasexuality. Jung speaks of animus and anima; Tibetan texts speak of dpa' bo (Sanskrit: vīra, dāka) and mkha' 'gro ma (Sanskrit: dākinī). Jung is much more specific in claiming that this function must be symbolized contrasexually, whereas Tibetans would be just as content with a mkha' 'gro ma inspiring a rnal 'byor ma (female yoga practitioner) as a rnal 'byor pa.[96] However, the Tibetans would insist upon sexual symbolism for this function, as we read in the Vyaktabhāvānugatatattvasiddhi of Sahajayoginī Cintā (one of the grub chen): "That man may wake up to his true nature, pure in itself and without duality, (this invisible point) manifests itself in the shape of a man and of a woman."[97] Or as we read in the Hevajra tantra:

> Therefore twofold is the Innate (sahaja), for Wisdom
> (prajñā) is the woman and Means (upāya) is the man.
> Thereafter these both become twofold, distinguished as
> absolute (vivṛti) and relative (saṃvṛti). In man there
> is this twofold nature, śukra (relative) and the bliss
> arising from it.[98]

Or as the grub chen Kāṇha sings: "How can enlightenment be attained
in this bodily existence without thine incessant love, oh lovely
young girl?"[99]

One of the major functions of the anima and the mkha' 'gro ma is
that of inspiration. Much has been made of Jung's adaptations of the
literary motif called the "Beatrice figure," the feminine which in-
spires and leads men through various travails. The parallels here to
the function of the mkha' 'gro ma in the rnam thar of Nāropa, for example, is most striking. In so inspiring men to begin their symbolic
journeys, the call of the anima or mkha' 'gro ma may be shrill or
beatific. Just as the mkha' 'gro ma who summons Nāropa from his comfortable position at Nālandā is terribly ugly, revealing to him the
state of his mind and the qualities which he has neglected, so the
anima, Jung claims, is responsible for many neurotic disturbances in
life. It is these disturbances which lead one to psychotherapy; it
is the mkha' 'gro ma that leds one to the guru. We find the analogy
may be carried further: after one has become individuated, the anima
becomes a guide to the unconscious; after successful training with
the guru, the mkha' 'gro ma becomes one's patron and initiator. So
we find in both Jung and Tibetan materials an image of a disturbing
female figure, leading one to a guru or a psychiatrist (or in less
fortunate cases, to a mental hospital), who, by the process of psychotherapy or meditation becomes beneficent.

In one of Jung's excursions into the non-European area, he finds
the anima as a mana-personality, powerful and awesome, but somehow
conquerable. After such conquest, her power becomes reappropriated
and oneself becomes the mana-personality, as a magician, sorcerer, or
what have you. Analagous to this motif, we find the mkha' 'gro ma as
exceedingly powerful and the grub chen may call upon her power for
magical or other purposes. If the grub chen is exceptional (as in
the rnam thar of Padmasambhava and Mi la ras pa), he gains power over
the mkha' 'gro ma, becoming in turn their patron and teacher.

We also find the image of ongoing relationship carried through in
Jung's writings and Tibetan texts. Several grub chen are said to
take up residence with a woman; the majority of them are iconograph-
ically depicted with women. Jung tells us that since the anima is
unknowable in itself, we must remain in dialogue with it and other
archetypes, as an individuated person.

The mkha' 'gro ma appear to the grub chen in dreams (which could
also be said of Jung's anima), in visions and meditations (this also
could be said of the anima), real women such as Lakṣmiṅkārā and
Sahajayoginī (Jung speaks of "anima women"), and even as Kukuripa's
dog (for which we find no analogy in Jung's writings).

The inspiration of the anima or the mkha' 'gro ma is a call for
one to look inward. As such, she is the link between the conscious
and the unconscious. In appearing to consciousness, the anima calls
its attention to what has remained hidden; she is the door to the

unconscious.

In Buddhist terminology, one does not come across such a term as "unconscious," although the notion of kun gzhi (ālaya) comes close. One difficulty involved is the highly personalistic nature of the unconscious as understood in classical psychology. However, Jung's unconscious is not nearly so personal as is Freud's. Jung wants to reorient Western psychological thinking so as to become less personalistic. "Whenever a Westerner hears the word 'psychological,' it always sounds to him like only psychological" he writes in commenting on the difficulties in a Westerner approaching psychologically-oriented Buddhist texts.[100]

In considering the mkha' 'gro ma, we find the Buddhist taking a similar position. The mkha' 'gro ma, though psychic, are readily identifiable. We have seen a Buddhist describe a "private" (i.e., psychic) vision to a lama, which was at once identified and pronounced to be the devotee's yi dam. If one chose to speak in such terms as "private" and "public" realities, undoubtedly the mkha' 'gro ma, like Jung's archetypes, would be in the public domain. However, it is this very bifurcation of reality into private and public sectors that would be seen by Buddhism as an expression of the problem of self: belief in an objectifiable, external world is a corollary to belief in abiding reference point of its relation to consciousness, or ego. Such categories must break down somewhere along the Buddhist path, as Guenther observes:

> The yoginī who effects the integration of man is not an
> "object" but a participant in the drama of man's develop-
> ment that is enacted within and portrays itself as taking
> place without, so that it is often difficult to decide
> which is within and which is without. No wonder that this
> experience is spoken of as magical.[101]

In summary, then, when approaching the anima and the mkha' 'gro ma from a phenomenological perspective, we find more than accidental analogies. For example, the following ten attributes could as well be predicated of one as of the other:

(1) contrasexual appearance (much more emphasized by Jung
    than by the Tibetans)
(2) function of inspiring and leading
(3) appearance in dreams, visions and actual women
(4) source of power
(5) teacher and guide
(6) preliminary to therapy or meditation instruction
(7) wrathful and peaceful appearances; multivalence of
    image generally
(8) concreteness of image
(9) leading to transformation of the individual and
(10) psychogenic origins

However, when one considers how these phenomena are reflected upon, one runs up against enormous gaps. Furthermore, when Jung attempts to explicate Buddhism, or Eastern religions generally, we go even further afield. For example, at one place Jung writes:[102] "In the Eastern view the concept of the anima, as we have stated it here, is lacking, and so, logically, is the concept of the persona. This is certainly no accident for, as I have already indicated, a compensatory relationship exists between persona and anima." One might be so generous as to attribute such a claim to Jung's lack of familiarity with Buddhism and Buddhist texts. One might also attribute it to a pernicious "Orientalism" in Said's sense of wanton over-generalization.[103]

Such problems aside, we are left with a compelling, crosscultural portrait of a phenomenon of great import for human growth. It becomes obvious that both Jung and our tantric authors wished to call our attention to this phenomenon with great urgency. Such a phenomenon is sufficiently subtle to warrant its study from as many perspectives as possible, so there is no need to either bifurcate human thinking into irreducible "Western" and "Eastern" modes that cannot even meet in dialogue, nor assume that Jung was struggling to articulate something which classical Buddhists said better (or vice versa). We would offer that this phenomenon, called anima or mkha' 'gro ma, could be treated as a paradigm for comparative psychological study which neither reduces one perspective to another, nor sees the discourses of Buddhist and Jungian psychology as rigidly and artificially compartmentalized.[104]

NOTES

1. Herbert V. Guenther, Treasures on the Tibetan Middle Way (Berkeley: Shambhala, 1971), p. 103, fn 1.
2. Carl G. Jung, Two Essays in Analytic Psychology (Princeton: Princeton University Press, 1972), p. 221.
3. 'Phags pa shes rab kyi pha rol tu phyin pa rdo rje gcod pa zhes bya ba theg pa chen po'i mdo bzhugs so (Vajracchedikā Prajñā-pāramitā Sūtra) (Dharamsala: Tibetan Press, n.d.), fasc. 8a.
4. Jung, Two Essays, p. 304.
5. Carl G. Jung, Psyche and Symbol, ed. Violet de Laszlo (New York: Anchor Press, 1958), p. 9.
6. Jung, Two Essays, p. 299.
7. Carl G. Jung, Psychology and Religion (New Haven: Yale University Press, 1972), p. 40.
8. James Hillman, "Anima I," Spring (1973): 97-132; and idem, "Anima II," Spring (1974): 113-146.
9. There are obvious dangers in confusing any male-defined notion of "femininity" with actual women, as powerfully demonstrated by Mary Daly, Gyn/ecology: The Metaethics of Radical Feminism (Boston: Beacon Press, 1978), passim. It is not my purpose here to expunge Jung's thought of sexist elements, of which there are many. Issues involved in such an effort have been indicated by Naomi R. Goldenberg, "Jung After Feminism" in Beyond Androcentrism: New Essays on Women and Religion, ed. Rita M. Gross (Missoula: Scholars Press, 1977), pp. 53-66.
10. Jung, Two Essays, pp. 160-161.
11. Ibid., p. 201.
12. Hillman, "Anima I," p. 123.
13. Jung, Psychology and Religion, p. 91.

14. Ibid., p. 35.

15. See Jung, Two Essays, p. 192.

16. Jung, Psyche and Symbol, p. 8.

17. Emma Jung, Anima and Animus (Zürich: Spring Publications, 1974), p. 65.

18. June Singer, Boundaries of the Soul: The Practice of Jung's Psychology (New York: Anchor Press, 1973), p. 231.

19. See Jung, Psychogenesis in Mental Disease from The Collected Works of C.G. Jung, vol. 3 (New York: Pantheon Books, 1964), p. 41.

20. Jung, Psychology and Religion, p. 114.

21. Jung, Two Essays, p. 227.

22. Ibid.

23. Ibid., p. 228.

24. Ira Progoff, Jung's Psychology and its Social Meaning (New York: Anchor Books, 1973), p. 63.

25. See Jung, Collected Works, vol. 17, p. 339; vol. 9, p. 335; and Hillman, "Anima I," p. 115.

26. Jung, Two Essays, p. 221.

27. Jung, Psychogenesis in Mental Disease, p. 41.

28. Jung, Psyche and Symbol, p. 19.

29. Jung, Collected Works, vol. 8, p. 439, and cf. pp. 964, 419, as cited by Hillman, "Anima I," p. 114.

30. Richard Wilhelm, trans., The Secret of the Golden Flower: A Chinese Book of Life (New York: Harcourt, Brace and World, 1962), pp. 111-113.

31. Jung, Psychology and Religion, p. 102.

32. For one the Grub thob brgyad cu rtsa bzhi'i lo rgyus, (Caturaśīti Siddhi Pravrtti), by Mi 'jigs pa sbyin pa dpal (Abhayadattaśrī), bsTan 'gyur, Peking edition, rGyud 'grel, vol. lu, fascs. 1-68a, Otani number 5091, in an edition published as The Eighty-Four Saints of Buddhist (sic), Varanasi: E. Kalsang, 1972. We shall also be using the Grub thob brgyad cu rtsa bzhi'i gsol 'debs (Caturaśīti Siddhābhyarthanā), by rDo rje gdan pa (Vajrāsana), bsTan 'gyur, sNar thang edition, sNgags, vol. nu, Otani number 4578.

33. Especially the modern work by Khetsun Sangpo, rGya gar pan chen rnams kyi rnam thar ngo mtshar pad mo'i 'dzum zhal gsar pa (Biographical Dictionary of Tibet and Tibetan Buddhism, vol. I, The Arhats, Siddhas and Panditas of India) (Dharamsala: Library of Tibetan Works and Archives, 1973).

34. Herbert V. Guenther, trans., The Life and Teachings of Nāropa (London: Oxford University Press, 1963); Bhupendranath Datta, trans., Mystic Tales of Lama Taranatha (Calcutta: Ramakrishna Vedanta Math, 1957); Jacques Bacot, La Vie de Marpa le 'Traducteur' (Paris: Libraire Orientaliste Paul Guenther, 1937); W.Y. Evans-Wentz, ed., Tibet's Great Yogi, Milarepa (London: Oxford University Press, 1969); Keith Dowman, trans., The Legend of the Great Stūpa and the Life Story of the Lotus Born Guru (Emeryville: Dharma Publishing, 1973); and Helmut Hoffmann, The Religions of Tibet (London: George Allen & Unwin, 1961).

35. Lama Anagarika Govinda, Foundations of Tibetan Mysticism (New York: Samuel Weiser, 1972), p. 53.

36. See my book, Buddhist Images of Human Perfection: The Arahant of the Sutta Piṭaka Compared with the Bodhisattva and the Mahāsiddha (Delhi: Motilal Banarsidass, 1982).

37. I am indebted to my former student at Temple University, Mr. Steven Goodman, for developing this typology during an independent study course in 1975.

38. Guenther, The Life and Teachings of Nāropa, pp. viii-ix. See also pp. 24-25 for the textual account wherein the mkha' 'gro ma terrifies and abuses Nāropa and admonishes him to give up the pretense of his learning and seek his Vajrayāna guru. Reading this compelling tale, it is not difficult to see why the first accredited Buddhist college in the Western world was named for this grub chen.

39. Datta, Mystic Tales, p. 65.

40. Sangpo, rGya gar pan chen rnams, p. 161.

41. Bacot, La Vie de Marpa, p. 33.

42. Evans-Wentz, Tibet's Great Yogi, Milarepa, pp. 144-145.

43. Garma C.C. Chang, trans. Hundred Thousand Songs of Milarepa (New York: Harper Colophon, 1962), pp., 35, 64.

44. Evans-Wentz, Tibet's Great Yogi, Milarepa, pp. 88, 305.

45. Guenther, Treasures on the Tibetan Middle Way, p. 103, fn. 1.

46. Govinda, Foundations of Tibetan Mysticism, p. 192.

47. rDo rje gdan pa, Grub Thob, passim.

48. Sangpo, rGya gar pan chen rnams, p. 159.

49. rDo rje gdan pa, Grub thob, p. 3.

50. Grub thob brgyad cu rtsa bzhi'i chos skor (Tibetan wood block text, Library of Tibetan Works and Archives), fascs. 154-157.

51. Datta, Mystic Tales, pp. 54-55.

52. Sangpo, rGya gar pan chen rnams, pp. 384-385.

53. Ibid., pp. 161-162.

54. rDo rje gdan pa, Grub thob, p. 4.

55. Ibid., p. 7.

56. Sakya Geshe Thukjey Wangchuk, A Short Historical Outline of the Sakyapa Sect (Dharamsala: Imperial Printing Press, n.d.), p. 5.

57. David L. Snellgrove, ed. and trans., The Hevajra Tantra: A Critical Study, 2 vols. (London: Oxford University Press, 1959), p. 9.

58. Hoffmann, The Religions of Tibet, pp. 142-144. See also Sangpo, rGya gar pan chen rnams, pp. 586ff.

59. The smyon pa teaching is not restricted to Tilopa by any means. The grub chen Mekopa is held by the tradition to be among the foremost of these "mad drunkards." See Sangpo, rGya gar pan chen rnams, pp. 695-696, where Mekopa sings:

To one's mind, the wish-fulfilling gem,
Worldly and transworldly are seen as particular aspects.
As apprehension and nonapprehension are not two.
Steadfastly look at the state of that mind.
How comes the notion of dualistic apprehension?
As there is no inherent existence in that state,
None of the dharmas are formed,
The nonapprehension of which is found
By desireless deception.

60. Hoffmann, The Religions of Tibet, pp. 143-144.

61. From a discussion with Herbert V. Guenther.

62. Snellgrove, The Hevajra Tantra, I.i.9.

63. Ibid., II.iii.67. For a lengthy discussion of the psycho-physical nature of female and sexual symbolism in the tantras, see Snellgrove's introduction to the text, pp. 33-39.

64. Lama Anagarika Govinda, "Principles of Buddhist Tantraism," Bulletin of Tibetology II, no. 1 (March 1965): 9-16.

65. W.Y. Evans-Wentz, ed., The Tibetan Book of the Great Liberation (London: Oxford University Press, 1968), pp. 131-133.

66. Sangpo, rGya gar pan chen rnams, pp. 587-589.

67. Mi 'jigs pa sbyin pa dpal, Grub thob, pp. 51-57, trans. Nathan Katz and Kelsang Yeshi, "The Hagiography of Nāgārjuna," Kailash: A Journal of Himalayan Studies V, no. 4 (1977): 269-276. See also Mircea Eliade, Yoga, Immortality and Freedom (Princeton: Bollingen Foundation, 1958), pp. 344-345.

68. On the equivalence of these terms, see Stephan Beyer, The Cult of Tārā: Magic and Ritual in Tibet (Berkeley: University of California Press, 1973), p. 47; and cf. Snellgrove, The Hevajra Tantra, p. 135.

69. Nalinaksha Dutt, "Synopsis of Taranatha's History," Bulletin of Tibetology VI, no. 2 (July 1969): 26.

70. Beyer, The Cult of Tārā, p. 314.

71. Ibid., p. 342.

72. Dutt, "Synopsis of Taranatha's History," p. 19.

73. Mi 'jigs pa sbyin pa dpal, Grub thob, pp. 115-119, trans. Nathan Katz, "A Translation of the Biography of the Mahāsiddha Indrabhūti with Notes," Bulletin of Tibetology XII, no. 1 (February 1975): 25-29.

74. Datta, Mystic Tales, p. 51.

75. Ibid., pp. 18-19; and Evans-Wentz, Tibetan Book of the Great Liberation, p. 165.

76. Chang, Hundred Thousand Songs of Milarepa, pp. 50-63.

77. Grub thob brgyad cu rtsa bzhi'i chos skor, fascs. 154-157.

78. Katz and Yeshi, "The Hagiography of Nāgārjuna," p. 274.

79. Evans-Wentz, Tibetan Book of the Great Liberation, p. 171.

80. Govinda, Foundations of Tibetan Mysticism, p. 56.

81. Chang, Hundred Thousand Songs of Milarepa, p. 126.

82. Evans-Wentz, Tibetan Book of the Great Liberation, p. 179.

83. Dowman, The Legend of the Great Stūpa, p. 17.

84. Evans-Wentz, Tibetan Book of the Great Liberation, pp. 188-189.

85. Evans-Wentz, Tibet's Great Yogi, p. 309.

86. Hoffmann, The Religions of Tibet, pp. 59-60.

87. Evans-Wentz, Tibetan Book of the Great Liberation, pp. 130, 142.

88. Ibid., p. 177.

89. Chang, Hundred Thousand Songs of Milarepa, pp. 13, 118.

90. W.Y. Evans-Wentz, ed., Tibetan Yoga and Secret Doctrines (London: Oxford University Press, 1967), p. 146.

91. Snellgrove, The Hevajra Tantra, I.x.36.

92. Beyer, The Cult of Tārā, p. 47.

93. Govinda, Foundations of Tibetan Mysticism, p. 194.

94. Saraha, Dohā-kośa, v. 84-87, trans. David L. Snellgrove in Buddhist Texts Through the Ages, ed. Edward Conze (New York: Harper Torchbooks, 1964), pp. 235-236.

95. Although I did attempt something of this sort in "Anima and

mKha' 'gro ma: A Critical, Comparative Study of Jung and Tibetan Buddhism," The Tibet Journal 2, no. 3 (Autumn 1977): 13-43.

96. See Evans-Wentz, Tibetan Book of the Great Liberation, p. 121.

97. Quoted in Herbert V. Guenther, Yuganaddha: The Tantric View of Life, 2nd ed. (Varanasi: Chowkhamba Sanskrit Series, 1969), p. 87.

98. Snellgrove, The Hevajra Tantra, I.viii.27-29.

99. Quoted in Guenther, Yuganaddha, p. 43.

100. Carl G. Jung, "Psychological Commentary" to The Tibetan Book of the Dead, ed. W.Y. Evans-Wentz (London: Oxford University Press, 1960), p. xxxviii.

101. Herbert V. Guenther, trans., The Royal Song of Saraha: A Study in the History of Buddhist Thought (Berkeley: Shambhala, 1973), p. 50.

102. Jung, Two Essays, p. 192.

103. Edward W. Said, Orientalism (New York: Vintage Books, 1979), pp. 31-72.

104. Substantial portions of my essay, "Anima and mKha' 'gro ma" are included in this piece with the kind permission of The Tibet Journal and Mrs. Yangzom Tsarong, the managing editor.

Contributors

Gustavo Benavides studied psychology at St. Marcos University, Lima,
Peru; Religionswissenschaft at Freie Universitat, Berlin; and
Buddhism and comparative religions at Temple University, from which
he received his Ph.D. He also pursued Sanskrit studies in Benares
and has taught at St. Marcos and Temple. His research interests involve the language of mysticism, especially in Nāgārjuna and
Nicholaus Cusanus.

Richard J. De Martino received his B.S. from C.C.N.Y. and Ph.D. from
Temple University; he also studied Zen Buddhism with Daisetz T.
Suzuki and Shin'ichi Hisamatsu in Japan. In 1960 Dr. De Martino co-
authored, with D.T. Suzuki and Erich Fromm, Zen Buddhism and Psyco-
analysis, and edited "Conversations with Paul Tillich and Shin'ichi
Hisamatsu" in The Eastern Buddhist (October 1971, 1972, 1973). Dr.
De Martino is associate professor of religion, Temple University.

M.W. Padmasiri de Silva received his B.A. from University of Ceylon
and Ph.D. from the University of Hawaii. Among his publications are
Introduction to Buddhist Psychology, Buddhist and Freudian Psychology, Tangles and Webs, and Value Orientations and Nation Building.
Formerly Visiting Fulbright Professor at the University of Pitts-
burgh, Naropa Institute, and University of Colorado, Dr. de Silva is
professor and head of philosophy at the University of Peradeniya, Sri
Lanka.

George R. Elder received a B.D. in Church History from Union Theolog-
ical Seminary, and Ph.D. in Tantric Mahāyāna Buddhism from Columbia
University. Dr. Elder is currently assistant professor in the
Religion Program at Hunter College of the City University of New
York.

Jan T. Ergardt received his B.D. and Dr. Phil. from Lund University,
Sweden. He is author of the book Faith and Knowledge in Early Bud-
dhism. Dr. Ergardt is currently docent in the Humanities Faculty at
Lund University.

Herbert V. Guenther holds Ph.D. degrees from Munich University and
Vienna University in Indian philosophy and linguistics. He spent

many years in India, teaching at Lucknow University and the Sanskrit University at Varanasi. His major interest is in the area of Buddhist philosophy and, specifically, psychology on which subjects he is the author of many books, such as The Life and Teaching of Nāropa, Buddhist Philosophy in Theory and Practice, Philosophy and Psychology in the Abhidharma, and numerous articles. Dr. Guenther is head of the Department of Far Eastern Studies at the University of Saskatchewan in Saskatoon, Canada.

Steven Heine received his B.A. from the University of Pennsylvania and Ph.D. from Temple University; his dissertation was on the notions of time according to Dōgen Zenji and Heidegger. Dr. Heine is currently a Fulbright Research Fellow at Tokyo University, studying Dogen's poetry and the role of aesthetics in his philosophy.

The late Rune E.A. Johansson studied psychology and languages, among them Sanskrit and Pāli, at the University of Lund, earning his licentiate degree in psychology. Among his publications are Psychology of Nirvana, Pali Buddhist Texts and The Dynamic Psychology of Early Buddhism; he has also translated into Swedish the Dhammapāda and Sutta Nipāta, as well as writing numerous articles on experimental psychology. Dr. Johansson was a research psychologist at the Research Institute of the Swedish National Defense until 1976. He died shortly after completing his article for this anthology.

Stephen Kaplan earned his Ph.D. at Temple University. He also studied Sanskrit and philosophy at Benares Hindu University, psychiatry at the Temple University Medical School, and neuropsychology at Stanford University. He is currently assistant professor of religion at Manhattan College in the Bronx, New York.

Nathan Katz received his Ph.D. from Temple University, and has been a Fulbright-Hays Research Fellow in Sri Lanka and India. He is the author of Buddhist Images of Human Perfection, editor of Buddhist and Western Philosophy, and has written numerous essays, translations, and reviews for scholarly journals. Dr. Katz is assistant professor of Indo-Tibetan and comparative religions at Williams College.

Akihisa Kondo received his A.B. from Tokyo Imperial University and his M.D. at Tokyo Jikeikai School of Medicine. He was the only Japanese student to have worked with Dr. Karen Horney. Dr. Kondo is a practicing psychiatrist in Tokyo.

Peter D. Masefield holds a B.A. and Ph.D. from the University of Lancaster. He has translated Dhammapala's commentaries on the Petavatthu and Vimānavatthu for the Pāli Text Society, London. Dr. Masefield is visiting fellow at the University of Sydney.

Mokusen Miyuki received his Ph.D. from Claremont College, and is the author of the book The Secret of the Golden Flower: Studies and Translation, as well as numerous articles on Buddhism and Jungian psychology. Dr. Miyuki is professor of religious studies at California State University, Northridge; faculty member of the Institute of Buddhist Studies, Berkeley; faculty member of the C.G. Jung

Institute of Los Angeles; and a Jungian analyst.

The Venerable Chögyam Trungpa, Rinpoche, is the eleventh emanation of the Trungpa Tulku. Before the Chinese occupation of Tibet, he was abbot of the Surmang monasteries. Before emigrating to the United States, he studied comparative religions at Oxford University and founded the Samye Ling meditation center in Scotland. Currently he is president of Naropa Institute and spiritual director of meditation centers throughout Europe and America. He is the author of numerous books and articles, including Cutting Through Spiritual Materialism, The Myth of Freedom, and Meditation in Action. He is currently engaged in translating Tibetan texts from the bKa' brgyud lineage such as The Rain of Wisdom and The Life of Marpa the Translator.